The Great Mistake

CRITICAL UNIVERSITY STUDIES

The Great Mistake

How We Wrecked Public Universities
and How We Can Fix Them

Christopher Newfield

JOHNS HOPKINS UNIVERSITY PRESS   BALTIMORE

© 2016 Christopher Newfield
All rights reserved. Published 2016
Printed in the United States of America on acid-free paper
9 8 7 6 5 4 3 2 1

Johns Hopkins University Press
2715 North Charles Street
Baltimore, Maryland 21218-4363
www.press.jhu.edu

Library of Congress Cataloging-in-Publication Data

Names: Newfield, Christopher, author.
Title: The great mistake : how we wrecked public universities and
    how we can fix them / Christopher Newfield.
Description: Baltimore : Johns Hopkins University Press, [2016] |
    Series: Critical university studies | Includes bibliographical
    references and index.
Identifiers: LCCN 2016012781| ISBN 9781421421629 (hardcover :
    alk. paper) | ISBN 9781421421636 (electronic) | ISBN 1421421623
    (hardcover : alk. paper) | ISBN 1421421631 (electronic)
Subjects: LCSH: Public universities and colleges—United
    States—Finance. | Education, Higher—Aims and objectives—
    United States. | Higher education and state—United States. |
    Privatization in education—United States.
Classification: LCC LB2342 .N49 2016 | DDC 378/.05—dc23
    LC record available at https://lccn.loc.gov/2016012781

A catalog record for this book is available from the British Library.

*Special discounts are available for bulk purchases of this book. For
more information, please contact Special Sales at 410-516-6936 or
specialsales@press.jhu.edu.*

Johns Hopkins University Press uses environmentally friendly book
materials, including recycled text paper that is composed of at least
30 percent post-consumer waste, whenever possible.

What do you do when you know that you know
That you know that you're wrong?

—Sun Ra, "Face the Music"

Contents

Acknowledgments

It's been wonderful to have written so much of this book on the academic road, and to have written it in part because of the people I've met during a long series of speaking invitations about the university's fate. Among the most valuable of these visits have been those with groups working on the university with at least one foot outside of it, often without official status. I owe particular thanks to: Edu-Factory for bringing me to Università La Sapienza in Rome; Sauvons la Recherche for their invitation to Toulouse; l'Institut Méditerranéen de Recherches Avancées in Marseille; Projet Foreduc at the Université de Paris X-Nanterre; the Society for the Study of New and Emerging Technologies participants in Darmstadt in 2010; the Los Angeles MLA counter-conference in 2011; HUMLab at the University of Umeå, Sweden; the EPOKE seminar at Aarhus University's Danish School of Education; the Social Science Centre in Lincoln, United Kingdom; the organizers of the MLA Subconferences 2014–2016; and the Vampire Slayers Project at San Francisco State.

In 2011, a fellowship at the University of Cambridge's Centre for Research in the Arts, Social Sciences, and Humanities (CRASSH) allowed me to start thinking about how my work on various topics might turn into a book. Many thanks to the members of our research group on the future university, CRASSH director Mary Jacobus, Ellie Shermer for punting and talking, and especially to Susan Larsen for company and theater and for getting me there in the first place. That term I first met Stefan Collini, Joel Isaac, and Paul Ryan, who have continued to help my thinking about the higher ed environment.

A series of lectures that led to particularly enjoyable and illuminating conversations were set up, in chronological order, by Bob Frodeman, Les Back, Priscilla Wald, Asli Tekinay, Eva Hartmann, Carolyn De La Peña, Bruce Burgett, Lauren Goodlad, Robert Knapp, Marcia Kay Klotz, Henry Giroux, Pat Morton, Jim Lee, Scott See, Meredith McGill, Peggy Kamuf, David Theo Goldberg, Doug Morgan, Winfried Fluck, Sieglinde Linde, Patrik Svensson, Sabine Sielke, Catherine Cole, Ron Strickland, Ann Bermingham, Daniel Mitchell, Ann Cvetkovich, Jonathan Elmer, Sarah Blackwood, Greg Niemeyer, and Jenna Ng. The book took its final cyclical form through discussions that took place after my lecture at the Consortium of Humanities Centers and Institutes' Annual Meeting in April 2013 at the University of Kansas, and I am grateful to Victor Bailey for both the invitation and extraordinary hosting. From there another round began, thanks to Shuchi Kapila, Sue Wright, Brenna Bhandar, Nora Hanson, Helen Small, Constance Penley, Jenna Joo, Laura Pulido, Matthew Wickham, Sarah Misemer, Sara Guyer, Richard Grusin, Teresa Mangum, Matthew Santos, Robert Watson, Anne Barron, Amanda Anderson, Colleen Lye, Howard Brody, Judy Taylor, Laura Goldblatt, Cris Shore, Daniel HoSang, Will Callison, Martina Kohl, Elisabeth Schäfer-Wünsche, António Magalhães, Fiona Hollands, Mike Neery, Lisa Hajjar, Davina Cooper, Jo Williams, Matthew Sparke, Eric Sandeen, Margie Ferguson, Crystal Bartolovich, Timothy Melley, Angela Segler, and Scott Thomas. These generous individuals and their astute colleagues were my teachers and continuously renewed my education on the state of universities across North America and Europe.

In California, I was regularly inspired by a UC faculty-staff-student-activist-analyst crew that included Amanda Armstrong, Michael Buroway, Julie Carlson, Aranye Fradenburg, Peter Krapp, Celeste Langan, Catherine Liu, Bob Samuels, James Vernon, the UCSB Faculty Association Executive Board, and particularly Wendy Brown and Colleen Lye. I'm sorry I can't thank the UC staff members who, worried about employer retaliation, wrote to me about internal affairs on condition of anonymity. Bloggers have had to fill a news void between airbrushed official communications and a downsized independent press; many thanks on this count to Dan Mitchell at the UCLA Faculty Association blog, Bob Samuels again, the folks at Reclaim UC, the mysterious Cloudminder in California, and to Nick Fleischer, Richard Grusin, Chuck Rybak, and Sara Goldrick-Rab in Wisconsin. Ongoing thanks to Stanton A. Glantz, the unshakable advocate for the public status of the University of California, for his example.

While I was writing the book, three research groups offered intellectual and moral support. One was the Online Study Group I formed at UC Santa Barbara to investigate the Age of the MOOC that was decreed across the land: thanks to David Theo Goldberg, director of the UC Humanities Research Institute, for funding it, and to researchers Xiao Hu, Giselle Jaude, and especially the die-hards Jenna Joo, Cameron Sublett, and Alexandra Splan. After the MLA Subconference in early 2014, I fell in with a group of wonderful graduate students and younger faculty to work on designing an alternative university. The reason, as one put it, is, "we want a precarity we chose and not a precarity handed down to us by our declining institutions." The Autonomous U group assured me that better educational systems still lie over the horizon and that they will draw on the idealism that attracts people to higher education. Thanks to all participants and particularly to core animators Laura Goldblatt, Nora Hanson, and Thea Sicar.

Finally, as I was writing the first draft of this book in late 2013, the European Union Marie Curie Initial Training Network, called Universities in the Knowledge Economy (UNIKE), invited me to give a talk at their first meeting in Copenhagen. Intellectually, I never left. UNIKE formed a continent-wide higher education research consortium with graduate fellows from every part of Europe and representation from East and Southeast Asia. Among the many contributions of its encompassing sociointellectuality to my thinking has been a clear sense of the government-corporate-NGO postsecondary educational "ecosystem" of which the university is only one part. If any group has helped suspend my churchy centrism toward the university as the unique site of advanced learning it has been UNIKE, through its multicentered collaborative interactions rooted in a series of weeklong workshops at a range of sites, even as its reigning ethos has been the renewal of the public university as a free social force. I am reluctant to single out individuals in this distributed group effort, but am particularly grateful to: UNIKE's faculty partners at Bristol, Roehampton, Ljubljana, and Porto; the Auckland, Copenhagen, and Porto site teams; the Theme 6 crew that first formed as "the angry group"; the Nyhavn last-drink crowd who refused to help me write these acknowledgments; Chris Muellerleile; and especially Susan Wright, UNIKE's PI who put it together and kept it going while conducting inspiring research. My summary of the UNIKE effect is sanity and enlightenment. The effect continues.

This book was written with the help of a sabbatical from UC Santa Barbara in 2013. I'm grateful to my recent department chair Bishnupriya Ghosh.

Ruth Wilson Gilmore helped me with conversations over many years and offered crucial last-minute input, as did Aashish Mehta of global studies at UCSB. Michael Bérubé gave the project a good shove at an important time, and the research of Andrew Ross and Doris Sommer helped propel it. In England, I've benefited enormously from higher ed conversations with Helen Small and with Andrew McGettigan. McGettigan's work on post-2010 changes in UK university policy is a superb and extremely rare effort to picture the university's formative financial structures for the staff and publics it effects. I'm grateful to Jeffrey Williams for comments on the manuscript and for his university writing over the years. A while back he coined the term "Critical University Studies," started a book series on the subject with Greg Britton at Johns Hopkins University Press, and asked me to coedit it with him. Jeff and Greg made it possible to finish this book—Greg did an excellent job of demanding it. I'm also grateful to the editing crew for their patience and skill.

My most involved intellectual relationship in university studies is with my coeditor of *Remaking the University*, aka blog husband Michael Meranze, with whom I exchange a couple of dozen links and commentaries nearly every day. I met Michael over a year after he started coediting the blog with me. I arrived late from the airport for a talk at the UCLA History Department, dragging my suitcase down the hall looking for the room, when I suddenly heard words that seemed familiar, because, I realized, they were from my paper, which was being read for me in an unknown voice. The voice turned out to be Michael's. I entered and hugged him, he recoiled, and we've been together on e-mail ever since. His influence is so pervasive in my thinking about universities that it's sometimes hard to separate his thoughts from my own.

In Santa Barbara, my friendship with Ricki Morse has been one of the most sustaining and important of my life, and it has helped float this book, among many other things. It was while writing this book that I came to realize clearly that my optimism about the power of education descends directly from my mother, Marilyn Morgan, a UCSB alumna and former teacher.

Most of all, endless thanks to Avery. I don't know how she stood all the university talk, but most of its conditions and content would be unthinkable without her.

Many to whom I owe thanks are unnamed here, and to them I apologize. Everyone named and unnamed is obviously blameless for my mistakes.

Part I: Introduction

Holding Back Public Colleges

This book addresses the dominant mystery of higher education today. How have US public colleges and universities come to struggle with their recent glory—the combination of broad access and high quality? How did we get public university tuition that is far too high even as students seem to be learning less? How did we get increased tuition and decreased learning just when we most need new capabilities to rebuild a multiracial middle class in the age of outsourcing and automation?

My answer to these questions is the opposite of the conventional wisdom. The conventional wisdom says that US public colleges have been weakened by public funding and public sector thinking. The conventional wisdom says that public colleges will never again have the public funding they used to assume, so they must economize, commercialize, marketize, and financialize. They must be closer to business and be more like business. They must focus on multiple revenue streams. Universities have, in this view, been protected from the market economy and must move teaching and research toward workforce demands and economic needs. Nearly all senior university officials, whether or not they like this model, feel obligated to adapt to it. They assert that the marriage of public and private funding is a happy one. Higher tuition, student debt, continuous fundraising, corporate partnerships, online learning, and the rest don't damage the public mission but sustain it through changing times.

This conventional wisdom is wrong. In reality, public colleges and universities have been following this commercialization script since 1980 or so, responding to the same political and corporate demands that we hear today. Today's problems do not reflect a failure to introduce market thinking but the effects of its long-term presence. I show that what everyone now laments—high student costs, stagnating educational benefits, and destabilized public college finances—flow not from public but from private sector practices. What I call the American Funding Model is indeed broken, but it has not been broken by too much public funding, public service, and public slack. It has been broken by too much private funding and service to private interests. This book shows how this breaking has taken place and how undoing this failed experiment can start to set things right.

In describing the commercializing mechanism that is damaging higher education today, I use the increasingly familiar term *privatization*. I define this word in the next chapter, but in general it means what it sounds like—replacing public with private partners, purposes, and interests. The problems with this trend are financial and educational at the same time. Submitting public universities to private sector standards hasn't increased their overall wealth and made their education more efficient. It has increased their costs and shifted resources from the educational core. I show how privatizing public colleges has made them more expensive for students *and* impaired students' learning. Private sector "reforms" are not the cure for the college cost disease—they *are* the college cost disease. They set up a *devolutionary cycle* that shifts resources away from education while raising rather than containing costs.

When I describe damage or benefits, I am not thinking about budgetary abstractions but about student learning and basic research relevant to a rapidly changing world. The combination of learning and research has a unique social value that occurs at the requisite advanced level only in the special institutions known as universities. Unfortunately, funding cuts, tuition hikes, and conflicting political and corporate demands have for many years destabilized the public colleges and universities that teach three-quarters of all college students. More fundamentally, they have lost their ability to explain their social benefits, although these are greater than the private benefits they also confer. Academia's senior managers have helped two generations of policymakers to overvalue the private benefits of higher education, which has given an artificial, unmerited advantage to the forces of privatization over those of the public good. In this book I identify the *price of privatization* in the wake of the 2008 financial crisis and outline how the situation could be put right.

A Continuous Downgrade

The most influential commentary on universities now focuses on cutting their costs by using more technology while applying business sector controls to their educational activities.[1] The familiar combination of technology and corporate management is the hammer that has turned every educational problem into a nail. In fact, society's actual educational problems are not helped by market-oriented, cost-focused managerialism. This book is about how these standard private-sector practices damage public higher education.

The situation is urgent because global economic and social changes have made standardized mass education obsolete. The world's problems used to seem containable through normal science, conducted by people with advanced competence and known methods in established disciplines. Today's problems—climate change, overgrown financialization, and continuous warfare, to name three—require interdisciplinary expertise, hybrid methods, and continuous creativity on the part of the whole population. Universities are the only social institutions devoted to helping the rising generation master coherent parts of the vastness of human knowledge *and* acquire personal capabilities that will renew themselves throughout their lives. Universities are the only social institutions devoted to disinterested research (always tied to context and human interests but *not* controlled by financial goals). Universities are the only social institutions that put student learning and cutting-edge research together for the full spectrum of society, helping graduates become de facto researchers in their lives and their communities. And yet, in the period when public universities need to upgrade instruction and research while inventing new ways of combining these, they are being asked to cheapen and dilute themselves instead.

Cheapening public universities will only make them less effective for society. The same is true for their impact on individuals. The corporate world used to provide relatively secure career pathways to competent college graduates. Now college graduates are asked to have customized know-how and creativity that will help them forge their own paths. Even without this economic pressure, each student should be able to learn who she is and what she is particularly good at doing. But now this economic pressure is a driving force, and one partial response is to develop special capabilities that will help keep her from being turned into an interchangeable part.

These demands are a very mixed bag—new problem-solving capabilities combined with more precarious white-collar jobs—but they reflect changes in worldwide economic policy that universities do not control. We are asked to absorb the lessons of books like *Average Is Over* and *The Global Auction* that show commodity skills to be of declining value in the rich countries whose white-collar workers now compete with their counterparts in lower-income countries.[2] The clear lesson is that generalized *creativity learning* is the necessary (though not sufficient) condition of prosperity and justice. And yet public universities are being pushed relentlessly toward offering a cheaper version of the mass commodity learning that was thought to be sufficient for non-elite students during the rapid growth of college attendance after World War II.

In an effort to help reverse this disastrous trend, I show how conventional economic thinking is forcing public college education in the wrong direction and suggest how to get it back on track. We need research learning, we need it to be individualized, we need it to be free of debt and political restraints, and we need it on an enormous scale. We won't get it by privatizing our public universities, reducing their resources, and making them more market friendly.

I am also writing this book because for twenty-five years I have had a front-row seat at the continuous effort to make the public university more like a business. As a research professor who spends much of every working year in the classroom, I have seen firsthand how privatization is blocking public universities' ability to design the higher levels of learning that society needs. I know that most of the popular discourse about cost diseases and technological fixes has and will continue to make things worse, not better. Privatization is not an appealing word or a concept that most of us like to ponder, but it is changing our educational world and shrinking our future. This book tries to help anyone and everyone think about it.

Troubles of a College Family

Before we get into the details, I'll present the symptoms of the privatization disease through a second-person address to an imaginary parent who is a composite of many with whom I have spoken. As a group, parents have been miseducated into thinking that tuition hikes are inevitable, that financial aid takes care of all needy students, and that public funding cuts haven't damaged the educational core. Unfortunately, none of these conventional claims is true.

For starters: your children were very good students in their racially diverse high school. They were not perhaps in the 0.7 percent that will go to an Ivy League or Ivy-type private research university, or in the 2.4 percent that will go there or to an elite liberal arts college.[3] But they were in the top tenth or fifth of their high school class, are energetic and intelligent, and have big plans for having good lives while helping humanity. Your kids are mixed race and could check the Hispanic box. You manage apartment buildings and feel middle class on some days but not on others. Your ex-spouse is a teacher and hopes to get her master's degree when the kids are out of the house. In your state college days in the late 1980s, your family situation might have allowed the kids to write application essays about overcoming racial discrimination and hardship, but everyone you know can tell similar stories these days, so you don't think it means much anymore. You're very worried about cost. Since you and your spouse finalized your divorce five years ago, your $74,000 salary, though well above the national median, hasn't gone very far.

Each of your kids has a couple of lower-income friends whom you have known for years to be very bright, but who were counseled at home or at school not to go to a four-year college. Several of them went to work after high school, planning to attend college in a year or two, and some went to a two-year college and stopped their education there.

When your daughter was a junior in high school, you took two weeks of vacation time to take her to public and private colleges outside the region where you live. Someone at work gave you a copy of *Colleges That Change Lives*, a book about the large number of liberal arts colleges that offer individual attention to help students develop special capabilities and to understand what they want do with them. You visit several of these in what your daughter calls "Greater Portlandia"—Reed College, Lewis & Clark, Whitman College, Evergreen, Seattle University—and she likes them quite a bit. But visits to their financial aid officials convinced you that paying their freight would be a hard prospect. It would force you to take out parental PLUS loans, of which you hadn't heard until the college tour. Since your daughter is the eldest of three, you don't see how you can take out tens of thousands of dollars in parental loans for her without hurting the other two.

Your daughter is in the top 5–10 percent of her class (and has 98th percentile SAT scores). She applied to several wealthy elite colleges that could afford to give her grants rather than loans. But ultimately—after dangling on the wait list of one she especially liked—she doesn't get into any of them. You decide together that she should go to a public university in the state where you reside. You know that its tuition has tripled since 2000, but at $13,500 a year it is still about a third of the sticker price of the liberal arts colleges she liked, and the web site of her preferred public university campus advertises freshman seminars and personal attention for students.

So when your daughter is admitted to this well-ranked public research university, you think the equation is solved—until you get the paperwork. You are assured it's a good financial package, but you add up the total cost of attendance and are not happy with what you see. You discover this total minus her financial aid leaves a funding gap of $9,200 a year. Although politicians now continuously rail against excessive tuition and student debt, they aren't doing anything practical about it either, beyond some modest reforms. The idea still seems to be that you should go borrow the missing money, since you and your daughter can surely pay back $22,000, $27,000, or perhaps even $73,080 for a good BA—per child.[4] But your daughter's financial aid already mixes loans with grants, and if her after-tax income is about $10.00 an hour at an off-campus job, she will need to work sixteen hours a week through the whole school year just to keep her borrowing under control.

But this is the best deal that you can get, and a BA is now the ante into the economic game even if it doesn't offer a winning hand. Thus your daughter enrolls in this very good public research university a few hundred miles away. Although the immediate cuts of the Great Recession are past, she discovers that a quarter of the catalog courses she wants to take are now rarely offered and that she will not be able to get into some of them until her third or fourth year, when she has more seniority at registration. Many of her new friends want to get out of college in three years to save money. This is feasible because top scores in high school AP courses mean they count for college credit. But these students are taking courses because they are available, not because they add up to an intellectual sequence. If your daughter holds out for a curriculum that will help her develop a coherent expertise, she is likely to take five or even six years to graduate. You look up graduation rates for her public university and see that it has a solid 81 percent rate—after six years, not four.

She goes to college, she comes home after the first semester, and in the process of talking it all over you review her schedule. You see that her first semester selection consists of general education (GE) courses like "Introduction to American Political Systems" and "Introduction to Archeology." Each class has between 100 and 600 students, her professors don't know her, and her teaching assistants (TAs), though competent and well intentioned, have too many students—seventy-five per TA, per term—to give her much individual feedback. Her advisor is a senior undergraduate who knows the GE requirements backward and forward, but she can't help your daughter shape a coherent academic program that reflects her personal interests and intellectual goals. "What happened to the freshman seminars?" you ask. "There aren't enough," she said. "They can't pay professors to teach them, so only a few offer them on top of their regular work."

When you ask your daughter about what these courses add up to, she says that everybody's schedule looks like this. "You have to get requirements out of the way," she explains, "and the major starts later." "Does anyone ask you about your academic goals?" you ask her. She laughs and says, "Daddy. It's public school!"

At the end of her sophomore year, after two years of a cafeteria-style selection of mostly interesting courses the additive academic effect of which remains unclear, your daughter has decided to major in molecular biology. She wants to go to medical school, or maybe do research—one of her professors described her own research with such enthusiasm that this has become an option. "What topic might you research?" you ask her. "I could work on some chemical interactions in the hypothalamus in my professor's lab," she replies. "Are you interested in that?" you inquire. "Not that exactly." "What are *you* interested in?" you ask your daughter. "I don't know yet," she replies, "I'm only a sophomore." You let it drop.

Your son, meanwhile, has started at a community college (CC) for his first two years, which has open admission and very low fees. He has always been more interested in making things than studying them, but with an intellectual turn: he built a complicated tree fort in a neighbor's yard when he was nine, but only after drawing and redrawing designs for a month beforehand. He has been a citizen of Maker Nation from childhood and wants courses that combine architecture with sustainable landscape design. CC seems like the natural place to look for these.

But he got a letter from the local CC in the spring of his senior year in high school saying that his units would cost 30 percent more than in the current year. Toward the end of the summer, he discovers that two of his fall entry-level required courses have been canceled, and that he will have to wait until spring to take them. Your son decides to take a "gap year" and keep his part-time job working in a computer repair shop, where he is learning by helping the technicians while reading about the history of landscape design in his free time. He gets a second job with a landscaper who has a background in stone masonry, and for the moment his higher education is do-it-yourself.

You hear about a couple of books that say that college students aren't learning higher-order cognitive skills in four years because they aren't assigned enough reading, that they don't write many papers, and that they study half as much as your generation did. On top of that, while many students spend too many hours working for tuition, rent, and food money, others pour most of their nonclass time into their extracurricular and social lives, as though college were a lifestyle choice.[5] This fits your daughter's descriptions of her school, where the haves and the have-nots experience college very differently. You feel lucky that your daughter developed as much direction as she has.

Now at the end of her third year and in the biology major, her grades are very good—she's turning out as well as you could have hoped. She is selected for a summer program for pre-med students with an interest in biomedical research. Cosponsored by a pharmaceutical company and an Ivy League university, it offers advanced undergraduate courses that are hard to get at her campus. It brings together strong students from private and public research universities. After a week in the program, she calls you. This is a great program, she says, but you should see the private university kids. My roommate is from Stanford. Most of her courses were discussions or seminars with regular professors. She's been writing papers in cognitive science since her second year, not just taking tests. Professors read what she writes and give her feedback! She has a faculty advisor who helps fit courses together. She takes courses that give her specific knowledge that fosters her research interest. She was told as a freshman that if she wanted to be able to travel as a scientist she should not just study but become fully functional in her second language, which is

Mandarin, and she's been taking Chinese every semester for all three years. This coming year she's doing study abroad in Shanghai. "Daddy," your daughter cries, "I'm just not competitive!"

Your son has finally gone to CC and is getting ready to transfer to a four-year college. He has battled to get into required courses and is applying with a hodgepodge of subjects that you can't quite figure out. He assures you that the courses on everybody's transcript don't add up to much. He's also taken several of his courses online from home.

A professor friend sends you a scholarly article that says the "American Funding Model" has hit the wall and that trying to rescue this old system is making things worse.[6] When state funding was high, the article states, poor and middle-class students could finish college in spite of the sky-high tuition at private US universities, since state funding kept public college fees very low. Now, the article says, low public funding *equals* high tuition *equals* high student debt *equals* lower access *equals* lower college attainment—period. The author insists that it's time for parents and everyone else to pull their heads out of the sand and face the system's need for rebuilt public funding—if political and business leaders are still interested in having a middle-class society.

The article's funding math is a bit tedious, you find, but you ponder its claim that there is a causal connection between privatization—the shift from public funding to private tuition and donations—and a decline in US college attainment. You mark this quotation:

> The evidence of U.S. educational decline is now unmistakable. For the first time in its history, younger people are *less* educated than their baby-boom parents. The American university's "college completion rate" (counting only those who started college) is now 56%, or 29th of the 30 OECD countries. California, one of the world's wealthiest places, has seen one of the world's most astonishing declines in college achievement. The state's continuation rate, the proportion of students starting college who complete it, fell from 66 percent to 44 percent in just eight years (1996–2004). California's rank among states in investment in higher

education declined during the same period from fifth to forty-seventh, according to Tom Mortenson, a higher education policy analyst. The state has cut its investment in higher education by close to 50 percent since 1980, forcing tuition increases like the 60 percent rise at the University of California from 2004 to 2008, which was followed by a 32 percent rise between 2009 and 2011. Meanwhile, half of California's K–12 students are now eligible for the federal school lunch program, up from one-third in 1989. As Mortenson notes, these students will have no personal resources to cover the costs of attending college, which at UC is nearing thirty thousand dollars a year. The U.S. is experiencing an educational meltdown whose effects, if unchallenged, will lead to an abandonment of its younger generations that is unprecedented in its history.

You think about your own kids as you read this. Are they going to get pulled under by a vortex of bad decisions that lock in decline?

You read about online college courses and MOOCs, or massive open online courses. You had once talked your son's best friend out of taking the expensive version of these from a for-profit provider, but these MOOCs are supposed to be free. Some new companies are offering them, and they are endorsed and even funded by the country's most prestigious universities—Harvard, MIT, Stanford, Penn, Duke, and others. Your kids could never get into these schools, and if they did you couldn't afford their tuition. But now they can "take" courses offered by those famous schools' most famous professors. Some companies are selling certificates of completion—a kind of course credit. You tell your son about them and he says, "My online courses were OK. But I would never take one in my major. The feedback from the students is too easy, and the prof exists only sometimes on email. Some kids are there because they can cheat. It's like a talking textbook with a chat room. I could read a textbook, though this was sometimes more fun."

You start to wonder about what has happened to the whole public higher ed system. Your daughter is a great student, but she will graduate a year late without a coherent set of methodological skills and without an identifiable expertise in a subject area. If she wants to do knowledge work in a company, she will need months or years of additional specific training. If she wants to do research she will need another five or, more likely, ten years of graduate education and postdoctoral positions, and the same goes for practicing medicine. As it is, she will likely stay a couple of economic tiers below the elite school students that she told you had a leg up on her because they receive greater per-student investments.

Although you don't actually have the time, you decide to dig a little into the professional higher education literature. You buy a book that has a mixture of academics, administrators, and public officials writing about an issue that matters to you, *Getting to Graduation*.[7] In one chapter, you read a passage that fits with your experience of your kids' educations:

> College systems need to be simplified to reduce confusion among students and to alleviate the need for complex counseling. Administrators and faculty need to focus on designing coherent programs and working to get students into those programs as soon as possible. Technology must be intelligently exploited to provide information and to track student progress (and lack of progress) in real time. Reformers need to turn their attention, much more than in past initiatives, to pedagogy, instruction, and professional development. Finally, faculty (including part-time faculty) . . . need to be more broadly engaged in reform efforts.[8]

This sounds right to you: programmatic clarity, directness, simplification, coherence, and counseling, all leading to real knowledge and skills in each student. You look for chapters about the policies that will make this happen. What you find instead are two disappointing things. First, you read generalities that sound to you like improving graduation by making graduation easier: "We must broaden our definition of what 'counts' in our measures of degree attainment. Second, we must look to the sub-baccalaureate sector as a place to make gains in the number of students who earn a credential."[9] Even worse, the book is rife with admissions that the warnings and policy changes of recent decades have produced no educational gains. You feel that the authors don't really believe in their preferred policies. You pay particular attention to this problem in the financial aid chapter, which calculates that over $150 billion in annual financial aid expenditures may increase attendance at the country's colleges by 3 or 4 percent—or not at all, since the authors write, "we have to make significant assumptions to get a positive rate of return on these programs."[10] None of the book's completion measures look like they will improve individual intellectual development on a mass scale.

You have some bitter thoughts. Why, you wonder, do we struggle with the tax funding of public colleges our kids take five to six years to get through and that don't give them methodological and subject expertise they can name and put to use right away? What are we paying for if they have to take whatever courses they can get, and cobble together a do-it-yourself curriculum whose parts don't mesh for lack of course availability and academic advising? Why are they graduating with $20,000 to $30,000 in student debt when they can't identify specific intellectual achievements, ones that fit with their interests or with society's needs? If the outcomes of public colleges are so uncertain, why not shrink the public college system drastically, save a lot of tax money, and get "as good or better" results with online technology?

Wandering around online one evening, you find someone who wants to do exactly that—the author of a book called *The End of College*.[11] The idea seems to be to convert college to a large volume of certificate programs and put most teaching online. Great, you think. Just when the US population needs to be massively smarter, some expert wants to get rid of the public colleges that were supposed to help everyone do that.

You stop reading, with a sense that the higher education policy world has created massive problems for itself and has no idea how to fix them. You and your kids, you think, are on your own.

Why I Wrote This Book

When I first began to study universities as a system around 2000, I was as surprised as anyone that we seemed to be throwing away the efficiencies of public provision for higher education. I was surprised that the visible financial problems of families like these didn't cause a change of course. I've written this book to explain how we've gotten to a place where the public university's unique product—low-cost, no-debt, high-quality university learning on a mass scale, or *mass quality*—now seems both impossible and unnecessary. We did, as a country, create the mid-twentieth-century version of mass quality after World War II when we were poorer and more racist than we are now. Yet today a generation of political, business, and educational leaders has somehow decided that mass quality is out of reach. We know that no country has a large middle class without 'mass-scale higher learning, and that this in turn depends on minimizing individual cost. We did learn to offer high school for free at a time when mass high school graduation made all the difference. And yet most people aren't fighting to hang onto low-cost public colleges and their power to *democratize intelligence.* That is the Great Mistake.

Much of my effort here is devoted to getting us beyond a bunker-like wall of denial about our current situation. This denial built itself from off-the-shelf components of modern corporate life: the eclipse of internal debate by image management, incomprehension of the value of public goods, a complacent faith in technological disruption, and a *lack* of faith in the intelligence of everyday smart people.

I focus on a diagnosis of the problem in this book—on the *how* we got here rather than on the *why*.[12] I put the problem in the form of a self-reinforcing cycle. I call it a *devolutionary cycle,* or a *decline cycle.* I do this because the crisis within public universities has been caused not by any one privatization decision—to admit more non-resident students or to borrow to build new buildings to be funded by projected start-up company revenues—but by their interaction. I focus here on the pieces of the cycle and how they work together to form the doom loop within which public colleges everywhere are now struggling. Resource shortages and the scramble to cover them have hurt our ability to take the rising generation, not overwhelmingly white like its public university forebears, and help them attain the higher-order creative capabilities they need to face the future. In the book's conclusion, I outline a cure. I don't offer detailed policy suggestions, but show that the decline cycle that seems irresistible can be reversed if we undo some key economic and cultural assumptions.

This book is based on several aspects of my own experience during a quarter-century in which I have taught 10,000 students in every format. It emerges from my expertise as a scholar of US culture—I work in the American Studies tradition that combines literary, historical, political, and sociological analysis, and, in my case, financial analysis as well. The book also draws on the better part of a decade I spent as a member and then the chair of academic senate committees on planning and budget both on my own campus and at the University of California system-wide office. These roles have given me firsthand experience with the academic-managerial thinking that I analyze here, as well as access to financial data that don't circulate outside of the realm of senior officials.

As the 2008 crisis began to decimate budgets and give senior managers a reason to consolidate their authority, I ramped up a blog, *Remaking the University*, edited with my partner, the historian Michael Meranze, where I have since written 750 posts in an attempt to interpret the unfolding situation to colleagues, friends, and a wider public. I try to bring this combination of hands-on experience and back-office expertise to bear on the crisis that has changed the features of the public university since 2008.

The book is particularly for parents and students like those in my sketch above. They are the brains who arrive in society by the millions, and whose collective enlightenment is the only thing that will solve the planet's problems. Social, political, and economic movements are essential to bringing the right forces to bear. But so are public colleges and universities that offer great research and teaching unbound by the conventional wisdom of elites and unrestricted by ability to pay. The capacity to offer mass quality to entire generations is what our devolutionary cycle may cost us. This book is intended as part of the struggle to reverse it.

The Price of Privatization

I've suggested that the American public university is failing the current generation. Here we are going to start getting into *how* this is happening. The public university is failing not because it spends too much money on its core activities of teaching and research, but because it spends too little on them. This is in spite of the fact that students are paying more tuition and taking on more debt to get something out of college. What I am calling the American Funding Model (AFM) is producing the worst of both worlds—costs for students that are too high and spending on instruction and research that is too low.[1]

Negative Trends

The problem has been building for three decades. This period has seen policymakers shift the real costs of higher education from society to students. The most recent figures from the State Higher Education Executive Officers Association, which has long tracked these things, show that state appropriations for public colleges and universities declined by 25 percent in constant dollars between 1989 and 2014. During the same period, *net* student tuition doubled.[2]

Politicians and university leaders have mostly persuaded themselves that no harm has been done. States still spend a huge amount of public money on higher education, they say; we tied high tuition to high financial aid, they say; poor students aren't hurt, they say; college is the best investment you can make, they say. To be $25,000 in debt for a UC Berkeley education is nothing, one senior University of California official recently said to me, so students should "suck it up."

The view that cuts to public funding don't hurt students or educational quality is wrong. During the past thirty years of shifting costs from public funds to student tuition, the United States has destroyed a global lead in educational attainment that it had held since the nineteenth century.[3] The United States is now nineteenth of twenty-three countries in the proportion of entering university students who successfully graduate. It ranks thirty-eighth out of forty-three countries covered in a standard international sample in aggregate progress in attainment over the past generation.[4] At the same time, despite assurances that access for poor students is being protected, twenty-four-year-olds in the lowest quartile of income have college graduation rates of 10.4 percent, or about one-seventh that of students in the top quartile.[5] Poor students who *do* graduate do not borrow less than affluent students because of the nation's generous financial aid, poor students borrow as much as do affluent students but with far less capacity to pay it off.[6] As we will see, the decline of public funding is causally connected to the simultaneous stagnation of attainment.

Two other socioeconomic trends have affected the value of an American public college education. The first is the long-term shift from mass production to customized production that coincided with the rise of the "knowledge industries." This shift began in earnest in the 1970s, and it asked blue-collar and white-collar workers to solve problems not explained in the instruction manual, and to make new rules rather than simply follow existing ones. They were to behave more like artisans and less like assembly line workers.[7] Faculty, staff, and students are aware of these changes, but adapting to them costs money that public universities don't have—even where senior managers are willing to make creativity learning a goal. Throughout this period, the main ambition politicians have had for their universities is that they spend less money on each degree. Public universities have always spent less per student than their private counterparts through factory-style efficiencies such as large lectures, mechanized grading, minimal personal contact between students and faculty, and, for four decades, increasing use of contingent instructors. But saving money on higher education makes it *less* suited to a knowledge economy by forcing its standardization. The rise of online instruction through the MOOC (massive open online course) wave of 2011–2013 was the most ambitious attempt to extend existing cost reductions without hurting instruction, but it failed.[8] Today's students need more personalized instruction, not less, and yet public universities are decreasingly able to offer this.

The second trend is economic: the breaking of the relationship between rising productivity and increases in mean compensation. From 1945 to 1975, a student could go to college, gain knowledge to increase his or her productivity, and assume that this increased productivity would be rewarded by increased pay. Throughout the 1980s, 1990s, and 2000s, worker productivity continued to increase, but pay did not.[9] This means that when policymakers obsess about making sure that college "pays," they ignore the fact that it is business that doesn't want to pay for productivity gains, not college that fails to increase productivity.

This is a problem with American economic policy, not with higher education. But it does mean that students who follow conventional economic rationality should want to pay for college *only* when it gets them up off the productivity median by giving them above-average skills. This is exactly what public universities are decreasingly able to do.

Bipartisan Austerity Blindness

There's a mystery to the nation's inability to trace the relative decline in university attainment to lower public investment. The solution starts with understanding our diversionary consensus on the subject.

Two broad groups think they have the *how* of university decline more or less sown up. The first, more conservative, group attributes rising prices and falling outcomes to variations on the Ronald Reagan theme of "waste, fraud, and abuse." They argue that government grants and subsidized loans have allowed universities to raise prices with impunity and encouraged many students to enroll in college who don't deserve to be there. President Ronald Reagan's secretary of education, William Bennett, is thought to be the origin of the idea that the availability of government grants and loans allows colleges to raise their prices with impunity because they know the government and the lending industry will cover them. Many commentators have elaborated this vision of a bloated sector insulated from market discipline and therefore overspending on gold-plated student facilities and self-indulgent faculty research.[10]

The second group points to cuts in public funding that have forced public colleges to compensate with higher tuition. The spread of this argument in the media is a relatively recent development: even senior managers did not generally accept it in the decade of the 2000s, at least in my University of California experience. But by 2010, the problem of public cuts had become conventional liberal wisdom that was said to explain ever-rising university tuition, class shortages, weaker degree outcomes, and other problems.

Both the conservative and liberal explanations could offer startling examples. Throughout the Great Recession, the University of California sustained an extensive capital projects campaign by doubling its debt and pledging increased tuition income as collateral.[11] Small private colleges have made massive speculative investments in infrastructure to launch themselves into the national limelight.[12] On the other side, financial companies who had helped grow student loan debt managed to get Mitt Romney, as the 2012 Republican presidential candidate, to promise to restore their former prominence in the student loan industry.[13] The 2016 Republican campaign renewed the assurance that the finance industry would again intermediate between students and their universities.[14] Standard data show massive, repeated nationwide cuts by the very legislators who complain about course bottlenecks and flawed academic priorities.

There was plenty of overlap and player swapping between these two teams. After 2010, differences over specific issues like the role of for-profit colleges (positive for most Republicans, negative for most Democrats) were overshadowed by agreement about the need for permanent austerity for public higher education. California was Exhibit A, where the Democratic governor Jerry Brown and the legislature's Democratic leadership subjected all public college segments to one-year cuts as large as those of the Republican predecessor Arnold Schwarzenegger, and carried on a budgetary squeeze without end in exchange for such small state funding restoration that the university systems would require a decade to make up what they had lost in a year.[15] After the Democratic Party acquired a supermajority in the California legislature in 2012, they made austerity permanent. On the national level, the Obama administration showed no interest in significant reinvestment in public colleges other than some improvement in the most underfunded part of the system—the community colleges.

The interaction of the two dominant parties continued the stagnation in public college funding. The consensus wisdom was that college overspending, university mismanagement, a lack of mission focus, and insufficient use of technology were at least as important as public funding cuts in contributing to the sector's growing mediocrity. The result has been a pervasive sense among politicians and business leaders that the public university just isn't a domain where they want to reinvest.[16]

Unfortunately, the austerity framework continues to damage teaching and research in the historical moment in which they need to become much better. The core fallacy of the austerity consensus is that there isn't enough money in the economy or the public sector to fund public colleges as they once were. A budget committee I chaired had demonstrated the fallacy of this belief in 2006: in California, college funding as a share of state personal income was well below previous levels, and even in good years this funding level had not been reinstated. When the California governor said in 2012 that personalized instruction would mean increasing spending on UC far beyond anything seen before, he apparently did not know that he could have doubled UC's state funding and still have stayed below the per capita higher ed tax spending of the 1990s.[17]

The same holds on a national level. The country's citizens have reduced their per-student tax outlay for public colleges by about 25 percent since the mid-1980s.[18] What they are doing instead is spending more of their money on individual college tuition and greatly expanding student debt.

Let's look at some budget arithmetic. In fiscal year 2013, state and local governments spent just under $79 billion on higher education.[19] This was about 10 percent below 2007–2008 levels. (In 2014–2015, the total was $86.3 billion, still below previous levels.)[20] In 2013, returning state funding to its 2008 level would have required an additional $6 billion or so—as a minimal baseline that would *not* allow for enrollment and cost increases, or any quality improvements. Perhaps the real additional need is closer to $20 billion, which would allow public universities to offer real quality enhancements for all public university students on the grounds that they are facing a higher creativity standard in the current economy. Both subject mastery and creativity are vital traits for the less-well-prepared students whose improved attainment is the key, we are told, to the country's overall performance.

Regardless of the precise number, the range of $6 billion to $20 billion in additional funding is a small share of aggregated state revenues of about $847 billion.[21] It is also less than the *new* share of public funds acquired by private lenders during the 2000s, when "the private [for-profit] sector's slice of federal aid money grew from $4.6 billion to more than $26 billion."[22] The country is spending plenty of money on education. It's just not spending it to improve public colleges. In reality, *triple* the state funding lost during the Great Recession could be covered by redirecting federal money from America's worst colleges, the for-profits, back to America's public colleges, which struggle every day to provide the basics of higher education that meet the needs of the current century. The austerity consensus allowed policymakers to distract themselves from the educational damage their continuous cuts have been creating.

The Id Theory of Public Spending

The further mystery is why the austerity consensus has held up so well. Leaders in both parties came to agree that universities shelter themselves from market forces and are therefore inefficient—that they have contracted a "cost disease" through their tradition of being faculty centered and student focused. The solution to the cost disease, they affirmed, was to replace hidebound academic methods with business strategies that respect students as consumers and that treat parents, the public, and loan companies as investors. This would allegedly bring commercial discipline to faculty who have used professional standards to make excessively independent decisions about teaching and research. Most politicians, business executives, and academic managers now assume that professional autonomy impedes educational efficiency. In this view, freedom from commercial discipline *is* the problem, and the imposition of it is the solution. Though the left wing sees government and public investment as basically good, it too sees colleges as opaque and perverse and in need of permanent austerity. I think of this view as liberal Reaganism, and it came to frame Democratic Party policy.[23]

A good example of this conventional wisdom was a nine-part series that the *Washington Post* ran in late summer 2013, under the title "The Tuition Is Too Damn High."[24] This was a major news outlet's most serious effort in years to get beyond the clichés and to understand the drivers of college costs. Everyone was rightly upset about costs. Lumping all types of colleges together, tuition increased 297 percent between 1990 and 2012, or twice the increase seen in health care costs.[25]

The *Post* series correctly explained that, in terms of basic salary returns, a bachelor's degree was still worth the money, and second that faculty salaries were not the reason that tuition is "too damn high." The series also found two genuine reasons that it *is* too high.

The first is "administrative bloat," where administrative personnel have grown at ten times the rate of full-time tenure-track professors.[26] The second is the "amenities race"—the alleged Vegas-style leisure facilities said to attract full-tuition students, and, less famously, the expensive research facilities that universities build to compete with each other for science talent and grants.

The *Post* series then went on to spoil its analysis. It did this by tracing the overhiring of administrators and the overbuilding of campuses to a primal desire to "raise all the money it can and spend all the money it raises." The authority for this claim was Howard R. Bowen, an economist and college president who invented an alleged law that came to be called Bowen's Revenue Theory of Costs. In 1980 he wrote, "At any given time, the unit cost of education is determined by the amount of revenues currently available for education relative to enrollment." Cost, he claimed, is *not* determined by need, technology, efficiency, and market wages and prices, but by income.[27] Regardless of the thin evidence Bowen originally offered of revenues defining costs, the dismissive cynicism of the "law" helped it acquire the status of a universal truth that could be deployed to explain virtually any spending increase. For Dylan Matthews, the serious cub reporter who wrote the *Post* series, Bowen's "law" applied to what he saw as the worst cost offender, the public research university, whose behavior he summarized with the phrase "just throwing money around and getting it from wherever."[28]

The inevitable conclusion was that public officials spend a lot because they have lots of other people's money. The combined habits of public sector and academia create a permanent "cost disease" that academics themselves will never cure. But this explanation rests on a mystical regression to a quasi-unconscious instinct to spend unless controlled. It gets there by ignoring the actual cost drivers that make up the privatization cycle. The conclusion is always the same: public sector spending is the problem, and market discipline is the solution. In this standard view espoused by liberals as well as conservatives, societies need to implement the systematic *businessing* of their higher education systems.

This perp walk of a public service has become a familiar ritual over the past fifty years. But here the authorities have arrested the wrong suspect. Their causal claims are incorrect. As I will show, administrative bloat and excessive amenities are symptoms not of an out-of-control public mission but of the *suppression of the public mission* in favor of relentless market competition for star faculty, affluent students, eight-figure donations, and everything else that might contribute to a continuously improved place in global rankings. The fundamental driver of college costs is the market competition that typifies private industry. Turning universities into private businesses is not the cure for the college cost problem, but rather its cause.

In this book I identify the real culprit that has made public colleges worse and more expensive at the same time. The real culprit is the turning of higher education into a business. We could use the term *businessing,* but it is awkward and not specific enough—many business practices are useful to universities, like complex accounting or construction management. We could say *financialization.* This has been an important mechanism, but it is not the main one. It is not the process most directly tied to the major changes the public university has undergone. *Marketization* is another possibility, yet is also incomplete, and doesn't capture the forms of accounting and managerial control that create pseudomarkets in some parts of university life. We could also say *commercialization,* as this is a more familiar and natural term. Commercialization is more the effect than the cause of university changes, however, and is also too general for my purposes.

The geographer Ruth Wilson Gilmore suggested *externalization* to me as the term that expresses how the private sector treats universities. A business can treat a university like a commons that it can use for free or at a discount and thus externalize, say, research costs, onto the university budget, which for public universities largely comes from student tuition and state taxpayer funding. One example is the business getting free or nearly free ideas for products; another occurs when higher education is converted to job-oriented training that a business sector can use for little or no cost—these costs are a negative externality for the university. Gilmore is right that externalities can be created by both private and public entities, and that funding mechanisms involve a variety of negative externalities that universities are now obliged to fund. But I will emphasize the private–public contrast as the fundamental driver of the devolution that I am discussing here.

In short, the problem to be exposed is the *means* by which colleges and universities have been commercialized, and that is *privatization.* Specific effects that people bemoan, like administrative bloat, are the symptom, not the disease. Privatization creates hidden costs that are rarely mentioned.

As I'll explain, privatization has become the main process whereby business practices are brought in, not to support but to restructure teaching and research. Privatization is a mode of governance and a control mechanism. It is raising rather than lowering the cost of public higher education. It does this through particular practices I'll identify, and also through the negative interactions among the series of these practices that create a *devolutionary cycle.* This cycle has trapped public universities in unsustainable budgets that cost students more money every year. This cycle is the real answer to the question "Why does college cost so much?"[29] College does cost too much, but that is not because public universities have a cost disease. Public universities have a *privatization disease.* They have been paying the high price of privatization.

Privatization Defined

Dictionary definitions of privatization generally refer to the transfer of ownership from the state to private parties. The increasingly common assumption has been that the private sector is more efficient than the public sector, and will therefore provide the same or better service at a lower cost to the customer.[30] One famous case was the wholesale transfer of state-owned industrial companies into private hands in the 1990s in the former Soviet Union.[31] Another was the privatization of British railroads through the Railways Act of 1993.[32] A third was the UK prime minister David Cameron's plan to sell the government's portfolio of student loans to private investors, which would have involved taxpayer subsidies to support investor profits.[33]

In contrast, US public universities are not being sold to private investors. And yet funding, influence, and mission have gradually shifted toward private interests.

As I use the term in this book, *privatization* begins with the presence of private influence in public functions. In the privatization of public universities, property does not move from public to private hands, as it often has. Instead, control shifts from public officials to private interests. To complicate matters further, this shift of control is incomplete, and usually involves power sharing. Privatization enables market relations to eclipse collaboration for common benefit, but without replacing collaboration. The privatization of public universities is a complicated pastiche of mixed modes, which is why so many people can plausibly deny that it is happening. And yet privatization is the central technique through which the relationships people have with each other in complex organizations shift from collaborations to transactions, sometimes, but not necessarily, mediated through price mechanisms. These transactions are often competitive, which most officials assume to be a source of efficiency. Formal university structures persist. Privatization puts new wine in old bottles.

The most obvious example of privatization is charging tuition to cover educational costs that used to be paid by the state. Through the tuition payment, students come to pay for a good that the professor is to deliver. The good's quality is assured by the status of the student as a paying customer, since the direct personal cost incentivizes her to demand value for money, unlike the traditional public university student who gets the goods for free. Anglo-American culture has been trained to regard the maximization of pecuniary gain as a natural behavior that can regulate education more efficiently than professional standards of personal goals. This culture largely blinds us to the nonmarket and social potentials of any social practice, including higher education. Privatization does not eliminate these nonmarket and social benefits, but hides them. This is why I have had to describe its operation in the long form of this book's devolutionary cycle. Before we get started, I need to identify five dimensions of privatization.

The first dimension concerns the *cost* of public higher education, which shifts from society as a whole to students and their families, that is, from tax-based state funds and grants to tuition payments and loans. When a relationship-based system is converted to a market, resources move toward those willing and able to pay for them. This goes beyond a market setting of prices to a managerial power to allocate resources toward those who can pay more and away from those who can pay less. In practice, privatization usually increases the inequality of educational resources. The American Funding Model has been doing this brilliantly.

The second dimension consists of outsourcing activities to external agents such that *revenues* go to for-profit vendors rather than to the university. These have historically meant noneducational activities like food services, student health care, and specialized financial analysis. When overused, outsourcing costs the university money, creates dependency on outside entities, and sidelines the educational core.[34]

The third dimension of privatization is shifting governing control of public higher education from public funders, particularly state legislators as representatives of the citizenry, to private funders of specific activities. In universities this is generally informal and takes forms like wealthy philanthropists indirectly steering research toward their area of interest with a gift, or corporations that, over time, moves a department toward applied research or future products with a series of sponsorship agreements. The influence of outside sponsors has further impaired university autonomy since the then-president of the University of California, Clark Kerr, complained about the influence of government agencies in the early 1960s.[35] This influence has spread and intensified as public university finances have worsened. It now comes from a range of private entities as well.

The fourth dimension involves the *mission* of public higher education. Privatization advocates generally dismiss the public value of educational gains, and downplay or ignore the many ways universities develop individual *and* group capabilities with *non*market benefits for the individual and the wider society. One nonmarket value for individuals is the better health that correlates with higher levels of education. Better health has a social value in lower aggregate health care costs and greater collective happiness, optimism, and interest in tackling and solving complicated problems. We think happiness is nebulous and subjective, but its absence appears in phenomena like rising mortality rates among some parts of the US population.[36]

Another nonmarket value is the impact of college knowledge and cognitive skills on social problem solving. This is an intangible yet indispensable benefit that transforms the lives of college graduates and of their societies. The capacity to solve problems has a non-market existence that conventional cost-benefit analysis overlooks. Some scholars have tried to correct this blindness. A leading example, Walter W. McMahon's *Higher Learning, Greater Good* (2009), calculated that the private market benefits of higher educa-tion are considerably smaller than the nonmarket and social bene-fits.[37] But policymakers and university leaders ignore or downplay these nonmarket benefits, helping to create fake efficiencies, false economies, and educational decline.

A fifth aspect of privatizing the public mission involves redefining the educated person. The student, teacher, or researcher becomes less the self as traditionally seen by most of Western philosophy, especially Kant, as pursuing its own developmental ends for its own sake, and more an economic subject, sometimes called *Homoeco-nomicus*. This shift involves reducing the full range of personal goals to the economic. Most forms of individual progress are non-economic, to become happier, clearer about the meaning of one's own life, less emotionally confused, more creative, more coherently prepared for meaningful work. Privatized universities encourage graduates to think of their main purpose as the maximization of their own economic self-interest. The converting of public funding into higher tuition focuses the student on assuring her future income to cover higher costs and debt.

University privatization now also converts students and univer-sity staff into a newer type of *Homoeconomicus*, one that is con-cerned not simply with maximizing its economic returns but with maximizing itself as *human capital*. The political theorist Wendy Brown defines this type as a dominant political rationality within neoliberalism, one in which market relations shift from "exchange to competition." She argues that "all market actors are [now] rendered as little capitals (rather than as owners, workers, and consumers) competing with, rather than exchanging with each other. Human capital's constant and ubiquitous aim, whether one is studying, interning, working, planning retirement, or reinventing itself in a new life, is to entrepreneurialize its endeavors, appreciate its value, and increase its rating or ranking."[38] Education in general and higher education in particular are society's main sites for the systematic development of personal human capital. The privatization of public universities is inducing the majority of the US college population to define their education as human capital maximization, rather than as personal development or even as skill development for purposes of exchange.

Privatization thus affects five aspects of education: costs, revenues, governance, mission, and the subjectivity of those involved. When we avoid the reductionism that has typified the economic debate, we can see that privatization not only changes accounting and finance, but also shifts individual subjectivity and group interactions. It modifies the structure of feeling of a department, a major, a university, and even the entire sector.

We can think of the current situation as *half-way privatization*. States still own their universities' physical plants and contribute operating funds to campuses run by trustees that are generally appointed by the governor or legislature. And yet private interests have partially decoupled statutory authority from effective power and gained greater access to, or influence over, the university activities that might benefit them. Although the public continues core support of public universities through tax appropriations, attention and praise have shifted to the effects at the margins of private donors and sponsorships. The public is in general the dumb money that creates value only when *leveraged* by the entrepreneur.[39]

Crucially, the general condition of the private sponsor's involvement is that it receives a share of public subsidies. This rarely takes the form of transferring public assets into private hands, which is why the conventional understanding of privatization is too narrow. Instead, it involves private entities getting discounted use of faculty and graduate student expertise and labor and of research results, which may indirectly involve discounted use of publicly funded staff and facilities.

The upshot is that public colleges and universities are not being trimmed via short-term crises or even somewhat downsized with long-term austerity. Privatization is subjecting public universities to a permanent redesign. Officials are turning great universities into unfocused businesses that, among other things, subsidize multiple private parties whose condition of involvement is generally to take more than they give. I will show how privatization is helping to make core educational activities mediocre—and more expensive.

Using and Not Using the Term

But isn't it possible that privatization might actually improve public universities by making them more efficient and saving them money? Yes, of course it is. Many private contractors have expertise that the university does not, and they can often be hired at lower cost than that of hiring these skills permanently into the university. Every day, universities contract with private vendors to do a range of things that these complex institutions need to have done. This is often a win-win situation for the university and for the businesses that provide an effective service.

But a large number of private contracts do not add up to privatization as I am using the term here. Contracting as such does not subordinate the university to private sector principles and practices. Privatization, in contrast, does do this, in the five dimensions I've just outlined (costs, revenues, governance, mission, and subjectivity). Privatization eliminates nonmarket benefits from cost-benefit analysis, skews the calculations of efficiency, and warps the expenditures, revenues, and governance of these institutions.

In my experience, most public university officials dislike the word *privatization* and don't want to use it. In a conversation I had well into the financial crisis, a prominent academic administrator privately lamented the negative impact of "years of neoliberal economic policy" on the university's public mission, which he believed had shifted popular attitudes toward markets and away from public goods. And yet he has gone on record saying that his public university was more public than ever before, regardless of high tuition, many more non-resident students, an obsession with cultivating wealthy donors, and a new bias toward study programs that could generate profits. Many such officials regret the powerful conservative shift that began with Margaret Thatcher's and Ronald Reagan's rise to power in the late 1970s and early 1980s, and that continues to frame economic choices. Many regret the culture wars that trashed academic knowledge and that cast the private sector as the only efficient corrective. They may refer to research showing that much of the public doesn't know that the public services they do want are government services, symbolized by the apocryphal line, "keep your government hands off my Medicare."[40] Most academic managers are conversant with shorthand for the new status of universities in Western societies—the corporate university, the financialized university, the "triple helix" university, and the stakeholder university, among others.[41]

Most university administrators are also familiar with perspectives that overlap with mine, and in particular with the analysis of "academic capitalism" that was brought to prominence by Shelia Slaughter and Larry Leslie in their landmark 1997 book with that title.[42] Many recognize the rich social science literature about the commercialization or marketization of universities in the United States and around the world, much of which sees the university's embrace of market forces as the most important change in higher education since 1980. Many senior managers share the interest of scholars in understanding the global forces that have changed the university sector in recent decades.[43] This research convincingly shows that universities are more affected than ever before by market forces, special interests, economic goals, and the globalization of trade in goods and services. Recent research identifies universities as just one species in a rapidly growing ecosystem of regulators, consultants, vendors, think tanks, and commercial businesses that are defining higher education in their own business terms.[44]

But I part company with those managers and scholars who see privatization as inevitable, on the one hand, or beneficial, on the other. As much as I have learned from economists who analyze privatization trends, I disagree when they are either fatalistic or enthusiastic about the shifting of the funding burden from public to private sources.[45] Recent research has shown that economic policy reflects the preferences of economic elites rather than a sea change in popular opinion.[46] University leaders have no good reason to attribute the shift toward privatization to such a sea change.

The fatalism of policy economists and university managers has made privatization plausible to the wider public. This fatalism assumes, in effect, that society doesn't see the nonmarket value of higher education, so they can leave these values out of their efficiency equations. Such managers aren't only failing to put up the necessary political fight for the university's nonmarket public impact, which leaves propublic forces to their own devices; they are also reducing the overall value of their institutions by omitting the nonmarket portion of its "product." In doing this, they allow private market values to set up and dominate cost-benefit calculations, which understates nonmarket private and overall public benefits. This encourages the privatization they say they oppose.

In short, I use this book to show that the broad, long-term rise of academic capitalism is driven by privatization as it works its way through the public university system. Its most visible effect, coast to coast, has been students *paying more to get less*. But that is not where its effects end. Privatization is a policy choice that has been installed over many years and through countless specific choices by decision makers in business, government, and academia: it does not express a popular groundswell. It is for this reason reversible. And it must be reversed—for the sake of student learning, research support, university solvency, and the public good—all of which are being wrecked by the privatization cycle.

The Devolutionary Cycle

Our central mystery is why public universities don't succeed like they used to. The solution I'm going to make plausible is that they have declined not because we have protected them from private sector models, but because we have exposed them all too well. Public universities have eagerly adapted business methods, and this has cost them.

This solution begs a further question: Why didn't policymakers see the evidence of decline and trace it to public funding cuts and attendant reliance on private revenues like tuition? And further, why would university leaders buy into this consensus, or at least not be able to fight it? Why didn't the crisis of 2008 lead them to reckon with the American Funding Model's problems? The answers here, as we will see, involve a bipartisan consensus about privatization that was largely endorsed by university leaders.

A wide range of actors played interacting parts in creating conceptual gridlock about public colleges. Any one decision was likely to have made sense at the time: we do not need to posit the ill intentions or stupidity of major actors to find the sources of negative effects. But their interaction has caused great damage. Nearly all of these decisions were made in response to external conditions and were constrained by them, and yet those conditions were cocreated by university faculty and senior academic managers.

In driving the devolutionary cycle, privatization does not operate as a unified idea, script, or formula that produces the same outcome across the range of circumstances. It acts as a common sense that silently preselects and sorts data, identifies options that can be

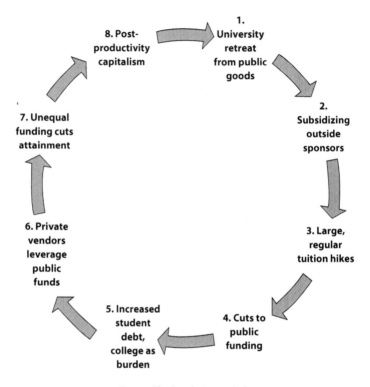

Figure 1. The Devolutionary Cycle

ignored without debate, and blocks the rethinking of core assumptions. Privatization has kept the reconstruction of the public sector from seeming necessary and possible to the decision makers in the best position to make that happen. It functions as an ideology in the broad sense, as the unconscious or unthought beliefs that frame and precondition policy choices. It is also an ideology in a sense made familiar by Marxist analysis, in which it repackages dominant economic agents as irresistible creators of the general good. Because of this reputation for social virtue, privatization has had an influence over public university operations that its internal inconsistencies and negative effects might otherwise deny.[1]

Though its every ensuing decision does not reinforce academic capitalism (which is itself not a unified thing), privatization has become the public university's political unconscious, in which non-economic educational means and ends lose their autonomy and become half-submerged in economic goals. Our challenge is to describe the workings of the nonhomogeneous cluster of activities called privatization behind the claims that it brings efficiency and progress to public universities. Our challenge is to do justice to the cycle's specific practices and effects without assuming tight causal coupling or getting lost in the details.

I've clarified the relationships among the various practices by simplifying them into a loop (figure 1), a *devolutionary cycle*, or a decline cycle (I use the terms interchangeably here).

This cycle structures the book. The cycle is not linear in the way that it is pictured here: Stage 6 affects Stage 2 as well as Stage 7, and so on. But each stage identifies key elements in a cycle that represents their dominant causal impacts. Let's get a feel for the cycle before we start our in-depth tour.[2]

Stage 1: University Retreat from the Public Good

American policymakers came to see primary and secondary education as a universal public benefit early in the twentieth century. Over the course of the century, more came to think the same way about two-year and four-year public colleges. To some extent they were influenced by labor, socialist, and civil rights movements, all of which stressed inclusivity as the hallmark of progress and of a good society. After World War II, they were influenced by economic arguments that emphasized the value of a highly skilled workforce to the creation of wealth and American global leadership. A midcentury consensus developed around the idea, rarely named as such, that primary, secondary, and now tertiary education were public goods, and, furthermore, that they were most efficiently funded with public monies. The low cost of public goods increased rather than limited their use, whether the good was a farm-to-market road network, free flu vaccination, primary school, or four-year university. This theory worked. For example, as the idea of free public high schools spread throughout the United States, Americans were increasingly likely to start and finish high school.[3]

The United States became a world leader in educational attainment in the nineteenth century, and implicit public good practice spread from high school through college. US society tacitly accepted the idea that "teaching is not a business."[4] Every child would receive an education of roughly equivalent quality to that of every other child on the basis of membership in the community (citizenship, residency, etc.) rather than on the basis of ability to pay. Racial and gender bias locked in skewed attainment throughout this period, but by the 1960s were (too slowly) also yielding to civil rights pressures. Civil rights and public good assumptions were symbiotic, to the extent that education was a public good the market transaction (educational service in exchange for private payment) was to be removed from the decision of whether a student would be admitted, advanced, and graduated. The effects were transformative: the largest expansion of high school and, later, of college credentials in the history of the world. Both levels of education were a major source of economic prosperity and democratization.

The implicit theory was that higher education had private *and* public benefits: there was a private market benefit to the graduate—higher lifetime earnings—*and also* private *nonmarket* and *social* benefits that helped the whole society, including nongraduates.[5] More college graduates meant a better society and economy and not just higher pay for individuals. Society was therefore justified in bearing the cost of public colleges itself. The presence of a private benefit did not undermine public funding, but supported it.

After 1980, several things happened at once. US economic dominance began to slip. The white middle classes responded to growing economic uncertainty by voting to cut their taxes, which began to weaken all public infrastructure. The youth population both grew and became increasingly multiracial, and, in many school systems, minority majority. Not coincidentally, the public good understanding of higher education came under systematic theoretical and political attack. Theory came from think-tank and academic economists and practice came from politicians, who began to ask public colleges to charge tuition and allowed them to raise it in step with their private counterparts. Of course they did not justify this change on openly racial grounds, by saying, for example, that free college was good for white people but that black and brown youth must pay. They narrowed the value of college to the individual's private investment in their future earnings while stigmatizing public benefits, particularly racial equality via race-conscious admissions, as attacks on private interests. By concealing the public value of continuously expanding college attainment, conservative intellectuals gave the public and its politicians an apparently objective reason to cut state support.

Stage 2: Subsidizing Outside Sponsors

Gradually and imperceptibly, public universities lost their obligation to organize themselves to maximize the university's social benefits. They stopped insisting on the general funding of each and every student's education. When a society values public goods, across-the-board quality in services like education, transportation, or health care is expected. But in the 1980s and 1990s, with the university's social value increasingly obscured, universities put more value on a narrow subset of activities, particularly those that seemed to offer financial return on investment.

State funding to universities had suffered its early shocks in the 1970s, and from that point on it was easier for universities to justify an emphasis on what were later called multiple revenue streams. One now-familiar example is the state university that admits more nonresident students who can pay up to triple the tuition paid by residents of the state. These higher tuition charges improve the university's net revenues, but the lower percentage of resident graduates reduces its public value to its state.

A similar shift took place in research. Implicit public good theory directed public universities to conduct public benefit research regardless of private returns to the university itself. The leading instance was military research during the Cold War. Universities lost money on this research—and lost money on all later research in science and technology. They had to subsidize indirect research costs with their own funds. But this was a public service that they were expected to perform, and public universities could afford to subsidize it with Cold War levels of state funding. As state funding declined, research costs became harder for universities to cover. An ever-increasing share of extramurally funded research had to be supplied by spending the institution's own funds.[6]

Although universities tried to keep their eye on research with the most academic merit, the financing of research became a silent burden, and interest naturally gravitated toward work that seemed to promise a financial return (via patents, industry partnerships, or spin-off companies). While the up-front gross revenues looked good, and were used to rank the university's research stature, the net revenues were usually negative. Many assumed that private firms would recognize the commercial value of university research and greatly increase their support for it, but in fact the share of academic research and development financed by business stayed flat.[7] Because American universities have always been intertwined with business, most citizens assumed that they made money on those businesses, from medical centers to Division 1 sports.[8] This was generally true only if the costs of internal subsidies were ignored.

Willful blindness about cross-subsidies directed policymaker attention in the wrong direction. Many traced the university's cost disease to high payroll and benefits, since universities are labor intensive and they seemed to outsiders not to care about reducing these costs. But universities had long been converting most of their instructional workforce from permanent to contingent positions. The effect was that real average faculty pay hadn't increased in decades. During the first extended period of steady tuition increases, 1971 to 1983, average faculty pay actually fell 14 percent.[9]

A key driver of tuition hikes is the large need for institutional funds created by high-status activities that lose money for the institution. The average sponsored research loss for universities is about twenty cents on the dollar, which universities must supply internally.[10] The figure for public research universities is twenty-four cents on the dollar, which is double the percentage outlay at private research universities.[11] Routine annual research losses can be as large as the worst multiyear state funding cuts. University of California officials, for example, have traced their tuition increases to the billion dollars the state cut from its budget during the post–2008 financial crisis.[12] But in just one of those years, UC lost $720 million on sponsored research.[13]

Sponsored research, fundraising, and partnerships also increase administrative growth, which occurs when complicated institutions get even more complicated by adding new activities and businesses in attempts to generate new funds. One study found that, between 1975 and 2011, the amount of full-time tenured and tenure-track faculty grew 23 percent, while the amount of full-time nonfaculty professionals grew 369 percent.[14] Many of these new administrative positions are expensive, since management that faces outward toward private sponsors tends to staff up to match their corporate counterparts and to compete with the private sector for managerial talent. University resources have shifted from educational to noneducational personnel to meet privatization goals, and this has driven up institutional costs in the process.

Thus, in a tragic irony, the shift from a public good to a private understanding of university teaching and research did not improve the universities' finances, but hurt them.

Stage 3: Large, Regular Tuition Hikes

As costs and loses increased, public universities joined their private counterparts in raising tuition two to four times faster than the overall inflation rate. Public university expenditures were already rising at well above the rate of consumer inflation before the state cuts began in earnest. During specific years of major public cuts, public universities often did hike fees to fill the new budget holes. The deeper question is why public colleges keep finding themselves in this position. A key answer is the costs of privatization that we saw in Stage 2: losses on supposedly self-supporting activities were steady or increasing.

Public universities began to judge their tuition by the level set by private universities, who have a sticker price of three to four times more than their public counterparts. Viewed from a public goods perspective, the lower tuition (about $9,000 on average for four-year publics in 2013) is an unmixed benefit for both the individual and society. Low prices can be maintained through a deliberative political process with public purposes in mind. As the assumptions behind privatization pushed the public goods view aside, the normal price became a market price defined by market leaders, elite private universities like Stanford and Princeton. Many public university officials now see low tuition as leaving money on the table. Privatization pushes costs up and encourages tuition increases to match it.

Tuition hikes are supposed to come *after* "cuts to public funding." The standard line today is that massive and regular state funding cuts have forced public universities to raise tuition far more than they would like. New tuition revenues replace lost public funding. So Stage 4, the public cuts, should in the standard view come before this one because they drive tuition hikes.

Public funding cuts have indeed done enormous damage to public university finances. But they are not the prior cause of tuition hikes. Tuition hikes preceded and were independent of the most serious cuts. Public colleges and universities raised tuition about 50 percent during the 1980s in constant dollars, and another 38 percent in the 1990s, when real state funding actually increased slightly.[15] By the time major state cuts had been routinized in the 2000s, public colleges had taught legislatures that they would use tuition increases to escape the worst effects of funding cuts. Politicians could use this lesson to justify state cuts, since tuition hikes would make up for them.

Stage 4: Cuts to Public Funding

This has become one of the most visible stages in the public university doom loop. All over the country, states have not only cut their funding to public colleges and universities, they have cut *this* funding more than funding to other parts of state government.[16] They cut these funds during economic downturns but did not restore them during upturns.

After 2008, states inflicted some of the largest cuts to their higher education systems in history. As of this writing, years later, all but a handful of states maintain college funding at a lower level than before the crisis began. Some of the largest funding deficits appear in large states (Florida, down 30 percent; Michigan, down 28 percent; New Jersey, down 24 percent; North Carolina, down 25 percent; Ohio, down 22 percent; Pennsylvania, down 31 percent; Texas, down 23 percent; Virginia, down 25 percent) and states with important knowledge sectors (Massachusetts, down 36 percent; Minnesota, down 24 percent; Oregon, down 38 percent; Washington, down 28 percent; Wisconsin, down 22 percent, with an additional cut of 5 percent in summer 2015). California, Illinois, and New York look relatively healthy by having kept their net cuts in the 10 to 20 percent range. States like Arizona (down 48 percent), South Carolina (down 42 percent), Idaho (down 37 percent), and Louisiana (down 43 percent) may have delayed the arrival of full-blown knowledge sectors for another generation.[17]

In some cases, states are not only *not* restoring college funding as their economies improve but are continuing to cut. Current cuts leaders include many of the previous champions listed above. Whatever lip service they pay to the problems of granting insufficient numbers of bachelor's degrees and the resulting skills gaps in their state's knowledge economy, many state politicians no longer believe that the quality of their public colleges depends on high levels of public funding. Many are convinced they can maintain quality while holding down tuition by forcing restructuring and the increased use of technology.

In reality, ongoing cuts are the bitter fruit of two university practices: a long-term willingness to raise tuition, which taught legislatures that universities could replace cuts with the user fee called tuition; and the failure to explain the irreplaceable role of public funding.

Stage 5: Increased Student Debt, College as Burden

Steady tuition hikes and public funding cuts shifted college costs onto students. The timing was terrible—public college tuition jumped at a time when most students and their families had been experiencing long-term wage stagnation—after the housing bubble's wealth effect had disappeared. Without having increasing incomes to cover increased tuition, students increased their borrowing at an extraordinary rate—by over 500 percent in the first decade of this century.[18] After the 2008 financial crisis, caused in part by housing debt, tuition hikes and public cuts drove a boom in student debt. This growth accelerated after 2008. Much of it can be explained by the increase in tuition itself, which is a central mode of privatization. Legislatures and universities acted as a team of rivals, to shift the funding of public colleges from the overall society to the private resources of the individual student. Another large piece of this debt growth can be traced to the halfway privatization of two related publicly supported sectors. The first is the federal student loan complex, which shifted relentlessly from grants, which students do not pay back, to loans, which they must pay back, and which also, until recently, moved from direct federal loans to private sector loans that were far more expensive to the student. The second sector is the public university financial aid system, which took advantage of the growing acceptance of private debt to build this debt into its funding packages. Politicians, bankers, *and* university officials have tacitly worked together to generate the student debt explosion. Each entity has profited from this increase in the private revenues students are required to pay. This debt is the single most obvious damage that university privatization has done to the public good.

Stage 6: Private Vendors Leverage Public Funds

The previous stages in the devolutionary cycle exert pressure on university financing and reputation. The search for new private sponsors (Stage 2) increases net losses as well as gross revenues and pulls staffing and funding away from the educational core. When universities hike tuition to cover their rising costs (Stage 3), they teach state legislatures that they can cut with impunity (Stage 4) and force students to increase debt (Stage 5).

Although universities have gone forth and multiplied every kind of private fund, their balance sheets don't look better than they did before. Many have made ends meet, as students were loading up on debt, by taking on institutional debt of their own. At public colleges, it rose 45 percent per student between 2003 and 2012.[19] As a result, public universities are more desperate than ever to display major cost savings and look to the services of private firms to do this.

The most prominent example of these, the scalable massive open online course (MOOC) companies of 2012–2013, claimed to have solved academia's cost disease by putting Silicon Valley information technology into the college classroom. Online technology was supposed to deliver more learning for less money. Unfortunately, administrators at dozens of universities signed partnership agreements with MOOC companies with little input from faculty, before either educational or financial claims had been proven. MOOCs flopped educationally, and their alleged cost savings remain entirely unproven. This episode showed that universities were so eager to push costs off their books that they were willing to put educational quality at risk, even as they were subsidizing private businesses. This search for vendor-based savings continues, further eroding investment—and confidence—in the public university's educational core.

Stage 7: Unequal Funding Cuts Attainment

The decline in funding for, and focus on, instruction has generated clear results. In 1980, the United States was a world leader in bachelor's degree attainment. Thirty-five years later, it has fallen to the middle of the pack. Attainment has increased steadily in one US income group—the richest 25 percent of students, who can often pay for college out of pocket and who disproportionately go to the richest schools. For the rest of the population, particularly the bottom half by income, attainment has stagnated throughout the privatization period.

Privatization was simultaneous with the stagnation of attainment, but was it privatization that caused stagnation? The answer is yes. Overall attainment rates are being held back by bad performance in lower-income groups, which is where privatization has its most negative impacts. It rations access to college by ability to pay and limits high expenditures to wealthy, selective colleges generally attended by affluent students. The great majority of lower-income students go to less selective colleges that spend a fraction per student of what selective colleges spend (both private and public). These poorer colleges have lower graduation rates because they have fewer resources to support student learning. Privatization discourages broad, general provision that supports correct funding of colleges with large numbers of students who cannot afford to cover most, or even some, of the cost of their education. Privatization mandates push funding toward those students who are already likely to succeed. Privatization defines as inefficient the egalitarian funding that supports educational attainment across the entire society. The sidelining of public good definitions of public universities leads to declining US educational performance.

Stage 8: Universities Build the Post–Middle Class

Across all debates about good and bad fields of study, political bias on campus, and the rest of it, public colleges had one universally understood benefit: a better *collective* economic future for all whose productivity they increased. During the 1945–1975 period, universities took for granted a social contract in which regular smart people would expend effort and forego full-time work income to attend college, thereby developing knowledge and know-how that increased their productivity. When they entered the workforce, their increased productivity would be recognized with rising wages.

This bargain held for thirty years, but in the mid-1970s began to fall apart. From that point on, most people who increased their productivity through education did *not* receive market payment for that increase. Income and wealth growth skewed toward upper brackets and associated with a narrower range of mostly technical postcollege vocations. More fundamentally, income and wealth became less associated with labor and its expertise and more with investment income and capital gains. The often-public colleges that furnished generic capabilities offered a good that, thanks to a range of policy changes, became economically less valuable than it had been in the past. On the other hand, the mostly private and highly selective colleges that furnished customized skills and elite social networks offered a good that retained its private value.

The larger economic trends were obviously outside the university's control. But the university always had the option of calling tirelessly for the social recognition of university-based forms of productivity that would have bolstered their graduates' claims to a growing wage. The university had the option of proclaiming the economic, political, and ethical value of equal development across racial and national differences in a fractured society embedded within vast migrational flows around the world. The university had the option of advancing cultural as much as technical knowledge and explaining its power to create collaborative subjectivities and democratic capabilities in the teeth of mounting inequality. Most of all, the university needed to explain the enormous, nonprivatizable, social value of these abilities in an economy that downgraded general productivity in favor of key specializations and social networks.

Unfortunately, those who spoke for the university as an institution did none of these things. They no longer explained that they offered general development to all, and that this now required replacing commodity skills with customized capabilities. The public university was decreasingly the institution that created a broad, multiracial middle class. It was increasingly the institution that helped divide the middle class between the high-end sectors that continued to thrive and the generic sectors that did not.

Though the larger trend was the result of public policy, public universities did not offer a countercyclical education; they generally accepted these changes that undermined their own economic value.

They marginalized faculty and students who advocated a socially egalitarian view of the knowledge economy. They struggled to deliver distinctive capabilities. They gave up on creating a knowledge society in which everyone would fully participate. And as they came to seem less on the side of general advancement and less able to deliver individualized education, they lost ground with ordinary citizens. The latter naturally wondered why they were offering public support for institutions that focused on private benefits for the shrinking percentage of applicants who managed to get in. The university's retreat from public benefits damaged their independence as institutions. It damaged their intellectual ability to see over the horizon to the next economy and society and not just adapt to the current one. The retreat damaged their financial solvency, as it undermined the case for public good provision on which public universities depended to offer high-quality education on a mass scale. The public university could not be heard arguing that it absolutely had to offer mass quality. What good were the educated masses in a tech age when all the valuable workers could fit onto the Google bus?

We have reached the last stage in the privatization cycle, but it continues to spin. The shrinking of public benefits (Stages 5–8) feeds back into the first stages of the loop, reducing public resources. The broken link between increases in productivity and wages erodes confidence in educational benefits, which suppresses interest in public provision. And on it goes, reinforcing the retreat from public goods and from public funding and encouraging more intense overtures to private interests, which in general leverage public universities rather than support them (Stages 1–4).

This devolution is rather depressing. My purpose is to show that it is completely unnecessary. I have written this book to help us understand what has happened to these vital social institutions, to restore hope and the desire to act on it. Each stage is imposed and unnecessary. Each stage consists of a major mistake. The Great Mistake that retreats from the public foundation of public universities, and thus from the democracy of intelligence, rests on the mechanics of an imposed resolution. I conclude the book by showing how each stage can be reversed.

There is plenty of bad news in these pages: the bad news is that these stages taken together have debilitated the educational quality and the finances of higher education. There is also good news: each stage can be undone, and the decline cycle can be reversed. The result of this reversal would be a higher education system focused on transformational learning for all and possessed of the public resources able to deliver this.

Part II: The Eight Stages of Decline

The University Retreat from Public Goods

It was my first Academic Council meeting, in the spring of 2005, and I thought the set-up was strange. The members of this council were the chairs of major committees and campus faculty senates for the University of California's systemwide Academic Senate. We were senior, tenured faculty members from every UC campus and discipline—medicine as well as sociology, computer engineering as well as dance. In effect, we represented over 9,000 tenure-track faculty at ten campuses. We faculty members sat around a large U-shaped table. At the top of the U, at a separate table, sat the university's three senior officers: the senior vice president for business and finance, the senior vice president for external relations, and the president of the university. The part that seemed strange was that the three officers gave prepared statements to the faculty. The faculty asked questions, but did not make prepared statements to the senior officers. The senate did not gather information from its thousands of members and present this data about issues on the far-flung campuses to the top executives, but instead received the executives' perspectives—which we generally did not transmit back to the campuses. There was no conversation about our common problems, no sustained discussion of a particular topic. Shared governance, I said to myself, looks a lot like an internal press conference.

A Privatization Compact

There was a second oddity that took me a number of meetings to notice. That was the specific official vision of the university's social role that was delivered by the senior vice president for external affairs—our top PR guy. He was both reserved and pleasant and spoke in a way that was simultaneously authoritative and serene. He had come up through the fund-raising and public relations side of the university system and had no research or teaching experience. This nonscholarly background posed no obstacle to his rise to the top of the national technology policy establishment: he would go on to preside over UC's National Laboratories before moving to a top post at the National Academy of Sciences. In 2005, he was stating month after month that the American population no longer believed that a college degree was a public good. The public, he stated, had decided it was a private good, and university funding was now going to reflect that reality.

The faculty senate members didn't pay much attention to this testimony. We heard the same thing every month, and we were all habituated to the idea that Californians, like other Americans, didn't want to pay taxes. The opposition to higher taxes was the VP's main evidence for this alleged epochal shift away from the public good notion of the university.

In retrospect, I realized that this was the most important single claim made in our senate meetings—society at large now saw the public university as a private good that moved students toward better future pay. Policymakers had been implementing private good practices in higher education for years, but these were specific changes that did not announce themselves as part of a transformation of public opinion.[1] Without quite realizing it, I was watching this idea cement itself as common sense in the Office of the President of my leading public university and then turn itself into a self-fulfilling prophecy. Once cemented, private good dogma allowed senior managers to see the fight for full restoration of public funding as futile, and excused their failure to give it the old college try.

The year 2004–2005 saw an epochal policy outcome of this managerial retreat from the public good framework. The heads of the University of California and the California State University signed a "Higher Education Compact" with Governor Arnold Schwarzenegger that committed them to raising tuition 7 to 10 percent per year from 2005–2006 through 2010–2011 in exchange for a state funding increase of 3 to 4 percent per year.[2] In addition to annual tuition hikes of twice the rate of state funding increases (and triple the rate of consumer inflation), the universities agreed to "continue to seek additional private sources and maximize other fund sources available to the University to support basic programs."[3] In exchange for minimal funding restoration in the wake of a 33 percent reduction in per-student funding in the previous three years, the universities agreed to privatize core revenue streams.[4]

This Higher Education Compact displayed the classic features of university privatization. First, neither party described it as "privatization" and rejected the word whenever it was applied. This prevented open, honest policy discussion of the effects of the new funding model. Second, the compact was focused on backfilling prior cuts in public funding, so it guaranteed increased costs to students without any guarantee of educational improvements. Next, it obligated the universities to leave no stone unturned and no suitor rejected in the tireless search for private donors and sponsorships. Further, it enforced austerity during growth years by refusing the restoration of cuts made in bad years. State funding was to remain below the growth of higher educational costs and below personal income growth in the state.

Ironically, privatization didn't actually offer basic revenue stability. On this point, my senate budget committee made sure senior managers and the UC Regents were aware of this problem in the 2005–2007 period by writing and presenting a report to the Board of Regents that described privatization as a recipe for long-term austerity.[5] Since the compact formally committed the two university systems to annual tuition increases, the state had built-in headroom to take money away again. When a crunch came, this is exactly what happened. Halfway through the compact's stated period, Governor Schwarzenegger used the financial crisis of 2008 to abrogate the compact and deliver a one-year cut to both university systems of 20 percent. The compact offered the universities no protection for public funding when they actually needed it. UC predictably imposed a one-year 32 percent tuition increase (for 2009–2010), and hiked tuition each year until a new governor, Jerry Brown, cut UC again and then imposed a tuition freeze. Ten years after the compact was signed, privatization had achieved one thing—doubling student tuition—without achieving any of its official goals: stabilizing revenues, ending institutional deficits, or improving educational quality.

Did Public Goods Become Unpopular?

The voting public didn't anticipate these changes. Nor did they go through a philosophical conversion to define higher education as a private good. Privatization came from senior politicians and their business allies, not from the general public. It came into being in California and elsewhere in the state through a process that has been confirmed by recent research in political science and told in a particularly lucid way in a book called *Winner-Take-All-Politics* (2010).

The authors, Paul Pierson and Jacob Hacker, noted a shift around 1980 in the "Republican 'brand' and self-image": "Ronald Reagan placed lower taxes at the heart of the GOP agenda and economic message, supplanting the emphasis on budget balance and incremental change of a previous Republican generation." The success of the Reagan tax cuts in 1981 came on the heels of the triumph of California's Proposition 13 in 1978. Advocates of cuts in taxes and public services managed to convince most of the media that these ˌreflected a nationwide populist revolt against government spending. In fact, Pierson and Hacker wrote, 1981 was the "legislative high-water mark of the Regan presidency."[6] Antitax advocates created an illusion of popularity not by winning hearts and minds but by capturing the political process.

Antitax activists had learned some lessons from their prior disappointments. Their fervent commitment to tax cuts was not new, but their strategy was. Put crudely, their efforts shifted from creating broad public support to recruiting and monitoring politicians. These groups came to play a key role in producing like-minded candidates—or at least candidates who faced strong incentives to behave as if they were like-minded—and in radicalizing tax politics. Two groups were at the heart of this effort: Grover Norquist's Americans for Tax Reform (ATR) and Stephen Moore's Club for Growth (CFG).[7]

Political organization was one mechanism for inventing the alleged popularity of the post–public good notion of policy. Another was the systematic concealment of the real impact of tax cuts, which was to redistribute wealth and income to the top of the economic food chain. In 2001, long after private good orthodoxy seemed fully entrenched, the manipulation of perception was still a full-time political job. I quote the authors at length because we still have such a poor general understanding of the artful construction of the supposed antigovernment majority:

> These tax cuts were popular in only the narrowest sense. Polls suggested that voters doubted that they would benefit personally, doubted tax cuts would have a positive effect on the economy, and overwhelmingly agreed that the tax cuts were unfairly distributed. If pollsters asked citizens to set tax cuts against other possible priorities, like spending on popular programs or deficit reduction, tax cuts typically finished last. Privately, the Bush administration acknowledged as much, with an internal Treasury Department memo warning bluntly, "the public prefers spending on things like health care and education over cutting taxes."
>
> Still, something beats nothing. If voters were asked, "Do you want a tax cut?" they were inclined to say yes. All this meant that the GOP needed to keep control of the conversation, making sure that tax cuts were not put in competition with other possible courses of action. Fortunately, the growing cohesiveness of the party in Congress, and the strong hand of its leaders, helped assure tight agenda control. The question would be kept simple: tax cuts, yes or no.[8]

Greatly exaggerating the democratic distribution of the tax cuts helped align the other major piece of political machinery: the cooperation of the Democratic Party. The Democrats played the role of the reliable enabler of a tax cut program they were happy to let the Republicans lead. As the Democrats "first accommodated and eventually embraced the winner-take-all economy," they could no longer make their traditional case for the relatively egalitarian economics that had helped created the postwar boom while supporting at least limited social justice.[9] Though Republicans led the policy-making,

> Democrats, by contrast, were more likely to be implicated in the part of winner-take-all politics that we have termed drift. As economic change undercut existing public policies designed to limit inequality and insecurity, Washington's dominant response was to do nothing. Since the Democratic Party was where we would expect some kind of response to come from, its failure to act is a central part of winner-take-all politics. . . . Drift allows policy change to occur silently, through what political scientists have termed "nondecisions"—that is, without visible legislative choices. Drift is far less likely to attract the notice of voters, who pay only sporadic attention to politics and have limited information about policy. For cross-pressured politicians in a tight spot between voters and interest groups, drift is often the easiest and safest solution.[10]

What I was hearing in my meetings in 2005 was academia's senior-manager justification of policy drift toward privatization. UC's top officials were also in a tight spot between the public educational mission and private interests. They got busy naturalizing their view that the university's future was with private interests. Drift was easier, and in the short run more lucrative, than battling a wealthy and successful illusion machine that was busily putting public goods at the disposition of private forces. There was no voter shift away from public goods, but there was an abandonment of the political fight for them by academic managers who followed the drift of their counterparts in the Democratic Party.

Debt without Work

Drift was a boon to the public university's administrative layers, but it was a disaster for many students, including the nontraditional students Democrats claimed to serve. After a few years of hearing that the era of the public good was over, I was interviewed for a film about declining public colleges by a woman I'll call Teresa. Teresa is a filmmaker from East LA who studied at the University of California at Berkeley. When the interview was over, I asked her how she got interested in declining public colleges.

"Well partly because going to UC Berkeley changed my life. I wanted to see if the cuts would keep it from having the same impact on others. And then there's my family. They tried for-profit colleges instead."

"Oh, interesting. What happened?," I asked.

"Well, there's my sister-in-law, Gail [not her real name]. She'd been a bookkeeper for a long time, and her company went out of business and her new office was run by some guy she didn't like. Gail had always wanted to teach kids anyway, but had her kids early and hadn't finished college."

"So she looked for teaching credential programs?"

"Yeah, she tried. She was pretty motivated. She might have to take a pay cut, she thought, but her kids were older now and she could have a career she wanted and make a bigger contribution to society. She talked about the bad things happening to the kids in her neighborhood who left school, or even to a lot of the ones who stayed in."

Teresa laughed at how the terrible economy made college degrees seem both indispensible and pointless. At least that's what I read into her laugh. "Anyway, she thought she could make a difference."

"So did she try Cal State LA or Fullerton, places like that?"

"Yes, but they wouldn't take her into the teaching program without a B.A. Getting her B.A. would mean re-enrolling in college. Gail didn't have the time or the money and didn't want to wait."

"Plus she was still working."

"She was, so she looked at other places to go. She heard about a private university that offered teaching credentials for nontraditional students. Once they got her name they didn't leave her alone. She liked the outreach materials, which talked about helping returning students from all walks of life. They promised her a teaching certificate without having to go back to college. Plus they said they had full financial aid packages adapted to any student's financial means."

"I think I know the rest of the story," I said.

"Well, it's not too unique. Gail's financial aid actually meant all loans. She got her teaching credential in less than two years while continuing to work, but left school nearly $50,000 in debt. Plus it was just in time for the crisis, when teachers were getting fired rather than hired. The other thing though, was that schools didn't think she had a 'real' teaching credential—it wasn't from a recognized university program, so no one really wanted her anyway."

"Great," I said to Teresa. "Did she find a job?"

"Not in teaching. She stayed at her bookkeeping job, but now she has a big monthly debt payment to add to her other bills, and really for nothing."

"She'll look for teaching jobs when the economy gets better though?

"She looks now and then," Teresa said. "But she can't risk quitting her job because of the loan payments, and the school would just fire her if the economy gets bad again."

The Opposite of Public Good

How typical is Gail's story? And how did the American higher education system generate this rotten result?

First, the story is quite typical, according to abundant data showing that for-profit colleges like the one Gail attended have the worst outcomes in the United States.[11] For starters, the industry fought a federal requirement to show that at least 35 percent of a college's graduates can make payments on their student loans.[12]

For-profits have the nation's highest dropout rates and the lowest graduation rates.[13] They charge high tuition and produce the country's highest levels of student debt.[14] When the Project on Student Debt analyzed federal data for the Class of 2012, they found that 88 percent of students at for-profit institutions had loans, and that their average total debt ($39,950) was 43 percent higher than that of graduates of not-for-profit public universities.[15] A US Senate committee investigation headed by Senator Tom Harkin got a similar result: it found that when students leave public community colleges to get two-year degrees at for-profits, the share with loans increases from 17 to 95 percent. For four-year students like Gail, the proportion with loans goes from 44 percent at publics to 93 percent at private for-profits. Students at for-profit schools—12 percent of all students—also account for nearly half of all student loan defaults.[16] These are undesirable and unsustainable debt loads for the economically vulnerable students that for-profits say they help.

Once for-profits have pocketed student financial-aid revenues, do they spend as much as possible on teaching, and spend more efficiently than the public sector? Clearly not. A federal government report found that they allocate one-third of the amount per student that their public counterparts spend.[17] Although the average annual cost of a two-year degree at a for-profit is $17,500, annual expenditure on instruction is $2,050.[18] This means that for-profits devote nearly 90 percent of their student revenues to "overhead"—which likely sets a new record for teaching inefficiency. In addition to the expenditures listed below, for-profits also spend lavishly on executive compensation, which has been so high as to place the sector under long-term federal investigation.[19]

For-profit advocates have sometimes tried to explain these institutions' poor performance by blaming their financially underprivileged and less-prepared students. The CEO of the Washington Post Co., which had been propped up by the profits of its commercial educational subsidiary, Kaplan, said at a 2011 stockholder's meeting, "If we are to be guided only by those factors—student graduation rates and how much debt they incur—we would probably close down all, or almost all, of the institutions of higher education—whomever they may be run by—that serve poor students."[20] This statement implied that for-profits put student learning first, and put their government loan receipts into instruction. The US Senate investigation found otherwise.

In fiscal year 2009, the education companies examined by the committee spent:

- $4.2 billion, or 22.7 percent of all revenue, on marketing, advertising, recruiting, and admissions staffing.

- $3.6 billion, or 19.4 percent of all revenue, on pre-tax profit.
- $3.2 billion, or 17.2 percent of all revenue, on instruction.

This means that the companies together devoted less to actual instruction costs (faculty and curriculum) than to marketing and recruiting or to profit.

The CEOs of for-profit education companies "took home, on average, $7.3 million in 2009."[21] In contrast, in the same year, the president of a public community college earned on average $165,000, or about 2 percent of his illustrious for-profit peer.[22]

The goal of for-profits is not educational value, but selling educational services for shareholder profit and executive wealth. In contrast, public colleges offer an educationally far more efficient model for providing access to degrees. Clearly we are not cutting public colleges because private sector higher education is cheaper and more efficient. And yet even as we starve public colleges, we continue to send public subsidies to the for-profits that engage in price gouging of both their students and the federal taxpayer.

The Department of Education has wanted to keep for-profits from getting nearly all of their money from government student-aid programs.[23] To this end, it has a rule that for-profits cannot receive more than 90 percent of their total revenue from federal student aid. After 2008, even as states made cuts to cope with revenue shortfalls, and the federal deficit grew, the number of for-profit colleges getting most of their revenue from the government continued to grow.[24] A *Barron's* investigative series concluded:

> Elevated sticker prices by the privates have given cover to for-profit schools, including University of Phoenix, owned by Apollo Group (APOL), Bridge-point Education (BPI), ITT Educational Services (ESI), Washington Post's (WPO) Kaplan University, and Career Education (CECO), a capacious umbrella under which to nestle. The schools live off of Pell grants, federally backed student loans, and, increasingly, the GI bill for veterans. Thus, they derive as much as 90% or more of their revenue from such government money, so they concentrate their recruiting efforts on the less affluent in order to qualify for such government largess.[25]

Similarly, the Senate committee that investigated for-profits con-cluded, "Some for-profit schools are efficient government subsidy collectors first and educational institutions second."[26] Higher educa-tion's private sector is less efficient than its public equivalent, and this low-efficiency private sector would not exist without taxpayer support.

For-profit colleges like Gail's exemplify the gap between what privatization says and what it does. The model says it serves students that the public sector won't serve, and uses market forces to lower costs. The model says that market forces assure educational quality: if the education is bad, the student-consumers will stop buying it. In contrast, the privatization model does require the company to put its revenues before educational or social benefits. It requires the com-pany to raise costs to students to maximize profits off the top, which also removes funds from education and directs them to investors, shareholders, and executives. The model does also require the for-profit sector to extract public subsidies—in this case, the public loans and loan guarantees that form up to 90 percent of for-profit revenues.

Specific policies based on long-term lobbying efforts made possible this combination of high private profits, low educational quality, and major public subsidies. The policies themselves rest on the weakness of the public good standard, while in turn reinforcing that weakness. Senator Tom Harkin had to be a lonely crusader to make any headway. He had to buck bipartisan common sense. Though the sector's enrollments declined after Harkin's investigation, some institutions are shrinking or shut, and though the sector's regulatory framework is improving, its business model and underlying princi-ples persist with little change.[27]

Public Good as American Mainstream

Populations around the world have at least a vague sense of the role of public goods in creating just and sustainable development. In the United States, African American and Native communities have advocated for public goods for centuries. The same is true for anar-chist and socialist traditions, for various forms of social democracy, and, more recently, for feminist and ethnic studies traditions, which frequently define progress and development as communal or collective processes that do not function when divided up into thousands, or millions, of self-regarding individual endeavors. The fact that a public goods vision crosses so many national, cultural, historical, and political boundaries suggests the power, adaptability, and range of the concept, even as the American Right seeks to stigmatize it by describing it as a radical Left ideology.

In fact, these social traditions *avoid* the common policy mistake of narrowing the meaning of public good to its standard definition in economics. I state as follows the social definition of a public good that I use in this book: a public good is a good whose benefit continues to increase as it approaches universal access. One example is public health. Your ability to avoid a lethal virus depends both on your own access to preventative measures *and* a similar access for as many other members of society as possible.

In contrast, economics defines a public good, to cite a particularly concise version, as "a good that is both non-excludable and non-rivalrous in that individuals cannot be effectively excluded from use and where use by one individual does not reduce availability to others."[28] A common example is unpolluted air. Your breathing of it neither prevents others from breathing it (non-excludable) nor makes clean air less available to others (non-rivalrous). Though this may sound like little more than a technical restatement of the common-sense definition of a generally accessible good, it profoundly distorts the social understanding of a public good.

In reality, most public goods are both excludable and rivalrous. Growing up in Los Angeles, my ability to enjoy somewhat less polluted air rested on my parents' ability to afford a house close to the Pacific Ocean's onshore airflow. My high school classmates who lived in Glendale were excluded from West Side air by the scarcity of both clean air and affordable housing. My parents' ownership of their West Side house meant that my friend Chuck's parents could not own it (private homes are rivalrous goods). The ownership of thousands of houses like my parents' drove prices beyond the means of most

Glendale residents (private homes are excludable goods). The L.A. housing market controlled access to the public good of relatively clean air. The common case is that the interaction of multiple goods in a capitalist economy makes most public goods excludable and/or rivalrous.

Higher education is a good example of a public good socially defined. The overall social benefit increases as more people have it. In addition, the value of each individual's education is not decreased when others are also educated (non-rivalrous). Getting educated, however, takes place in a rivalrous economy. One person's acceptance to Reed College does in fact prevent another from going to that college, and the same is true in the aggregate. People are routinely excluded from public higher education by having their applications rejected or being unable to pay the full costs, or for a combination of these and other reasons. Public higher education is a public good, and yet it has the features (rivalrous and excludable) of a private good. As a (quasi) private good, higher education is something that orthodox economics says is most efficiently managed by markets. This mistaken definition of public good puts higher education in a bind: its value increases as access becomes universal, and yet it is to be governed by markets that selectively allocate scarce resources.

I would call higher education a *dual good* or a *double good*. It has obvious private good features like increasing a graduate's future personal income, and it has an equally obvious public good status that means market governance will be inefficient. Any good that is subject to market pricing and private purchase is subject to scarcity, which reduces its general public impact. We don't care so much about the scarcity of private goods like Rolex watches or horseback riding lessons, which lack obvious social benefits. We always care about the scarcity of those public goods that come close to having the status of a human right, that seem essential to quality of individual life, or that are fundamental to increased social welfare.

Once we acknowledge that public goods are often rivalrous and excludable, even as their value increases as use approaches universality, we come to a further complication: neither their full value nor their full cost can be recovered by any individual or group funder. The individual who bought a car with a catalytic converter in 1975 did not *directly* reap the monetary value of that many hundreds of dollars invested. But she did reap health and other benefits *indirectly* through her investment in league with millions of other people. The failure of private good microeconomics to correctly estimate the value of public goods was noted in the mid-twentieth century. Neoclassical economists like Kenneth Arrow and Milton Friedman started to agree, in spite of divergent social philosophies, that converting certain goods, like information or education, into (rivalrous and excludable) commodities for private purchase would result in their underutilization.[29] So the final point here is that public goods depend on public funding to have their desired impact, which is broad, even universal availability.

Whatever the struggles of economists with this idea, education thinkers have long understood it. One example was Andrew D. White, who helped set up the land-grant mechanisms that enabled the founding of Cornell University and who later became its first president. In 1862 he wrote that the university he envisioned would be "a place where the most highly prized instruction may be afforded to *all—regardless* of sex or color." He added that to "admit women and colored persons into a pretty college would do good to the individuals concerned; but to admit them to a great university would be a blessing to the whole colored race and the whole female sex—for the weaker colleges would be finally compelled to adopt the system."[30] White wanted both inclusion of disfavored populations *and* the principle of inclusion spread throughout the higher education system. Universities had individual benefits, but these were paired with public benefits that increased as they approached universality—as is typical of our "dual good." These public benefits depended entirely on the kind of vast public provision that White was helping to organize.

Historians, cultural critics, literary scholars, writers, and many others readily grasp the claims about public goods made by a rich array of liberation and democratization theorists and activists. What is less well understood is the extent to which mainstream US economists have now verified the public benefits of public goods. As the financial crisis was becoming an economic crisis in 2008 and 2009, two books by prominent scholars made the case.

The better known of the two books was *The Race between Education and Technology* (2008), a title that would give a non-economist little idea that it analyzed two centuries of economic effects of public education in the United States. But Claudia Goldin and Lawrence F. Katz documented the US educational lead over the systems of all of its economic peers.[31] By 1950, the United States had almost double the secondary school attendance rate of Europe. Then, the American generation born in the 1930s acquired a similar advantage in college completion over other high-income countries.[32] That midcentury cohort had about double the bachelor's degree rates of England, Japan, and France (26.2 percent in the United States versus 16.1 percent, 13.7 percent, and 10.5 percent, respectively), and a 50 percent advantage over Germany and the Nordic countries. Only Canada and New Zealand were in the United States' league, and lower-income countries lagged dramatically.[33] During these growth years the American university became widely popular and attracted a previously unimaginable proportion of the population, particularly among World War II veterans and students with no college graduates in their family.

Goldin and Katz documented a systematic correlation between higher levels of education and higher levels of labor productivity. They estimated that "advances in education across the twentieth century account for almost 15 percent of the labor productivity change," and that the actual role of education "must have been considerably greater" than this (it is hard to account for a myriad of indirect effects).[34] International correlations between income and educational levels are also striking: over the course of the twentieth century, "almost all countries with incomes greater than the United States in a particular year have a secondary school enrollment rate that exceeds that attained in the United States for that year."[35]

Goldin and Katz confirm that the relevant phenomenon was "*mass higher education in the twentieth century*."[36] They identified its six core features:

(1) Public provision of education, thus the establishment of common schools; (2) numerous and small fiscally independent districts, thus decentralization and competition; (3) public funding of schools, thus a free education for all; (4) nonsectarian public schools, thus the separation between church and state in educational finance and control; (5) gender neutrality in access to public education, thus a public education regardless of sex; and (6) an open and forgiving system, thus mass education.[37]

Contrary to what you may have heard in contemporary political talk, the American mainstream came to associate progress with high-quality education that it grounded in (white) egalitarian access guaranteed by public provision. In previous research, I found these concepts bound together in nineteenth-century humanism and in twentieth-century middle-class democratic values, which presumed theories of social development focused on the welfare and virtues of the increasingly multiracial middle classes.[38] Regardless of whether one uses statistical or cultural analysis, what one finds in the United States was an educational boom aimed at mass effects through an egalitarian vision, rooted in public sector funding and organization.

Orthodox economic analysis confirms and deepens the findings of cultural study: the superiority of American educational attainment was grounded in its egalitarianism, which was rooted in public funding. Public funding was, in turn, made possible by an implicit, pervasive understanding of secondary and then tertiary education as a public good—one that could decline into rivalry and exclusion without public support.

Egalitarianism was never the overt goal of the decades of massive public college development: the United States was too devoutly individualistic, too antisocialist, and too unclear about the social foundations of general welfare. However, the postwar generations knew that inequality had repeatedly led to failure for American society. It was the hallmark of the brittle precursor Americas of the 1850s, 1890s, and 1920s, which had led to disaster and temporary decline. In contrast, both prosperity and democracy required broad intellectual equality. Obviously everyone did not have the same mental capabilities, but, implicitly, *everyone's* capabilities should be developed to the highest level. In *Unmaking the Public University*, I labeled this goal *mass quality* in higher education. In a democracy, it was not a luxury; it was an essential public good that, to offer its full social benefits, required public funding.

Demolishing Private Good Supremacism

A second major education economics book of 2008–2009 received far less press attention than it deserved. This was Walter W. McMahon's *Higher Learning, Greater Good: The Private and Social Benefits of Higher Education*, a comprehensive, meticulous study that generated quantitative metrics for the full spectrum of university benefits. McMahon's core claim appeared in the subtitle: higher education has social as well as private benefits, all of which must be taken into account. But this is the blandest way to put an analysis that stands the mainstream policy view of college's value on its head and undermines the standard case for privatization.

Although there is much drama these days about how students and their families need more data to make cost-benefit analyses of colleges' value, McMahon cites studies showing that the private benefits are the one thing that people *do* know.[39] On the other hand, students, parents, politicians, business leaders, lobbyists, and others know next to nothing about *nonmarket* private benefits and social benefits overall. A political and media discourse that focuses almost entirely on workforce readiness and future earnings has helped render every other benefit invisible. The list of known additional benefits is long: better health; increased longevity; better education and cognitive development for one's children; more happiness; better control over family size, consumption, and savings; better working conditions in higher skilled jobs; noncash amenities at better jobs; more access to lifetime learning; and reduced obsolescence of one's own human capital, among others.[40] And those are only the *private* nonmarket benefits.

McMahon described *five* additional modes through which universities add value to the society around them: *indirect* private market benefits; *nonmarket* private benefits, both direct and indirect; and social benefits, also both direct and indirect.[41] Unless all six types of benefits are assessed and added together, calculations of the value of college will be too small. They will also grossly overstate the share of total higher education benefits that are private market benefits.

Understanding true total benefits requires understanding several standard concepts that run afoul of the conservative policy framework, which overfocuses on the isolated, self-directed status of the economic individual. It also, inexplicably, considers collective life to be a fiction. The classic example is Margaret Thatcher's dictum, "There is no such thing as society."[42] In contrast, one necessary mainstream economic concept is the indirect effect, "defined as those that operate through some other variable. Examples . . . include the contribution of higher education graduates as they serve . . . on city councils, county boards," supply most of the donations to charitable boards, vote more frequently, supply the research and development departments of corporations, and so on.[43] Another key concept is *externalities*, which in this case are "benefits realized by others in the society that are not realized by those who do the investing in education, whether it be students, families, or researchers."[44] The qualities and efforts that a college graduate brings to the world at large are externalities in relation to her private market benefit of a salary that is higher than it would have been had she stopped her education in high school, or in relation to her *private* nonmarket benefit of being qualified to work for a knowledge-based company whose higher margins allow it to pay the higher rent in an urban area that makes her postwork errands more pleasant.

Externalities also work the other way around: the college graduate benefits from the education received by all the other people whose capabilities make her firm possible; researchers benefit from the educations of earlier scholars on whose work they build, and so on. These phenomena are well known in the social sciences, and are studied in various forms—the social "spillover" effects of intellectual property and the "regional advantage" from concentrations of highly qualified people whose educations were funded by multiple states and countries, and so forth. Total educational value is a function of direct, indirect, market, nonmarket, private, and social benefits, all overlapping and working together.

What happens when you put the "dark matter" of nonmarket, indirect, and social benefits back into the higher ed equation?[45] One thing that does *not* happen is that you go out on a progressive political or theory limb. In reality, you can stay on the solid ground of orthodox human capital theory as developed by Gary S. Becker and Robert E. Lucas because the initial Lucas production function already defined output as in part dependent on educational externalities.[46] The thing that does happen when you include dark matter, if you're a quantitative economist like McMahon, is that you estimate the monetary value of each mode of value and add them together.

The details of the calculations were elaborate and they required that he synthesize the research of scores of scholars according to detailed criteria that I pass over here. The results were surprising. McMahon estimated the private market benefits of a college degree to be $31,174 per annum in 2007 dollars. This is the type of value assigned to degrees as an estimate of "return on investment" for college attendance by services like Payscale or magazines like *Forbes* (McMahon's methods are more complete). However, the *non*market private benefits had a value of $38,080 per year, an amount actually greater than the private market value of having graduated from college.[47] When McMahon totaled the social benefits, direct and indirect, they came to $31,180, which is almost exactly as much as the private market benefits to the individual.[48]

In other words, the personal monetary benefit of a college degree is, in this calculation, only about one-third of the overall value. The dark matter that is excluded by conventional claims that college has become a private good is about two-thirds of the total value. Slicing the categories differently and using different methods of calculation, McMahon found that "total externalities come out to be 52% of the total benefits."[49] These overlap with private benefits, so that the graduate's personal return would be much lower were these externalities to be reduced through intensified efforts to privatize returns and/or to stop investing in any activities that seem to spill over to other individuals.

In sum, standard calculations of the value of college are completely wrong. They miss about two-thirds of its overall value. The standard calculations have given an undeserved and mistaken boost to the case for privatization by making private benefits seem a much larger share of the total than they actually are.

An example of the misvaluing that artificially bolsters the privatization case was a book by two business school administrators, *Public No More* (2013). The authors made the political assumption that the era of public funding was over forever. They paired this with a behavioral assumption that public subsidies create inefficiencies that high tuition will end. They also made the economic assumption that the value of a college education can be set by the price customers are willing to pay.[50] Even were we to agree with most economists and business professors that value and price are the same thing, the value that this student-customer would be pricing is the private market value that she expects to receive as a return on her personal investment. McMahon has shown that this is a fraction of a college degree's total value—again, about one-third of private plus public value, but also only about half of the market plus nonmarket value. So the tuition price a student is willing to pay will always be lower compared to the degree's full value, even if we assume (which I don't) that the tuition cost is a fairly accurate estimate of its monetary value to her. A privatized public university, if its necessary income is derived from the private market value for each graduate, will *always* be underfunded. This has been the case for much of the two or three decades when the "not as public as before" experiment has been run across the country. *Public No More*'s solutions would guarantee underfunding.

Privatization was a central issue in McMahon's analysis. He acknowledged that it is motivated by the view that "those who benefit should pay," and by a belief that it will increase efficiency.[51] But his book showed that nearly everyone is mistaken about who benefits— it's not just the individual graduate but also every member of society. His book also showed that nearly everyone is mistaken about what is real "efficiency" in education. It's not just internal efficiency, in the sense of holding down unit cost; it also means "external efficiency," which is "how well the outcomes relate to social benefits expected by society."[52] Maximizing efficiency therefore cannot consist of making everything as much of a private good or private transaction as possible. McMahon insisted that privatization can make the university *less* efficient. Privatization can express market failure, in which the lack of accurate information about the full benefits of the education leads to mispricing and, in the case of a good whose value is at least half social, the underproduction of college education.[53] In higher ed, privatization expresses the near-total ignorance of policy leaders about nonmarket and social benefits. Even where privatization expresses a desire for greater efficiency, it is a recipe for market failure.

McMahon calls for the half of college benefits that are social to be publicly funded.[54] As his book went to press, privatization was steadily moving public funding below that point.

Willful Blindness to the Public Good

As the costs of the 2008 financial crisis were spreading across society, many progressive education analysts tried to protect the public university sector from massive damage. They argued that these universities' missions depended on public funding, that short-term savings would produce long-term general damage, and that the low- and middle-income people losing income, homes, and jobs during the crisis couldn't take another massive shift of college costs from society's broad back onto their broken ones. They argued that policymakers should contain the damage within the banking system that had started the crisis, not transmit the losses to the public sector in the form of cuts and permanent austerity.

These progressives could have drawn on the books by mainstream economists that I have discussed. Goldin and Katz showed that all levels of education greatly improved economic health when constructed as a public good. McMahon showed that the public benefits of higher education were larger than the private benefits, and much larger than private market benefits. The Goldin and Katz book was widely reviewed, but generally to say that education had fallen behind technology and we now have a skills gap. Had Goldin and Katz been linked with McMahon, a solid two-part position could have been established that *only* strong public funding had historically created the general capabilities that enabled economic health (Goldin and Katz), because most educational benefits were nonmarket, indirect, and social, and thus escaped private market calculations (McMahon). Both works were at bottom antidualistic: McMahon broke private and public benefits apart to quantify them, but showed how interwoven they actually are, and Goldin and Katz showed that individual and social prosperity increase together with universal education. University presidents might have used public good arguments to build a coalition of progressive analysts, orthodox economists, worried scientists, fearful parents, and concerned students to confront politicians and businesspeople who were busily cutting the public sector to bail out banks.

Though public universities were powerful, exciting, enriching, noble, and economically defensible as public goods, their defenders mostly showed what good sports they were in taking their downsizing medicine.[55] Officials occasionally cited reports showing the university's multiplier effect on the local economy. But no administrative comment that I ever heard offered an explanation of the university as a public good in which the *entire* population participated. Nor did officials ever explain why public funding was specifically required to fulfill this public good. Instead, senior managers across the country narrowed their explanations of the university's function as a way for individuals to increase their salaries—one-third of a college education's total value—and as a service to business.

In overselling private goods and downplaying the public, what did university officials do to the status of their own universities? Three effects must be mentioned. We will meet each of these again later in our devolutionary cycle.

First, university managers tied their institutions to a *declining* private good: middle-class salaries. Most graduates struggled to find jobs, and businesses continued to deal with economic problems through outsourcing, layoffs, and short-term hiring strategies that college graduates could not transcend. Even after the financial crisis, public universities stayed hitched to a corporate economy that was no longer delivering for their graduates.

Second, university leaders undermined their ability to deliver the *emerging* private good, which was not standardized job preparation but creative capabilities on a mass scale. Social thinkers had for decades predicted the end of good jobs for well-trained rule followers. This was a major theme of Alvin Toffler's megahit *Future Shock* (1970), and of Michael J. Piore and Charles F. Sabel's *The Second Industrial Divide: Possibilities for Prosperity* (1984), which argued influentially that the firms best surviving new post-1970s conditions were relying not on mass production but on "flexible specialization," which in turn required widespread craft production skills. Such arguments appeared regularly—David Harvey explained (1989) that the "post Fordist" economy doomed traditional standardization; David M. Gordon showed that "corporate bloat" was hurting wages and productivity by overmanaging employee creativity (1996); and Giovanni Arrighi detailed (2007) how the "Western pathway" of capitalist development, which replaced human skill with energy-intensive technology, was in decline.[56] Wealthy private universities and liberal arts colleges got the message and proliferated seminars and, later, design labs to make learning both active and individualized. They increased their costs alarmingly, but they also increased the value of the human capital they produced.

Meanwhile, public universities were stuck defending their costs without stellar educational products to excuse them, and endured cuts in state appropriations while claiming to be successful cost cutters. They were not funding improvements in educational quality that responded to the need for higher-order, flexible, creative capabilities in their graduates. McMahon was indignant about this mistake. He called "cost disease" analysis a fallacy whenever it is applied to the activities in which the university specializes. Yes "the costs are higher," he noted, but so is the productivity that comes from them, "so if the outcomes were measured properly, the true unit costs are no higher and may in fact be lower."[57] But public universities did not measure even the private market outcomes properly, or really try to explain how knowledge workers needed more complex, more flexible, more diverse, more imaginative capabilities than ever before, and that this costs more money than ever to deliver. They did not tie budgets to quality of human capital, even in the narrow domain of private market goods, and let their rising costs remain an aggravating mystery of bloat and inefficiency.

Finally, in failing to make the strong case for their social, non-market, and indirect benefits, public university managers weakened their case for public funding. The key feature of public funding is not that it comes via taxes from society as a whole, though that is the sole workable source, but that it does not require privatizable returns as a justification. Instead, public funding evaluates itself through largely nonmarket and public benefits. Standard cost-benefit analysis fails to capture the bulk of the public university's value, which occurs through spillovers to present and future societies, and which permeates activities far from the university. The private good model sees the social, nonmarket, and indirect benefits of the university as losses rather than gains, since they are not recouped by the funder or traceable to specific expenditures. Only a public good case can make total university benefits visible and thus justify high levels of public investment. But this case has been all but non-existent.

In spite of these positions, public university leaders know perfectly well that their quality depends on public funding and public support. The downplaying of the public good is less ignorance than "willful blindness," which in the British legal tradition refers to a case where someone should know something that he claims not to know. An example is someone who, when caught carrying drugs for a third party, notes that he had not opened the suitcase and did not know what was in it. A policymaker may also "willfully shut his eyes to the fact" that he is making a policy decision whose short-term benefits will be outweighed by long-term loss. As the author of a book-length study of the subject has noted, willful blindness begins, not in conscious, deliberate choices to be blind, but in a skein of decisions that slowly but surely restrict our view. We don't sense our perspective closing in and most would prefer that it stay broad and rich. But our blindness grows out of the small, daily decisions that we make, which embed us more snugly inside our affirming thoughts and values. And what's most frightening about this process is that as we see less and less, we feel more comfort and greater certainty. We think we see more—even as the landscape shrinks.[58]

This is what has happened to key senior managers within public universities. Their claim that the voters now saw the university as a private good was willful blindness—a comforting excuse for the failure of the university to appeal to the public, a failure that stemmed from its refusal to deploy mainstream economic findings about education's large public benefits and say how they overshadowed individual and corporate gain. University leaders might have used McMahon's 52 percent figure for social benefits. They might have gone beyond it, by noting that even the private market benefits stemmed from public practices past and present. They could have argued that treating total benefits nondualistically, as an inextricable mixture of public and private, justify something closer to 100 percent public support.

Instead, officials stuck with the private individual and commercial benefits. They made privatization seem far more efficient than it actually was. They made the price of privatization invisible.

Subsidizing Outside Sponsors

With the public university's social benefits placed largely out of view, its private benefits could be freely exaggerated. This in turn allowed the pursuit of private returns to dominate efforts to help the university's finances. Few argued that expanding private revenue streams would help the university's educational or social mission directly, and yet nearly everyone assumed they would help the university indirectly by increasing its total net revenues. But this indirect benefit of privatization did not generally occur. Private revenues helped the specific programs they were targeted to help. As we will see, these revenues often cost the university money, generating net losses for the university's educational core.

A Struggle for Printer Paper

I'd started my blog, *Remaking the University*, as a diary that helped me sort out my ongoing thoughts about the topics of my book *Unmaking the Public University*, which had come out in 2008. As far as I could tell, nobody knew the blog existed, except when I'd commented on how rape charges brought against the Duke University lacrosse team had affected local faculty of color, and somebody's web bot prompted a slew of cranky comments from lacrosse-loving Blue Devils.

This anonymous phase didn't last too long. The blog took off during the big California funding cuts of 2009, when it became a kind of statewide faculty news service about the crisis. It developed a readership outside of California and covered national issues, as it continues to do. I began to get quite a bit of mail, some of it confidential disclosures of backstage problems at public university campuses across the country. I heard something about all problems great and small.

In the latter category, a senior scientist at one of the world's leading public research institutes wrote to me:

> Last week a reporter called my institute to talk to an expert for a story to go in the local paper and on a national website. Since I was the most relevant expert, the reporter was referred to me, and he left a message on my work phone. I tried calling back, but the system would not let me because it was a non-local number. I could have called long-distance by using an index number for a sponsored research project, but it didn't seem appropriate. So I used my personal cell phone. A couple months ago I used my personal cell phone to talk with a reporter from the NY Times, and my minutes inadvertently ran over the monthly allotment.
>
> I asked my chair if I could get an index number for long-distance calls talking with news media. After all, I was directly asked by the Institute to do this. But—as you may have guessed—there is no money for that sort of thing.

The institute in question is one of the most highly respected of its kind in the world. You'd assume it could cover long-distance phone calls from its operating budget. But since the financial crisis surfaced in 2008, I have gotten many e-mails like this. Many complain of a lack of everyday infrastructure that lowers their productivity and shifts responsibility for a range of small costs to their grants or their own funds. Teachers in underfunded urban schools have for years been buying books, pencils, chalk, and the like for their students when the school's budget runs out. Since 2008, some top researchers at the most prestigious public universities have faced a similar lack of equipment they consider part of core infrastructure. Their grants bring in so much money, so why can't their department or college pay for their long-distance calls?

Let's get a sense of the basics of public university budgeting by looking at a revenue chart for the College of Liberal Arts at the University of Minnesota (figure 2). This college has only one department, psychology, that functions as a laboratory science and that is

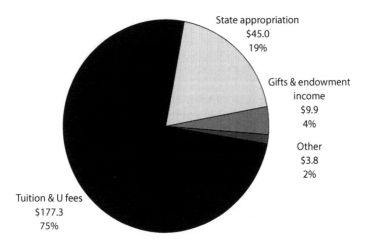

Figure 2. College of Liberal Arts revenue, FY 2013, University of Minnesota ($ millions). *Source:* Kelly O'Brien, "CLA Budget 1001—Part 1: Basic Revenue & Expense," College of Liberal Arts, University of Minnesota, January 23, 2013, accessed May 19, 2014, http://blog.lib.umn.edu/cla/enews/2013/01/cla-budget-1001—part-1-basic-revenue-expense.html.

therefore eligible for large-scale extramural grants.[1] The rest of the lineup consists of liberal arts disciplines in a broad sense: fine arts, literature, languages, music, philosophy, history, linguistics, cultural studies, area studies, ethnic studies, plus the mainline social sciences (anthropology, communications, economics, political science, sociology), and major vocational variants like the journalism school and a department of media and public relations. As is still typical for such colleges, its revenue is almost entirely dependent on state funds and student tuition, which together come to 94 percent of the total.

The gigantic tuition slice is also increasingly typical of state colleges after the 2008 cuts: three-quarters of the budget comes directly from student funds, and this share now overwhelms the contribution of the taxpayers, which has fallen to under a fifth of the total. The college can generate this amount of revenue from tuition because (in FY 2013) in-state Minnesota students paid gross tuition of $13,526.[2]

Gift income is small—4 percent. And even smaller is "other," whose identity we will discover shortly.

Bearing this in mind, here's another example of a research equipment problem, not from the University of Minnesota but from a major scientific research institute. Some of the terms here will be unfamiliar, but bear with me and I'll explain them below.

> This past week I needed some new printer paper and ink so I got some from the campus bookstore and charged it to a particular federal grant I've been working on a lot recently.
>
> A couple of days later my office manager informed me that the federal agency administering the grant has strict rules against buying office supplies and suggested that I charge them to a different grant administered by a more lenient agency. She explained that general office supplies are not permitted as direct charges on federal awards but instead are supposed to be treated as Facilities and Administration (F&A) costs. Even though indirect cost (IDC) recovery [ICR] is collected on my grants for the purpose of covering F&A costs, it turns out that there is no pool specifically set aside for providing office supplies to principal investigators (PIs). So I need to use whatever discretionary funds I can scrape together to provide my own office supplies in support of federally-funded research, not to mention teaching and service.
>
> How can I get those discretionary funds? About the only way I can do so is to work on a sponsored project during the academic year and pay part of my salary from a grant. My unit will then set aside what they would have paid as salary (but not benefits) into a discretionary funds account (after applying a 10% tax).

This scientist is describing a standard shell game. It doesn't rise to the level of the absurdities in *Catch-22*, but it structures the daily lives of research faculty. Lots of money gets deducted from an investigator's grant before she ever sees it—as "indirect cost recovery," which includes "facilities and administration" expenses (IDC and F&A). But the university, which retains the IDC and F&A, won't use it to pay for the researcher's routine background expenses. And the funder on the main grant won't let "direct cost" funds pay for it either.

That's the catch-22, and the manager encouraged the PI to bend the rules to raid an innocent separate grant, which is vulnerable because it has more flexible terms. (I am happy to note that six years after I got my first report of this issue, my source wrote to say that this specific problem has been resolved by creating a small pool of shared internal funds that is not subject to individual cost accounting.)[3]

This is a good time to recall two central premises of privatization. The first is that private sector management increases efficiency, and the second is that having more market activities increases net revenue. Sponsored research—research funded by off-campus parties—is Exhibit A for this argument. It is widely regarded as a profit center for the university. The more big-ticket scientific research you have, in this theory, the more money you make. Academic leaders often talk, especially to the public, as though increasing research activity is a way to increase their net cash flow. They try to hire scientists who will get more grants, which supposedly earn more money for the campus and put the operation firmly in the black. For a time, one public university, Texas A&M, rated all faculty members on the income they generated for their campus, counting extramural research grants as gross income.[4] But the idea that sponsored research makes profits for the university is a myth. This myth has confused everyone about the nature of the university's financial problems. And when used as a reason to privatize, the real economics of research discredits privatization rather than supports it.

Two Kinds of Research Costs

To see why I say that, let's look in more detail at what a federally funded scientist has to do to buy printer paper. The scientist applies for a federal research grant. The application process is already enormously time consuming, both for her, the lead writer of the very long, detailed application document, and for her institution, which provides accountants and other personnel to put the complex application together. One multiyear National Science Foundation application for which I served as a lead author ran to sixty single-spaced pages, the size of a novella you wouldn't want to read, and that was considered by our scientist partners to be compact. Even if the application is successful, as ours was, preparation costs cannot be deducted from the grant. All such applications must be supported by institutional funds.

If the grant comes through, the total amount of funding has two pieces. One covers "direct costs," which pays for the salaries of people working on that grant's specific research, as well as for its unique equipment, travel costs, and similar activities focused on that project. The second piece of the overall funding goes to covering "indirect costs" (IDC), which means supporting research infrastructure that many different grants use: accountants, compliance personnel, research building mortgage and maintenance, general utilities, or, to make a long story short, facilities and administration costs (F&A).

So our scientist buys her printer supplies and charges them as an expense on a research grant. This makes sense to her, since she is no doubt using the printer to produce data printouts from that research, drafts of conference papers reporting on that research, and research e-mails that need to be read carefully. And like all printers, it is used for other things as well—administrative memos, material from other grants, class materials for the scientist's graduate seminar, a newspaper article about a British comedian who called for social revolution on the BBC that the scientist reads at lunch, and so on. So the federal government has reason to consider printers to be part of F&A costs—as background infrastructure rather than dedicated equipment for a specific grant. These and similar rules are set forth in infamous Office of Management and Budget (OMB) Circular A-21. The staff member no doubt had this in mind when she told our scientist that the feds consider paper and cartridges to be shared infrastructure that should not come out of a grant's direct costs.

The catch is that no individual lab or scientist has direct access to IDC funds. That money is paid directly to the university, whose central administration retains it and distributes it as it deems necessary. It could give all of the IDC money to the lab that generated it, so they could buy paper and cartridges and telephone service and much more besides. Or it could give all of that funding to the scientist's department. But universities never do these things. They use IDC to cover a wide range of expenses incurred by the overall research enterprise—everything from office furniture to electricity to outside consultants making engineering drawings for a building remodel to paying the mortgage on new research buildings to the recruitment and retention of research faculty who need multimillion dollar labs.

The official explanation usually sounds like this, from the budget director for the University of Minnesota's College of Liberal Arts. Recall the pie chart above. "In FY 2012, the college brought in $3.7 million of ICR revenue on its $14.9 million of sponsored expenditures. A portion of these funds are utilized at the collegiate level to cover costs associated with maintaining necessary research infrastructure, and a portion of these funds are directed toward the relevant academic units to support the infrastructure needed at the department level."[5] We now know that the "other" source of revenue at the College of Liberal Arts consisted almost entirely of indirect cost recovery on research funds, largely from a handful of college departments led by psychology. We know that in the case of this college it comes to 2 percent of the total revenue stream. This is not a lot of money to maintain "necessary research infrastructure" at both the college and departmental level. Maintenance can include laboratory start-up costs for arriving scientists or lab upgrade offers to retain faculty being recruited to other universities. Minnesota's CLA does not contain the most expensive laboratories, which are found in fields like chemistry and materials science. That is lucky, because one hire and one retention case in those disciplines might have consumed all of the college's $3.7 million in ICR funds.

Each extramurally funded grant brings some amount of indirect cost funding, which is meant to pay for overhead in the broad sense. And its actual use is indeed broad. Administrations generally convert ICR into unrestricted funds—which is permitted by federal regulations—and then use them to cover the wide range of expenses I just noted.

There's a puzzle here, because these research activities bring in large amounts of money. Let's repeat our question: Given the tremendous sums involved, why can't the successful scientists who generate them assume that these revenues, much of which go directly to their university, are enough to cover printer paper, phone calls, and every other incidental expense?

Running Losses on Research

The explanation appears here and there in sentences scattered through official reports on the research enterprise. For example, the National Science Board (NSB) expressed concern about public university finances with a report titled *Diminishing Funding and Rising Expectations: Trends and Challenges for Public Research Universities* (2012).[6] It described revenue sources, which were divided into four roughly equal quarters: (1) net tuition from students; (2) state and local appropriations; (3) federal appropriations, particularly for research; and (4) auxiliary enterprises, particularly hospitals. On research funding, the report noted, "The Federal Government has been the primary source of funding for academic R&D for over half a century. Federal funding for S&E [Science and Engineering] R&D continued to increase at an average of 4.8 percent (constant 2005 dollars) from 2000 to 2009 when it provided 59 percent of academic spending on S&E R&D."[7]

This is a familiar kind of comment, in which the federal dollars seem to be flowing just fine. But in a break with tradition, it was followed a few pages later by a much more unusual passage.

> Institutional funds from universities and colleges comprise the second largest source of funding for academic R&D, accounting for $11.2 billion of the $54.9 billion of academic spending on S&E R&D in 2009. Since 1991, the overall share of university support for research has remained stable. However, the actual costs to institutions during this period have increased three-fold in current dollars, with compliance costs representing a large component. Institutional funds are directed toward institutionally financed research expenditures, including infrastructure, such as buildings, laboratories, field stations, facility renovation, cyberinfrastructure, and unrecovered indirect costs and federally mandated cost sharing.

Research universities make these investments to support current and future academic S&E R&D, both independently and in partnership with the Federal Government and others.

Institutional funds are partly used to cover unreimbursed costs of federally funded research resulting from Federal limitations on reimbursement for the indirect costs of research. Federal funding for academic research includes both direct and indirect facilities and administrative (F&A) costs. The F&A rate is used to reimburse universities for expenses associated with funded research, but that are not easily identified with a specific project. According to the NCSES Higher Education R&D (HERD) survey, unrecovered indirect costs of academic R&D reached $4.7 billion in FY 2010.[8]

The rare public admission is this: between 9 and 20 percent of the cost of *externally* funded research is supported *internally* by universities themselves. (I will defend the higher number later.)

This subsidy has grown over the years. It was closer to 10 percent in the 1960s and 1970s, but the university's share of research costs gradually doubled and has been fairly constant at around 20 percent since the early 1990s.[9] The report notes that the actual dollar amounts coming from universities have tripled during this time. The reason, rarely discussed in public, is that universities are required to fund a full range of advanced infrastructure and support activities, outlined above, for which outside sponsors will not pay.

Prior to the financial crisis and the new round of state funding cuts, federal agencies had taken a hard line against full reimbursement of indirect costs. For example, the Government Accountability Office (GAO) reviewed the Department of Defense's (DOD) reimbursement policies in 2007. It found that DOD reimbursed IDC at very close to the rate requested by the university in question; it had a much better record on this point than the National Institutes of Health. The GAO nonetheless recommended that the 26 percent reimbursement cap on facilities and administration costs be revisited and perhaps increased. But this recommendation was rejected by the Office of Management and Budget (OMB), on the ground that "the administrative cap has helped the schools to be more efficient with their administrative effort and more disciplined with spending in administrative costs."[10] The OMB ignored the implication that the main effect of this kind of "discipline" was to force universities to subsidize federally funded research.

There is huge variation around this average internal subsidy for research.[11] It averaged 19 percent in FY 2011 and was a bit over 22 percent in FY 2013, suggesting that the internal subsidies continue to get worse.[12] As this book was entering production, the NSF released figures for FY 2014 and reported, "The universities' own funds used for R&D (institution funds) rose 5.3% to $15.8 billion in FY 2014 and have been the fastest-growing source for the past 5 years. Institution funds now constitute 23.5% of total R&D, rising from 22.4% last year and from 19.5% in FY 2010."[13]

Johns Hopkins University has the largest annual R&D expenditures of any university in the United States—about $2.17 billion. In 2013, it spent $88.3 million of internal funds to support this (up from $78 million in 2011), or 4 percent of the total (up from 3.6 percent in 2011). The number two university in terms of total R&D expenditure is the University of Michigan at Ann Arbor, at about $1.4 billion. But it spent over $445 million of its own funds to support this research (up from $363 million in 2011 on a minor increase in total funds), or a remarkable 32.4 percent of the total (up from 28 percent in 2011). The University of Washington at Seattle, in the number three position, apparently spent 6.5 percent of its total via internal funds (up from 5 percent two years before). Number four, the University of Wisconsin-Madison, had a very high 35.4 percent of its expenditures come from internal sources in 2013, which is nearly double the proportion of internal subsidies in 2011 (19.85 percent). For number seven, Harvard, 26 percent of its research expenditures were funded internally. Similar variations appear in the University of California system, with number 5, UC San Diego, contributing 14.3 percent of the total from internal funds (up from 9.8 percent in 2011); UC Berkeley spending 21 percent (up from 17.2 percent in 2011); UCLA at 18.2 percent (up from 16.3 percent in 2011); UC Santa Barbara at

15.6 percent (down from 16.3 percent in 2011); and so on. The University of Chicago (number fifty-four in volume) spent 9.5 percent of its total through internal funds. On the other hand, Michigan Tech paid for 46.3 percent of its total R&D out of its own coffers. (This small increase from the already very high 44.5 percentage of 2011 saw it improve its ranking by just seven places, to 168.)[14]

In mid-2014 the Council on Governmental Relations (COGR), a leading research university lobby, produced a good primer on the differences between private and public university funding and then got into some of the gory details of research costs. The report confirmed that universities' internal funds are the fastest-growing source of research funding and that the universities' share is large. The total university contribution has grown again since the NSB and NRC reports, from $11.2 billion to $13.7 billion per year.[15]

Over the period from 1976 to 2012, the share of R&D expenditures assumed by colleges and universities had grown faster than any other category of support. University spending nearly doubled to 21.6 percent of all R&D expenditures in 2012 from 12.0 percent of all R&D expenditures in 1976. (A recent study of research losses in England generated a similar figure—losses of 24.5 pence on the pound.)[16]

Such data never appear in the publicity that universities understandably lavish on their faculty for their success in winning sponsored research contracts. Faculty can easily work seventy hours a week or more teaching, researching, administering that research, and looking for money so they can continue their research. The funding rates for many federal agencies are under 20 percent, and some are closer to 10 percent, so an award is the result of a highly competitive and sometimes exhausting effort. The effort of many unsung staff members and graduate students is also required. The result is often the trumpeting of an aggregate figure of all campus grants—"UCLA researchers bring in $966 million in contracts and grants awards," read one typical headline.[17] Success is typically measured in gross income. This is America, after all, where the dollar is king.

But there is much more to the story. The year in which that UCLA headline appeared was a crisis year for the University of California and for many other public universities. Their public funding was being cut, and major tuition increases were causing student hardship and political backlash. UC undertook an elaborate self-study under the auspices of the "UC Commission on the Future." One of its working groups, on "Research Strategy," uncovered news that led to a very different headline—not "UCLA Researchers Bring in $966 Million," but "UC: Millions Lost in Research Costs from Grants."[18] How do we explain the contradiction between these headlines?

The answer is simple. The two headlines are reporting two different accounting categories. The first counts *gross* revenues. The second refers to *net* revenues—what is left over after expenses are paid: "In recent years, the University has received over $3.5 billion per year in extramurally-sponsored research grants, of which over $780 million per year is designated for indirect costs such as facilities support and research administration."[19] So far so good. This was an overall research revenue figure of which UC faculty and staff could be proud. The report continued: "But the actual indirect costs of extramurally-funded research are estimated to be $1.5 billion. It is therefore critical that the University increase its rate of indirect cost recovery, since it can no longer afford to substantially underwrite the infrastructure costs of conducting research."[20] That was an understatement. The report found that UC's *gross* research income of $3.5 billion translated into a *net* research loss of $720 million. The University of California, arguably the most successful public research university system in the world, in that year *lost* 20.6 cents on every dollar of extramural research.

The UC Commission on the Future study produced a brief flurry of calls to reduce these losses. On most campuses, the losses instead got worse. This was typical of the national pattern. An essential part of this pattern was the difference between public and private university shortfalls, which was pointed out in a study in *Nature*.[21] The article is accompanied with the graphic shown in figure 3.

FOOTING THE US RESEARCH BILL

With state support falling below 10% of total research funding, public universities are increasingly relying on institutional funds, and student tuition fees in particular. The effect is less pronounced at private universities, which rely more on federal research dollars and can have large endowments.

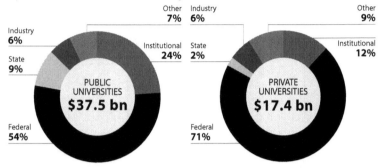

Research and development funding source as a percentage of total (2009)

Figure 3. Comparison of internal university subsidies, private versus public. *Source:* Eugenie Samuel Reich, "Thrift in Store for US Research," *Nature* 476 (August 25, 2011): 38.

The institutional bands in the figure signal the problem. In that year, private universities paid 12 percent of their research costs out of their own funds. Public universities conducted twice the quantity of R&D for the country—and spent twice as much per dollar of research of their own money. It is important to recognize that not all internal research spending at all universities exists to cover extramural research losses—I will return to this point. But the strain on internal resources has been enormous. Since public research universities have far smaller average endowments as a group than do their private counterparts, we are looking at a structural irrationality in which the larger and poorer group of research universities—the publics— shoulders twice the subsidy for research in percentage terms. State funds shrank again after this chart was created, which further increased public university research losses.

Meanwhile, the financial crisis was pressing universities to stem their very real research losses. The largest of research universities, the University of California system, resolved in 2010 to increase its

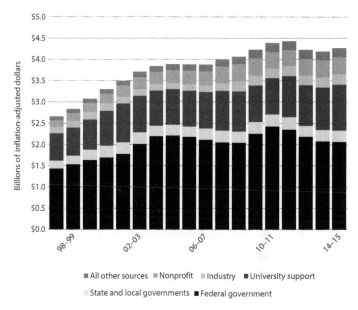

Figure 4. Bar chart for 2016 accountability indicator 9.1.1, research expenditures by source. *Source:* University of California Office of the President. Used with permission.

recovery of indirect costs by $300 million a year. The results appeared in the University's Accountability Report (figure 4).

The third band from the bottom of the bar in the figure represents institutional funds. In FY 2010, 25.4 percent of the University of California's research funding came from university funds, a figure already over the national average. Initial figures for FY 2013 showed that the UC share had risen to 29.3 percent.[22] From a high in FY 2011, federal and state research income declined in the three subsequent years. Industry and nonprofit funds stayed largely flat. The university's internal support increased 19 percent, and then appears to have increased again in FY2014 (figure 4).[23] This is a high rate of internal subsidy for extramural research. It diverts funds from instruction and from research that has few outside sponsors, particularly in the arts, humanities, and qualitative social sciences (which I call SASH for short, slightly rearranging the letters). Although industry funding for academic research is lionized in press releases, the university in any given year spends four times the industry share of its own money supporting research, with no credit given to the students and state taxpayers who provide it.

I am reluctant to get into the weeds on research budget detail more than I already have, but one university budget veteran who read a draft of this chapter thought this was a mistake. In a letter to me, she wrote,

> I think you give short shrift to the very real overhead that any campus must pay: utilities, a building's financing, insurance (especially for wet labs), and huge sunken costs called start-up packages to recruit new faculty members. Sometimes the full costs of a hire is tens of millions, and if the PI [principal investigator] leaves and takes post-docs and lab grants elsewhere, the campus is sitting on a big debt. My vice-president for research once told me that his experience in two states is that on average it takes 22 years for a hiring institution to completely amortize STEM startup packages. Let's say he exaggerated and it's only 11 years. Still, that's a real issue for a research campus.
>
> As for ICR, all faculty want to see the money come to them, and so the very real ICR is multiply oversubscribed. The culprit nobody talks about here is the industry that farms out R&D to research institutions for pennies on the dollar. If our industry partners actually paid for the training going on in labs, for all the expenses of running fume hoods and transgenic mice and supercomputers, we'd have a fair partnership.[24]

Research projects minimize costs to themselves by maximizing costs to the university, and the two are in a tension. I offer this kind of localized commentary because we lack systematic public data on the subject.

What we do know: it is simply not possible to say "why college costs so much" without understanding that one of two indispensible core activities of the university, research, *loses* large sums of money for the university that conducts it. In 2012–2013, the University of California spent $928 million in "university support" for research.

Had it been suddenly able to avoid these losses, UC could have replaced the full amount that the state had removed from UC's annual budget after 2008.[25]

It's worth noting that corporations would generally not tolerate this kind of loss-making arrangement. But universities do, in exchange for other things—scientific networks, professional partnerships, industry goodwill, and various kinds of sponsorships and gifts. Universities do get real benefits in this way. But they do not appear to outweigh the institutional costs, even when we count intangible goods, and in any case they don't pay SASH or STEM research bills. This disparity between corporations running research in the black and universities running it in the red is a logical consequence of half-way privatization, which allows private interests to externalize costs to the university and gain access to public resources below cost, which they can then use to help generate their future private returns.[26]

Who Covers Research Losses?

Who does provide the university's "institutional funds" that it needs to support research? (By support research, I mean cover the unsponsored and unfunded indirect costs of sponsored research: direct costs are generally funded by the sponsor.) Private universities have endowment income and large fund-raising programs to cover some of it, and high tuition for most of the rest. Public colleges and universities have two main sources of institutional funds: state appropriations and student tuition.[27] For public universities, nearly all educational activities other than direct research costs are funded by a combination of students, who pay through tuition, and state taxpayers, who pay through fees. Research universities generate enormous revenues through their medical centers and other auxiliary enterprises. Those are non-educational expenses, and are not part of the core budget.[28]

At public universities, the portion of core funds that is sometimes called "expenditures for education" includes the "institutional funds" that support research. These come almost entirely from students and the public. The shares can be seen in an official UC graphic (figure 5). Ignoring the changing relative share of general funds and tuition,

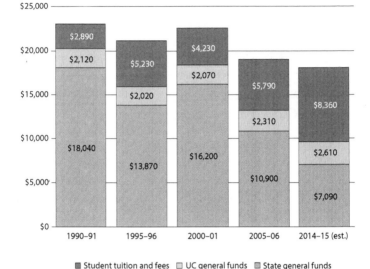

Figure 5. Per-student average expenditures for education, universitywide, 1990–1991 to 2014–2015, selected years. *Source:* University of California, *Annual Accountability Report 2015,* Indicator 12.5.1, accessed March 18, 2016, http://accountability.univer sityofcalifornia.edu/2015/documents/pdfs/Acct%20Report%202015%20Web.pdf.

which I will discuss later, we can see that about 90 percent of core operational funding for this relatively affluent public university comes from those two main sources, student tuition and state funds.[29] Since some UC General Funds come from nonresident tuition and application fees, the student share is higher than it appears. Although there are exceptions, I retain the precept that campus educational activities (again, excluding the direct costs of sponsored research) are funded by the three sources listed above, with the vast majority coming from tax funding and student tuition.[30]

What this means is that university research is subsidized by state taxpayers and by undergraduate students. Does student tuition subsidize research? The answer is yes, it does.

The problem with this situation is not that these subsidies, which are called *cross-subsidies*, are inherently wrong. To the contrary, these subsidies are commonplace and justified by the public benefits of research results. They are also justified by the private benefit to the student of attending research-intensive universities. At these institutions, students work with faculty who are at the forefront of their part of the knowledge world. They have access to the research process, which helps them to develop creative capabilities sooner rather than later. One can argue that the public *and* the student receive more benefit from an education in which instructional funding subsidizes research in the same environment. Though the costs can and should be separated so we can see who is paying for what and how much, the cross-subsidy is completely legitimate in principle—as long as it is acknowledged *and* shared in an equitable way.

Unfortunately, these things don't happen. Cross-subsidies are opaque to the payers, not openly negotiated, and damage some fields to help others. These problems have become more acute as tuition has increased. Now that students pay half or more of core budgets (Stage 3), and assume that their tuition is supporting their education, meaning that a student majoring in, say, theater would expect her tuition to support intensive teaching in history, theory, and studio training of the kind she needs, the redirection of some portion of theater's budget to an unrelated field like chemistry raises new ethical and efficiency issues. One can see why officials would try to avoid these awkward discussions, but the avoidance makes the problems worse.

Official university statements often hide the truth by claiming that big STEM departments subsidize their poor relations in other divisions, usually the humanities and social sciences. Some typical publicity reads as follows:

> MYTH: *UC [the University of California] doesn't really have a budget problem because it has so many different fund sources it can dip into.*
> FACT: UC's budget is made up of many different fund sources, but most of them are restricted to specific uses and cannot be applied to other purposes. A federal grant for laser research can't be used to fund a deficit in the English Department. A payment for a surgery in a UC hospital can't be redirected to fund graduate students.[31]

This language suggests that laser research runs a surplus while English loses money, so unprofitable English might be tempted to go to the laser lab for some surplus cash. In fact, laser research will, like other sponsored research, lose an average of twenty cents on the dollar. It does not run a profit that is available to give to English.

What about English department research—doesn't it lose twenty cents on the dollar as well? Let's compare the dollar amounts (figure 6). The bottom chart in this figure is a blowup of the lower two-fifths of the bottom one-fifth of the first chart because the research expenditures for social science and arts and humanities research are so tiny. In addition, comparing arts and humanities research to the social sciences renders the former nearly invisible: arts and humanities research is even cheaper than social sciences research by close to an order of magnitude. And the social sciences costs are already minute in relation to the STEM fields.

Like other arts and humanities departments, English has no sponsored research losses to subsidize because it has in effect no sponsored research. When it does have sponsored research, it has almost non-existent equipment needs. Like other arts and humanities departments, it asks for, and receives, close to zero infrastructural support. English does not, contrary to the official statement, have a research deficit that a science lab might be called on to fund.

The big research fields are not only unable (and unwilling) to subsidize English and sociology: they are generally unable to support their own research losses with instructional profits. For example, Arizona State University, a booming public research university, spent $405 million on research in FY 2013, which put it in fifty-third place nationally. Of that total, about $201 million came from the federal government and almost $150 million came from its own institutional funds.[32] This means that ASU paid for 37 percent of its overall research expenditures out of its own pocket. That is a very high proportion. How does ASU come up with $150 million of its own money for research?

The traditional answer is to assume that everybody incurs these costs and everybody pays taxes of various kinds to cover them. In my

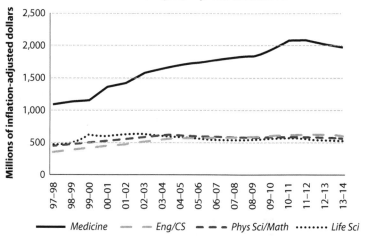

Medicine, Eng/CS, Phys Sci/Math, Life Sci

— *Medicine* ~~~ *Eng/CS* – – *Phys Sci/Math* ••••••• *Life Sci*

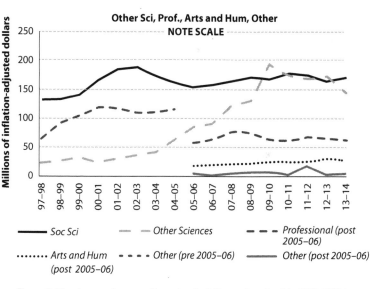

Other Sci, Prof., Arts and Hum, Other
NOTE SCALE

— *Soc Sci* ~~~ *Other Sciences* – – *Professional (post 2005–06)*

••••••• *Arts and Hum (post 2005–06)* – • – • *Other (pre 2005–06)* ~~~ *Other (post 2005–06)*

Figure 6. Direct research expenditures by discipline, universitywide, 1997–1998 to 2013–2014. *Source:* University of California, *Annual Accountability Report 2015,* Indicator 9.3.2, accessed March 18, 2016, http://accountability.universityofcalifornia.edu/2015 /documents/pdfs/Acct%20Report%202015%20Web.pdf.

conversations with STEM faculty over the years, I've found that they feel that they are paying for everyone else. This view reflects a reality of their research lives: their university removes the money the funder designated for indirect costs—typically around a third of the total award—and yet, as we saw with our opening example, they can't buy printer paper with it. From the investigator's point of view, "their" money is taxed away by the university's central administration and never comes back.

But this perception disguises quite a different reality. The reality is that all the money that the administration took out of the grant for indirect costs did in fact go to cover those costs—and it still wasn't enough. As it happens, we have ASU administrative data showing the real pattern (figure 7). Starting on the left-hand side of the figure, we first see engineering, and then the natural sciences and life sciences. These are disciplines whose faculty overwork themselves to get large extramural grants, and their enormous effort and outcomes should be honored and funded. But we are discussing cost, not value, and their extramural grants do not cover their full costs. ASU's three big divisions ran a net loss of around $40 million for their campus in FY 2010. That loss had to be covered by some other unit.

It's possible that ASU has auxiliary enterprises that contribute to the core campus budget, but the main source for these shortfalls will be profits in other divisions.[33] Looking at figure 7 again, what we see is that social sciences, business, the teachers college, and the humanities, added together, run a profit of about the same $40 million that engineering and the sciences lose. The normal process of balancing the campus books involves moving money *from* education, humanities, business, and the social sciences, which earn "profits," *to* science and engineering, which run losses.

To repeat, I am not saying that this cross-subsidy is inherently wrong. Mutual support is essential to the welfare of the whole. I am saying that universities use revenues from one core mission—instruction—to cover losses in their other core mission—research. This means that departments that teach a lot of students and perform little sponsored research are called on—via their student

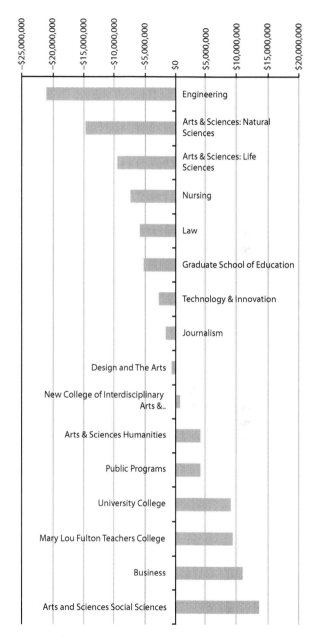

Figure 7. Difference between revenue and direct expenses by college, ASU 2010. *Source:* Original in author's files from administrative source.

revenues—to subsidize departments that produce routine annual research losses. I am saying that under everyday budget practice, the arts, humanities, social sciences, and nonbench professional programs like education and business tend to *subsidize* bench sciences, engineering fields, and, under some conditions, medicine. Under normal conditions, research universities rob Peter to pay Paul—where Paul is research in general and STEM in particular, and Peter is undergraduate students in general and SASH students in particular. Finally, I am also saying that concealment of this reality has damaged university budget policy, confused policymakers about expenses, hurt the human sciences (arts, humanities, and social sciences), and weakened public support. These are privatization's material costs.

Breaking the Silence on Cross-Subsidies

The fault here lies not with science but with our funding system. And yet this system—based on cross-subsidies—is almost never publicly discussed. I started learning these basic facts in 2001 through my work on planning and budget for my university's academic senate, where I was lucky to be mentored by people who understood the budget plumbing.[34] I published a chapter on cross-subsidies in *Unmaking the Public University* in 2008, just before the financial crisis emerged, and published variations on the cross-subsidy theme in a range of venues.[35] A few other scholars, in some cases well-known education economists who might presumably have the ear of policymakers, have made similar efforts.[36] How have these efforts fared?

In the category of budgetary truth tellers, I nominated the analyst Jane Wellman as most likely to succeed. After spending decades in university finance, she helped found the Delta Cost Project on postsecondary educational budgeting and began to circulate important findings in 2008, leading to the important report *Trends in College Spending* (2009).[37] On September 8, 2009, she testified at the first meeting of the UC Commission on the Future, an operation established to deal with implications of the latest round of massive state cuts.

Among many important points she made to this high-level board, Wellman stated clearly that universities function through cross-subsidies—that it's normal for less expensive programs to subsidize more expensive ones.[38] She didn't spell out which departments are expensive, but noted that undergraduate education has helped to pay for graduate education. This was fine, she said, when 80 percent or more of the cost was paid by the state, so that no undergraduate wrote a check to a graduate student. With falling state support, that's exactly what undergraduate students do.

Wellman made a related point about research: the federal government has not been paying for the costs of its research for some time, she said. This means that students are increasingly paying for the costs of overhead. Research is not a free lunch, she noted: somebody has to pay for that. That somebody, to repeat, is the undergraduate student, paying in the form of their state funds and tuition money. These points were spelled out in a Delta Cost Project Fact Sheet that was posted around the same time.[39]

Wellman had made the point even more explicitly just a few days before, when quoted in the *New York Times*. She flatly contradicted the image of the English department that runs deficits: "An English student . . . is generally a profit center. 'They're paying for the chemistry major and the music major and faculty research,' Ms. Wellman said. 'They don't want to talk about it in institutions because the English department gets mad. The little ugly facts about cross subsidies are inflammatory, so they get papered over.' "[40] The picture of money flowing *from* English and music *to* engineering and chemistry is hard to miss here. There was hope, this early in the crisis, that the reality of research losses and social science profits would begin to penetrate budget mythology, particularly among board members with total authority over those budgets.

But, at least in California, officials busily muddied the budget waters. UC president Mark G. Yudof continued to invert the subsidy facts in public statements. On the *PBS NewsHour* in late November 2009, he asserted, "Many of our, if I can put it this way, businesses are in good shape. We're doing very well there. Our hospitals are full, our medical business, our medical research, the patient care. So, we have this core problem: Who is going to pay the salary of the English department? We have to have it. Who's going to pay it in sociology, in the humanities? And that's where we're running into trouble."[41]

Yudof got the relationship exactly backward and spread the fiction on national television that the humanities and social sciences are financial basket cases. The reality is that they are net donors, but this reality was concealed by a senior manager who had just been selected by *Time* magazine as one of the country's top ten college presidents.[42]

Faculty irritation ran high. Yudof's statement was rebutted in some detail by an English professor, Robert D. Watson of UCLA, first in a letter on December 14 of that year and then in a *Chronicle of Higher Education* article. Since it gets to the heart of the problem, I cite it at length.

> If you count what patients pay for treatment as income earned by a medical center, but do not count what students pay for literature courses as income earned by the humanities department, the hospital will surely look like a much smarter business. You might therefore appoint those productive health-care administrators to a death panel (called a universitywide planning committee) on lost causes like the English major.
>
> But, according to spreadsheet calculations done at my request by Reem Hanna-Harwell, assistant dean of the humanities at the University of California at Los Angeles, based on the latest annual student-credit hours, fee levels, and total general-fund expenditures, the humanities there generate over $59 million in student fees, while spending only $53.5 million (unlike the physical sciences, which came up several million dollars short in that category). The entire teaching staff of Writing Programs, which is absolutely essential to UCLA's educational mission, has been sent firing notices, even though the spreadsheet shows that program generating $4.3 million in fee revenue, at a cost of only $2.4 million.
>
> So, the answer to "Who's going to pay the salary of the English department?" is the English department. It earns its own salary and more,

through the fees paid by the students it teaches. These profits will only grow as tuition increases ...

That isn't an eccentric calculation. Of the 21 units at the University of Washington, the humanities and, to a lesser degree, the social sciences are the only ones that generate more tuition income than 100 percent of their total expenditure. Cary Nelson, president of the American Association of University Professors, recently cited a University of Illinois report showing that a large humanities department like English produces a substantial net profit, whereas units such as engineering and agriculture run at a loss. The widely respected Delaware Study of Instructional Costs and Productivity shows the same pattern.[43]

Yudof replied to Watson and claimed to embrace his view: "I have long made the case that, with undergraduates all paying the same fees, the humanities indeed can be seen as cross-subsidizing science, engineering, and similar departments."[44] In reality, Yudof had been making the opposite case, and this statement turned out to be a plug for differential tuition—for charging engineering students $1,000 or so a year more than history majors. But the letter was a step in the right direction. Would the humanities get a better budget deal?

Awareness of the general research problem did improve. After 2010, universities began to argue in technical venues that insufficient public funding was harming sponsored research. Locally, the UC Academic Senate published a report that confirmed ICR shortfalls, and its findings were conveyed to UC president Yudof on May 6, 2010.[45] The UC Commission on the Future confirmed the very large research losses I described earlier. The federal agencies began to chime in, as noted, when in 2012 the NSB and the National Research Council (NRC) of the National Academies each released reports lamenting and quantifying the extent to which universities were increasingly on the hook to pay for extramural research from their own internal funds, thus diverting money from necessities like instruction and maintenance.[46] Universities started to negotiate increases in their official indirect cost recovery rate. To take another example, UC Davis's rate is to increase in several steps from 54.5 percent in 2013–2014 to 57 percent in 2017–2018.[47] Estimating a shortfall of twenty cents on the dollar, this increase will take care of 15 percent of the problem. This is better than nothing. But it is not enough.

The 2014 COGR report I referenced earlier concluded with some bureaucratic fighting words: "The university subsidy is a legitimate issue and one that should be addressed honestly and constructively by all stakeholders. [Forcing] universities to fund real, unreimbursed costs through non-federal revenue sources [makes them] potentially reduce investments in core missions and infrastructure. Ultimately, this impairs a university's ability to strategically plan and invest in its future research enterprise."[48] In other words, concealing true research costs has hurt the university while also hurting research. A high-level organization was now explicitly saying that unrecovered research costs "are a financial burden with severe implications for the future productivity of research universities."[49] This was progress.

Do All Institutional Funds Subsidize Sponsors?

Little of the new attention was directed toward qualitative fields. The same is true for funding. Figure 6 showed that *extramural* funding for "Arts and Humanities" was at most 1 percent of the funding totals for the University of California. The national pattern is more or less the same.[50] As total federal R&D funding approaches $40 billion a year, the humanities receives about $400 million.[51] Although private giving to "arts, culture, and humanities organizations" is charted in the many billions a year, the research revenue streams follow a kind of 1-percent rule: the humanities fields that grant 10 percent of bachelor's degrees, and that must address all the major questions of human society and culture, receive about 1 percent of national research funding.[52]

Yet this is the treatment we expect within privatization culture for disciplines with no calculable "return on investment" (ROI). Even the losses on STEM research fit into the privatization framework in that their advocates could attach a speculative positive ROI to future developments somewhere down the road. No pecuniary projection could be made for a critique of racial capitalism, an analysis of homophobia in Hollywood cinema, research on conveying scientific data on climate change through environmental photography, or a new edition of the works of Henry David Thoreau. We will see later that such work in the arts and humanities has large nonmarket benefits, both private and public, but conventional ROI calculations put them beyond the privatization pale.

On the other hand, what share of institutional funds goes to supporting research in the arts, humanities, and qualitative social sciences (SASH) fields, rather than to subsidizing losses on externally funded research? This is an important question for these fields, because somewhat under two-thirds of humanities funding comes from academic institutions.[53]

Universities need to support extramural research with outlays for their myriad indirect costs, and also need to pay for research that is not supported by outside sponsors, including virtually all SASH research.[54] The unreimbursed costs of extramurally sponsored *and nonsponsored* research accounts for the $15 billion that universities spent of their own money on research in FY 2013 (out of a total of $67 billion)—up from $13.7 billion the year before.[55] How much of this money goes to qualitative "SASH" research for which little or no external sponsorship exists?

The National Science Foundation tries to figure out how much money goes to these various research categories through the HERD survey cited in note 12. The COGR report cites its findings as follows (for FY 2012): "Of the $13.7 billion, 56% ($7.7 billion) was in the form of direct funding for faculty or student research projects, 9% ($1.3 billion) was devoted to cost sharing, and almost 34% ($4.6 billion) represented unrecovered indirect costs."[56]

At first it seems as though more than half of university research expenditures supports the research of its own faculty and students. A third goes to cover costs incurred by sponsored research that are not covered by the sponsors. Another tenth goes to cost sharing, which always involves sponsored projects. Summing up these figures, we might at first conclude that 44 percent of institutional funds subsidizes extramural sponsors, while 56 percent helps faculty fund internal research projects. All of these costs are within the normal scope of research university activity—and, to get pious for a second, form much of its obligation to society.

But is this breakdown correct? The COGR report suggests it is by singling out the $4.6 billion as the main subsidy burden universities bear. Other documents tell different tales. Bear with me: we need to take a walk in the weeds.

The COGR report itself offers a case study that listed University-Funded Research at about 28 percent of the institutional fund contribution, or *half* of the *average* for "direct funding for faculty or student research projects" in the HERD survey.[57] In the UC case we already discussed, its statement of losses suggested that sponsored research caused the *entire* shortfall that the institution had to cover with its own funds.

Official accounts thus generated at least three different stories about the extent to which research universities subsidize outside research sponsors:

A. One third (or at most 44 percent) of institutional funds goes to subsidizing costs of sponsored research. Policy could have reduced the university's expenses here: federal agencies appear to pay their corporate clients' costs in full while not providing the same service for universities.[58] Still, in this case, 56 percent of a university's internal funds goes to nonsponsored or "internal" research for faculty and students. (This reflects the NSF average.)
B. A quarter of institutional funds goes to nonsponsored research. That leaves three-quarters supporting extramurally sponsored research. This is the COGR case study.
C. More or less *all* institutional funds go to filling in these short-falls in sponsored research funding. This is the result implied by the UC Commission on the Future.

Which story is correct? The best answer, unfortunately, is all of them, depending on the university. Wealthy private universities may well be close to A, spending most of their internal funds on their own faculty's nonsponsored projects. Less wealthy privates and some major public research universities may be close to B. Together these two stories say that half to three-quarters of internal research funds are used to cover losses on already-sponsored extramural research, rather than to support good research that lacks outside funders.

The case of C, in which nearly all institutional funds subsidize sponsored research, may be right for public research universities like the University of California. It is an average of very different research campuses, some with old endowments and medical income, others with unique local conditions like ground rents from commercial property, and still others that are heavily dependent on student enrollment funding. Its campuses are fairly typical of the spectrum of large public research universities.

To check whether option C could be true, in which almost no internal funding goes to nonsponsored research of the type that typifies the arts, humanities, and qualitative social science fields (SASH), I offer some calculations based on figures for one campus, UCLA. There are many numbers in the next few paragraphs. If this is too much, you can skip to the end of the section. But I think it's worth hanging in there. One reason we never get decent answers about research costs is that even this amount of budget detail can't get a public hearing.

UCLA is the wealthiest UC campus and has an unusually large endowment, diverse revenue streams, and various private funds. Its humanities division runs a teaching revenue surplus, and a 2009 report found that humanities teaching generates an ROI of 11 percent (as did the social sciences division, in contrast to a 4 percent ROI for life sciences and negative 5 percent for the physical sciences–on instruction only).[59] Federal statistics state that UCLA spent $177 million in "Institutional Funds" on research in FY 2013.[60] When the NSF breaks out UCLA expenditures by discipline, "all non S&E [Science and Engineering] fields" received just under 6 percent of the total in that year. (The NSF's definition of "Non-S&E Fields of R&D" covers most *qualitative* disciplines [SASH].)[61] The same table shows a range at UC campuses: UC Berkeley, with its powerful, venerable SASH and social science disciplines, spent nearly 9 percent of its institutional funds on non-S&E fields. UC Santa Barbara spent nearly 18 percent (most likely because of one large social sciences grant funded from an NSF engineering program). On the other hand, UC San Diego spent 2.2 percent and UC Davis spent 0.9 percent of institutional funds on non-S&E fields. These figures give scenario C plausibility, and UCLA looks like a reasonable middle case in this university system.[62]

Unfortunately for those of us who would like to avoid still more minutia of university budgeting, this "non-S&E" figure for institutional funds is not the same as the figure that supports nonsponsored research, that is, SASH research that has significance but no external financial support. If around 60 percent of institutional funds are used to cover direct costs, then UCLA spends 60 percent of 6 percent, or 3.6 percent of its institutional funds on direct funding for non-S&E research.

This assumption is a bit of a stretch, however, because less non-S&E research is extramurally funded, which means it needs less coverage of indirect costs. So I've run another kind of calculation to see if the 3.6 percent figure is in the ballpark—and it verifies our scenario C.

UCLA has formally recorded institutional funds expenditures from its Academic Senate Committee on Research, which in 2013–2014 dispensed about $1.4 million in travel and research support. (This is the same figure as in 2007–2008, and is down from $1.9 million in 1996–1997. It is a 50 percent reduction from $2.87 million in 2014 dollars.)[63]

UCLA thus spent less than 1 percent of its institutional funds on faculty research internally peer-reviewed by the Academic Senate—and some of this would have been used to top up extramural grants rather than supporting independent research.[64] About 63 percent of the Committee on Research (COR) funds went to SASH disciplines that have few extramural funders. This is 0.09 percent of total campus research expenditures. It is a half a percent of the internal funds that UCLA spends on research.

The campus's financial schedules break down research spending into several categories.[65] A bit more than $41 million is classified as research expenditures that come from two types of "unrestricted" funds for all of the schools outside of the medical enterprise.[66] Restricted research funding is nearly $197 million (funds covering the direct costs of extramural research are "restricted" to the grant that generated them).[67] I posit that restricted funding is roughly equivalent to the revenues the university receives extramurally to cover direct research costs. I also posit that the two types of unrestricted funding, which together include something under half of all indirect cost recovery, are funds available to cover indirect costs. If any money is left over, it could fund internally initiated research that lacks an extramural sponsor.

Here's my next step: UCLA's indirect cost recovery rate in 2012–2013 was 54 percent for on-campus research. Eighteen percent of its research funding came from internal campus funds, which, unless we learn otherwise, I interpret as running an 18 percent loss. Assuming that UCLA covers all its research losses each year, it will need 72 cents to pay the indirect costs on every dollar of research ($54 + 18$). So I would expect "unrestricted" expenditures to be 72 percent of "restricted" expenditures just to cover the actual indirect costs of research. Any unrestricted funds *beyond* 72 percent of "restricted" could be used to fund nonsponsored research (outside of that funded by the campus Council on Research).

UCLA's major nonmedical units would need to spend $141,497,000 to cover the indirect costs that extramural pays for plus the additional 18 percent that they don't. But the combined total of the two categories is $40,975,000, or 29 percent of my estimated full indirect costs. This requires UCLA to come up with $100 million to cover indirect costs for nonmedical research. Some will come from ICR, and some from institutional funds. But we can reasonably posit zero *departmental* support for internally generated research that is *not* part of a special individual faculty budget obtained through recruitment and retention. We have provisional confirmation that this large and well-off public research university spends next to none of its institution funds on internally generated faculty research (scenario C).

Let's dig down one more layer with the budget model I've posited here, knowing that accounting categories don't work the way we need them to, and look at some centers, institutes, and departments.[68] On the departmental level, STEM faculty are completely justified to complain that they never see the research overhead money (ICR) that their grants generate. The department of chemistry and biochemistry at UCLA gets to spend 7.3 percent of its restricted ("direct" for my purposes) monies through unrestricted funds. For chemical engineering it's 6.5 percent, for earth and space sciences it's 2.3 percent, and so on. On the other hand, English spends 135 percent in unrestricted funds of what it receives in "restricted" funds, suggesting some campus subsidy for its research—this is nearly double our 72 percent threshold for full cost recovery on research. History's figure is 310 percent, philosophy's is 97 percent, and East Asian languages and cultures' is 202 percent. The actual amounts are much smaller than in the STEM departments—particularly in proportion to the student enrollments that generate these unrestricted numbers. But there seem to be small pockets of surpluses (more than 72 percent of restricted funding). What do these surpluses add up to? The total surplus of fields that spend more "unrestricted" research funds than (72 percent of) restricted funds comes to $4,215,000.[69] Nearly all of these are SASH fields, and their expenditures on internally generated research (according to my convention here) is about 2.4 percent of UCLA's overall institutional fund expenditures on research ($177 million).

This is not a complete picture of internal research funding at our best-case public research university, UCLA. But it puts the estimated portion of institutional funds *not* spent covering extramural funding shortfalls at less than 2.5 percent of the total (adding COR and the "surplus" unrestricted expenditures together). This figure is close to the 3.6 percent derived from NSF data. Both lend plausibility to the

UC Commission report that rounds the percentage of institutional funds that cover unreimbursed indirect costs of extramural research to 100 percent. UCLA is much closer to our scenario C than to the two others, in which a quarter (scenario B) or over half (scenario A) of these internal funds sponsor new, internally generated research, including SASH research.

We can now make several provisional generalizations. First, public universities, particularly in the wake of state funding cuts, are likely to be in category C, in which more or less all institutional funds for research must subsidize extramural grants.

Second, a very low percentage of these institutional funds go to the SASH disciplines that are almost completely dependent on them for funding.

Third, humanities research is therefore most likely to thrive or survive at wealthy private universities and a few flagship publics. To speculate gloomily for a moment, public research universities may be drifting toward quasi-irrelevance in the sociocultural disciplines on which global problem solving depends.

Finally, this model flunks the test for funding research in public good disciplines that cannot attract investment oriented toward pecuniary returns. Privatization's core logic discriminates against the human sciences. It also makes it harder for the middle- and lower-income students who disproportionately attend non-elite universities to have access to humanities research. Many people have worried that the humanities as a *research* field will become a luxury good found mostly at wealthy private universities. This brief budget study of a best-case public university scenario, relatively wealthy UCLA, suggests that their worries are justified.

The Private Gave, and the Private Hath Taken Away

Does all this really matter so much? Did all of this research need to be done? What about the assumption at the heart of neoliberalism's private good view of social infrastructure—that public funding is always replaced by private money where the public function meets the rigorous cost-benefit standards of the private sector? In other words,

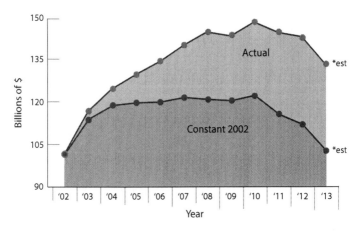

Figure 8. Federal R&D investments since 2002. *Source:* American Society for Biochemistry and Molecular Biology, *Unlimited Potential, Vanishing Opportunity: Nondefense Discretionary Science 2013 Survey* (2013), 6, accessed November 2, 2013, http://www .asbmb.org/uploadedFiles/Advocacy/Events/UPVO%20Report%20V2.pdf.

the private sector will adequately fund anything really worthwhile that the public sector was doing before. If privatization makes the SASH disciplines second class, perhaps that's the way things oughta be. Business will step in to pay for the STEM research that, in its careful, market-oriented judgment, deserves support.

Part of this view is true. Public investment in R&D has certainly been going down (figure 8). In the three-year period 2010–2013, inflation-corrected science funding fell by 20 percent.

But do we see evidence of the theory that the private sector will pick up the slack in STEM research? Did US business help fill in the ebbing tide of public research support? The chart in figure 9 gives one answer. Throughout the three decades of declining state funding for public universities, US industry sponsorship of academic R&D has been essentially flat. It has never risen above 7 percent of the total overall. This pattern has remained unchanged after 2008, even while funding shortfalls have increased, funding rates in many fields have fallen to 10 percent of applications, and two-thirds of scientists in a recent survey say they have "had difficulty receiving grant fund-

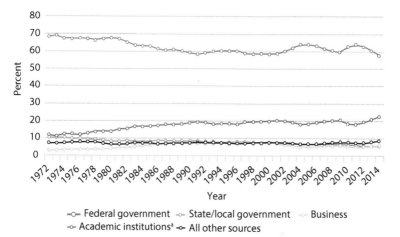

Figure 9. Academic S&E R&D expenditures, by source of funding (FYs 1972–2014).
Source: National Science Foundation, *Science and Engineering Indicators 2016,* fig. 5-1, accessed May 6, 2016, http://www.nsf.gov/statistics/2016/nsb20161/#/report/chapter-5/expenditures-and-funding-for-academic-r-d.
ᵃ Academic institutions' funds exclude research funds spent from multipurpose accounts.

ing" since 2010.[70] Although one organization predicted an increase of over 25 percent in industry funding of academic R&D for 2012, it noted that 98 percent of industry R&D funding remains internal to industry.[71] The following year, the industry increase had not materialized.[72] The COGR reported in 2014 that "private industry" funding for academic R&D peaked at 7.8 percent of the total in 1956. It declined from 7 percent in 1996 to 5 percent in 2012.[73] The federal share of R&D declined, and the gap was made up not by the private sector but by the universities themselves.

We have a very awkward situation for defenders of privatization. As public funding is cut, it is the universities that must spend an ever-greater share of internal money to cover extramural funding shortfalls. Meanwhile, the private sector is keeping its share of federal R&D funding while not increasing its spending at universities. Business helps to insure that though universities perform about half of the nation's basic research, they receive just under a quarter of overall federal R&D funding.[74] While universities spent $15 billion of their own money supporting research in FY 2013, business contributed $3.5 billion, or about one quarter as much as universities themselves. In some important cases the ratio can be ten dollars of institutional funds for every one dollar of business funding, as at established flagships at Ann Arbor, Michigan, and Madison, Wisconsin, and rising Sunbelt flagships at Gainesville, Florida, and Tucson, Arizona.[75]

When the private sector does fund academic R&D, it typically minimizes its indirect cost contribution at well below federal rates. Back at the University of California, a senate report summarized the situation like this:

> Federal ICR rates are a ceiling for private grants and contracts; corporate sponsors negotiate lower overhead rates. Indeed, given the competition for research funding, UC may see itself forced to accept lower overhead rates to stay competitive in a race to the bottom for private sponsorship of research. This negative spiral may explain why an increasing share of UC research support is declared as gift rather than as grant or contract, subject only to flat-tax foundation fees but not to appropriate overhead assessments (5% or 10% rather than around 1/3 of total support granted). If state resources are being diverted from teaching and other campus needs to development offices in the hope of bringing private funds to campus and to manage complex projects, then accepting research sponsorship that covers little or no share of the associated effort in administration, space, equipment, and utilities, will continue to take more resources from the UC budget than it brings in.[76]

In other words, losses were generated in chasing private research sponsorships in which success meant further losses. The 2008 crisis seems to have intensified money-losing sponsorships.

Privatization thus delivers six separate blows to research. Business has steadily shrunk its commitment to *basic* research, requiring universities to pick up the slack.[77] Business has generally not supported increases in either the share of existing public R&D funding going to universities (which would reduce business's share) or tax increases that would expand the overall public R&D pie. (Some high-tech companies that depend heavily on R&D, like Apple, are leading tax avoiders.)[78] Third, business has not increased its funding of academic R&D as a share of either the academic budget or its own, requiring universities to compete for shrinking public R&D funds. Next, when business does send money the university's way, it systematically underfunds indirect costs. It forces universities to spend more institutional funds covering research losses rather than helping to reduce these university losses. Outside sponsors in effect force students and taxpayers to cross-subsidize their research, and many of these students are in SASH fields that lack research funding in the first place. Finally, privatization erodes the nonsponsored research that is of particular social and cultural relevance.

In short, privatized research funding is not a way that public universities can cost-share with the private sector. It is a way for the private sector to extract value from the public. For-profit companies behave rationally when, rather than making philanthropic donations to the university's research, they use universities to *leverage* other people's money for their own benefit.

The Effects of Philanthropy

This is a moment in the discussion in which philanthropy may come up as an apparent refutation of the problems with private revenue streams. Private giving seems like an act of overwhelming generosity to the university recipient, and there is no doubt that specific gifts have been of enormous benefit to specific programs. Many academic resources—sometimes entire schools within universities—would not exist without initial, substantial gifts from generous donors. My own department has an undergraduate mentorship program that would not exist without a donor, and it is very hard not to like gifts that support new skills and creative excitement. Philanthropy can, in fact, raise the level of aspiration of mid-level programs, attract stronger students and faculty, and help the reputation and ambiance of the whole institution. University officials are naturally reluctant to show ingratitude toward generous donors, particularly as public revenue streams have steadily declined. For this and other reasons, the potential negative impacts of the philanthropy system have largely escaped scrutiny. Philanthropy is often treated as free money—the proverbial gift horse whose mouth you do not look into. Reviewing lists of eight- and nine-figure gifts can create the impression that public universities could fund-raise their way out of their serious shortfalls, if they just put their minds to it.

Even if federal grants lose money for the university, don't gifts make up for some or all of that? In fact, there are financial, institutional, and intellectual costs to philanthropy that are rarely openly discussed.

The main exception to the blind eye turned toward philanthropy's drawbacks has been the specific gifts that threaten academic freedom. These occur when donors seek to buy direct influence over academic content by endowing programs or professorships. A classic example has been the Charles Koch Foundation's funding of academic programs, including the Program for the Study of Political Economy and Free Enterprise at Florida State University.[79] A faculty committee that examined the gift memorandum found that "this issue is not about the study of free-market economics. It is about outside control and undue influence over the academic endeavors of the FSU Economics department and about abatement of faculty control over the curriculum of the Economics department." Such outside control included Koch Foundation influence over the selection of teaching personnel, student fellows, curricula, and other matters.[80] This type of direct donor intervention is important, since it involves individuals or foundations trying to use their wealth to change faculty research and teaching. But there has been a fair amount of mainstream press coverage of direction intervention, and I will sidestep it here.[81]

Donors may also seek to control an institution indirectly. This is a routine part of gift structuring: focusing on developing one discipline or unit on a campus rather than all the others. Philanthropy is not the general provision of basic research, with questions and directions defined by a diverse body of researchers, but is targeted at issues and applications of interest to donors. Some policy analysts are increasingly concerned that a few disciplines receive much more funding than others—biomedical research as opposed to researching how to achieve equitable voting mechanisms in multiracial societies. In addition, donors may "pick winners" among goals and methodologies, with the experts in question forced to follow the money and operate, at least in project selection, as hired hands.[82]

Indirect influence has become more pervasive with the rise of "advocacy philanthropy" or "philanthrocapitalism." The concepts are associated with unusually wealthy foundations—in higher education, the Gates and Lumina Foundations are leading examples—who seek specific outcomes in exchange for their funding while also reshaping the institutions delivering those outcomes. They often involve a noblesse oblige, which is expressed with unusual directness in the book title *Philanthrocapitalism: How the Rich Can Save the World*.[83] The premise of philanthrocapitalism is that big social problems cannot be solved with existing public institutions, since the public institutions are part of the problem, or even its source. This type of philanthropy, when it focused on K–12 education, did not give money either directly to underfunded schools or to researchers studying them, but to third parties creating new mechanisms of measurement, accountability, assessment, and governance that could remodel the schools themselves. If remodeled governance did *not* fix the schools, then they could be closed, and new, privately run schools put in their place.

A similar premise animates advocacy philanthropy in higher education—it is not the public funding cuts but the public institutions themselves that have become inadequate. As the authors of one study of advocacy philanthropy put it, "There has been a shift in the focus of foundations toward issues of completion, productivity, metrics, and efficiency—foundations are focusing on broad policy issues, including the ways in which higher education systems are arranged, their funding structures, how they are held accountable, and how they manage their data systems."[84] These philanthropists no longer trust universities to reform themselves and give much of their money to "intermediary organizations" that can create and inspire external standards and practices. "While some foundation money continues to go to specific higher education institutions, increasingly foundation grants are being awarded to systems of higher education, states, and policy organizations."[85]

In short, philanthropy that seeks indirect influence over universities may also seek structural control by enacting long-term organizational change. The inequality of resources between wealthy foundations and public colleges is matched by the foundations' superior confidence in their ability to decide correctly how universities could be better run. Philanthropic relations may not now presume the excellence of the college that receives the gift, but instead its deficiency. In this way, universities may be more like the recipients of charity in the Victorian sense than it sometimes appears. The goal of such charity is not to enhance the recipient's resources, but to change it, so it needs—or at least asks for—fewer of them.

Put another way, when university officials say that today's private fund-raising can partially *replace* public funding, they reverse cause and effect. They imply that cuts and austerity came along, and that leads to philanthropy that appears to compensate for austerity's worst effects. But advocacy philanthropy leads to austerity: austerity, in the sense of "doing more with less," is a core goal of metrics-based philanthropy. This is why one analyst of philanthropy concluded that "the focus of the Gates foundation and its partners on public higher education could further institutionalize the divide between the roughly 72 percent of American students who attend public colleges and the 28 percent who attend private colleges, even if it improved economic mobility between the lower and middle classes."[86] Philanthropy that aims not to increase poor colleges' resources but to more rigorously control them will continue their impoverishment.

But what about the majority of direct gifts that don't attach strings to the funded activities? Surely these gifts can help replace public funding?

Unfortunately, the answer is no again.

For starters, the scale of philanthropy is far too small. Headline gift numbers can be very impressive, but the cost of raising this money needs to be subtracted from the return. Fund-raising cost indices (FRCIs) or calculations of the cost to raise a dollar (CTRDs) suggest that 20 percent is a reasonable ballpark guess about overhead costs, which the institution must deduct to determine its net yield. Although this kind of number would help everyone understand the real returns of philanthropy, I have never seen a university make this calculation public.

Next, the amount of a gift that we might see in a headline is capital, not the interest on the capital that creates the revenue stream. The annual revenue a gift generates is thus something like 5 percent of the headline figure. This enormous gap between the overall gift and its annual revenue has startling consequences as to the scale at which philanthropy might serve to supply a large public university's operating expenses. For example, in the mid-2000s my academic senate budget committee calculated the endowment that the University of California would need to get its general fund allocation back to where it would have been had this allocation kept pace with the growth in state personal income after 2001. "By 2010–2011," we wrote, "the sum that would have to be generated by private fundraising to achieve 2001–02-level operating revenues is about $1.35 billion per year." At normal rates of return, "the endowment that would have to be raised would be nearly $30 billion."[87] While we were reviewing these calculations, we joked that California would restore state funding once it realized the alternative was to nationalize Harvard University's entire endowment and move it west. In the ten years since, the gap between UC's actual state revenues and the state income benchmark has grown to $2.5 billion.[88] UC would now have to nationalize Harvard and Yale together.

This might seem so obviously absurd that no one would ever make the mistake of saying private giving *could* replace lost state funding. In fact, fund-raising is invoked every day as compensation for public cuts, even if no one says the numbers are equivalent. Indeed, no one says gross fund-raising = lost state general funding, but that is not the way the fund-raising vision distorts financial management. It distorts it by diverting attention away from the endless political effort required to maintain public funding at the levels that excellent teaching and research require. The fund-raising vision makes this tiring, expensive, frustrating effort seem less essential. If we can get some laboratories and undergraduate seminars and PhD dissertation fellowships by fund-raising rather than by lobbying the legislature, why grind through the corridors of a dusty state capitol only to be told by legislative staffers that they might consider allocating another 2 percent—if you cut executive pay or get rid of your defined benefit pension? The prospect of philanthropy—not to mention the superior locations and company at donor events—makes it easier for public university officials to give up on rebuilding public funding. But philanthropy will never surpass its role as just another "nickel solution" for public university budgets—adding 5 percent or less to overall operating funds. In figure 10, philanthropy is the small third band from the top, staying flat from year to year.

The scale of philanthropy is unsuited to the public mission, even on the level of the individual program. Nike chairman Phil Knight made big waves in early 2016 when he announced that he was giving $450 million to found Stanford's Knight-Hennessy Scholars program, which would bring the best and brightest from around the world to study at Stanford.[89] Press coverage likened these scholarships to Oxford's famous Rhodes Scholarships. After Stanford's contribution of $300 million, the total scholarship endowment became $750 million. This meant that Knight-Hennessy became the 130th largest university endowment in the country, about the size of the endowment of Bucknell University, which is itself a fairly posh school with over 3,500 undergraduates, or one-tenth of the enrollment of Cal State Fullerton. The new Knight-Hennessy endowment is twice that of the University of Wisconsin system.[90] And yet this colossal gift goes to cover full cost of attendance for a total of one hundred students for three years, or three hundred students at a given time.[91] One of the biggest gifts in higher education history will graduate about half as many people as my English department does every year, where we have a total instructional budget for thirty-two faculty

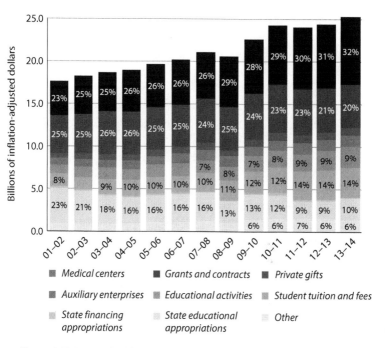

Figure 10. University of California revenues, by source, universitywide, 2001–2002 to 2013–2014. *Source: UC Accountability Report 2015,* Indicator 12.1.1: Revenues by source, universitywide, http://accountability.universityofcalifornia.edu/2015/chapters/chapter-12.html#12.1.1.

members of about $5 million. The reason that a gigantic gift yields a micro outcome is because of the 5 percent rule: 5 percent annual return on this large overall endowment will generate $125,000 per student per year. This is quite a bit more than the $9,000 or so my department spends on each of our majors each year, but it is not enormously more than what a private research university normally spends per student (about $90,000 on average).[92] In short, the Knight gift to Stanford is effective as targeted elite training but irrelevant on the scale of democratic higher education. The donor and the university in fact did make clear that public education was not their goal: they intended to form a global leadership elite.[93]

While we are on the subject of the academic effects of the Nike shoe fortune, we can consider a further limitation of philanthropy. The vast majority of university charity goes to a small set of special interests in an institution rather than to the institution as a whole. For example, the Knights have given generously not only to Stanford but also to the University of Oregon. But of the $1 billion the Knights had donated to charity prior to the Knight-Hennessy gift (on an estimated net worth of $19 billion), only $34.7 million went to non-medical public university academics. The figure rises to $76.4 million by counting their gift to UO's athlete tutoring center.[94] Most of their gifts have gone to medicine and athletics.

In this way the Knights are typical of major donors in steering their gifts toward favored recipients rather than operations as a whole. As another example, the largest donor to that major public flagship, the University of Michigan at Ann Arbor—Stephen M. Ross—recently gave $200 million "to significantly transform the student experience at the business school and athletic campus." The gift was to be split between those two areas.[95] The great majority of significant gifts are to the health sciences (representing half of all giving to UC), sports, and business programs. Very little philanthropy is unrestricted: at UC it is 99 percent restricted.[96] With the partial exception of the arts, the sociocultural fields represent a drop in the bucket of all philanthropy.[97] Development professionals often say that one gift leads to another and that a major gift to theoretical physics, for example, will encourage gifts to multiply across all the disciplines. It is doubtful that this actually happens: athletic giving may "crowd out" academic giving, according to one study. (However, another study by the same authors found that giving areas were symbiotic.)[98] Whether or not giving to favored areas actually lowers giving elsewhere, it does not seem to be encouraging giving to less favored disciplines, judging from the imbalances in the amounts flowing to different areas.

In other words, philanthropy does not support the vision of the public college as teaching all subjects to all kinds of people that goes back at least to the Morrill land grant legislation of 1862. Philanthropy also may not support most forms of innovation, since it favors already-identified high achievers and prominent disciplines as likely to harbor yesterday's breakthroughs as tomorrow's. Breakthroughs frequently come from avant-garde, experimental, or apparently marginal topics that a typical non-expert donor is likely to overlook. In addition, *innovation* must be understood to include arcane knowledge with no commercial potential that exists almost exclusively in universities—the archaeology of ancient Sumeria, the study and preservation of indigenous languages, the analysis of microbial ecosystems in the polar regions. Why should the existence of such study be at the mercy of a donor class, whose expertise comes largely from tech, commerce, and finance? We risk losing the full range of knowledges created and taught in public universities by applying the notion that philanthropy can make up for cuts in taxpayer funding.

This breach of the mission of general development appears in the lopsided philanthropy distribution across different types of institutions. When the Council for Aid in Education reported fund-raising results for 2015, the giant headline total of $40 billion (not following the 5 percent rule!) was followed by the notation, "The top 20 fundraising institutions together raised $11.56 billion, 28.7 percent of the 2015 total." The top twenty list consists entirely of the Double Ivies, as I call the Ivies plus similar private research universities like Stanford, Northwestern, Duke, NYU, and USC, and a handful of public flagships (the University of Washington, UCSF, UCLA, the University of Michigan, and UC Berkeley, all, except for Berkeley, with medical schools). A review of a list of major gifts over time shows the fairly small set of repeat beneficiaries among universities.[99] Assets show a similar skew. A Moody's report found, "The 10 richest institutions held nearly one-third of total cash and investments at four-year schools in fiscal 2014, while the top 40 accounted for two-thirds."[100] Another study found that the weighted mean endowment per student for the top half of colleges and universities (excluding the top 10 percent) was about 1.5 percent of that for the top 1 percent of university endowments.[101]

Even the familiar "the rich get richer" narrative doesn't quite capture philanthropy's shutting out of the relatively open-access public colleges that serve the vast majority of low-income students and students of color.[102] The problem can be illustrated by comparing UCLA and Cal State Fullerton. They are located in the same metropolitan area. They serve about the same number of students, with the major difference being that UCLA is as selective now as Harvard was a generation ago. But UCLA's endowment is about $2.3 billion, while CSUF's is $42.5 million.[103] The several thousand regional colleges and two-year community colleges that educate the majority of the country's college students have effectively zero endowment resources to bring to bear on their students' education. Philanthropy does not grow the general provision for public colleges, but simply mirrors existing differences in resource inequality. It is a good way of raising educational revenues in a plutocracy, but not in a democracy.

For these reasons, philanthropy is a third-rate solution to public higher ed's austerity-induced revenue problems. Tax-based public funding would be far more equitable and efficient. Tax reform would generate far more income for colleges and other public infrastructure needs than does voluntary giving. In one typical year, 2011, wealthy donors "contributed on average 1.3 percent of their income to charity," meaning that philanthropy generates far less revenue for public institutions than would the closing of tax loopholes, the taxing of capital gains at the same rate as income, or the oft-threatened stripping of wealthy private universities of their tax-exempt status.[104]

By 2015, enormous gifts to already-rich universities were for the first time in history receiving some negative reviews. The new era was informally launched by famed *New Yorker* writer Malcolm Gladwell's angry tweeting against hedge-fund billionaire John Paulson's $400 million gift to Harvard—"It came down to helping the poor or giving the world's richest university $400 mil it doesn't need. Wise choice John!" Or "Paulson to Harvard: is there a way to give back without actually giving anything back?"[105]

Some federal officials aren't much happier than Gladwell. The chairs of the Senate Finance and House Ways and Means committees signed a letter requesting information about the expenditures of large endowments: "Despite these large and growing endowments," they wrote, "many colleges and universities have raised tuition far in excess of inflation."[106]

Efficiency actually dictates increasing tax receipts and college allocations, holding tuition down or reducing it, and publicly funding not only the general but also the special programs that now require private donors. Since the ability to do independent research is a core skill in a twenty-first-century knowledge society, it shouldn't take a donor giving a million dollars to a custom mentorship program to generate the revenue to pay for one graduate student to help twenty undergraduates get properly trained. Since these general skills are a public good, public money should be there for that. On top of the intellectual and social value, it would also save society money in the long run.

The economic rationality of increased public funding (and tax rates) won't come easily, given the benefits of philanthropy to the donor. There's the pleasure of fame and glory, of course, in which major donors become VIPs who outrank long-term staff and faculty. There are the rates of voluntary giving that are far lower than tax rates. In addition, donations to nonprofits like universities are tax deductible.

Another benefit to the donor—and a price of privatization—is the access the private gift receives to institutional and/or public funds via the university. In the Knight gift to Stanford, the donor's $450 million is matched by $300 million from the institution. Knight required that the $500 million he donated to the Oregon Health & Science University be matched by $500 million from others. A list of his gifts is a list of leveraged investments: giving $10 million to a $25 million building campaign created the William W. Knight (Knight's father) Law Center. In 2006, "Knight gives $105 million toward the $345 million, eight-building Knight Management Center at the Stanford Graduate School of Business." In 2011, "Knight pledged $100 million to help repay the bonds for the construction of the 12,541-seat Matthew Knight Arena. State-backed bonds worth $200 million financed design and construction of the arena." And so on.[107] In most of the Oregon cases, Knight received 100 percent naming rights to buildings and programs for contributing a minority stake of the overall cost, with the rest of the cost furnished by the uncredited public taxpayer.

Another example is the Peter and Melanie Munk gift to the University of Toronto in 2009 to found the Munk Centre for International Studies. The Munks were to provide $35 million over eight years—the largest gift in U of T history. But the Ontario government was kicking in $25 million, and the university was contributing the interest from an endowment of $39 million that it had dedicated to that purpose. In effect, the Munks were leveraging $64 million in public funds with their $35 million, or getting nearly $100 million in capital for a contribution of a third of that—which in turn allowed various stipulations and forms of control that created an outcry on campus.[108]

In general, when donors give to universities, they often cover only part of the costs of the project associated with their name, requiring universities to cover the rest of the costs with their own money. A further instance is the Luskin Conference and Guest Center at UCLA. What began as a UCLA alumnus's gift to the School of Public Affairs wound up including a $40 million donation to build a 282-room conference center and hotel. The conference center and hotel, however, cost over $160 million. Initial reports were that "the remaining $120 million of construction costs will be financed by bonds that are expected to be repaid through rental and room revenue."[109] The UC Regents documents specified that the university would borrow $112 million of the funds, with additional funds from "housing reserves ($7,225,000), and campus funds ($3,200,000)."[110] This is a standard privatization scenario in which private donors, the Luskins, are credited with funding a $160 million building for one-quarter of the actual cost, with the rest provided by public funds—grants or loans against future revenues—that remain the dumb money that makes it all possible. Privatization has helped lower the status of the public money and made the public officials secondary to the point that they couldn't build a gateway facility like this on their own, but require the private sector leadership of a minority interest to put the project in place.

In short, philanthropy extends the tendency of private funding to cost public universities money, while wrongly convincing onlookers that it makes public funding less necessary. While philanthropy does not support higher ed's inclusive and egalitarian public mission, it *does* enable public universities to legitimate the authority of private interests.

The Distraction of Technology Transfer

If research loses money, and fund-raising has many hidden costs, what about the business activity associated with academic technology transfer? Technology transfer refers to a process whereby university inventions are transferred to industry to be developed into useful and lucrative products for the marketplace. The process is generally perceived in a linear way, as moving from laboratory invention at the university, to disclosure, to technology officials on campus, through the patenting process which, if successful, allows the university to license the patent to a company for royalty income, or to support the creation of new spin-off businesses that, in the ideal case, turn into Google. Sometimes this linear model is called "from bench to bedside."

Years after the financial crisis began, federal research funding was flat in real terms, while university subsidies continued and, in cases like UC, increased.[111] Senior managers continued to seek philanthropic gifts that, even in their targeted areas, could not provide research subsidies because in most cases they required subsidies of their own. And yet there were no signs of a paradigm shift away from seeking money-losing sponsorships. Elsewhere I have written at length on tech transfer (note 113); my remarks here are deliberately brief.

For example, in 2013, the university gave authority over the patenting and licensing process of UCLA's publicly sponsored research to a private group of business leaders.[112] The income from patenting university research is generally disappointing—usually in the low single digits as a percentage of research revenues.[113] But officials did not interpret these low returns correctly. The market benefits of research disclosures are generally less than the total value of research, which includes nonmarket and social value. The classic example of social value is the polio vaccine, which its inventor, Jonas Salk, put directly into the public domain, without charge, to increase its immediate widespread use.

Instead, UCLA privatized the management of the patenting processes by taking it away from university officials. A reporter tried to get to the bottom of this scheme and turned up evidence that its advocates had made past personal returns on university inventions that far exceeded the returns to the university itself. It was possible that these private interests were now trying to do the same thing on a larger scale. This article also suggested that these businesspeople were unaware of the extent to which their past practice of private investments in UCLA intellectual property had created losses rather than gains for the university.[114] UCLA officials were unwilling even to speak to the reporter who wrote the story, suggesting that they were unwilling to entertain any doubts about the public benefits of private intellectual property management, or to subject this privatization of the management of publicly funded research to public debate.

Valuing academic research in market terms creates a cascade of effects that turns the devolutionary cycle. It skews funding away from basic and toward commercial science, increases overall costs, understates research's social benefit, and harms sociocultural fields. Walter McMahon showed that the indirect and nonmarket benefits of research are large, and then explained why these benefits cannot be reduced to tech transfer.

> The rule of law (democratization, human rights, political stability as studied in political science, law, and history), . . . advancing trade (foreign languages and business), and . . . social capital (journalism, criminology), [flow from sociocultural] fields, [which therefore] also contribute to economic growth, albeit indirectly. Fields like engineering and business

administration make fewer of these indirect contributions; most of their contributions to growth are direct. In contrast, most of the indirect benefits to economic growth come from research and graduate programs in liberal arts . . . as well as from law, social work, education, and labor relations.[115]

Even this confined list suggests the size of nonmarket and social benefits omitted by our national fixation on monetary revenues via STEM commercialization. One could respond, "well, we can have all these kinds of fields, some whose benefits are more indirect that others," and we can—in theory. But in practice, commercial STEM costs are so much higher than the "indirect benefit" fields' costs that, as we've seen, they tend to crowd them out.

When McMahon tabulated costs per article across disciplines at the University of Illinois, the differences were shocking. Psychology spent twenty times more per article than philosophy. Microbiology spent 100 times more per article than English. The fields producing indirect private and public benefits are squeezed by the "direct benefit" fields for which returns can, in theory, be monetized and privatized. Their *actual* private returns are always underwhelming, and yet their pursuit, as mandated by privatization culture, shrinks the much larger total returns of research across all fields.

Maintaining the University's Losses

In reality, these problems are entirely solvable. Academic budgeting could be made less opaque and mystifying. We could detach ourselves from the image of profitable science and recognize the need to fund science's full range of indirect and public benefits. We could develop multiyear plans for full research costing, in which every public and private sponsor of extramural research must pay the entire cost to the campus in question. We could reduce the intramural injustices of exploitative cross-subsidies that shortchange SASH fields that are already relatively poor. We could face down political hostility from politicians who already cut funding for research they dislike, and who might cut further when they learn that their favorite thing about science, its alleged profits, have been exaggerated.

All of these changes would be difficult, for paradigm shifts are never easy.[116] But privatization has created deep budgetary liabilities that force public universities to use students and taxpayers to cover them. Unless universities reorient themselves around the nonmarket private and social benefits of research, privatization will continue to undermine university budgets, while enforcing the second-class status of research for the public good.

Large, Regular Tuition Hikes

There was a time when you could play word association with a member of the public, say the word "college," and *not* have the person respond with "student debt" or "tuition hikes." Those days are gone, perhaps for good. Nothing says "college" to the American public today like a pile of loan applications or a hockey-stick line on a tuition chart (figure 11).

Since 2008, it has become hard to find media coverage that does *not* mention high tuition as part of any story about a university. The high cost of college has tainted nearly everything colleges say about themselves. A rising sense of college unaffordability has soured the public mood. Many otherwise neutral onlookers have become scoffers and doubters about university intentions and have sided with political crackdowns that they would have avoided in more confident years.

But can we really trace these huge tuition hikes to the subsidies for outside sponsors we examined in Stage 2? Aren't these hikes far too large to be explained by anything other than state funding cuts?

After 2008, the term *tuition bubble* entered public discourse.[1] The term resonated with the dot-com stock bubble, which had burst in 2001, and with the housing bubble, whose bursting was a major cause of the 2008 crisis. In all these cases, prices had risen far faster than incomes, and buyers had used easy credit to fill the gaps. The sky-high sticker price of college tuition made headlines when, in June 2010, its silent partner, student debt, passed the total amount of US consumer credit card debt for the first time. In an address at the University of Texas at Austin in August 2010, Barack Obama paired his call to lift

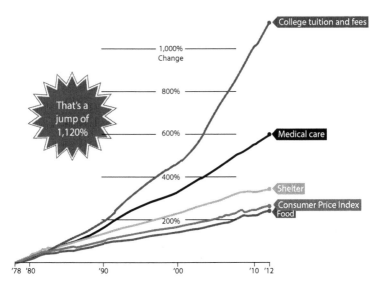

Figure 11. Tuition increases outstrip all others. *Source:* Ilan Kolet, "College Tuition's 1,120 Percent Increase," *Bloomberg Businessweek,* August 23, 2012, http://www.bloomberg.com/bw/articles/2012-08-23/college-tuitions-1-120-percent-increase.

US college graduation rates with a critique of continuous tuition hikes.[2] The national media now wanted to know, why is tuition so damn high?[3] As he geared up for his 2012 reelection campaign, Barack Obama drew a causal connection between colleges' skyrocketing tuition charges and the country's stagnant college attainment rate.[4]

The assertions about rocketing tuition mixed private and public universities together. Tuition increases had been led by the privates. Public universities charged the same real tuition in 2010–2011 that their private counterparts had charged twenty years earlier.[5] But whatever thanks public colleges might have received for keeping tuitions lower than privates' were blocked by the post-2008 environment, in which some public universities jolted their students with the largest one-year tuition hikes in living memory, exemplified by the University of California's 32 percent increase for 2009–2010.[6]

Everyone also had a theory for why tuition cost so much. I discuss the most important theories after we look at the tuition increases themselves. I'm sorry to report that none of the major theories of tuition hikes understand the big costs at the heart of the university mission that we looked at in the previous chapter. These theories wrongly treat privatization as free, rather than as what we have seen it to be—a cost to be borne by the institution being privatized.

Which Causes Which?

The basic fact is that the United States has the highest average college costs in the world, with the partial exception of Japan.[7] Overall, educational costs would be even higher in the United States if it were not that one-third of college enrollments are in two-year schools, which have the lowest fees.[8] The United States was thirteenth out of fifteenth in affordability at the lower number (Japan and Mexico were worse), but the tuition in the quality US sector was two to three times higher. There is little doubt that four-year US college prices are on a planet all their own. By 2014–2015, six years after the financial crisis, published tuition and fees at private, nonprofit universities had risen 12 percent to $31,231.[9] Public university tuition rose an average of 29 percent in the same period.

For years, universities have been raising their tuitions faster than consumer inflation. After 2008, the lid blew off. One think tank in Washington, DC, produced a particularly gruesome image of the results (figure 12). More than half of state universities increased tuition by 20 percent or more. All percentages are on top of inflation, during a period of job loss and wage stagnation. And again, all figures are reduced by low-cost two-year colleges.

Although public college tuition was still less than a third of that at private colleges, the average five-year increase of 27 percent shook public confidence. This was a special problem among lower-income students who were most likely to see costs as a reason not to attend university.

Why did public college tuition shoot up? After 2008, the prime suspect became state funding cuts. From the mid-1980s to the present,

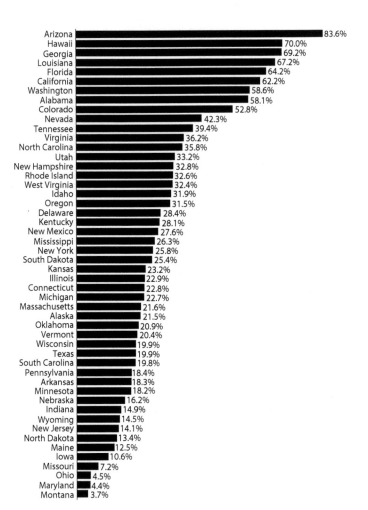

Figure 12. Public college tuition increases by state for four-year colleges, 2008–2015.
Source: Michael Mitchell and Michael Leachman, "Years of Cuts Threaten to Put College Out of Reach for More Students," Center on Budget and Policy Priorities, May 13, 2015, fig. 5, http://www.cbpp.org/research/state-budget-and-tax/years-of-cuts-threaten-to -put-college-out-of-reach-for-more-students.
Note: CBPP calculations using data from Illinois State University's annual Grapevine Report and the State Higher Education Executive Officers Association. Illinois funding data is provided by the Fiscal Policy Center at Voices for Illinois Children. Because enrollment data is only available through the 2014 school year, enrollment for the 2014–2015 school year is estimated using data from past years. Years are fiscal years.

states have on average reduced their per student allocations, in constant dollars, by 25 percent.[10] The state cuts have been levied at public college systems whose quality was fragile and uneven. The cuts have been terrible and destructive, have damaged state universities, some irreversibly, and will reduce their social benefits for the indefinite future. As I was completing this book, seven years after the financial crisis surfaced, cuts were continuing in thirteen states.[11]

And yet before we join the pundit conga line claiming that state cuts *caused* public college tuition hikes, we need to understand that the causality is indirect, structural, and reciprocal—it has always flowed in both directions.

State cuts did not start in 2008, but have been part of a de facto public policy for decades. They have been loosely correlated with the rise and fall of the economy, but we cannot assume that tuition hikes arose directly from recessions and ensuing state cuts.

In 1980–1981, four-year public colleges charged 47 percent as much as their private counterparts. Lower public tuition was a crucial element of the affordability of the country's expensive college system. This gap between public and private tuition charges had narrowed by only 2 percent by 2010–2011.[12]

This also means that private university tuition increases of two to four times the rate of inflation have for decades been matched, on average, by similar increases at public universities. Though the spectacular jumps in tuition came during economic downturns, when states had a good reason and a good excuse for cutting state colleges, public universities were already raising tuition at the same overall rate as their private counterparts. The base was lower and the real dollar increments were smaller, but public tuition rose regularly and at a rate that was higher than overall inflation. These increases took place in good years and bad, under a whole range of economic conditions.

A useful illustration of the issue appears in figure 13, which I took from a newspaper report on the State of Washington's treatment of its flagship campus, the University of Washington at Seattle. What we see is a startlingly direct swap between public and private funds.

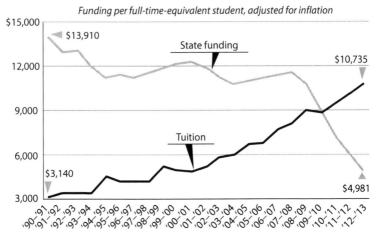

State funding goes down, tuition goes up

The University of Washington has seen a sharp decline in state funding in the past four years. Tuition now surpasses state support.

Funding per full-time-equivalent student, adjusted for inflation

Figure 13. Relationship between tuition charges and state funding, University of Washington, 1990–2013. *Source:* Katherine Long, "The Budget Breakdown: Trimming Higher Ed May Erode Job Opportunities," *Seattle Times*, January 19, 2011, http://www.seattletimes.com/seattle-news/education/the-budget-breakdown-trimming-higher-ed-may-erode-job-opportunities/.

Over the twenty-year period covered here, per-student state funds fell to about one-third of their 1990–1991 level, corrected for inflation. Over the same period, student tuition tripled.

You might have started to look at this chart by reading the headline. The headline asserts the normal causality: first state funding is cut, then the state university reluctantly raises tuition. But this causality is assumed, not shown, and a closer look says that something else is going on.[13]

For example, in the twelve years between 1990–1991 and 2002–2003, real tuition at the University of Washington doubled, for an increase of $3,000. But by that point, state funding had fallen by about $2,000 per student, or approximately 15 percent. Although tuition hikes were triggered by economic downturns and bad budget years, like 1993–1995, the long-term pattern suggests that, prior to the 2008 crisis, the university was hiking tuition independently of state cuts.

I do not want to minimize the thoughtless damage inflicted by state legislatures on their colleges and universities. Politicians' obsession with cost savings comes after decades in which states have been cheapening their colleges. Even when legislators recognize that they have underdeveloped their university systems, they generally refuse to offer new money to fix the problems they created.[14] Nationally, state funding per student has declined about 25 percent in real dollars over twenty-five years—while real Gross Domestic Product per capita was increasing by two-thirds.[15] This is a disgraceful disinvestment that has been driven by politics, ideology, and greed rather than by any concern for the educational levels of post–baby boom generations. State spending "efficiencies" are hardly a new idea, but have been a coercive state practice since the end of the Reagan presidency. They have made it difficult, if not impossible, for public universities to maintain the same output even defined in orthodox human capital terms. Legislatures show no sympathy for the hardships they cause by using public universities as a piggy bank during downturns. The failed dialogue between state leaders and university officials remains a problem for the health of the sector.

That said, do we have clear evidence that the causality runs unilaterally from public cuts to tuition hikes? The University of Washington went through periods in which state funds were not cut but tuition went up anyway. Another problem with this causality is that net tuition revenues per student—tuition after financial aid is returned to the student—doubled during a period when educational appropriations declined "only" 25 percent.[16] State funding per student was much higher than tuition at the start of the period, which explains some of the difference in the percentage changes of the two factors, but we are still looking at tuition increases that are disproportionately larger than the state cuts. Some public officials now reject the claim of university officials that their tuition hikes were caused by cuts. In one case, in California, the State Assembly

Speaker accused the University of California of profiting from state cuts.[17] University bookkeeping is murky enough to allow such charges to circulate indefinitely and to be invoked for political purposes at the drop of a hat.

My claim is that public cuts are neither the only source of tuition hikes nor, over time, the *main* source of the cuts. The general pattern has been this: public universities raise tuition at the same rate as privates, with some independence of the timing of state cuts and sometimes with a net gain in revenues rather than a simple fill-in for cuts. Universities do this to cover the costs of *privatization* as well as the costs of state cuts. We can see this as we look beyond state cuts to understand tuition hikes.

Circular Theories of Expenses

First, we must review a set of common theories that share my view that universities raise tuition independently of government cuts, but that get the causes wrong. One of these, which I described briefly in the chapter "The Price of Privatization," is called the Revenue Theory of Costs and says that universities raise as much money as they can and spend all the money that they raise.

This theory's main source, Howard Bowen, explained the syllogism in 1980: "Each institution raises all the money it can. Each institution spends all it raises. The cumulative effect of the preceding . . . laws is toward ever increasing expenditure."[18] This sequence offers a convenient explanation of higher education spending: universities take whatever they can get and spend as much as they have. The practical corollary is that cutting funds to them will do little if any harm. Many state governors appear to act as though they believe the Revenue Theory of Costs to be true and that budget cuts will in reality do no damage.[19]

What did Bowen see as the drivers for his theory? There are two: idealism and competition. In Bowen's words, "The dominant goals of institutions are educational excellence, prestige, and influence."[20] Universities take educational excellence as a self-evident good. Since universities think they spend money on good things, they don't mind spending more money. Universities do this good in competition with other universities, who are also doing the same good things. It's expensive to keep up with the Joneses by trying to attract the best students and faculty at all times, which means having the best facilities for both, which means spending as much money as one has to have the best facilities. Intellectual and educational quality is hard to measure, so university rankings come to represent outcomes in prestige competitions. Most elite universities have held their positions for decades, in some cases for centuries, so attempts to move up the ladder are at worst futile and at best enormously expensive.

Just as Freud identified a third psychic force that was neither ego nor superego, Bowen offers us an institutional id behind the relentlessness of rising prices. It functions somewhat like Freud's, in that it is profoundly self-regarding and not self-regulating. The id-driven university is not thinking of the welfare of its students, parents, society, or citizens, but acting from its boundless appetite for greater stature.

Though an economist, Bowen offered a psychological theory of primal profligacy, and it appeals even to sympathetic non-academics because it is a drive-based explanation for a phenomenon that behaves like a drive—tuition that rises through thick and thin, bust and boom. One journalist who made hay with it was Dylan Matthews, who, as I mentioned in Part I, devoted a ten-part series in the *Washington Post* to explaining why "The Tuition Is Too Damn High."[21] Matthews singled out research universities for special condemnation. While their poor relations at the community colleges raised tuition to make up for state funding cuts, public research universities increased overall revenue "by $5,793 per student, almost double the increase in per-student spending." What this meant, Matthews concluded, is that "public research universities could have kept tuition stagnant and still had $2,651 more per student to work with, which could finance a good share of the actual spending increase." Instead, their spending just went up and up and up. Matthews's explanation was Bowen's university id: "They wanted more money than that, so they increased tuition too."[22] Private research universities have an even worse unconscious urge, increasing spending three times more per full-time student than their public cousins, or $12,435, during the period 2000–2010.

The tuition punch line in *this* theory is that research losses, administrative bloat, or the amenities race are not root causes. The root cause is the will to spend as much money as possible. Big student service staffs and Vegas-style amenities helpfully sponge up the kind of high spending that supposedly attracts students and tuition. One of Matthews's subheadings was "Just Throwing Money around and Getting It from Wherever."[23] The tuition is too damn high because higher ed is compulsively profligate (except the community colleges, which are destitute). Although colleges should cut expenses to keep tuition down, the "moral character of college and university administrators may be somewhat lacking, to put it politely." And so, our mild-mannered guide concluded, "universities could be spending far, far less than they are now without any corresponding decline in educational quality."

This conclusion is both groundless and destructive—groundless in that it offers no evidence that something like 100 percent of increased spending is wasteful, and destructive in that it claims that funding cuts don't hurt quality. Neither Matthews nor any of his sources have pieced through spending patterns to develop an estimate of wasteful increases. They did not consider the need to cover research or partnership losses of the kind we discussed in Stage 2. Instead, they invoke the id to spend, which serves to tarnish every spending decision made by hundreds of thousands of senior university officials, without needing to look into any of them in detail. Though this dismissal of all new allocations has no basis in fact, it serves a powerful political function, which is to justify funding cuts on the phony grounds that they do no harm.

A more troubling example of this thinking came from the thoughtful author of a book about public university budget crises called *Saving Alma Mater.* I say "troubling" because the cynicism arises not from a journalist trying to piece together a storyline from writings he is encountering for the first time, but from an experienced public university administrator who cares deeply about affordable public colleges. James Garland was clear that public colleges are defined not by extravagance, in point of fact, but by the opposite—grinding austerity, oddly coupled with ever-rising tuition charges.

> I was president of Miami University during half of the fourteen-year period when the university's tuition increases grew 18 percent per year, and even though the state appropriation increases were minimal, we still saw significant yearly increases in our total revenues. Each year at budget time we would look at our costs, and it was always discouraging to see how they grew. Energy costs, health care costs for employees, maintenance expenses, and salary raises—all of these kept climbing in a relentless upward march. . . . Thus during those years, the university implemented hiring freezes, clamped down on operating budgets, and took other difficult steps to keep our books balanced.

Garland offered the public a vital reminder of the reality of public college resources in post-1970s America. Opulence is the exception, and austerity is the rule. Cost inflation and austerity go infuriatingly together.

He then continued in a different vein.

> But what we never did in all those years, and what public universities almost never do, was try to save money by becoming more productive. It never occurred to us, for example, that public corporations also face increases in health care and energy costs, that they also want to give salary raises to their employees, and that they also need to maintain their physical plants—and that successful corporations can do all of these things without increasing prices of their goods and services at a rate any higher than the inflation rate. In point of fact, public universities are among the least efficient enterprises in America, and the burden of that inefficiency is borne on the shoulders of Americans who desperately want to educate themselves and their families and have no other options.[24]

Garland claimed that public universities lack efficiency and don't really care. Since *he* cared, and audited everything all the time, the problem was most likely that his audits ignored, among other things, the subsidy losses we looked at in Stage 2. The charge of innate inefficiency covers up conceptual mistakes in budget analysis.

Perhaps Garland's book provides no evidence of gross inefficiency and indifference because he took for granted a idea from public-choice economics that asserts public entities to be prone, more than private ones, to rent seeking, meaning they will always protect revenues rather than lower costs. And yet this is an aversion to efficiency that, in my twenty-five years of experience as a professor, five of which were spent as a faculty planning and budget chair for my campus and then the UC system, I have never seen. The private sector is the permanent public university superego, as big as the head of the projected Wizard of Oz, and our administrators, much like Garland, compared everything we did to what we imagined Stanford, Google, or Genentech were doing. The result was unceasing doubt about the value of existing staff and faculty activities, accompanied by significant staff layoffs and reorganizations and a weakening of academic infrastructure. Throughout my career, there has been *no* discussion about a teaching, research, or administrative program that was *not* controlled by the cost debate.

Obviously this was also true at Garland's Miami University, since he imposed seven years of nonstop analytical accounting on the entire campus. His motive for this was fine: universities used to lack data about the cost of more senior seminars or faculty governance that they did need to collect and consider. But collecting better data is one thing and assuming permanent inefficiency is something else. Are institutions like Miami University or U Mass-Amherst or UNC Chapel Hill or Cal State Northridge or UC Berkeley that are no longer able to wash windows and wax floors really less "efficient" than, say, health insurance companies, or hedge funds, or private universities? Unfortunately, the Revenue Theory of Costs entitles its holders to exactly this kind of blanket assertion of universities' indifference to productivity. Their "proof" lies in the a priori assumption that increased spending equals increased waste.

Garland proceeded directly from his assumption that public colleges are grossly inefficient to his solution, which was to expose public universities to markets. His premise was that universities were *not* exposed to markets, and Garland showed that less selective local colleges enjoy some monopoly pricing power over students whose family and work commitments prevent them from leaving the area. This is a special exception from the fact that private and public colleges alike engage in relentless market competition for each other's students and prize faculty—only the most elite brands are partially immune.[25] And yet the pervasive presence of market thinking in public college management does not prevent Garland from invoking the market as his solution.

> The concept underlying [my] proposal is to introduce competition into the equation by expanding taxpayer options for education. If students have other choices, then public universities lose their quasi-monopolistic status, thus freeing the enormous power of market forces to shape their organizational behavior. When an organization depends on a market to provide the money that is its lifeblood, then it will do everything possible to satisfy the needs of that market. If it fails to meet those needs as well as its competitors do, the organization cannot long survive. However, if an organization is buffered from market forces by government subsidies, third-party payments, or other sources of revenue that are not tied to its performance, as is currently the case in public higher education, then it will naturally focus its energy on sustaining those revenues rather than serving market needs.[26]

Garland assumed that the academic spending id is insulated from market relations, though this is what he was supposed to prove. He also assumed that the cure is market discipline. He did not acknowledge that universities are already engaged in competition on multiple fronts, or that market "discipline" can easily *increase* costs though competition in its many modes—imitation, duplication, overbuilding—or that his university, like all second-tier public universities in the country, was constantly scrambling to move up, to be noticed, to get better students, to attract famous faculty—all of which costs money.

Matthews and Garland represent the consensus terrain on which public universities are analyzed in the policy world. I called it liberal Reaganism.[27] It is a liberal view in the sense that it sees the public sector doing good things, but Reaganite in its assumption that the public sector is defined by waste, opacity, and inefficiency in its blissful ignorance of market forces. We could also call this view "neoliberalism," which similarly assumes that social relations and human motives are inefficient while market relations are not. Neoliberalism defines markets, as Philip Mirowski has explained, as "an ideal processor of information."[28] Democrats as well as Republicans now accept this belief, and it runs from Bowen's "revenue theory" to current anger about college costs. It means that public universities are routinely derided as intrinsically extravagant and inefficient without the logic or evidence to support such an accusation. It means too that public colleges' all-consuming—and costly—struggle to be efficient will never change the *perception* of inefficiency, no matter how cheapened public education becomes.

The Costs of Competition

The kernel of truth in the Revenue Theory of Costs is not "spend all you can" but "compete all the time."

Universities are marked by "patterned isolation" among their academic disciplines, few of which have any direct communication with others.[29] The senior managers who preside over their compartmentalized departments do not have a unifying vocabulary with which to measure value across them. The default lingua franca is money, so that the value of teaching is measured by student enrollments and the value of research is measured by the cash value of extramural grants. The same rule governs private fund-raising—a department may attract a donor interested in curing multiple sclerosis, protecting deep sea ecologies, or reversing concentration of ownership in the film industry, and that department's research may gravitate in that direction while making a claim on the university's internal funds. Something similar happens with recruitment and retention, in which a faculty member with an outside job offer can extract research funding or other benefits by asking for a match of the offer. Both teaching and research are heavily influenced by persistent resource competition in academic life.[30]

Bowen's revenue theory works better if we recast it as a theory of academic competition. A major cost driver is faculty doing what the entire system of resource incentives demand that they do, which is display continuous *entrepreneurialism*. The overall effect on a research campus is that each of fifty or sixty departments will have ten good ideas every year for new courses to offer, new minors, new subfields the department should research, new funding sources that should be tapped with novel projects, new faculty that should be hired away from rivals, new social or scientific problems that should be addressed today. Of those ten ideas, the department may agree to put one forward. Contrary to the stereotype of faculty traditionalism, most faculty are writing new research proposals and dialing for new dollars much of the time. Budget officers should be so lucky as to have traditionalist or even "deadwood" faculty—it would help them stay within austerity budgets. The mythical faculty members who like to repeat exactly the same thing each year do not need more money each year. Real-life entrepreneurial faculty do.

The university's best recipe for overspending is for 10 to 20 percent of its fifty departments to be really successful at getting grants, starting new programs, and teaching new courses. The administration will endure a steady rain of deserving initiatives that, if funded, could double the budget every five years. The driver, to repeat, is academic hustle. The driver is not profligacy but entrepreneurship. The driver is the desire to teach, to learn, to research, to know more, to have more impact, to do everything better—to succeed at everything. Success is really expensive.

The entrepreneurial imperative has come to govern teaching and research, which it subjects to the requirements of market competition. Everyone agrees that universities compete constantly with each other for the best faculty, the best students, and the best donors.

University managers and faculty alike have become as obsessed with rankings as sports fans, and build the facilities to attract the faculty that will earn the grants that will entice the philanthropy—and this cycle never ends. Faculty regularly apply for federal grants whose acceptance rates are somewhere between one in five and one in ten. As the odds worsen, they apply even more.[31] Administrators solicit public funding increases and donations to support this activity. This includes constructing new buildings and, in some cases, new campuses, such as the University of California at San Francisco's whole new campus at Mission Bay near the city's waterfront. Between 2011 and 2021, the University of California expects the state to cover only one-third of the cost even of state-eligible buildings, meaning that campus ambitions will create large budgetary holes that will require "nontraditional" funding methods and engage everyone in a perpetual scramble for cash.[32]

The outsized growth in tuition via increased research expenditures, not to mention via administrative growth, hospital costs, Vegas gyms—*every single category* of *non*-instructional spending that many faculty actually protest—has been driven by free-for-all competition for market position. The huge costs and spending perversities are incurred by academic administrators, it's true, but they are incurred as all institutional actors engage in a scramble for mostly private revenue streams in the wake of repeated public cuts.

The Revenue Theory of Costs thus gets the real situation backward. The theory assumes that the problem with universities, especially public ones, is that their desires are unregulated by the market forces that discipline corporations. The solution then becomes to impose market forces, which always take the form of cuts from above.

In reality, the problem with universities is that their desires are governed by the market forces that require them constantly to pursue external funding. As public funding for public colleges is cut, entrepreneurial competitiveness is jacked up, which ratchets up costs to support everything from accountants for grant application budget writing to lab upgrades to the construction of new buildings.

Public cuts have not only reduced revenues; they have increased costs and specifically hiked the costs of entrepreneurial competition. These can be divided into the costs of losing competitions and the even higher costs of winning them. In developing the research and teaching programs that will attract funding, entrepreneurial staff and faculty drive up costs—costs that, as we saw in Stage 2, are not covered by research revenues.[33] Public cuts cause tuition hikes in this restricted and indirect sense: they force expensive entrepreneurial competition in resource markets.

The Illusive Cost Disease

One possible response to my claim here is to say, yes, entrepreneurship is expensive and its successful version even more so. But universities have only half the market picture. They are good at seeking revenues and raising costs, but bad at controlling them. Market discipline is the missing piece of the puzzle here.

To put this claim another way, Bowen's revenue theory should be supplemented by "Baumol's cost disease." The concept is generally traced back to a 1966 paper by the economists William Baumol and William Bowen (as opposed to the Howard Bowen we have been discussing) and has been debated continuously ever since.[34] The main argument is that, while costs may fall over time in industries like manufacturing, where labor is replaced by technology, industries that continue to use high quantities of labor will not see their costs fall in the same way.

Baumol and Bowen's famous example was a string quartet: one cannot improve the productivity of a quartet performing a Beethoven piece by using only two or three musicians; at the same time, musician wages are higher now than in the nineteenth century. Both of these facts reduce or even eliminate productivity gains in labor-intensive industries. Universities that depend on skilled faculty and staff labor thus cannot match the cost reductions that one sees in manufacturing. University cost increases will always exceed measures tied to the prices of manufactured goods like cars and smartphones.

A college can of course keep costs from rising through cuts, but in a recent update Baumol notes: "a reduction in the amount of time put into a personal service is likely to make the service worse. . . . an increase in productivity in health care or education—that is, a rise in the number of patients or students treated or educated in a given amount of time—is difficult to attain without an accompanying decline in quality."[35] Services that require intensive personal involvement cannot easily be cheapened through technological changes that increase productivity. What happens instead is lower quality. Alternatively, maintaining quality as high-skill wages increase will steadily drive up costs.

How important is Baumol's cost disease to rising tuition? One recent attempt to quantify its impact puts it at just under one quarter of overall cost increases.[36] The explanation is often associated with excessive salaries for senior managers and for faculty, particularly the star STEM faculty who can exploit bidding wars for their services among different universities.

The explanation does not hold up for the overall mass of faculty salaries. These generally grow at one-half to one-third the rate of tuition increases.[37] More importantly, universities have steadily lowered the proportion of teaching staff who are full time, tenured, or tenure-track faculty.[38] Non-tenure-track faculty have lower salaries and teach more, which significantly lowers the cost per student of the instruction universities have delivered. The American Association of University Professors has long been tracking salaries and proportions of adjunct instructors. They have concluded, "AAUP data clearly indicate that full-time faculty salaries have not been driving up the costs of higher education over the last three decades."[39]

The Delta Cost Project noted that the situation was even worse in public colleges: "In public institutions, spending for instruction saw the greatest relative declines during the 2003–2008 period, with absolute cuts in this category during the first part of this period in all public sectors. Spending rebounded after 2005, although in all sectors, the instruction share of spending was lower in 2008 than both five and ten years prior."[40] Overall faculty costs have been subject to three decades of cheapening, particularly in the public sector, and are not the source of tuition hikes.

If Baumol's cost disease does not operate in the most literal sense, in which the relentless rise in high-skill labor drives up costs and tuition, does it operate in some other way?

An answer came from two economists, Robert B. Archibald and David H. Feldman, who used an analogy with health care to explain that cost increases in services are driven most fundamentally by improvements in a "standard of care."

> A new piece of medical equipment may allow a physician to do more accurate imaging, leading to fewer mistakes in designing the care a patient will receive. The new imaging equipment likely will be more expensive than the old. But if it produces better outcomes for patients, it improves the quality of care. Patients will want to have it, and physicians will want to use it, so it will be used. In addition, physicians have an ethical and legal requirement to meet standards of care that evolve over time. When the new imaging technology's superior proficiency is clearly demonstrated, the standard of care will require its use. At that point, physicians will have no choice but to use newer techniques, even if they are more expensive. They cannot choose to continue to do things the old way simply because the old way is cheaper. Nor can they offer budget procedures for the price conscious. They have to adopt the new and supposedly better technology, or they will face a malpractice suit.[41]

Education is a service that resembles health care. Once you discover a better method, you have two choices. You can figure out how to give it to everybody. Or you can give it to those who can pay privately, while retaining older, cheaper methods for the rest, even though they are now associated with second-class care.

Americans get door number 2 in both health care and education. Privatization does not prevent more affluent patients or students from getting the best available. To the contrary, since its general rule is "pay to play," it can concentrate resources among the richest customers and provide a still-higher or more rapidly improving standard for them. The US health-care system, in the hands of private providers and their models of market discipline, has excellent results at the top, very mediocre results overall, and exceptionally high overall costs. It is a premier example of the price of privatization.[42] As we see later, the same skew in resources is reducing outcomes in US higher education. The point here is that rising costs in services are tied *not* to constant waste but to rising quality.

Separating waste from improvement is a complex task that requires empirical study and administrative work, not the bandying of slogans. Walter McMahon noted that in "human capital-intensive industries," higher costs bring higher "human capital outcomes," which reveals "the fallacy of the 'cost disease' when this widely misused concept . . . is applied to human capital-intensive activities."[43]

Information technology offers a familiar example of cost increases that grow not because the institution is protected from market forces but because it is incessantly responding to them.

> In the second half of the 1970s and into the 1980s, the ways people accessed computers changed. The first step included remote access through terminals distributed across campus coupled with mini-computers in laboratories and on the desks of selected computer users. This required a certain amount of wiring of the campus. With the advent of the personal computer and the Internet, the entire campus needed to be wired, including dormitory rooms, classrooms, and faculty and staff offices. Wiring campuses for high-speed Internet access required very large expenditures. Finally, more recently students and faculty have migrated to laptop computers and access the Internet through wireless hubs.[44]

Any university that failed to wire, rewire, and dewire would have fallen behind in perceived quality of service and become uncompetitive. As a result, "the expensive effort to wire campuses . . . was followed almost immediately by an equally expensive effort to make campuses wireless."[45] The shift to wireless didn't make anyone more efficient in the sense of lowering costs. It may have improved educational quality—this is a complicated question—but, in any event, it was "market discipline" that demanded these repeated expenditures in order to not fall behind the competition. Everybody reacted to market signals and ponied up the funds.

We are getting closer to understanding the real sources of rising college tuition. Costs are driven by a rising standard of quality in a competitive environment. The new equipment and methods required to achieve higher quality force new expenditures. Were universities actually protected from market forces, as many critics suggest, they could pick equipment and methods adapted to their specific needs and ignore the rest. A college might decide not to shift to campuswide wireless technology, for example, on the grounds that they do not want students online during lectures anyway and want Internet experience to be a specific activity performed at a desk, rather than a ubiquitous temptation for undergraduates who need to read seven-hundred-page Victorian novels and redo problem sets until they understand them. But, in reality, universities are driven by market competition to imitate and duplicate the equipment and methods offered by their peers. The unavoidable costs of meeting a rising standard of quality are increased by market competition.

Quality and competition overlap and are not easy to distinguish in practice. The correct conclusion is that cost increases are not driven by Bowen's "spend all you can" or by Baumol's "cost disease"—both are mere symptoms—but by a rising care standard pressured by market competition. The quality goalposts keep advancing. Competition further increases spending. Meanwhile, as we saw in Stage 2, decades of privatization have forced universities to continue and even deepen large losses on their outside partnerships, making it that much harder to keep up. State governments are reluctant to appropriate large increases to universities even in the best of times. In this context, large tuition hikes are a consistent temptation, since they moot the need to separate necessary from merely competitive or imitative improvements. State cuts destabilize a budget model that was already out of whack, encouraging universities to make their tuition move again and again.

The Tuition Liberation Front

Still, since postwar state funding built some of the world's greatest public university systems, we might logically assume that their executives would fight tooth-and-nail for public funding as their *only* viable foundation. We might assume they would make the points we've been discussing here: fund-raising and research revenues do *not* increase general operating revenues that support mass quality. The only alternative to adequate public funding increases are large, regular tuition hikes. The arithmetic is not complex, and senior managers with their many publicists could make a lucid case.

This is certainly what I was expecting when I started going to the University of California Office of the President (UCOP) for regular meetings during the second major multiyear period of public cuts (2002–2005). Several of the senior faculty members on my committee, the University Committee for Planning and Budget, pressed UCOP budget executives, month after month, to explain clearly to the public and the politicians that public funding was essential to the combination of access and quality for which the state's public universities stood. These senior managers no doubt understood the argument. But they were steadfastly unwilling to make it out loud to officials in the state capitol of Sacramento. As I've already noted, they claimed the public no longer saw college as a public good. They did not want to be seen actively mobilizing the public against any representatives who continued to hack away at the UC, CSU, and community college systems. This meant that cutting deals with the state governor, Democrat or Republican, was the only option left. After Arnold Schwarzenegger's victory in a recall election in 2004, the university was also dealing with a hostile governor's office.

One of my faculty colleagues finally got tired of the deadlock in which the university's own leadership seemed unable to explain public funding. UCSF professor of medicine Stanton A. Glantz, a veteran of battles for public opinion about the health effects of tobacco, commissioned a public relations firm to make a series of sample ads that UC could place in state newspapers (figures 14 and 15).

Figure 14. Sample campaign ad 1. *Source:* Jono Polansky | Onbeyond LLC.

HOW THE STATE BUDGET WILL TAKE TWO YEARS OFF HER LIFE.

She earned her place at a California university in the fall of 2004. But enrollment cuts mean she won't get one. Budget cuts also mean fewer classes when she *does* enter university, stretching the time it takes to graduate, already more than four years, closer to six. Together, class and enrollment cuts could take two years or more off this generation's promising future. Can students and their families afford to lose so much time? *Can California?* Please call Governor Schwarzenegger's Sacramento office at 916-445-2841 or email him at governor@governor.ca.gov. Tell him there's really no time to lose.

CALIFORNIA'S PUBLIC COLLEGES and UNIVERSITIES

Keep California's promise.

Figure 15. Sample campaign ad 2. *Source:* Jono Polansky | Onbeyond LLC.

The point of such ads was to spread the following syllogism far and wide:

1. The state's public colleges and universities serve the population as a whole by offering affordable quality. All qualified students receive a top-tier education, not a second- or third-rate education pegged to their second- or third-rate ability to pay.
2. Cuts to state funding have damaged public university quality, reducing their public service.
3. Quality can be protected through large tuition increases. But these reduce affordability.
4. Only public reinvestment offers affordable quality.

But neither these nor a number of similar ads saw the light of day. UCOP declined to use them or to advocate for public funding in a single-minded way. Individual campuses also stayed silent. Regents and campus foundation members didn't pitch tax surcharges or state revenue increases. Given this silence on the specific powers of public funding, voters might be forgiven for thinking that replacing some public funding with moderate tuition increases would do no harm.

As it turned out, this is exactly the program that was being prepared by university officials with the Schwarzenegger administration. In May 2004 our faculty budget committee learned on the same day as everyone else that funding and tuition were to be governed by a multiyear Compact for Higher Education. This would end the cuts to state funding (16 percent in that round), and then increase state funding 3 percent per year for two years and 4 percent in the third year. This was just a bit more than inflation, and would get UC back to nominal 2001–2002 public funding levels by 2008–2009.

As I noted earlier, the university partners, UC and CSU, agreed to raise tuition each year by 7 to 10 percent for undergraduates, with 10 to 20 percent annual increases for graduate students.[46] The universities thus offered to move toward private sources for revenue in exchange for an end to public cuts. They also got public funding growth that was too low to make up for previous cuts, much less fund quality improvements.[47] The compact was great for the Schwarzenegger administration, since it pushed more higher education funding off the state ledgers and reduced pressure to reverse the tax cuts the governor had implemented on his arrival in office. For university officials, the compact implemented halfway privatization, which many of them felt was the best of both worlds—they kept most of their public money, but they had a permanent reason to direct their faculty toward raising private funds. The shift from public to private money was built into the agreement.

The public revenue loss was large, but so was the conceptual loss. University managers had to defend their deal. Since it consisted of rebuilding public funding at about half the rate of required tuition increases, they were unable to trumpet the benefits of public funding. They in effect had accepted the conservative position on the virtues of privatization and sacrificed their ability to explain the state's essential role to the public.

There was also a political loss. Without a popular understanding of the role public funding played in sustaining mass quality, the university systems were more vulnerable to public cuts in the future. They would not be able to rally voters to defend public funding whose benefits they had actively suppressed as part of their compact. Sure enough, when the financial crisis surfaced in late 2008, Governor Schwarzenegger unilaterally abrogated his compact and imposed a new 20 percent cut on public higher education. UC complained about this but then massively hiked tuition—32 percent for 2009–2010. A popular understanding of public funding would not have prevented cuts in a massive financial crisis. But it would have armed voters to demand a rapid funding recovery in the aftermath and to demand lower-to-no tuition hikes in the future. It may even have prevented a repeat of massive state cuts two years later by a Democratic governor, Jerry Brown, who saw that voters had been taught to hate budget deficits more than cuts to education.

Wisconsin provided another important example of a public university's failure to explain public funding. As the crisis was settling in, the head of the Madison flagship campus focused on gaining more autonomy from the state rather than on explaining why she needed more money from them.[48] The chancellor then departed for a private college, but the University of Wisconsin system head continued her initiative.[49] A few years later, the "autonomy" idea turned up as a proposal from Governor Scott Walker, where it was predictably accompanied by a call to cut the university system budget another 12 percent over two years.

In response, the University of Wisconsin's managers did not clearly state that such cuts would permanently damage the university.[50] The new Madison chancellor said they needed more time to implement the cuts and also said, in defiance of basic arithmetic, that autonomy would allow efficiencies that could compensate for the loss of state funding.[51] Administrative correspondence obtained by a newspaper showed that the university's senior managers were focused on getting their autonomy, even if it cost them a public funding cut.[52] The concept of public funding was a big loser.

Why did public university officials, in California, Wisconsin, and elsewhere, not use the 2008 crisis to explain the absolute necessity of public funding to improve educational quality, and improve it without tuition hikes that would damage access? Why did they use the crisis to justify higher tuition? Their timing couldn't have been worse—in a recession that was liquidating much of the working-class and middle-class wealth that could have paid for college. Their hikes also paved the way for the backlash that, by 2015, had stuck many public universities with tuition freezes. Why did they make such a huge mistake?

Though the state cuts put enormous pressure on university officials, the deeper problem was their belief in, and responsiveness to, market forces. Most public university officials saw pricing through the lens of their market competition with peers and allowed the highest-status private universities to define market levels.[53] Public university officials came to judge tuition levels not by the level required to supplement state appropriations but by the levels set by private colleges, particularly at the prestigious end. One could imagine a culture in which normal tuition was a mean established by a mixture of public colleges—for example, California State

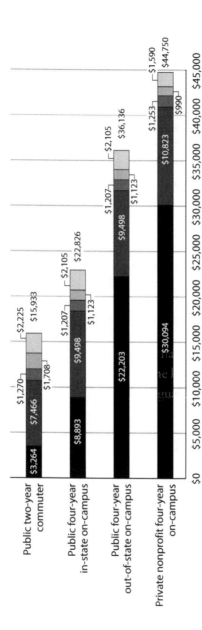

Figure 16. Average estimated full-time undergraduate budgets, 2013–2014 (enrollment-weighted). *Source: College Board, Trends in College Pricing 2013,* fig. 1, accessed December 7, 2013, http://trends.collegeboard.org/sites/default/files/college-pricing-2013-full-report.pdf.

University, the University of Oregon, Indiana University, SUNY Purchase—such that tuition levels at Harvard and Swarthmore would be seen as anomalous surcharges. Car buyers do not see the cost of a Bentley, Ferrari, Porsche, Range Rover, and Tesla as setting a market norm for car prices. They are recognized as luxury goods and placed at an extreme on the price curve. But higher education officials treated their equivalents—Harvard, MIT, Stanford, Yale—as the market standard to which they could benchmark public university tuition.

One can see how the thinking developed by looking at a College Board slide that compares private and public undergraduate budgets (figure 16). The public university receives between a third and a quarter of the private university's revenue per student. For decades, this didn't matter so much because of solid state appropriations in California, Illinois, Minnesota, North Carolina, New York, Washington, and elsewhere. But as these funds dwindled through the 2000s, I more frequently heard public university officials say that low tuition meant "leaving money on the table." They were looking at that $30,094 that private universities receive per student. This kind of thinking was enabled by seeing high private tuition as the norm rather than as the deluxe exception. The shift was subtle but powerful and became an unconscious support for privatization culture.

Privatizer-in-Chief

Sometimes a new administrative common sense can be established by the efforts of a few leading figures. This was the case in California, where an important ideological role was played by a pivotal senior manager of the 2000s, Berkeley law school dean Christopher Edley.

Edley was a progressive Democrat and illustrates an important part of our story, which is the extent to which Democrats and Republicans came to share a privatization consensus. Having spent his academic career in private universities, mostly at Harvard, Edley moved to Berkeley to take over its law school (then called Boalt) in July 2004.[54]

Before he started the job, Edley was asked by a Berkeley audience how he was going to support his ambitious intellectual agenda for the law school. He replied,

> I'm going to raise a lot of money. First and foremost, I'm going to work with the faculty and senior administrators to launch a planning process for a major fund-raising campaign within the next few weeks, not months. The strategic planning for this is not going to await my full-time arrival in July. But second, I hope to have an opportunity to work with the chancellor and the provost to help make the case to the broader public in California that the UC system in general, and Berkeley in particular, deserves the continuing and vigorous support of the public. I think that if we articulate a vision for Boalt of pre-eminence in the way I've described, we'll be able to persuade alumni and others that it's worth not only their enthusiastic support but their generous investment.[55]

Edley indicated that his focus was more private fund-raising, though public support could have a supporting role. His main motive became clear in another interview, in which he said his goal was to "raise the resources from alumni and others to compete with the best private law schools."[56] The driver was market competition with private law school rivals, measured by Berkeley law's ranking. Edley cast the state not as funder or partner but moocher (via allegedly using the law school as a "profit center") from which the law school needed to be freed.

Halfway through his first year, Edley announced in the *Los Angeles Times* that state funding was not enough to support excellence.

> I am not interested in privatizing Boalt Hall's mission. The university's overall mission is to provide public access to world-class excellence at a bargain price. . . .
>
> Yet the state is increasingly unwilling or unable to pay for excellence, so escalating tuition, partially offsetting neglectful appropriations, threatens to make the bargain a cherished memory.
>
> Tuition for California residents at Boalt Hall, where I became dean last July, is about $22,000. That is roughly two-thirds of what Stanford

and Harvard law schools charge, and double what Boalt charged just four years ago. Ten years ago, Boalt cost only a third of the top privates, and I regularly see alumni who, a generation ago, got three years of a world-class legal education for a total of $750.[57]

Edley's justified concern about public funding declines shifted rapidly to a call to raise Boalt tuition to the private sector market price. He described low public law school tuition as a kind of giveaway that hurt Boalt's market position. A reader would also assume that high tuition could replace public funds and make public funding restoration unnecessary.

There was a further twist that, in my experience, became an important part of administrative thinking about the public sector:

> Sure, private fundraising has been on the rise at Boalt and throughout UC for some years. The dominant alumni mind-set, however, is that surely the state is paying to sustain the access and excellence that make us great, when that is no longer the case. Boalt is probably typical of UC in that a decent proportion of alumni do contribute, but in amounts that are dwarfed by private competitors. Yale Law School, with an alumni body comparable to Boalt's, has eight times as many professional fundraisers, and also eight times the endowment income per student.[58]

In order to increase fund-raising from alums, Edley had to assure them that public funding would never recover. This project of minimizing the chance of public recovery took precedence over advocating for it—as a consequence of the exclusive focus on Berkeley law's market position.

As much as Edley focused in the press on voluntary alumni giving, he focused in the university on involuntary student giving in the form of tuition hikes. The UC Regents began discussing decoupling professional schools from undergraduate fees in 2005, with plentiful evidence from Chris Edley and other professional school deans. Their discussion document in November 2005 identified a few professional schools as especially deserving of extra tuition increments.

> A sustained program of fee increases over and above the levels proposed for other professional schools is recommended for the law and business schools at Berkeley and UCLA to begin to restore excellence and ensure broad accessibility. Accordingly, just as the proposed fee increases for the law and business schools at Berkeley and UCLA for 2006–07 are higher than those proposed for other programs, increases for these programs in future years also are likely to be higher—at least 10 percent per year and perhaps more if additional funds are needed to restore quality to those programs.[59]

The goal was to keep professional school quality from being dragged down with the undergraduate programs, especially at those four schools. The "Draft Guiding Principles for Professional School Fees" had six points, three of which allowed these fees to rise to market, defined equivocally as public university peers.[60] In January 2007 the Regents considered, and later approved, a policy that allowed professional schools to set fees to respond to, among other things, "market-based factors that permit University programs to compete successfully for students."[61]

With professional school tuition suddenly easier to increase, my budget committee became quite concerned that the Berkeley law model was going to spread to the rest of the university system. We were quite worried about a perverse effect I discuss in Stage 4, which is "tuition substitution"—the more you raise tuition, the less the state thinks you need public funding. This phenomenon was noted in many documents, though it was apparently ignored by the Regents and pooh-poohed by senior administrators when my colleagues and I raised it with them.

Edley presented his Berkeley law plan to my faculty budget committee in April 2007. His goal was for Berkeley to join the top five law schools again: it was apparently of the utmost importance that Berkeley move from top ten to top five status. Of the top ten that year, only Michigan, Virginia, and Berkeley were historically public. Though Yale spent three times more per student than Berkeley, the others were in Berkeley's ballpark, and yet market competitiveness, Edley insisted, required a shift to private funding and large annual tuition increases. This would happen every year, always, for the foreseeable forever. He projected that he would effectively have tripled tuition to about $45,000 per year by 2011 (with increased financial aid).

By then, the Academic Senate considered professional school fee hikes to be a done deal. But we asked Edley—in my case, pleaded with him—to make it clear to Sacramento and the Regents that this tripling of fees to "market" would *only* work for the "big four" professional schools and that if applied to undergraduates, would wreck UC overall, as well as PhD programs and professional programs whose graduates have moderate incomes. We asked him to call for public funding increases to save UC, even if he was talking down state funding to open donor wallets. UC is damaged, we said to him, when the Berkeley law dean says, "The alumni mistakenly believe that the state remains committed to providing a quality legal education for next to nothing. . . . But those days are over."[62]

Edley saw the point and agreed that the undergrad programs were nothing like his law school, but he charged out of the meeting proclaiming, "California is a failed state," and changed nothing about his policy or rhetoric. A year and a half later, the 2008 crisis surfaced, and a whole new round of cuts took rebuilt public funds off the table.

When the university responded to the new cuts in 2009— 20 percent on top of a previous 40 percent—with pay "furloughs" and other measures, a few of us authored a petition called "Stop the Cuts." We called for a freeze on the furloughs until the Regents could consider alternatives, and for a new anticuts lobbying effort with the state.[63] The petition received 2,800 signatures in a few days. Edley responded furiously. "The profound lack of knowledge reflected in the petition is utterly staggering," he began.[64] He went on, "The petition suggests . . . what? That masses of faculty and staff spend the time to become proficient in budget tradeoffs, and sensitive to competing values and goals? How practical is that? Delaying things in order to have another 20 town hall meetings and another 30 public speakers at a future Regents meeting will accomplish nothing substantive, and almost nothing in governance terms." It's true, we did call on faculty and staff to become informed about budget matters and for them to receive accurate, detailed budget information—for the first time in university history. But I took exception to Edley's suggestion that university officials had done all they could to increase public funding. I felt they had done all they could to raise tuition.

I wrote him back.

Dear Chris,
I barely recognized you in your angry ad hominem attack on the "stop the cuts" petition writers.

You and I have met once—when you presented Berkeley Law's financial planning to the Senate's systemwide committee for Planning and Budget (UCPB) while I was chair—but I remember you as a charming, rigorous persuader, and have always respected your passionate advocacy for your law school unit.

You may not be aware that I have written two books about universities as cultural, intellectual, and financial institutions, as well as many articles on the subject in the US and abroad. But I know you know the UC budget reports I co-authored, which did three things: 1) they correctly predicted the gravity of the current crisis at a time when UCOP insisted that everything was fine; 2) they showed that only undesirably high tuition increases could make up for chronic and now massive cuts in the state portion of UC's budget; 3) they called on UCOP and the Regents to make the public "ask" for a correct level of state funding.

The history is relevant here. Our Senate budget group calculated a reasonable recovery route as a return to the 2001 state funding effort for UC. In 2006–07 this meant we were down $1.1 billion from where we would have been had we continued to grow at the same rate as state personal income after 2001. The systemwide Academic Senate endorsed this recommendation for a return to the "2001 Pathway" through a UCOP/Regental deal with the legislature for a sustainable ramp-up. That was before the current crisis, when we could imagine this happening reasonably soon.

Then-chair of the Senate John Oakley and I presented the Futures Report and the recommendation to the Regents in May 2007. The next year, my committee wrote the Cuts Report, showing that the Governor was doing exactly the opposite of what UC required, which was to go beyond the worst of our four scenarios for reductions of public funding. That report recommended that UC set a minimum for state investment per student and not go below that. This would set a floor to the degradation of resources, after which we would reduce enrollments.

UCOP and the Regents ignored these formally endorsed recommendations. Even though we showed that the restoration of proper public funding is the only way to have a high-quality public research university with the widest possible access, I do not know of a single statement made by any UC official that has called for a major restoration of public funding. Instead, this was widely written off as a "non-starter," although it is exactly how Pres. David Gardner got UC back on track in the 1980s—massive, repeated general fund increases—and although we all know that you will never receive if you don't even ask in the first place.

You don't tell us about any of "zillions" of ideas that have been considered—and in failing to offer even one concrete instance, your response reflects the lack of transparency and the vagueness of the financial analysis that the petition signers are rightly concerned about.

But I do know about one idea that you have advocated publicly and with your characteristic energy and eloquence: the era of public funding is over. I also know about your main solution: you got permission from the Regents to raise the fees at some UC professional schools to market, and you have nearly doubled Berkeley law tuition to almost $36,000 a year (Stanford is $42,420). The in-state fee exemption has also disappeared, although I assume Berkeley law still receives a good multiple of state general funds beyond that received per student by the campuses.

This has protected Berkeley Law, but it is a doomsday scenario for UC as a whole. You help discourage UC from ever asking for correct levels of funding, even though you know that we neither can nor want the Berkeley Law solution of $20,000 rising to $40,000 tuition. We are caught in a trap that is in large part UC officialdom's own making, and so far, Chris, you are making it worse.

This year's cuts are a complete catastrophe for the University of California system. Please redirect your guns not at your own colleagues but at the downsizers who are degrading higher education for a now-minority-majority population at a time when we all need it the most.

It would be great to have you with us and not against us.[65]

I did not receive a letter from Edley. Entering Berkeley law students received letters from him, however—announcing another increase in tuition in the fall of 2009. Though Edley later left the deanship, his tuition hikes remain: by 2015–2016, in-state Berkeley law tuition was $48,655.[66]

State legislatures are responsible for the funding cuts that have done so much harm to public universities, and university leaders have episodically complained about them.[67] But as a group, academia's senior managers made several fatal errors. First, they did not admit to the losses incurred by necessary research, external partnerships, and related costs (Stage 2). Second, they failed to explain that most cost increases reflected quality. Third, they did not explain that competitive market rivalry within their sector costs money rather than saves it. Fourth, they did not develop procedures for separating the quality sheep from the imitation goats. Fifth, they did not insist that quality improvements are public goods whose wide use can only be supported by public funding. Finally, they buried these issues by regularly and routinely using their power to raise tuition, in good years and bad. This diverted everyone's attention from public funding's virtues and privatization's price.

The States Cut Public Funding

Oh, I don't blame myself.

—Noah Cross, *Chinatown* (1974)

State legislators know in the abstract that public funding enables the low tuition that is the backbone of college affordability and access, which in turn helps drive their regional economy. This has been US conventional wisdom since the land-grant college legislation passed during the Civil War. But economic downturns have always given states an excuse to cut colleges. The financial crisis of 2008 gave states the mother of all such excuses, and cut they did (see figure 17).

The only states to escape the initial carnage were in the midst of shale oil booms, and there were two of these. Thirty-six states cut their public college funding more than 20 percent in constant dollars. The only good thing about this was that this new round of cuts helped the media finally grasp the size and scale of public funding cuts.[1] For the ten years prior to the 2008 collapse, higher education budgets in California had grown more slowly than those of any program area other than job training—at about two-thirds the rate of the state average.[2] The cuts to higher education were larger than those to any other sector.[3] Democratic governors were almost as ready as Republicans to cut public higher ed. Jerry Brown cut the colleges and universities as much in 2011 as Arnold Schwarzenegger had cut them a couple of years before.[4]

Since the value of higher education was holy writ in the knowledge economy, why were state politicians so ready and willing to slash it?

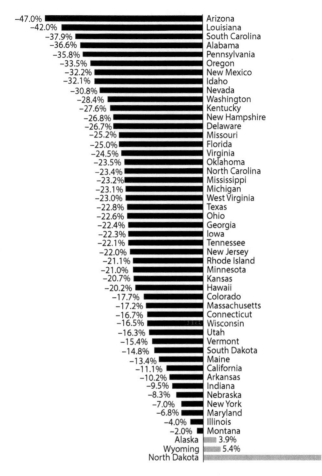

−47.0%	Arizona
−42.0%	Louisiana
−37.9%	South Carolina
−36.6%	Alabama
−35.8%	Pennsylvania
−33.5%	Oregon
−32.2%	New Mexico
−32.1%	Idaho
−30.8%	Nevada
−28.4%	Washington
−27.6%	Kentucky
−26.8%	New Hampshire
−26.7%	Delaware
−25.2%	Missouri
−25.0%	Florida
−24.5%	Virginia
−23.5%	Oklahoma
−23.4%	North Carolina
−23.2%	Mississippi
−23.1%	Michigan
−23.0%	West Virginia
−22.8%	Texas
−22.6%	Ohio
−22.4%	Georgia
−22.3%	Iowa
−22.1%	Tennessee
−22.0%	New Jersey
−21.1%	Rhode Island
−21.0%	Minnesota
−20.7%	Kansas
−20.2%	Hawaii
−17.7%	Colorado
−17.2%	Massachusetts
−16.7%	Connecticut
−16.5%	Wisconsin
−16.3%	Utah
−15.4%	Vermont
−14.8%	South Dakota
−13.4%	Maine
−11.1%	California
−10.2%	Arkansas
−9.5%	Indiana
−8.3%	Nebraska
−7.0%	New York
−6.8%	Maryland
−4.0%	Illinois
−2.0%	Montana
Alaska	3.9%
Wyoming	5.4%
North Dakota	35.5%

Figure 17. Percent change in state funding per student, inflation adjusted, FY 2008–FY 2015. *Source:* Michael Mitchell and Michael Leachman, "Years of Cuts Threaten to Put College Out of Reach for More Students," Center on Budget and Policy Priorities (CBPP), May 13, 2015, fig. 1, http://www.cbpp.org/research/state-budget-and-tax/years-of-cuts -threaten-to-put-college-out-of-reach-for-more-students.
Note: CBPP calculations use data from Illinois State University's annual Grapevine Report and the State Higher Education Executive Officers Association. Illinois funding data are provided by the Fiscal Policy Center at Voices for Illinois Children. Because enrollment data are only available through the 2014 school year, enrollment for the 2014–2015 school year is estimated using data from past years. Years are fiscal years.

From Tuition Hikes to the Austerity Consensus

We already know a key reason that states were willing to cut funding to universities: universities could and would raise tuition to offset their losses. So better to cut higher education than to cut Medicaid, income maintenance programs, preschool education, and similar services. When senior academic managers responded to funding cuts with tuition hikes, legislatures learned that their next funding cut would be offset in the same way.

This is a simple feedback loop that was well entrenched by 2008, even if university leaders were unable to acknowledge it publicly. We have already looked at an example of this cycle with Washington State. Senior managers insisted that state cuts caused tuition hikes. But the political causality ran the other way: *tuition hikes enabled and encouraged state funding cuts.*

The pattern of using tuition as a state-funding substitute had already begun in the 1960s in California, where Democratic state senator Al Rodda noted that Governor Ronald Reagan's insistence on charging some tuition for UC students meant not only a doubling of overall student fees between 1970 and 1972, but also a new "era of the politics of tuition." "We have abandoned a 101-year tradition which has been supported by fourteen Republican Governors and seven Democratic Governors. The Regents no longer have a principle of no-tuition to stand on. They will have to bargain on the tuition question and tuition will now become a part of the budgetary debates and deliberations each year."[5] In other words, after 1971, the California legislature would factor the university's power to raise tuition into its allocations. Similar patterns occurred in Michigan, Arizona, and elsewhere, as public universities, led by prestigious flagships, began to raise tuition annually for decades at a time.[6]

After 2008, more state officials pointed to tuition hikes as their reason for cutting. A former aide to Ohio governor Ted Strickland summed up this arrangement in that state:

In Strickland's first two years as governor [2007–2009], universities froze tuition rates in exchange for strong state financial support. In the [next] two-year budget, state spending on higher education was less robust, so colleges could raise tuition up to 3.5 percent each year. . . .

But even as Governor Strickland closed that gap, Ohio still is below the national average in state funding per student.

Read the tea leaves, and the universities are giving Governor-elect Kasich an out: cut our funding and we won't complain if you let us increase tuition more than we could under Governor Strickland. For a lazy, short-sighted legislature facing billions (and growing, thanks to Governor-elect Kasich's actions) in estimated deficits, cutting university and college funding while permitting those higher education institutions to offset those cuts with tuition increases is a relatively pain-free way to cut spending. The university presidents say we'll let you promote our partnership in economic development with the private sector, Governor-elect Kasich, and not complain about you cutting our state funding, but only if you allow us to return to the double-digit tuition increases under Governors Voinovich and Taft.[7]

Cut our funding and we won't complain if you let us hike tuition: this is the hidden contract between public university executives and their state officials.

Another example: in Pennsylvania in 2011, Governor Tom Corbett proposed "the largest single-year reduction in state support to public universities in the nation's history." His justification was that the state should direct "money to students rather than institutions," because "the money given to public universities in the past has not prevented tuition from rising."[8] He had a point—and an alibi for cuts.

In California, the Legislative Analyst's Office also built the university's power to hike tuition into state budgeting.

Unlike many other areas of the state budget that are constrained by constitutional or federal requirements, the Legislature has significant discretion over university and financial aid expenditures. At the same time, the universities have greater control over their total operating budget than most state agencies because they have the ability to raise additional revenue by increasing student tuition. These factors mean that expenditures on the universities and financial aid are very sensitive to future legislative actions and the systems' future decisions on tuition levels.[9]

The legislature assumes that the university will raise tuition to get more revenue whenever they can't get it from the state. The legislature factors this tuition power into their budgeting and does not see access or quality as dependent on high levels of public funding.

In case UC officials weren't noticing this link—"you university officials raise tuition, we legislators cut your funding"—State Assembly Speaker John Pérez came to a Regents meeting in January 2013 and spelled it out: "The possibility of increased funding right now: it doesn't exist. . . . There is no significant amount of money to backfill previous cuts. We've made roughly $900 million in cuts and you've increased fees 1.4 billion dollars. The [fee] increases were disproportionate to the level of disinvestment by the state."[10] Pérez was accurately citing California Department of Finance data (without factoring in the costs of financial aid).[11] From the state's point of view, UC turned a massive public funding cut into a $500 million profit for itself.

Later in the year, California's governor, Jerry Brown, promised officials that tuition hikes had been and would be held against them. In September 2013, he made this remarkable statement to the Board of Regents, which I cite at length:

> Maybe you need to make a more effective argument to be getting more than you're getting. But up there in the legislature there are people who are saying I want. And I can tell you as someone who's been watching this process for four decades, the desires are endless, and the desires have a way of transmogrifying into needs, and needs have a curious way of transforming into rights, and rights have a tendency to turn into lawsuits. And that's kind of where we are. Desire-need-rights-lawsuit. So we're trying to manage all that. Whatever it is, your desire-need-right-lawsuit machine, is not as effective as the inmates in our prisons. They have turned their desires into very effective rights that are being validated by the federal judiciary. We just allocated $315 million to buy more prison

beds solely, solely because of pressure from the three federal judges that are in charge of our prison system. So if you could find a way to [claim] deprivation of one of the Bill of Rights, because of funding inadequacy, you could sue the state, and we would have to pay you whatever you want, so maybe some of your clever Boalt Hall, UCLA, Irvine lawyers can figure out why your desires, although they may have turned into needs, have not yet evolved into rights. Because rights do get vindicated outside the democratic process, by the judicial process, which the politicians don't control.

Anyway I want to end this little detour by saying everything has to be on the table here. Whether it's enrollment growth or the faculty workload. Again, desires are endless, but which desires do we validate? When we say we, who's we? "We" is the Regents, it's the legislature, it's the governor, it's the people. It's a process of making collective decisions, through this messy democratic process. It isn't just oh we want to keep growing. Oh we want to expand. We want more market share at our medical centers. Or whatever the hell it's going to be. You gotta really—at least I am going to—look, ok, how do I balance that off against other things, and one of the other things is tuition. And this is remarkable when you look at UC compared to the Ivy leagues and other schools. The way the Pell grants, the low-income, the Cal grant, we're doing quite a lot. [*sic*]

And now the legislature, under the leadership, or pressure, depending on how you want to look at it, of the Speaker, is now going to add a middle class scholarship. That's going to be several hundred million dollars. That, on a yearly basis, is more than our increase to the university. Maybe had you been lobbying a little more powerfully you would have turned that into a direct investment in the university. But it's not going to turn out that way. It's going to turn out to be something called the middle class scholarship.[12]

In brief, Brown was saying that the university's recent tuition hikes were now directly costing it several hundred million dollars every year in state appropriations. The state's accounting had changed. In future years, the state would deduct from the university's state fund the state's cost for grants required to offset the university's tuition hikes. Tuition hikes, henceforth, would be an immediate cause of state funding cuts.

It's worth remembering that Pérez and Brown were leading the state Democratic Party in a period when, for a time, it had acquired a supermajority in both legislative chambers and could pass whatever higher education legislation it wanted. What it wanted, it turned out, was neither public funding restoration nor new tuition increases. Their rationale reflected a bipartisan national consensus that a postcrisis austerity could fairly be imposed on public universities in the wake of decades of tuition hikes. Repeat the tuition increases over many years, in most states, and throw in the post-2008 crisis and a nonrecovery for the working and middle classes, and the country now has an explicit, locked-in version of a formerly tacit feedback loop in which tuition hikes cause flat or falling funding rather than supplementing it. State officials could now use previous tuition hikes as a standing excuse for pushing higher education costs off the state books and onto the budgets of students and their families, while at the same time riding to the rescue of family budgets by crusading against tuition increases.

Advancing Education or Protecting Administration?

The second reason for the relentless public funding cuts is that university officials failed to tie public funding to *educational* quality. They allowed administrative functions and costs to feature in any public discussion of the role of state costs.

To clarify the impact of this default strategy, let's look at an alternative. As support for public funding softened, senior managers needed to make the public good case I analyzed in Stage 1. It might have gone something like this: the university's core public benefit is high-quality instruction for undergraduates. This is by no means the only benefit—graduate education and advanced research are equally essential. But the base funding for a public university is tied to the enrollments and/or degree completion of undergraduate students from our state, and we are obligated to offer top-quality undergraduate instruction on a mass scale. Our goal is to take our students, who are generally not the 1 percent, and give them skills that are functionally similar to the 1 percent that *is* educated at elite private colleges and universities. We do this for a multiracial society—in states like Texas, Arizona, California, and Florida we are doing it for minority-majority youth populations. This has private and public benefits, market and nonmarket outcomes: we create general intelligence for the workforce and also spread high-level democratic and cultural capabilities. We advance what we used to call "civilization," in a deep sense, which involves invention and discovery of new knowledge and the transformation of the rising generation that will need to solve novel problems through their collective, creative capabilities. Universities form "human capital," but this is an economistic term for liberating human potential into its full intellectual, political, and cultural maturity. Our university's aspiration is universalist, in that *every* graduate becomes able to work and imagine at society's highest level. Every citizen benefits from this democratization of intelligence. The university's aspiration is also individual and particularist, in that we help teach each individual how to recognize and analyze our state's complex, multiple identities and cultures in an atmosphere of respect and originality. Cultural capabilities are as important to us as technological ones. A research university integrates the levels of undergraduate, graduate, and advanced learning—and loses money doing it. It is society's only such institution.

How did we do at explaining this project? I cannot offer the result of a content analysis of thousands of public relations statements across the country, but I have followed the California case carefully for twenty-five years, and I offer a reading of one example that I see as both typical and foundational in the quarter century in which the state's public colleges and universities have struggled with repeated funding cuts. This document is from 1994, a year that fell in the midst of the first multiyear cuts period in California. It is a memorandum from the UC Office of the President about the elimination of executive leaves.[13] These "leaves" had received much press attention, since they suggested that UC was crying wolf about the damage done by state cuts. If you are so poor, the question went, why are you giving senior managers these long paid leaves?

After saying that President Jack Peltason had "decided to immediately discontinue all extended executive leaves because there is no longer a consensus on granting them," the memo discussed the larger budgetary context.

> Peltason said eliminating leaves might hurt UC's competitiveness with other universities that offer such leaves. But he said he made his decision because it is more important to focus debate on the long-term economic survival of the University than on continued controversy over executive compensation issues. The decision reflects debate and concerns raised both from within and outside the University, he said.
>
> "The University," Peltason added, "is something much larger and much more important than any single issue. It is the greatest hope we have of rescuing California from its formidable problems, and of giving our young people the best chance they will ever have to build a bright future for themselves. . . .
>
> "I don't believe that it is hyperbole to suggest, in fact, that the University of California is in a fight for its life. The potential losers are our children and their children. They stand to lose access to an affordable college education in this state. In fact, they stand to lose access to a quality public education at any price. We must also work to instill new public confidence in our stewardship, and we must be worthy of that trust." . . .
>
> In just four years, he noted, the University's nine campuses will have suffered $433 million in budget cuts—"the equivalent of closing the doors to Dartmouth."

Officials are defending their universities in exactly these same terms twenty years later. This memo offered a blunt, official warning that the state was attacking the postwar formula of low-cost quality college. In noting the enormous size of the cuts to public funding, UC's president claimed that access to a "quality public education" was in danger. But *how* were the cuts harming that quality?

On this issue the memo was silent. It tied the president's concern about competitiveness not to educational quality but to maintaining executive compensation. The memo did not explain that the real stakes were the quality of full-scale higher ed. The early 1990s saw the elimination of some support staff for faculty and students, real increases in class size, reductions in individual feedback, and other reversals of educational progress. All of these were invisible in senior management's crisis discourse. The memo did not state that mass quality meant spending a lot of money on *instruction* as such, or say what that money would do for students. It also did not mention that continuous quality improvement in instruction required continuous new investments in it—more technology, more training, more personnel. The university needed to explain its cost structure as the effect of its devotion to a *rising standard of care* for its students.[14] As we have seen, the deeper meaning of a service industry's alleged cost disease is "ever-improving quality" for the patient, client, or student. The university's core public benefit is this ever-rising level of intellectual development (via both research and teaching). This public good is also the *only* justification for large public expenditures on public universities. Senior management did not explain its cost structure as a direct and indirect public benefit that produced mass-scale intellectual advancement through labor-intensive instruction and research. They thus failed to make the core case against funding cuts.

The university was also fully engaged with the project of replacing public revenues with private funds through massive hikes in student tuition. The Peltason memo appeared midway through a period in which UC was tripling undergraduate fees from $951 in 1990–1991 to $3,086 in 1994–1995.[15] Affordability was certainly at risk, but this was as much the university's responsibility as the legislature's. At the same time, the university damaged any public focus on affordability—the most urgent public issue—by touting its financial aid programs and assuring everyone that access was being protected for those who couldn't pay. The memo undercut its own chicken-little alarmism with this promise that, even after the sky fell, student aid would continue to flow.

I remember wondering about the absence of plans to restructure administration when I read the memo the first time as a new assistant

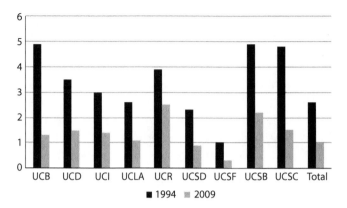

Figure 18. Ratio of ladder rank faculty to senior administrators (FTE) in 1994 and 2009.
Source: Ákos Róna-Tas, "Growth Trends in UC Administration," *Remaking the University* (blog), December 10, 2009, http://utotherescue.blogspot.co.uk/2009/12/growth-trends -in-uc-administration.html.

professor. In retrospect, the memo's omission of instructional needs predicted later, repeated defenses that protected the managerial ahead of the educational apparatus. For example, the recovery from the second multiyear cuts cycle ten years later (2002–2005) was hurt by a scandal involving then Provost M. R. C. Greenwood's role in the appointment of a friend and business associate to a staff job that paid \$192,100 a year, which came on top of the revelation that she had received about \$150,000 to move seventy miles from Santa Cruz to Oakland to take her new job.[16] It appeared to politicians and the public that the university was yet again crying wolf about its poverty, since there was always enough money to pay 1-percent-style salaries padded with special perks.

After the financial crisis surfaced in 2008, the sociologist Ákos Róna-Tas became interested in administrative growth on his campus, UC San Diego, and extended his calculations into a snapshot of growth for the whole system. In 1994, tenure-track faculty outnumbered senior administrators by five to one at Berkeley and UC Santa Barbara, and by somewhat lower amounts at other campuses. Fifteen years later, when classes were being cancelled, staff fired, and salaries cut, the ratio had dropped to nearly one faculty member per one senior administrator at the three big-city flagships, and to around two to one even at the poorer campuses. Although students are often blamed for administrative growth, supposedly because student services are so expensive, this study found that "institutional support" was larger than "academic support" and twice as large as "student services."[17] In other words, UC's first major funding crisis in the early 1990s signaled the start of an administrative boom.

In the wake of the renewed cuts as Jerry Brown was taking office in 2011, the independent budget analyst Charles Schwartz used similar administrative categories over a similar period to compare management growth to faculty growth and to overall employee growth (figure 19). Management grew at the same pace as overall employee growth at the start of the period. When the cut cycle of 1992–1995 ended, management growth took off on its own course. Throughout the two decades of public funding troubles, administrative employment grew at between four and five times the rate of general employment growth.

UC senior management did not dispute these figures. When they produced their own analysis of administrative growth at UC, they showed that three-fourths of UC personnel fell into the three main management categories. Though they found that faculty growth kept pace with growth of the student population, they explained the three to one ratio of non-academic to academic personnel by saying that "UC does much more than just educate students."[18] But without precisely tying these other activities to a higher standard of educational care, UC management continued to feed the impression that the university had no revenue problems that it couldn't solve by cutting some administrative growth—once it could no longer raise tuition.

Just a few months after the September 2008 market meltdown, the Delta Cost Project published a study that confirmed a national pattern similar to that found at the University of California: university administration grew even as instructional expenditures fell. "Direct instruction expenses have consistently declined as a proportion of

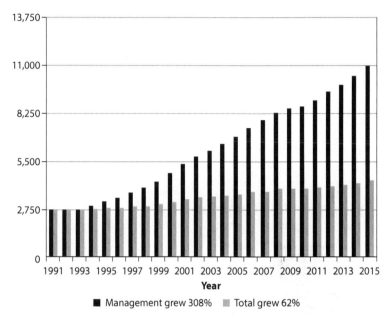

Figure 19. Comparison of management growth to growth of overall employment (FTE) for all of the University of California. *Source:* Charles Schwartz, "New Data on Management Growth at UC," *University Probe*, 2011, http://universityprobe.org/2011/03/new-data -on-management-growth-at-uc/#more-881; updated version provided via correspondence to author, March 4, 2016.
Note: Management refers to what UC calls the Senior Management Group—SMG—plus Management & Senior Professionals—MSP. Schwartz provides further details in his post.

education and related spending, relative to spending increases in student services, academic support, administration and maintenance."[19]

University leaders had endless opportunities to link restored or increased public funding directly to improvements in educational quality, ideally by linking instruction to research. I am not aware of a single public university administration that made a consistent, coherent case for the direct dependence of public university quality on strong *public* funding. Though senior managers may not have intended to defend the administrative cadres first, this was the practical outcome: administration grew through thick and thin, executive salaries climbed, public perception of public universities focused on executive pay and administrative bloat, and the problem of educational decline got lost. This trend has continued with only a brief pause throughout the post-2008 period.

Managers Silence Their Faculty

The post-2008 crisis was also a chance to explain the educational necessity of public funding. The media wasn't indifferent to the story. In 2009 they had discovered the mayhem produced by public university cuts: "California's financial crisis jeopardizes one of the world's finest universities," declared *The Economist*.[20]

The faculty already knew all this. At UC, when state funding was cut 20 percent in 2009, student tuition was raised by one-third and employee salaries were cut for one year by 4 to 10 percent via "furloughs" (unpaid, nonwork days). Departments all over the system deleted senior seminar requirements, eliminated discussion sections, increased lecture sizes, and reduced various kinds of feedback to students for lack of personnel. Administrative support for faculty was also cut back. On the one hand, this is more efficient. On the other hand, it is less efficient: it reduces student advising, research project budgeting, and other forms of essential collaboration, meaning faculty time is spread more thinly across more activities, many of which now involve neither teaching nor research, which in turn lowers educational results.

In the summer of 2009, many UC faculty wanted a strike or a walkout for one overriding reason—to communicate the damage caused by public cuts to the general public.[21] One possible action was that the first day of classes be converted to a teach-in about the concrete instructional effects of the 20 percent reduction in state funding that was being passed on to students that fall.

Faculty e-mail lists were full of examples of the educational damage that should be communicated to students and the world.

We have converted our required introduction to the major from a writing to a lecture course. We are going to teach the lecture next year without sections. We are expanding 30-student discussion courses to 90 students with a reader, whom we can't afford to pay to actually attend the class, so s/he will grade papers without contact with the students. The departments in our building are losing their individual support staffs, which are being pooled. Students will have no one working with our department from whom they can get help. Faculty can't advise on the major, and now staff can't either: it will all be peer advising? It was clear from our department meeting that faculty had no idea this was happening, were angry that they weren't consulted, think this will hurt them and their students, and don't see what we can do. We need to tell our students and the public that we the faculty are opposed to this, so they don't think the cuts are there to protect us while making them pay more.[22]

These examples were similar to those that arrived from all over the UC system. A faculty member at the Irvine campus reported as follows:

In BioSci, caps in some lecture sections are being increased from 343 to 444 with no discussion sections provided and, in others, 200 to 300 with no discussion sections provided. Engineering CEE60 has doubled its cap for both class size (30 to 60) and lab size (15 to 30). Anthro 2c lecture has increased its cap from 190 to 344; Anthro10/Socio10 has increased the cap from 125 to 160. In Math, four out of five General Education courses will have fewer sections this year. Econ, Linguistics, and PoliSci are increasing the number of students admitted to some classes by anywhere from 40 to 236 students per class. The cap for Dance 90a is going from 24 to 60; despite huge demand in 2008, Art 1a will be reduced from 5 sections to 1. Due to the reduction in the number of sections offered (from 59 to 50), demand will not be met in the Fall for 200 students who are wait-listed for Writing 39b, 71 students for Writing 39c. As of August 20th, the Humanities Core course had reduced the number of sections it offers from 45 last year to 32 this year. Access to research materials, computers, and other resources will be cut dramatically as well. As a result of state-mandated cuts, during the fall quarter, all libraries will only be open half-days on weekends; Langson Library will close at 8 p.m. Monday through Thursday, and at 5 p.m. on Fridays, significantly reducing opportunities for weekend study and research. The Libraries Gateway Study Center will only be open after 6 p.m. M–Th, and only 4 hours on F–Sa. Many students rely on Gateway computers to complete their course assignments. Library book orders are restricted to items required for instruction. The UCI Libraries are bracing for further reductions in services, collections, and personnel in order to contend with a $4 million budget cut. These reductions in hours, services, and acquisitions (echoed at other UC campuses) will significantly diminish faculty and student access to the latest knowledge in our fields, as well as students' ability to seek information and work in a quiet setting on campus.

In other sectors such as facilities and maintenance, anticipated layoffs (11 for Facilities Management and 35 for custodial workers) will not only create hardship for some of the lowest paid workers on campus, but will inevitably lead to an unkempt and potentially unsanitary campus environment: trash collection in campus laboratories has been reduced to once per week. As a campus that has been praised for its efficiency in maximizing existing resources in the past, UCI stands to suffer in profound ways from the new round of cuts—there is very little "fat" to be trimmed.[23]

Faculty opinion about striking was mixed, though most felt it was justified.

I do not think a faculty strike is particularly feasible. Let's face it, too many people do not have the stomach for this kind of action and the press would be quick to condemn it and where there is no solidarity, there is no effectiveness. We CAN control our enrollments, however, and that can be done through individual departments. Isn't it time we started making our own students the priority? And what do you think would put the fear of god in the administration? News headlines that because we do not have adequate resources to teach the students on this campus, we cannot do so. While we know this is true, why isn't it being reported? Because we are teaching them anyway. It seems to me that talk is cheap, and it fills the time. Real substantive action has to be taken. The entire world is modeling itself on doing far too much with not nearly enough. We reject that business model as a means of producing education. And yet if we accept this kind of treatment, we are embracing that model.

Everyone rejected the cuts model. Everyone acknowledged the reality that students were "paying more to get less." There was widespread faculty sympathy for the student protests in the fall of 2009 that attracted sympathetic press attention and sorrowful editorials.

My own feeling throughout this period was that senior managers at public universities could use faculty anger as leverage with business and political leaders. From time to time, I mentioned the line apocryphally attributed to Franklin Delano Roosevelt when he was being pressured by A. Philip Randolph to sign antidiscrimination legislation: "I agree with you. I want to do it. Now go out and make me do it." My assumption was that senior managers wanted to reverse public funding cuts and avoid tuition increases and could use internal unrest to strengthen their bargaining position.

Across UC, the faculty debated class cancellation, strikes, walkouts, and teach-ins for weeks. The idea was precisely to make the educational damage visible to the public (and to university administrators). At the end of July the systemwide Academic Senate endorsed a strategy that would use some of the furlough days (of required nonwork) to cancel some class meetings.[24]

Before the term could begin, the "make the cuts visible" faculty were blocked by a declaration from university provost Lawrence Pitts. Toward the end of August he informed the university, "we have decided that faculty furlough days will not occur on instructional days (days for which a faculty member is scheduled to give lectures, lead classes or workshops, have scheduled office hours, or have other scheduled face-to-face responsibilities for students)."[25] Not only did the central administration overrule the senate on a matter of faculty authority, instruction, but it pushed the damage the cuts did to students back in the closet—in the name of the welfare of students.[26]

What must have seemed to officials like keeping good order was a strategic disaster for the university in general and for its students in particular. As we have seen, senior managers had never offered a real answer to the pressing policy question of why a public university's operations, from executive salaries to classroom teaching, specifically required *public* funding. When the 2008 crisis hit university budgets, public university managers were still unprepared to describe the unique value of public taxpayer support. Tax dollars appeared in the role of "that which reduces tuition hikes." This role was important, but in a pinch it could be reduced or eliminated, usually with the promise that when things got better tuition could be frozen or even rolled back. University officials confused matters by using the term "businesses" to describe activities like clinical practices and stressing their profitability in the midst of an economic crisis. This reassured probusiness politicians and corporate leaders while publicizing that the university had resources not available to the public at large. This took pressure off both politicians and the taxpayers to maintain support.

When senior managers blocked class cancellations, they made the cuts *invisible,* and this focused all attention on tuition hikes. The huge student protests of November 2009 made further large tuition increases politically untenable. Students were understandably focused on price, particularly as average real wages fell, families lost jobs and houses, and the country took a big step toward its new status as post–middle class. What got lost in the debate about affordability was the constitutive relationship between high public funding and high-quality education.

What *was* so indispensible about public funding? Judging from the public university's own arguments, the answer was *nothing.* Put another way, university officials made Baumol's "cost disease" true—the state could cut funding, and this wouldn't hurt quality, and, if so, cuts would make the university more efficient.

In sum, when the administration silenced its educators, it reduced its own political weight, and more importantly, it wrecked the educational case for public funding. Public attention had been focused on excessive tuition hikes, which to most people appeared to feed administrative bloat, executive perks, and student amusements; meanwhile, the group best positioned to make the educational case, the faculty, were deprived of a public platform by their own administration.

The situation years after the crisis hit is that students and their parents have successfully held state politicians accountable for only half of the public university bargain. They have blocked further large tuition increases, which helps affordability, but they have not restored public funding, which would help restore and upgrade educational quality. When public university administrators minimized the educational damage of cuts, then neutralized their own internal experts on the topic, they made state cuts seem tolerable. In California, this paved the way for the repetition of cuts under the next governor—a Democrat—who would face no political backlash for cuts as long as he capped tuition. The "silence of the educators" has been a political and budgetary disaster. *This* part of public university decline was entirely self-inflicted by university managers.

Suppressing the Possible

We now have several answers to our question, why do public officials cut public outlays to the "knowledge factories" in our alleged knowledge economy? First, politicians have learned over decades that universities can raise tuition to backfill cuts. Second, university executives obscured the link between public funding and educational quality. Third, university officials have in crucial cases blocked and in general not supported the faculty explanation of educational quality that would attract public support.

One response to all this might be to say well yes, senior managers have not led with educational quality or unleashed their faculty, but this is because the fiscal situation is hopeless. States simply don't have the money for top-quality public universities anymore: state Medicare expenses during the public university's sixties heyday were zero, the population was younger, and the demand for services is much broader and more expensive than it was before. Since universities are just one of many worthy claimants, there's no point in getting more aggressive. The public university needs to stay on good terms with its state leaders and make modest claims in a time of diminished resources.

The premise of the politics of modesty—that states are broke—is wrong. In the midst of the doom and gloom of summer and fall 2009, a faculty member and the executive of a statewide faculty association wrote a paper that made a simple arithmetic case.

The authors, Stanton A. Glantz and Eric Hays, began by noting,

> It is widely recognized that large reductions in state funding and sizeable increases in student fees have eroded quality and accessibility in California's three-segment system of public higher education: the University of California, California State University and California Community Colleges. This report estimates what it would cost—through restored taxpayer funding or tuition increases—to restore the system's historic quality while accommodating the thousands of qualified students excluded by recent budget cuts.[27]

The authors followed an earlier Academic Senate report in establishing the year 2000–2001 as one in which the California higher education system was still close to the levels of affordability and quality that had built the university's reputation. They calculated how much public funding the three segments needed to return to that level, adding for inflation, and then determined how much it would cost for each segment to get back to that level by tuition hikes alone. The answer for the Cal State system was a tuition increase of over $2,000 to a total of $7,600 per year. For UC, tuition would need to rise nearly another $10,000 to a total of about $21,500. This would be for state residents and would do nothing more than return per-student funding to the level that had still existed in 2000.

These tuition levels would further privatize the university and compound its decline as a public good. So what if state funds were the sole source of the additional $5.7 billion the three segments would need to reach 2000 levels of state investment and lower tuition?

Tuition could be lowered by 60 percent at UC, 55 percent at CSU, and 68 percent at the community colleges. For example, UC tuition would be $5,364 rather than $13,200.

But wouldn't this cost the beleaguered taxpayer a fortune? The paper's breakthrough was to calculate the cost to the median individual resident.[28] To have 2000–2001's higher investment per student at that year's much lower level of tuition would in 2015–2016 cost the median taxpayer $31.[29] Restoring full quality and affordability for the nearly 700,000 students in these two systems would force the state median taxpayer to spend the equivalent of a holiday bottle of scotch.

Many commentators who have given up on good public university funding claim they want to avoid gouging the poor. It's not fair, they say, to tax the country's ever-growing, low-wage population for the sake of middle- and upper-class university students.[30] In reality, low-income citizens would pay *no* tax surcharge for this purpose. At an income of $17,000 a year they would pay an additional $5.13 a year. At $70,000 (about two-thirds of California incomes are below this), the additional payment to restore all three university systems, with 1.7 million full-time equivalent undergraduates, would be $158.03.[31]

Glantz and Hays's paper showed that full public funding is affordable for individual taxpayers. The real problem for this reinvestment is not that it would soak poor people but that it would soak the rich. Allocating payments strictly proportionately to income would mean that someone making just under $150,000 would need to pay an additional $404 to restore 2000-level quality to the public higher ed system. In the $300,000–$400,000 income range, where top 1 percent incomes begin and where many senior managers find their salaries, the extra charge would be $1,700.18. This is no more money for the 1 percent than five dollars is for a low-wage worker, but it produced sticker shock among the well-to-do.

Glantz and Hays were able to refute the financial and budgetary argument against restored university funding. They showed that the blockage was not really financial, but political. The California situation had already been brought home to me in 2007, backstage at a

UC Board of Regents' meeting. I had just delivered the first—and so far, the last—faculty analysis of the university's budget to the UC Board of Regents, and one point our research had made was that university funding had not been going up and down with the business cycle, but was in secular decline. At the time, university officials had not made this clear in their presentations to the board. I assumed that when the Regents saw that real-dollar funding had dropped enormously, corrected for enrollments, they would gear up to fight to reverse the cuts.

Having finished the presentation, I ran into the chair of the board's aide for UC affairs.[32] "Dick [Richard Blum] was paying attention," she told me. "I could tell because he put on his glasses to read your report while you were talking about it."

"Great," I replied. "How'd he like the part where we recommend that the Regents get public funding back on trend?"

"What do you mean?" she asked.

"Where the report shows that UC state funding is $756 million below the 2001 state income growth trend. We used this finding to recommend that we get back to income trend over the next four years."

"Oh that," she replied. "That's a non-starter."

Having hit a wall too soon, I tried one of those "not really a joke" comments that irritate my friends.

"But actually the general fund cut was a loan. That was UC's money. The state ran a deficit. We loaned them our money to fix their deficit. Now they need to pay us our loan money back!"

The aide managed a weak smile. "That's funny. But state money isn't coming back."

I have forgotten the friendly chitchat that followed, but not her statement that restoring state funding was off the table. In retrospect, it suggests that permanent public austerity was the high-level agenda even before the 2008 crisis gave governments an excuse to lock it in—for Democrats like Blum as well as for Republicans like Schwarzenegger. This marked a fundamental paradigm shift from public funding keyed to the business cycle to de facto privatization, in which new revenues would not return with the spring floods of a reviving economy, but would always come from tuition hikes.

Reversing the decline cycle with public funding is affordable. But we run up against a familiar additional reason for why it's not happening—a leadership narrative that says that the "era of public funding is over." Public reinvestment is well within the means of the American public, when structured as a progressive tax. Implementation would require overcoming the refusal of the wealthy to pay a proportionate share into the common public university system. That is a political campaign in which the current generation of university executives has not engaged. With this default, public universities became what Jerry Brown said they are: desires dressed as needs claiming rights, without the guts to become a lawsuit.

Increased Student Debt, College as Burden

We've passed through the first four stages of the public university decline cycle. We've seen how forgetting the university's value as a public good has cost public universities plenty. The cascade effects run from increasing expenditures in order to support and subsidize outside partners, to charging students more tuition to cover these costs, and to cutting or capping state funding through a potent mixture of austerity, ideology, opacity, pragmatism, and confusion. We have now arrived at another consequence of the devolutionary process: student debt.

Everyone knows the total amount of student debt is gigantic. And yet universities have managed to avoid blaming themselves and assessing their own role in creating the problem. Public and private colleges say that they subsidize every student, that they never cover their costs, and that any money they make on affluent students goes to cover the tuition of poor students who can't pay their way.

If the student rich subsidize the student poor, why has student debt ballooned in recent years? If the aid is so good, why are poor students as indebted as their middle-class counterparts? And to recall this book's central mystery, what larger social or economic agenda does the debt bubble serve?

I answer this last question at the end of my discussion of the decline cycle. The answer to the other questions is the tendency of privatization culture to see every university activity as a revenue stream that must be harvested to stave off the effects of permanent austerity. The streams include financial aid, which public universities run as a revenue business in the sense that the student's payment into the financial aid system lowers university expenses. Students who borrow have a "self-help expectation" that works something like a deductible in a health insurance policy: the university packages aid to cover student expenses past a certain point. In the case we'll review, students pay $9,200 per year on their own even if they have a very low family income. There is no evil intent, just the university maintaining one of its multiple revenue streams by using financial aid to capture some student outlays rather than reducing them to zero. Financial aid today reflects the privatization effect we've been discussing, in which universities replace declining public resources with private funds, in this case from students and their families via the financial aid process.

Debt as the Cost of Teaching

The topic of student debt produces epic bouts of hand washing. Debt, universities say, grows simply to cover educational costs. One example comes from a high-quality private liberal arts college, Dickinson College in Pennsylvania, which exonerated itself this way:

> At Dickinson, the *cost* of educating, housing, feeding and supporting a robust experience for one student inside and outside the classroom during the 2009–2010 school year (FY10) was $63,000. For the same year, the *price* charged to each student (for tuition, fees, room and board before any financial aid) was just under $50,200. That means that every student began with a "subsidy" of close to $13,000 for the year. . . . Beyond this price/cost differential that every student receives, a total of $32.4 million in financial aid grants was awarded by the College during FY10. 92% of these awards were based on demonstrated student and family financial need. The average award made from College funds in FY10 (not counting awards from state and federal programs) was approximately $26,450 per student.[1]

In other words, colleges make such huge financial sacrifices for their students that they should not be blamed for these students' debt problems. And yet the average Dickinson student needed to come up with $23,740 of her own money that year. If her family didn't have that, she would finish college with $95,000 in student loan debt.

Even the richest university on earth deployed this narrative of self-sacrifice for students. At the end of FY 2013, Harvard University's endowment stood at nearly $33 billion, up over 11 percent in that year alone.[2] This sum, supporting the activities of twenty-one thousand students, was three times the size of the aggregated endowments of the 122 universities of Great Britain, which enroll nearly 2.5 million students.[3]

And yet it still wasn't enough for Harvard. In the fall of 2013 the university announced a campaign to raise a further $6.5 billion, which would put its endowment well beyond the $40 billion mark. Harvard's own coverage suggested another motive beyond student support: "From any perspective, $6.5 billion is a lot of money. But Harvard was never going to cede bragging rights to Stanford (The Stanford Challenge, concluded at the end of 2011, raised $6.2 billion), not to mention the University of Southern California's current $6-billion goal."[4] It appeared that the fund-raising goal was set less by educational needs than by a rich college rivalry, one that highlights the costs of market competition. There was little said about the educational purposes to which the money would be put.

Though Harvard president Drew Gilpin Faust's address launching the campaign was a call to unlimited further glory for Harvard, it also invoked the costs of the residential student experience, noting that the 60 percent of students who receive financial aid pay an average of $12,000 a year to attend.[5] Twenty-five percent of the new funds were to go to financial aid and the "student experience," the campaign said, and another 45 percent to "teaching and research."[6] The claim was that the Harvard endowment needed to get to $40 billion in order to keep world-class quality accessible to the best students. Even the richest university on earth stressed the Herculean difficulty of subsidizing its students.

The steady message was that universities worked tirelessly to *minimize* their students' debt, at great risk to their own solvency.

Universities were claiming that the debt students did incur was unavoidable. They did their best to convince the country that under-graduate education was so expensive that universities always lost money on the deal. This reinforced the notion that they had a cost disease in their core teaching operation. The post-2008 backlash against colleges was fueled by mixing the student debt boom with the impression of uncontrolled instructional costs.

The Debt Explosion

Student loans have been around for decades, so it was easy to overlook aggregate growth, as the formerly pet-sized debt alligator now threatened to devour the host. But was this debt growth simply covering colleges' big new investments in teaching?

The data show that the answer was no. Over the course of the 2000s, colleges' and universities' instructional outlays were essentially flat—except when they dropped. Between 2000 and 2010, public research universities increased their instructional expenditures per student by 0.6 percent overall. Private research universities decreased theirs by 1.9 percent. Community colleges' instructional expenditures fell 6.9 percent.[7] Were student debt being used mainly to cover in-structional costs, it would have remained flat as well.

But of course debt did not stay flat. Average per-student debt (across all types of universities) stood at $17,550 in 2000, $23,450 in 2008, and $25,250 in 2010, an increase of 45 percent in nominal dollars in a decade in which real instructional expenditures did not increase at all.[8] The increase was 23 percent in adjusted dollars.[9] By 2012, it had increased again to $27,253.[10] By 2015, average loan debt had gone up again, according to a different source, to about $35,000 per student who'd taken out loans, or double its 2000 level.[11]

The debt burden for college graduates attracted enormous at-tention when, in late summer of 2010, the overall balance of student loans surpassed that of revolving credit (at about $830 billion versus $826.5 billion). Equally shocking was the growth rate of nonfederal or private student loans, whose interest rates could approach credit card levels of 18 percent. The *Wall Street Journal* reported the calculations

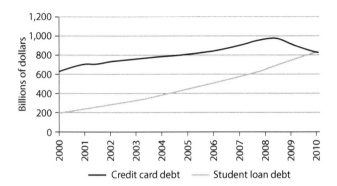

Figure 20. Relationship between credit card debt and student loan debt, 2000–2010 (total debt outstanding). *Source:* Mark Kantrowitz, "Total College Debt Now Exceeds Total Credit Card Debt," *Fastweb*, August 11, 2010, accessed December 31, 2013, http://www.fastweb.com/financial-aid/articles/2589-total-college-debt-now-exceeds-total-credit-card-debt.

Note: Kantrowitz uses revolving credit figures on the grounds that "As much as 98% of revolving credit is credit card debt." See also "Student Loan Debt at Graduation, Bachelors' Degree Recipients," in Mark Kantrowitz, *Proposal for Free College Tuition and Required Fees and Free Textbooks,* Edvisors, August 20, 2015, accessed August 27, 2015, https://www.edvisors.com/media/files/student-aid-policy/20150820-proposal-for-free-college-tuition.pdf.

of one expert, Mark Kantrowitz: "By his math, there is $605.6 billion in federal student loans outstanding and $167.8 billion in private student loans outstanding. He estimates that $300 billion in federal student loan debts have been incurred in the last four years."[12]

Kantrowitz produced a chart that told an extraordinary tale (figure 20): in the first decade of the twenty-first century, total student loan debt, uncorrected for inflation, had quadrupled.[13]

When I was invited onto a radio show discussing the issue in September 2010, I was struck by the host's incredulity regarding the debt's sheer size. A widely respected fixture of public radio, Warren Olney covered education regularly, but this debt bubble, as it would soon be called, had been pumped up behind the backs of nearly everyone. I found myself explaining that this money wasn't all going to colleges and universities because of runaway costs. It was the effect of a loan system that allowed the financial industry to take a growing slice of

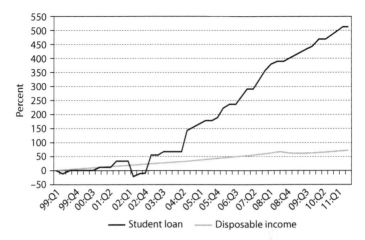

Figure 21. Growth in student loans compared to growth in disposable income (cumulative growth). *Source:* Daniel Indiviglio, "Obama's Student-Loan Order Saves the Average Grad Less Than $10 a Month," *Atlantic*, October 2011, http://www.theatlantic.com /business/archive/2011/10/obamas-student-loan-order-saves-the-average-grad-less -than-10-a-month/247411/.

the country's education money. "What do you mean?" he asked. "You save for college," I replied. "Then you send a big piece of your college savings not to your college but to your bank." Most of us assume that loans are a nonprofit service the federal government provides to students, and that the loan money supports core operations at the college they attend. This belief is out of date. In reality, student loans are part of the banking business in which the financial industry *and* the federal government turn a profit on the creation of student debt.

Anger about this debt fed on the stagnation of middle-class incomes that had been intensified by the crisis. A year after the student debt revelation, in the fall of 2011, the *Atlantic* magazine published a piece drawing attention to a chart that illustrated the dramatic and alarming story. The chart compared the cumulative percentage growth (not the grand totals) of disposable income to the growth in the balance of unpaid student loans (figure 21).

A period in which income grew at the same rate as student debt had come to an abrupt end around 2003, when student debt exploded. The article noted, "Student loans have grown by 511% since 1999. Meanwhile, disposable income has grown by just 73%. As this chart also shows, most outstanding student loan debt (82%!) was accrued by students over just the past decade."[14] Higher ed financial aid was, for the first time in US history, endangering rather than supporting the solvency of a generation of college students.

Multiplying Individual Debt

To help make the effects of the debt system real, a victim of unpayable student debt named Alan Michael Collinge published *The Student Loan Scam* in 2009. He collected stories of debt even more ruinous than his own, with which he began his book: "Over the course of earning three degrees in aerospace engineering at the University of Southern California, I managed to accumulate about thirty-eight thousand dollars in student loans. In 1998, when I graduated, these loans had grown to fifty thousand dollars, and I consolidated them with a friendly-sounding organization called Sallie Mae—an organization that at the time I believed was part of the federal government."[15]

Collinge found a good job with a modest salary at Caltech. A couple of years later, he decided to look for an industry job to improve his income and failed to get one. He then tried, as an unemployed person, to get economic-hardship forbearance on his loans until he could get a job. His appeal was denied, and his loans were placed in default. At the end of 2001, he received a payment claim for $60,000. Three years after leaving school, his balance had *increased* 20 percent, and he was in default.

After a year of working multiple jobs at minimum wage, Collinge's debt got worse. I cite his summary at length, because it is an example of the debt multiplier effect of penalties that helps explain the otherwise utterly bizarre 2000s debt boom.

> In the fall of 2002, when I returned from Alaska, I was shocked to find a bill from a collection company, General Revenue Corporation, for nearly

eighty thousand dollars. The company, a subsidiary of Sallie Mae, was collecting on behalf of EdFund, the guarantor. I was baffled: Who were these two new companies, and what was a guarantor? I wasn't in a position to ask a wealthy relative for assistance, and the fact that the company was demanding "immediate payment in full" greatly increased my apprehension.

This began two years of relentless collection activities. I was inundated with calls from various collection companies, and at the same time, I was contacting my loan holders and attempting to negotiate a reasonable settlement. I tried Sallie Mae first, then EdFund and the various collection companies they used, and finally the U.S. Department of Education. I told them I'd repay the principal and accrued interest and even offered to pay at an increased interest rate of 10 percent if only they would remove some of the penalties. I believed that I was proposing a rather lucrative settlement; Sallie Mae had already made well over twenty-five thousand dollars on my original thirty-eight-thousand-dollar loan—why should they need more?

However, at every step along the way, I was refused. I found that I had no negotiation power whatsoever for my student loan debts: bankruptcy does not eliminate them, statutes of limitations do not exist for them, and the standard consumer protections on other types of debt do not apply. Meanwhile, my loan balance was exploding.[16]

In four years, Collinge's debt more than doubled. It appears that, even without penalties, the lenders had a return on investment of about 66 percent in less than ten years, with no risk of default thanks to government regulation. Of the $63,000 Collinge was to pay, the split was 60–40 between the lenders and his university, meaning that the majority of loan proceeds went to the lender.

This was the *best*-case outcome for Collinge. His book collects stories of former students who also saw their debt double, triple, or even quintuple as the result of unemployment, medical treatment, or other ordinary setbacks that student loan regulations turned into permanent disasters.[17] And Collinge's own personal debt bubble was not done growing. It hit $103,000 in 2005, or about three-and-a-half times its original amount.

Even after the wave of publicity about student debt that helped propel the Occupy movement in 2011, student debt rose inexorably. In summer 2012 the New York Fed reported, "Since the peak in household debt in 2008Q3, student loan debt has increased by $303 billion, while other forms of debt fell a combined $1.6 trillion."[18] Between the surfacing of the financial crisis in 2008 and 2013, total student debt rose from $730.7 billion to $1.213 trillion, for five-year increase of 66 percent.[19] Aggregate student loan debt kept going up, and by 2015, student loans were the only loan category in which delinquencies continued to rise.[20] The highest mean and median loan balances were for borrowers under the age of forty. Default rates for students graduating in 2005, 2007, and 2009 were around 25 percent.

Converting Aid to Loans

What enabled this bizarre and untenable debt explosion? We have already identified two causes. The first is the continuous rise in tuition itself. Every year in the 2000s, tuition increased, on average, 3 percent per year at private and 5.6 percent at public four-year colleges.[21] By the end of the decade of the 2000s, tuition had increased 27 percent at private and 46 percent at public universities.[22] (These averages hide specific catastrophic increases, like the ten-year tripling of tuition at the University of California.) Students had steadily larger tuition bills that they needed to cover. Students had these larger bills at a time when the majority of American incomes were no longer rising. And yet overall tuition increases, even in conjunction with stagnant wages, do not by themselves explain the quadrupling of student debt.[23]

The deeper enabler was the decline of government *grants,* which in contrast to loans do not need to be paid back. Pell Grants, for example, covered about half the proportion of 2010–2011 tuition that they covered in 1979–1980.[24] Congress was in effect cutting federal grant allocations during the same period that the states were inexorably lowering operating funds. The result has been a large shift in the government's instruments from grants to loans—from two dollars in grants for every one dollar in loans in 1992–1993 to a one-to-one grants-to-loan ratio from the late 1990s to the present.[25] As we will see, this shift has been a particular blow to low-income students, as grants targeted to them received a smaller share of the federal budget, which went increasingly toward programs for which middle-income students were also eligible.[26]

Federal policy shifted from direct funding to universities, to grant funding to students, to a mixture of grant funding to students and indirect subsidies to loan companies who would then sell loans to students. Grant payments to students were partially replaced by a system of government-backed loans issued by financial corporations, who would profit from interest and fees on the loans while federal guarantees and, later, antibankruptcy legislation, shielded them from risk. By 2000, federal student loan payment policy had become a classic instance of privatization, in which public resources create and protect private revenues.

The shift began years before, during the Nixon administration, when the Student Loan Marketing Association (Sallie Mae) was created "for the purpose of encouraging banks, schools, and other lenders to make loans to college students; Sallie Mae would then purchase these loans, thus serving as a secondary market for them."[27] Sallie Mae acted increasingly like a commercial lender, growing both its market share and its political influence in the 1990s and embarking on a series of acquisitions of lenders and collection agencies in the late 1990s to early 2000s.

Congress needed to reauthorize the Higher Education Act of 1965 periodically, and after the election of Ronald Reagan in 1980, it made loans more common and collections more enforceable. The policy analyst Suzanne Mettler argues that in the 1980s political expediency was as important as ideology in moving loans to the center of federal financial aid policy:

> Gradually a new normal emerged over student aid, as annual budget skirmishes led to deterioration in the value of Pell grants and, indirectly, to the growth of student loans. Democrats pointed to rising tuition on college campuses and argued for increases in Pell grant levels. . . .

Conversely, officials in the Reagan and George H. W. Bush administrations and congressional Republicans, motivated by fiscal conservatism, worried about growing government deficits and sought to scale back Pell grant spending. The compromises between these positions did not decimate the grants, but they took the entitlement option off the table and left benefit rates dwindling in real terms and falling well behind average tuition costs. Politicians in both parties found common ground instead on the expansion of student loans because that only required them to lift borrowing limits and waive restrictions on who could borrow.[28]

Mettler suggests that the final turn toward the debt system came after Newt Gingrich's hard-right Republicans captured the House of Representatives in 1994. Bill Clinton decided to compete with tax-cutting Republicans, including 1996 presidential candidate Bob Dole, by supporting a new system of tax credits for college expenditures in the 1990s, which seemed to make increased college assistance compatible with tax cuts but whose benefits flowed mostly to higher-income families.[29] Although the 1997 tax credit program "was portrayed as a $40 billion national investment in higher education," it was a public subsidy for the purchase of commercial loan products offered by private financial companies.[30] ("ObamaCare" operates in the same way.)

One might think that these policies could form a reasonable public-private partnership of the kind that the administrations of Bill Clinton in the United States and Tony Blair in the United Kingdom had applied to many public services.[31] University administrators and faculty members have accepted the situation as a normal mixed-economy approach to funding a service that has both private and public benefits. But in reality, these shifts in financial aid amounted to a substantial privatization of federal subsidies that damaged the student budgets the system was designed to protect, while putting public resources in the service of private firms.

One driver of privatization was the relentless assault by banks, led by Sallie Mae, on the Federal Direct Loan Program that had been created in 1993 "to bypass the middlemen and loan money to college students directly, thereby saving taxpayers significant monies that would have otherwise gone to the banks."[32] Contrary to popular myth, government loans have lower costs and are more efficient than private-sector loans, and the Direct Loan Program proved this by rapidly beating Sallie Mae and regular banks for market share. Collinge reported, "In the first two years of operation of the Direct Loan Program, Sallie Mae lost about half of its market value, and Direct Loans grew to about 34 percent of the student loan market."[33]

The market success of the public loans triggered a relentless banking campaign to restrict them:

> Throughout the 1990s and into the beginning of the twenty-first century, the Republican Congress made repeated attempts to starve the Direct Loan Program by putting its funding into an account held at the discretion of Congress—making the program easier to kill. Congress also passed laws that made Sallie Mae's loans more profitable through enhanced subsidies, thus allowing them to be more competitive against the Direct Loans, although at a high cost to the taxpayer. Despite the fact that multiple studies confirmed that the Direct Loan Program was significantly cheaper for the federal government than other options, the Bush administration perpetuated "a slow strangulation of the student loan program," according to Barmak Nassirian, a highly regarded industry expert. By 2006, the share of the Federal Direct Loan Program had diminished to about 19 percent of the market.[34]

The banking attack on direct loans went beyond political lobbying. President George W. Bush appointed the former head of a bank lobbying organization to the number-two position in the Department of Education with control over the Direct Loan Program, and the program carried on under continuous attack from congressional Republicans, led by future Speaker of the House John Boehner.[35]

To enable the privatization of the public good of college for all, a series of public laws in the 1990s and 2000s stripped students of the normal consumer protections afforded all other classes of customers. Bankruptcy protection was eliminated. Student loan recipients were unable to refinance their loans after a first consolidation. Loan forgiveness for a major hardship was almost impossible. There was no compensation for lost "back-end benefits" from a loan resale.[36]

Far from using their private sector status to set up a competitive, open market system for providing loans, lenders used their legislative influence to restrict student choice. Once these restrictions were in place, lenders were free to impose interest hikes, unexpected and exorbitant fees, draconian default conditions, and massive penalties for those defaults. Students could not escape bad loans by finding a cheaper lender, and the result was the lender's power to fatten their bottom line and grow their stock price by multiplying the debt of a graduate on the basis of minor financial problems.[37]

In some cases, privatization involved using financial incentives to encourage university officials to steer business toward private lenders and away from direct loan programs. The Spitzer-Cuomo investigation in New York State established a list of "industry-wide findings," which included manipulating the university's "Preferred Lender Lists" to steer business toward the lender in question, among many others.[38] Universities were either unable or unwilling to keep student debt from ballooning in conjunction with bank influence over government loan policy.

The policy shift to loans had the desired effect of guaranteeing large profits for lenders from a captive mass of student debtors who were unable to reduce or escape their debt. These were monopoly rents in the classic sense: policy restrictions on consumer choice allowed lenders to receive revenues in excess of what they would have received in an open market—and far in excess of their costs or their risk, which, thanks to the near total prohibition on student loan forgiveness, was close to zero.

The system was extremely effective at achieving its silent goal of creating a vast student loan pool from which revenues could be extracted. As we have come to expect, privatization worked to increase returns to higher education's satellite industries rather than increasing educational resources for higher education. And it was students who paid for these returns.

The Debt of the Low-Income Student

The student debt system was so entrenched that debt growth inevitably continued unabated after 2008, regardless of the decline of the incomes and wealth that had supported it. In February 2013, investor demand was fifteen times greater than supply for one particularly unsavory instrument offered by Sallie Mae (renamed SLM Corp).[39] That summer, financial journalist Matt Taibbi found that student debt abuses were continuing, with the federal government and the lending industry having similar monetary incentives to trap students in debt—and default.[40] Progressive reformers did not push for the restoration of standard bankruptcy protections for student debt, but partial modifications.[41] The *New York Times* kicked off its 2014 higher education coverage with a story about student debt paralyzing adult lives, and could not find improved protections for borrowers.[42] And a federal report to Congress found that by the end of FY 2013, the government had earned $66 billion on direct loans issued between 2007 and 2012.[43]

Debt growth occurred in spite of the Obama administration's official concern about it. In 2010, the government passed legislation that eliminated fees to private banks acting as intermediaries, increased the Pell Grant ceiling to enhance the ratio of grants to loans, and took other steps to curb abuses.[44] In 2011 Obama issued executive orders allowing loan consolidation and other improvements. During his 2012 presidential campaign, Obama made a series of major statements about protecting college affordability.[45] In 2014 he proposed expansion of eligibility for the income-based repayment program, reduction of repayment from 15 percent to 10 percent of annual income (above a living allowance of 150 percent of the poverty line), and loan forgiveness after twenty years.[46] But analysts predicted that these measures would not reverse student debt's rising tide. They turned out to be correct.[47]

Social movements arose in the vacuum created by the inaction of elected officials. By the end of 2011, Occupy Wall Street had given currency to concepts like a student debt jubilee and student loan forgiveness. Scholar-activists like Andrew Ross of New York University sity continued to press the case for loan forgiveness, while Robert Samuels of UCLA and UC Santa Barbara argued for winding down the loan system by making tuition free.[48] Former students of the shuttered for-profit company Corinthian Colleges began a debt strike with the help of the Debt Collective, and in the summer of 2015 the latter could be found picketing the annual convention of the National Association of Student Financial Aid Administrators.[49] These movements cycled back into the political system. Massachusetts senator Elizabeth Warren championed student loan protections as vigorously as she had campaigned for Wall Street regulation. In 2015 President Obama called for free community college with a plan called "America's College Promise." A few months later, presidential candidate Senator Bernie Sanders proposed a College for All Act that would make all four-year public colleges free as well.[50] The desire for large-scale relief from the student loan burden had gone mainstream, and the call for free tuition was hard on its heels.

Given the national outcry, and the support of top-level Democrats for student debt relief, where did public university officials stand?

The 2006–2007 investigations suggested that at least some university financial aid specialists had been co-opted by the lending industry. For various reasons, they could not be counted on as a group to stick up for the interests of students.

What about university presidents and other senior leaders? They had generally followed the larger policy drift toward private revenues. In the 1980s and 1990s, academic leaders responded to changing aid programs by showing "little regard for whether students paid their tuition bills with federally supported loan dollars or grant dollars."[51] In the 2000s, academic leadership reactions ranged from fatalistic acceptance to active endorsement—not of debt relief but of "high tuition/high aid" policies. (I here shorten high tuition/high aid to HITHA.) In states like California, Michigan, Wisconsin, Illinois, and Ohio, which were for different reasons facing long-term public budget austerity, a university president faced a choice among three kinds of statements about the funding model underlying student debt.

1. *High-quality public universities require high public funding and low tuition.* This funding model protects a special combination of affordability and educational quality. Looking to the future, when economic growth and political rationality return, we'll rebuild public funding and cap tuition, or even roll tuition back.
2. *Public universities now have lower public funding and high tuition, but their quality is as good as ever.* We have made the new system as good as (1) by using high levels of financial aid to support low- and middle-income students.
3. *Public universities are better with high tuition/high aid.* The older low tuition model meant that poor taxpayers were subsidizing wealthy ones. HITHA protects quality while adding a form of social justice that low-tuition public universities had previously blocked.

Public university leaders who leaned toward (1) had to stand up to conventional political wisdom in America that assumed, wrongly, that the private sector was always more efficient than its public counterpart. Virtually none did, in spite of the public sector's proven achievement of rapid increases in college attainment with zero debt. The exceptions were generally reacting to new proposals for massive cuts, such as Louisiana State University president and chancellor F. King Alexander's successful campaign against cuts in 2015.[52]

Presidents who were engaged in the process of hiking tuition generally chose door number 2. They insisted that academic quality was being protected and that tuition hikes did not affect financially vulnerable students, thanks to high financial aid.

The classic example is again the University of California, which in the 2000s had a policy of returning 33 percent of tuition funds to financial aid. In 2011, UC president Mark G. Yudof took to Facebook to refute various myths about the university, including the myth that "only the wealthy can afford to attend UC."

> Last year, UC's average in-state tuition and fees were $11,300 per year. This figure places the university near the middle of its major public comparator institutions.

But 61% of all UC undergraduates receive need-based aid. At comparator institutions, it's around 30–55%. And once average grant and scholarship aid kicks in, UC's average net tuition was only $4,400—among the lowest of its comparator institutions.

The reason for this is that UC has *both* very strong state and institutional need-based grant programs.

The university's Blue and Gold Plan is among these. This program ensures that 100% of in-state tuition and fees is covered for all students who come from a family with an annual household income of $80,000 or less.

These students don't pay *one dollar* in tuition or fees.

UC also covered the 2011–12 fee increase of $1,890 for needy families earning up to $120,000 per year. In fact, overall, we estimate that the most recent tuition increase was covered for 55% of all UC students.[53]

Listeners were meant to conclude that high tuition was *neutralized* by high aid. Yudof's claim was that this system was *as affordable as* the previous high state funding/low tuition model had been (position 2).

The effect of this claim was to demobilize students and parents who might have objected to incessant, and sometimes enormous, one-year fee hikes. In California, student protests in the fall of 2009 and 2011 had embarrassed state and university officials. Coverage of one meeting at UCLA produced images of UC Regents fleeing on foot from students who were trying to talk to them. Although public university officials might have used student and parent anger to rebuild political support for public funding (position 1), they rejected this opportunity.

Politics aside, how did officials make the leap from summary data like that quoted above, based on averages, to *affordability*? How did they actually show that "high financial aid" made high-tuition public universities as affordable—or even more affordable—than they were during the period of low tuition?

The rhetorical mechanism is clear: a university president asserts that HITHA allows low-income students to have 100 percent of their core college costs covered by grants and that any borrowing starts at higher annual income levels, such as $80,000, at which families have some resources and can afford to pay back loans. Borrowing levels then increase only gradually, it is said, and in step with the student's capacity to repay. Perhaps it then tapers off for affluent students whose families can foot the full cost of attendance out of pocket.

Many financial aid officials no doubt work hard to make this story true, in spite of the way debt is structured into aid packages. Unfortunately, it is false. The rub is that students do not only pay tuition; they also pay to support themselves while they are in school. College is "affordable" only if the student can cover not only tuition but also the full "cost of attendance," which includes rent, food, clothes, books, and similar everyday expenses. (It does not include income lost while in school.) The reality is that most students cannot cover these overall costs without borrowing, which undermines affordability.

The University of California produced an Accountability Report that illustrated the problem. Figure 22 refers to how much students and their families have to pay out of pocket after tuition discounts and grants have covered as much of their costs as possible.

The lines in the graph represent the cost to a student after grants are subtracted. Note the two lower lines, representing, roughly speaking, lower-income ($0–50,000) and middle-class ($50–100k) students. Middle-income costs have risen 22 percent over the ten years from 2001–2002 to 2011–2012, and lower-income costs just under 10 percent (on top of inflation). In each case the out-of-pocket costs of attendance, *after* financial aid is spent, come to at least 20 to 25 percent of gross income. That is assuming the family has only one child in college at a time.

What we see, then, is that the HITHA model requires even low-income students to borrow. At a public university with in-state tuition, still set at less than a third that of elite private universities, and with one-third of tuition revenues going to financial aid, low-income students *still* pay about $10,000 a year. They will likely cover some of that by working for a wage while they are in school (half of all UC students work, and nearly one-third work eleven or more

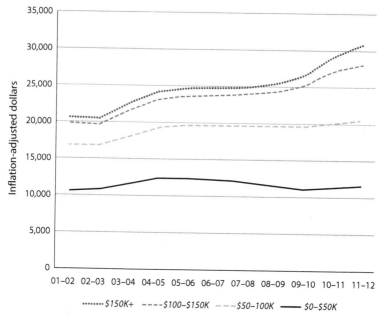

Figure 22. Net cost of attendance by family income, universitywide, 2001–2002 to 2011–2012 (constant dollars). *Source:* University of California, "Indicator 3.2: Net Cost of Attendance by Income," *Accountability Report 2013,* accessed January 5, 2016, http://accountability.universityofcalifornia.edu/2013/index/3.2.

hours a week—or nearly two eight-hour days per week while full-time students).[54] They will cover the rest of it by borrowing.

California is an important test case because historically it has been very well funded by the state and its three segments offer relatively lower levels of student debt than do most other public university systems.[55] But though low-income students borrow less than their high-income peers, their unmet need is surprisingly high—about $8,500 and $5,500 for UC and CSU students from the poorest families (with income under $30,000 per year). Amazingly, this income group has a $6,000 unmet need at community colleges.

Unmet need is somewhat higher for the next bracket ($30,000–$48,000 in the state calculations). The financial aid system has allowed unmet need to rise high enough so that even poor students are forced to borrow large amounts each year to attend the cheapest public colleges in their states.[56]

The national picture is the same. The result of significant unmet need, even among low-income students, appears in a striking chart from the College Board (figure 23). The height of the bars show median cumulative debt at different levels of student family income, grouped by type of university. At each type, the typical poor student has about as much cumulative college debt as an affluent student.

Supposedly generous financial aid doesn't mean that low-income dependent students borrow *less*. In reality, low-income students borrow *more* than affluent students. In the past, low-income students borrowed three times more than high-income students. The gap has narrowed because middle- and high-income student borrowing increased as tuition boomed, and yet, low-income students are still the bigger borrowers.[57] Their borrowing also increases with each additional year in school. Contrary to the HITHA premise, "high aid" does not make total costs for a four-year degree either flat or predictable for the poorest students. In one important sample these costs increased by 50 percent over four years.[58]

Whatever else HITHA is doing, it is *not* creating low-debt affordability for low-income students. Position 2, which claims that financial aid has protected affordability, is incorrect. The public university officials who espouse it are misleading policymakers and the wider public.

Building Debt into Financial Aid

Given the failure of the HITHA model to contain student debt, why didn't university executives reject it? They were right to be concerned about their own revenue needs after years of state cuts, but they did not join calls for rolling back tuition to 2000 levels as in the California "reset" plan, or to zero as in the College for All Act. To the contrary, when the economy improved, the University of California president proposed five years of 5 percent tuition increases as a way to make up for some of the previous cuts.[59] In states like Wisconsin, university leaders angled for the legal autonomy that would allow

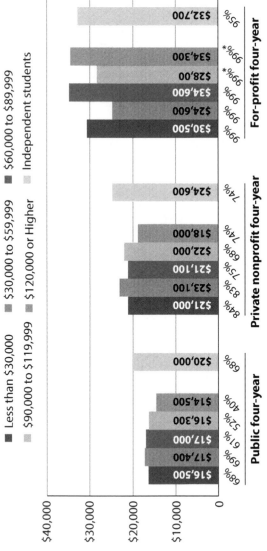

Figure 23. Median debt levels of 2007–2008 bachelor's degree recipients who borrowed and percentage with debt, by dependency status, family income, and type of institution. *Source:* College Board, *Trends in Student Aid 2010,* fig. 2010_9, accessed January 5, 2016, http://trends .collegeboard.org/sites/default/files/SA_2010.pdf.

them to raise rather than lower tuition. University officials may not have been prodebt, but they were generally protuition. In addition, they were learning that financial aid was an asset to be leveraged in the pursuit of private funding.

This is another area in which university budget practices are not transparent, and I offer a case study, again from UC, in place of a systematic survey of public data, which I have been unable to find. My own digging began in the fall of 2014, during a battle between administrative and student accounts of student finances.[60]

Students were objecting to the new university plan to raise in-state tuition 5 percent each year for five years. UC Office of the President (UCOP) officials continued their longstanding claim that generous financial aid protected all low-income, and most middle-income, students from tuition costs. For example, the UC Berkeley campus claimed, "California students from families with annual incomes under $80,000 will continue to have tuition and fees fully covered by financial aid, and the vast majority of California students from families earning less than $150,000 a year will see no increase."[61] That campus's immediate past chancellor, Robert Birgeneau, claimed that this high financial aid depended on high tuition, so that "frozen tuition means ever-increasing debt for low-income students."[62] Birgeneau escalated the argument from the second administrative policy position I discussed earlier, that high-tuition public universities are as good as their low-tuition predecessors, to position three—that public universities are *better* with HITHA, and in particular are better for low-income students.

While senior managers focused on *tuition*, students focused on their *total cost of attendance*. This is what they have to pay overall while they are in school. Grants can cover most or all of their tuition, and yet rent, food, transportation, health insurance, and so on run up the overall bill for attending UC. Regular folks watching the confrontations at board meetings might have wondered why the officials were so soothing while the students were so distraught. The explanation is that the officials and the students were talking about two different things.

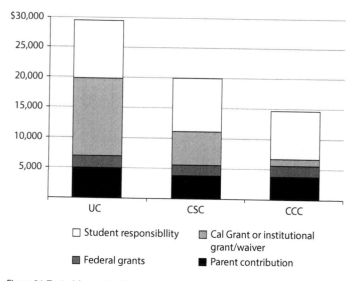

Figure 24. Typical financial aid package, State of California public university student, parental income of $60,000, 2013–2014. *Source:* Legislative Analyst's Office, "Financial Aid Overview," Sacramento, CA, March 13, 2014, accessed July 25, 2015, http://www.lao.ca.gov/handouts/education/2014/Financial-Aid-Overview-031314.pdf.

The state Legislative Analyst's Office had a chart that illustrated the experience gap (figure 24). For this sample student from a family earning near the state's median income, the university, federal, and state programs cover all tuition and some expenses.[63] And yet, in spite of fairly expensive aid, the student has to fill the large blank space of uncovered expenses on her own, totaling nearly $10,000 at UC and not that much less at CSU and the community colleges.

A bit of terminology will help us understand what is going on. "Student Responsibility" in the chart can also be called "Self-Help Expectation," or "Unmet Need," defined in a basic way as follows:

Cost of Attendance (COA) minus Expected Family Contribution (EFC) = Financial Need

Financial Need minus Financial Aid Awarded = Unmet Need

The first thing to note is that a university can say to a student, "we cover your full tuition" and still leave her scrambling to cover total COA, which here means filling a gap of between $9,000 and $10,000 per year. She will have to come up with loans or income from work.

Second, there is an ambiguity in the terminology. One might assume "Financial Aid Award" means grants. But in fact, universities "award" loans as well. They can, in this way, reduce a student's Unmet Need to zero, but only by inducing the student to borrow funds and/or to take on additional work. Financial aid offices can also include *parental* borrowing to close the gap of Unmet Need.

Since my example is from the University of California, I will follow its practice by calling the mixture of loans and work the student's Self-Help Expectation (SHE). Unmet Need is a better literal description of the situation university financial aid creates, but this is not how my case uses the term, so I will avoid it.

Next, where does the financial aid system expect the self-helping student to get this money?

Over the years I'd studied financial aid analyses off and on but had not done concrete aid calculations for hypothetical students. In addition, award letters to students are notoriously hard to interpret, which some observers believe is intentional, since it makes it harder for students to compare offers from different schools and choose a college on the basis of cost.[64] Financial aid "parameters" are apparently confidential, requiring input from financial aid officials to help with interpretation. I received help from an employee of my campus's financial aid office, who was nice enough to send me some examples and comments. This person created the following examples without disclosing the parameters, and I report the results without having the formula behind them.

These examples presume a family of four with one student in college and no assets, savings, or nonsalary income. They also assume the student does not have outside scholarships. The cost of attendance (COA) for UC Santa Barbara is given in figure 25.

Tuition is about one-third of total costs, which are close to $35,000 a year (higher than the statewide average we looked at in the previous example). A student can save about $4,000 by moving off campus,

Tuition	$12,192
Campus based fees	$1,674
Books and supplies	$1,391
Health care allowance	$2,569
Loan fees	$104
Room and board	$14,128
Personal expenses	$1,681
Telephone/cell phone	$395
Transportation	$724
Total	$34,858

Figure 25. The 2014–2015 undergraduate California resident university costs, UC Santa Barbara

putting off-campus COA at $31,000. I stick with the on-campus first-year student: How does she cover these costs?

Example 1: Total Family Income = $35,000
Expected Family Contribution (EFC) = $0

This is a low-income student. Her financial aid award letter (assuming on-campus housing) will break down like this:

$12,192   Cal Grant
$ 5,730   Pell Grant
$ 7,736   UCSB Grant
$ 3,500   Subsidized loan
$ 2,000   Unsubsidized loan
$ 1,700   Perkins loan
$ 2,000   Work-study

The student's COA is $34,858. Her EFC from her low-income family is $0, so her Financial Need is also $34,858. Her *grant* total is $25,658. She is left with a Self-Help Expectation of $9,200. She can supply $2,000 of that with a work-study job. She will still need to come up with $7,200 on top of that.

The student's award letter has her borrowing the entire $7,200 from three sources. Four years of this borrowing gives her a debt of $28,800. (In practice, annual loan offerings vary and generally increase each year.) If she took a second job to avoid half of the loan—by earning $3,600 per year—and she worked two eight-hour days per week at ten dollars per hour take-home pay, she would need to work 360 hours, or a day and a half per week, during the school year, while graduating with $14,400 in loans. This is a conservative estimate, as the *average* debt burden for a student in this income range is about $3,000 higher than this amount.[65]

Moving on, we see that a higher income eliminates eligibility for specific grants and loans.

Example 2: Total Family Income = $70,000
EFC = $7,820

$12,192	Cal Grant
$~~5,730~~	~~Pell Grant~~
$ 5,646	UCSB Grant
$ 3,500	Subsidized loan
$ 2,000	Unsubsidized loan
$~~1,700~~	~~Perkins loan~~
$~~2,000~~	~~Work-study~~
$11,520	Parent PLUS Loan

This student is no longer likely to receive a Pell Grant but can still get a Cal Grant (which covers full tuition). His COA is the same as the first student's, $34,858. His family is supposed to kick in an EFC of $7,820, so his Financial Need is $27,038 per year. His *grant* total is $17,838. He has a Self-Help Expectation of $9,200. Interestingly, this is the same expectation as for the low-income student. Student

2 is not eligible for work-study. His parents *are* eligible for PLUS loans, however, and on the basis of this and his $5,500 loan eligibility, the financial aid award letter he receives has the student and his family borrowing to cover both the EFC and his SHE.

Assuming his loan amounts increase and he accepts the maximum in each case, the cumulative borrowing for Student 2 is $5,500 + $6,500 + $7,500 + $7,500. This will leave the student with $27,000 in debt for a bachelor's degree. He could avoid $6,800 in loan debt by working sixteen-hour weeks during most of the school year, or avoid all of it by adding full-time summer work. He could also avoid $4,000 in expenses each year by living off campus. But if he wants to spend his time studying rather than working a job, as critiques of reduced student study time suggest that he do, he and his family together will have to borrow $27,000 + $46,080 ($11,520 in PLUS loans each year for four years) for a joint total of $73,080 for his bachelor's degree.[66]

Here's our last instance, with the highest family income of the three.

Example 3: Total Family Income = $100,000
EFC = $19,760

~~$12,192~~	~~Cal Grant~~
~~$ 5,730~~	~~Pell Grant~~
$ 5,898	UCSB Grant
$ 3,500	Subsidized loan
$ 2,000	Unsubsidized loan
~~$ 1,700~~	~~Perkins loan~~
~~$ 2,000~~	~~Work study~~
$23,460	Parent PLUS Loan

This student's family income is more than 150 percent of median family income in California. She has a kind of "middle-class scholarship" in the form of the UCSB Grant. It runs slightly higher than that for the student with $70,000 in family income, but she is eligible neither for the Pell nor the Cal Grant. Her family EFC is $19,760, so she has a Financial Need of $15,098 per year. Subtracting her Financial

Aid Awarded ($5,898) from her Financial Need yields her a Self-Help Expectation of . . . $9,200.

As with Student 2, she can cover $5,500 of that with her two loans and cover the remaining $3,700 with the balance of her parents' PLUS loan ($23,460 minus their EFC of $19,760 is $3,700). Or, her parents could take out a smaller loan and she could cover the balance by working a bit more than Student 1's sixteen hours a week for twenty-four weeks a year.

My financial aid source commented on this:

> To make up a third of her need [without borrowing], a student would need about 20 hours a week or more throughout the school year and that leaves very minimal time for academics and could also be a factor as to why students do not become involved in organizations or research on campus. That in turn could affect their attendance in grad school or programs like [study abroad]. It then becomes a question of "how much can I do in one day," and what gets left out is when a student has to work it almost always ends up affecting their educational goals.

Whatever she decides, Student 3 will graduate with $22,000 in loans after four years. Her parents will owe $93,840 on their PLUS loans, plus interest.

Putting these examples in the context of other research, this is how the situation seems to me. The unchanging size of each student's Self-Help Expectation is not an accident of an insufficient financial aid budget. It is built into the calculations. The parameters appear to be structured to generate an annual gap for all students—$9,200 at this particular institution. This includes poor students. This practice is sometimes called "gapping." It is defined as creating a gap between an accepted student's cost of attendance and his or her known resources. A college can be need blind in admitting students regardless of their individual finances while giving them financial aid packages that force them to borrow to attend. Estimates on the frequency of this practice vary, and if there is a national database for student gapping, I have been unable to find evidence of its existence. One survey found that 55 percent of colleges gap some of their admitted students, with 72 percent of private college admissions offices and 39 percent of public colleges doing this.[67] Another study found, "When colleges are asked if they meet the full financial need of accepted students . . . [o]nly 32 percent of public institutions and 18 percent of private institutions say that they make such a commitment."[68] Does the University of California gap *all* of its admits who can't just write a check for college? My source wrote, "I don't know the politics of the policies behind it. I just know financial aid offices are always leaving that 'gap' to be covered in loans or work."

When financial aid builds borrowing in, the impact on students is clear: covering a Cost of Attendance that assumes a $9,200 Self-Help Expectation requires plenty of work, or debt, or both. This is also true for low-income students, as the aggregate data confirm. In other words, a full-tuition scholarship is compatible with $15,000 in graduation debt. A "middle-class scholarship," as implemented by a campus-based grant, produces $22,000 in debt in these calculations. In order to hold down their borrowing, students may be tempted to work more than is good for their studies. Working too much reduces study time, which in turn lowers achievement. The financial aid system that builds in loans may damage student learning while also harming their finances.

Gapping is also bad for students' families. The most direct effect is that parents are taking on unprecedented levels of debt for their children. A $100,000 family income might suggest resources to support college, but in our cases the PLUS loans promise to soak all of that up. Student 3's parents take on close to 100 percent of their annual income in loans for one child's public university BA degree. A special program like UC Berkeley's Middle Class Access Plan (MCAP) would reduce Student 3's parents' debt by reducing the EFC from about 20 percent of annual income in that case to a maximum of 15 percent.[69] That would bring their debt down from $93,840 to $77,840. Such a program does not affect the debt of the other two students. Overall, parental debt doesn't seem to be reducing student debt, but to be added in on top of it.

This policy is also penny-wise and pound-foolish for society. States have used student debt to privatize more of the costs of college during decades when real wages haven't risen, without calculating the loss of human capital to their state. We've seen that college produces social as well as individual benefits. Lower public investment forces students to pay and borrow more. The result is that more student funds go to lenders rather than to universities, limiting their education budgets. Meanwhile, more student time goes to activities other than studying, which leads to reduced human capital and reduced social benefits. Together, these outcomes fuel the decline cycle that we have been observing.

Financial aid is also feeding back into that stage in the decline cycle (Stage 4) where state legislatures cut funds and then see no reason to reverse cuts when tax receipts improve. In the HITHA model, high tuition is to be accompanied by high financial aid, and universities often take credit for this. In reality, a large part of student aid at private, as well as public, universities comes from the federal government; at public universities, much additional aid comes from the states. Figure 26 shows the California case.

Fifteen years of UC tuition increases have increased Cal Grant outlays to UC by close to a factor of eight. Since the last academic year before the 2008 crisis, California has added a half-billion dollars to UC's financial aid budget. The state is on the hook for helping the university to address the core claim of the HITHA model, which is that high tuition with high aid will not damage affordability. This requires the state to increase its financial aid spending as tuition goes up, which simultaneously encourages the state to reduce its general fund outlays for UC operations by a similar amount. California governor Jerry Brown once explained this reasoning rather plainly to the Board of Regents: Sacramento is now putting money into student scholarships *instead of* making "a direct investment in the university."[70] As we saw in moving from Stage 3 to Stage 4 of our decline cycle, tuition increases now have a direct downward effect on state funding, feeding and being fed by Stage 5.

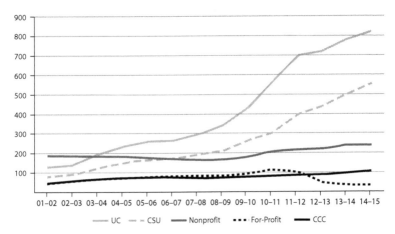

Figure 26. Growth in Cal Grant payments by segment ($ millions). Source: Legislative Analysts Office "Financial Aid Overview," Sacramento, CA, March 13, 2014, accessed July 25, 2015, http://www.lao.ca.gov/handouts/education/2014/Financial-Aid -Overview-031314.pdf.
Note: CSU = California State University; CCC = California Community College

But there is an upside to all of this—for the university. Its higher tuition is backfilled by the state. Meanwhile, the university can gap every student who needs aid, increasing its net revenues from tuition.

This generates real money for the university. Gapping saves UCSB $9,200 per student per year compared to the cost of meeting each student's calculated financial need to cover Cost of Attendance. Let's do some rough arithmetic. I'll assume a lower average Unmet Need gap across the UC system of, say, $8,500 per year. UC had 183,290 undergraduates in fall 2013, and about three-quarters of these had family incomes below $132,000 (a UC statistical threshold that includes nearly all students who are eligible for some financial aid). This suggests that the University of California can save about $1.17 billion in 2013–2014 by gapping all aid-eligible undergraduates rather than giving them grants.[71] A billion saved is a billion earned.

I've come up with a crude number: universities could improve these estimates by disclosing actual figures. My estimate does allow us to note the scale of the avoided spending: a billion dollars is

16 percent of the university's "core budget" spent on the campuses where undergraduates are.[72] It is about half of the difference between UC's current state funding and where the university's state funding would be had it kept up with state personal income growth after 2000–2001.[73] To use the health insurance analogy, this is the kind of corporate income that a large deductible allows.

If gapping financial aid is a widespread practice, then we must shift our thinking about the HITHA model. We should focus not only on how high tuition needs "high financial aid" but on how it enables *high gapping*. Gapping is discretionary, secretive, and hard to track, and yet in tandem with high tuition it supports exploding debt. Gapping appears on the university side, in contrast, as the university's power to increase its net returns from tuition revenues. To stick with our example, in the years after the 2008 crisis, UC grew its total tuition revenues to over $3 billion in 2013–2014, an increase of $1.4 billion.[74] (About one-third of that, as we've seen, came from the state through the Cal Grants program.) University policy is that it return a third of its gross tuition to financial aid, leaving it with $962 million in new net revenue by the end of that period. Were the university to have covered full Unmet Student Need, and if it gapped every student with financial aid, it would have lost all of its new net revenue in doing so. Instead, it preserved financial aid gaps as a tacit private revenue stream.

Students serve as revenue sources in other ways: housing seems to have become a major profit center, but it is beyond my scope here. In wrapping up our discussion of this stage I stick to tuition.[75] We first identified two sources of mushrooming student debt— continuous tuition hikes and government conversions of grants to loans, both of which benefitted private sector interests rather than education. Having looked at the financial aid practices of one major public university, we now have a third source of debt: the aid system's practice of not meeting all financial need and forcing some (un-known) percentage of students to supply more private funds to their university—more funds than they actually have.

In the clash between official reassurances and student anguish about tuition hikes, the students are right. The process of covering

Cost of Attendance has work, stress, and debt built into it. Putting the point more harshly, the HITHA system fuels the debt engine. We can now understand why Robert Birgeneau said that frozen tuition means "ever-increasing debt": universities can respond to frozen tuition with increased gapping, which requires increased student borrowing. It is also true that increased tuition means ever-increasing debt. The current financial aid system is structured to translate either flat tuition or higher tuition into higher debt. To repeat, the money the university avoids spending in grants can be spent on its own operations, while requiring students to make up the gap in work or loans.

Vicious cycles like ours are always fueled by negative interactions among choices that are individually rational. University managers are rational to say to themselves, "we can't afford to meet all student financial need, so they will need to borrow, but we will keep the borrowing to certain limits." They treat financial aid as a kind of financial pain management, of the university's financial pain as well as the students'. But this rationality does not apply to the overall system. The state once paid for the public good of education, and the university tried to keep students in school by minimizing student costs, which did not hurt university finances. The university also tried to maximize human capital outputs in teaching and research by "spending all that they make." Under the private funding model (that leverages reduced public funding), tuition goes up, student debt increases, states spend more public funding on financial aid, which inspires them to deduct this from their spending on university operations, and that induces universities to increase both tuition and the gap between student need and actual aid, which both further increase debt. As higher education is defined as a private good, the state and the university become antagonists, as do students and their universities. And everybody's costs go up.

Private Vendors Leverage Public Funds:
The Case of the MOOCs

The story thus far: Having hidden most of the university's public value (Stage 1), political, academic, and business actors came to expect public universities to seek private revenues and make money with them. This encouraged universities to ignore and conceal losses incurred by sponsored research, complex administration, and related activities (Stage 2). Universities covered their losses by increasing tuition (Stage 3), further privatizing their revenues, which signaled to state legislatures that public funding was dispensable (Stage 4). Public university tuition became high enough to induce significant student debt, which financial aid policy sustained in part to serve the university's revenue needs (Stage 5). Having lived for years with cuts, austerity, and uncertainty, and drained of internal resources for new investment in laboratories, libraries, arts and humanities infrastructure, and advanced technology, public universities were easy pickings for private firms that promised to use their technology to deliver more education for less money. Stage 6 brings the outsourcing of core educational functions to private firms—not because they provided better learning, but because their promise of more for less with private sector technology fit so well into the privatization paradigm.

The price of privatization, we've seen, was most directly experienced by individual students and families through the combination of rising tuition expenses and exploding debt (Stages 3–5). Anything that could reduce their costs would be of great public interest. One particular kind of vendor, providing massive open online courses (MOOCs), made news in 2012 and 2013 by claiming to have a fix for teaching costs. In California, a MOOC program was launched for remedial courses at a Cal State University campus after the state's governor was impressed with the cost and quality claims made in the *New York Times* by a company founder.[1]

The Dream and the Business

In the post-2008 period, the prize for best higher ed buzz goes to the MOOCs vendors. A *New York Times* writer was so impressed that she called 2012 "the Year of the MOOC." The term stuck, and MOOC momentum continued to build through the fall of 2013.[2] Observers were impressed by the potential size of a MOOC course, the apparent efficiencies, and the accompanying promise of radically democratized, fully globalized access to higher education. These scalable MOOCs were to reach the global masses that had been shortchanged, marginalized, or overlooked by their governments. When MOOCs found the missing billion learners, they would give them the best quality content and tools, not yesterday's hand-me-downs. There was huge excitement about Stanford University's spin-off companies Coursera and Udacity and about MIT's spin-off edX.[3] These firms were partnering with internationally renowned thinkers and teachers like Harvard's political science professor Michael Sandel and linking them to millions of "students." Poor villagers in a stereotypical developing country could learn government not from whomever happened to be the local part-time teacher but from one of world's great experts on civil society.

For reasons we have already analyzed and will analyze again in Stage 8, public colleges do need to offer today's students a higher quality, creativity-oriented education. Public college's social value will increasingly depend on its ability to help its millions of students master complex conceptual skills that will allow them to solve non-routine problems and guide their own projects: this would require offering active learning on a mass scale. The leaders of the new MOOC companies seemed to be addressing exactly this need, with a level of technology that colleges had not been able to deploy on their own. A leading example was Udacity cofounder Sebastian Thrun, who repeatedly described a "MOOC model in which students learn by solving problems, not by listening to a professor tell them how to solve them."[4] Cautious supporters of new technology from the traditional university sector, such as the president emeritus of Harvard, Derek Bok, were right about the limits of standard college lectures, which "leave little room for a thorough discussion of problems," for "collaborative efforts to solve problems," or for helping students "acquire habits of metacognition"—the capacity to reflect on how they are learning.[5] Online learning technology could give students a whole new range of opportunities to wrestle with material, learn it deeply, come up with new ideas, and prepare themselves for the global economy.

I share the educational dream that attracted so many to MOOC promises. The dream is easy to state: the huge majority of society getting the best university education, and getting it for free. Since I believe that only mass creativity can save the planet, I embrace any and all tools that will liberate humanity's brilliance on a universal scale, in every obscure or impoverished place where it languishes untended. I also agree with the educational technology (ed-tech) advocates who argue that a mass-produced, generic college degree is of declining value. Colleges have always tried to treat students as individuals, but public colleges have never been *funded* to do this. The ed-tech hope was that technology would now allow *mass specialization*, or the individualization of learning.[6] This would be teaching content and practice to each according to his or her need.

Promise and practice are two different things. Warning signs appeared at the same time as the MOOCs themselves. Ed-tech practitioner and enthusiast Cathy N. Davidson called 2012 MOOCs "horseless carriages," and invited students to help her invent the effective MOOC format that didn't yet actually exist.[7] MOOC company founders were all engineers, and they showed little awareness of the history of university teaching, of the existing literature on learning, or of the everyday reality of public college budgets under austerity. Too much MOOC virtue was established by fabricating a sinful pedagogical state for existing professors, who were said not to care about teaching or to have improved it since the Middle Ages.

I paid particular attention to the MOOC companies' business strategy. In the late 1990s I had been deeply involved with the day-to-day work of a similar kind of start-up company, this one focused on water treatment. They had a novel technology and interesting processes for developing it, and I had served as a cultural consultant. They taught me firsthand the start-up company habit of overselling a technology to attract investors, maximizing growth in market share regardless of the technology's field performance, while lobbying government agencies to build regulations around one's own products. Government pressure could be used to force customers to take you seriously—in our company's case, these customers were olive processors, hog farmers, milk processors, and other agribusinesses whose "non-point-source" pollution had been damaging aquifers. That pressure could encourage sales and revenues while we figured out how to make the technology actually perform as advertised. We confronted federal and state officials with a start-up company's garden-variety front-running of its real results, knowing they lacked the expertise to refute our exuberant claims—which we fully believed ourselves—that known performance problems were being solved even as we spoke. We would also remind regulators that they didn't want to be seen suppressing entrepreneurs with excessive due diligence. My experience with the late 1990s tech boom, combined with the current, nonstop marketing rhetoric from MOOC advocates, prompted me to warn our blog readers in March 2013 about false promises in the MOOC "shift from being an exciting experiment to being offered as a working solution to budgetary and access crises."[8]

Were MOOCs exaggerating their educational benefits in order to tap into a higher education market estimated to be a half-trillion dollars per year?[9] Their timing was right. Public college budgets were still depressed by years of cuts. Course offerings, class sizes, and graduation rates were often substandard, while student costs and debt were excessive. Senior managers at public colleges were desperate, having convinced themselves that public funding would never return to previous levels, and yet they often had to serve more students with less money, while being asked to turn a generation of "Race to the Top" test-takers into self-starters who could build careers out of internships and short-term contracts as they invented the industries of tomorrow. Managers were naturally interested in a product from the same Silicon Valley that had sold the nation on the idea that technology made most public services (and taxes) unnecessary—including everyday public colleges.

The conditions were in place for MOOC firms to *leverage* public funds with relatively small amounts of private capital. The term *leverage* had become well known in the phrase "leveraged buy-out" (LBO), in which a firm would borrow most of the money it was using to buy another firm (typically 90 percent), and use the target firm as collateral for the loan that could be paid off by selling parts of the acquired company. We discussed the leveraging of public universities in Stage 2: MOOCs were not going to leverage public colleges by buying them. But they could acquire a share of their revenue streams—that combination of student tuition and enrollment-based public funding—whose capture is one of our five key elements of privatization.[10] Nationally, public college instructional revenues totaled $81 billion in 2011–2012.[11] MOOCs could leverage their private capital with the far greater sums flowing through colleges and universities, and without buying anything up front. This offered the attractive prospect to strapped public colleges of gradually replacing even more tenure-track faculty with technology that could be managed by private MOOC firms off campus, for a reasonable fee.

The Double Promise

One source of the MOOC problem was that it was the most pretentious corporate intervention into higher education in recent history. Business leaders often imply that everything would be better if they were allowed to set the rules for all major decisions in the society. The philosopher José Medina calls this tendency "epistemic arrogance."[12] But they were outdone this time by a small group of computer science professors from a few of the world's most elite schools—Harvard, MIT, and Stanford—who declared their new companies to be the "single biggest thing in education since the printing press."[13] Even insiders were not using the term MOOC as late as December 2011.[14] A few months later, MOOC was the educational word of the year.[15] By 2013, the United Kingdom was also getting in on the act of defining MOOCs as the Great Disrupter—and the future—of higher education.[16]

What was the MOOC revolution? The answer isn't obvious if you just look at the product itself. The term refers to a multimedia course posted on a website that is accessible to anyone with a computer and an Internet connection. These had been around for two decades before they got the MOOC name. Electronic or broadcast learning had been in use for several decades before that. When the name was used before its Stanford incarnation, it referred to the connectivity MOOC or cMOOC, which had been associated with experiments in democratic and distributed higher education in Canada led by George Siemens, Stephen Downes, and others. Embedded in the theory of learning known as "connectivism," it stressed the value of peer-to-peer student interaction, student self-direction of learning processes, and project-based results.[17] cMOOCs were named as such around 2008, but connectivism had been in development for at least ten years before the MOOC wave hit in 2011. The emphasis was on "open" in the sense of accessible by anyone at no charge, and on a learning structure consisting of a flat social network that would enable self-organized, collaborative instruction.[18]

In contrast, the commercial MOOCs of 2012 were largely digitalized broadcast lectures on conventional course topics delivered by name-brand professors and "chunked" into bite-sized pieces of four to eight minutes, with interactive quizzes and related features. None of this was new to the 2012 generation of MOOC technology. Nor were the educational impacts obviously greater than what could be had through a conventional discussion course.

Four things about MOOCs fascinated the national media. The first was their enormous scale. Once 160,000 people signed up for a Stanford online course on artificial intelligence, it looked like MOOCs could tap a global mass market in higher education.

Second, advocates said that this mass market could be reached by adding tens of thousands of students for nearly zero additional cost. Traditional colleges had to build buildings and hire teachers, custodians, technicians, and administrators. MOOCs did away with all that thanks to the same digital miracle that allowed Facebook to add a million new users for next to nothing. The revolution sprang from thinking of education as an information and telecommunications industry in which the main obstacle to learning was the lack of digital delivery. Traditional colleges had come to depend on an expensive physical plant, and that was a needless bottleneck.

Third, investors were piling into MOOCs, for they seemed able to force higher ed finally to switch from a semiartisanal, relationship-based teaching model to digital delivery. edX was started with $60 million in capital from its partners MIT and Harvard, and Udacity and Coursera, the Stanford companies, had raised tens of millions apiece from Sand Hill Road venture capitalists.[19] MOOCs were free by definition, so the money would have to come later. In classic Silicon Valley style, the giant user base would come first. Once there were tens of millions of MOOC consumers around the world, monetization was sure to follow.

Fourth, certification of results could come from the companies' own data analytics rather than from an expensive, decentralized system of experts—professors in thousands of academic departments, regional accreditation agencies, and the like. In the age of Big Data, the recording of every user's every keystroke seemed like it could bring both individualized "adaptive learning" and validation of results to previously subjective and expensive processes.

These features were a call to action within the culture of privatization. In this culture, any service can be automatically improved by taking its everyday governance away from professional practitioners and giving it to private sector managers and technologists. Privatization had become conventional wisdom, and conventional wisdom is a cognitive shortcut that allows people to avoid the verification of analogies and cause-effect relations. Does being a brilliant modeler of driver behavior also make you an expert on college learning? Once the engineers that founded MOOC companies had positioned them-selves as disruptors, the *automatic* answer, via privatization culture, was yes. Did being an authority on algorithms make you an expert on teaching practices in the contemporary university, on the sociol-ogy of public colleges, on the range of today's college students and learning needs, or on budget and management issues as they affect teaching quality? The obvious answer to these questions is no. And yet the half-unconscious worldview I'm calling privatization culture made such questions seem unnecessary and even obnoxious. Their asking was generally limited to blogs.[20]

In spite of this strong cultural bias in their favor, MOOC fever wouldn't last unless the MOOC leaders were right about two core claims. First, their educational outcomes had to be "as good or better" than traditional face-to-face teaching. Second, their costs had to be lower, thanks to digital automation. The MOOC promise was that high teaching quality could be had at a new low cost through the miracle of digital design.[21]

This twin claim fit with the cost disease premise that helped drive the decline cycle—higher education is a private good that costs too much. It fit with the austerity economics that by 2012 controlled the public sector in the United States as in many other wealthy nations. It fit just as much with idealism about mass access to high-quality instruction for the world's hundreds of millions of potential univer-sity students who were ready to learn but who lacked universities. MOOCs promised private good personalization of instruction for a cost approximating free.

But were the paired claims to high educational quality at near-zero delivery costs actually true?

Claiming Zero Costs

Let's recapture the MOOC cost excitement. They were on vivid display at an event at UCLA in January 2013 called "Rebooting Higher Education." Sponsored by an organization set up to lobby for e-textbooks, 20 Million Minds, and run by a former president of the California State Senate, Dean Flores, it convened the heads of

Udacity, Coursera, Western Governors University, StraighterLine, and a few university-based online providers, with some end-of-the-day space for faculty comments.

Batting first and second were the founders of the twin Stanford companies. Sebastian Thrun of Udacity opened by claiming that MOOCs were going to do to universities what semiconductors had done to slide rules: "This is going to be the age of better, faster, and cheaper for higher education. I think we are the advent of discovering new technology and new pedagogies that will make higher education more accessible, more affordable, and [will] spread higher education to many more people than ever before."[22] Thrun was wrapping MOOC technology in the history of silicon devices and Moore's Law, under which the regular doubling of processor speed would be accompanied by the halving of price. When you liberate learning experiences from physical classrooms and face-to-face exchange, "almost everything changes," he said. One of the things that changes, he told *The Economist*, is the existence of so many physical universities, most of which will disappear. Correcting the original quotation in an e-mail to me, Thrun wrote, "in 50 years, 10 entities will provide 50% of higher education."

When her turn at UCLA came, Coursera cofounder Daphne Koller pushed further on the mass-production economics. Her partner, Stanford computer science professor Andrew Ng, had a machine learning class with six hundred students.

> When Andrew taught that class online, there were 100,000 students with that class. For Andrew to reach that same size audience, Andrew would have to teach at Stanford for 250 years. [With MOOCs we have the] ability to reach [that audience] at a cost of effectively zero dollars marginal cost per student. . . . Currently we have a little over 2.2 million students who have enrolled in 212 courses from these 33 very fine institutions that we were very fortunate to work with.[23]

As I noted before, this mass market was the galvanizing prospect. In discussion, Koller elaborated on the basis of the MOOC's enormous savings:

Our cost estimates are 25 to 50 thousand dollars for one of our courses and that doesn't include faculty time . . . that includes mostly TA support. We found that videographer time is not a huge expense because it's a commodity now and you can get it very economically but TA support for content is a fairly significant expense, which is why it costs 25–50 thousand dollars depending on how much support is required. But I think the important thing to keep in mind is that cost gets amortized over a much much larger number of students, both across iterations and within an iteration, and the marginal cost for students now comes down to under a dollar or very close to zero. . . . Yes the cost is high, but once you amortize them they are not that high after all. . . . You divide the cost that you would pay for the traditional face-to-face class not over a 100 students you are teaching but over 10,000 students you are teaching. Yes, so the fixed costs are there. The question is what's the denominator?[24]

At this point, Thrun demurred, saying "I'm not quite as bullish as my colleague Daphne in the sense that for $50,000 you can educate 30,000 students. The dropout rates are staggering and only highly motivated students join in." He agreed that "people matter. Instructors matter" to achieving educational quality. But the consensus among MOOC providers was that online was "much cheaper" than face-to-face, even if it wasn't free. Only a minority felt that "better faster cheaper" device engineering didn't apply to education. I found myself in this suspicious group.

Cutting Costs or Leveraging Public Money?

Let's start with *cheaper*. How do we know that online education saves money? During the Year of the MOOC, the coverage simply assumed it. MOOCs were technology, and technology supposedly always saves money. We were to picture processor price, not health care. Venture capitalists were investing tens of millions of dollars, and they only do that when they project huge profits associated with the tech-driven lowering of costs. There was also the general sense that college now costs so much that there *had* to be massive savings being left on the table. But tech would force "special interests"—faculty in particular—to change.[25]

Academic managers may have assumed that MOOCs were cheaper, but they seem not to have actually *known* that. This was because MOOC companies kept their business plans confidential. Public policy began to change on the basis of claimed savings that had no public records to back them up. The most famous of these policy changes was a California State Senate bill requiring the state's public universities to convert oversubscribed entry-level courses to MOOCs.[26] The formal explanation for this bill was to improve access. The implicit goal was to improve access while relieving the state of responsibility to reverse funding cuts. The discussion surrounding this legislation was long on assertions and short on financial evidence. Though the legislation was modified in response to widespread concerns that it would negate the University of California's constitutional autonomy, it remained a tribute to the MOOC companies' connections and prestige: they were attracting venture capital and getting themselves written into state legislation without providing educational or financial data to verify their claims, beyond awesome initial enrollment statistics. They had mounted what the musician Fela Kuti called a "power show."

In May 2013, after a year of data-free marketing claims that had generated dozens of contracts with leading universities, *Inside Higher Ed* reporter Ry Rivard obtained some contract documents for one widely publicized program. Georgia Tech had hired Udacity to create an entire MOOC master's degree. Rivard had had to file a public records request to get information about Georgia Tech's agreement with Udacity.[27] I then published an analysis of the Udacity spreadsheets, having gone through them in search of the promised savings.[28]

The contract, between Udacity and the Georgia Tech Research Corporation (GTRC), aimed to create a MOOC master's degree in computer science—described as "the first professional online master of science degree in computer science (OMS CS) that can be earned completely through the 'massive online' format." The hook was the low, low price—$6,630, according to Rivard, or one-seventh of the

$40,000-plus price of a face-to-face computer science MS degree at the same institution.

But when I looked for massive cost savings in the Georgia Tech-Udacity spreadsheets, what did I find? None in Year 1, when the program was planning to spend around $15,700 per year, per enrolled student, or about the same as the University of California spent for its students averaged together. This was disappointing, since partnering with a MOOC like Udacity was supposed to allow a university to skip development costs by using the existing Udacity platform, and go straight to the tech-based savings. But allowing for some ramp-up, what about Year 3?

There was confusion about Year 3 enrollments. Since the partnership was not collecting $6,630 per year but per degree, and the degree was estimated to take three years, the program would collect $2,210 a year in tuition. At that annual price, the $19 million predicted as Year 3 revenue would require 8,700 full-time students. But this figure was larger than the total number of computer science master's degrees granted in 2009–2010 in the United States.[29]

Were the program to hit these targets, it would spend about $1,655 per year per student, or under $5,000 per degree.[30] The cost is ultra-low for a master's degree, or for any other kind of degree. (The program reported actual enrollments for the end of Year 3, in spring 2016, as 3,358, which, with an estimated $14.4 million in program costs, comes to $4,288 per student per year, which would cause the partnership to lose $6,235 per student over the three-year degree term.)[31]

How would the online master's ever break even? The simple answer is that it wouldn't. Georgia Tech wanted a high-quality program, and the faculty working group called for a thirty-to-one student-to-TA ratio, which is fairly close to the ratio at a good public university. Each year, each student would get a total of twelve hours of personal attention, or thirty-six hours over the three-year program. And yet the program's initial cosponsor, AT&T, expected 100 percent online instruction. Either the program would have 290 "course assistants" (with the thirty-to-one ratio), or eighty-seven, who at forty hours a week could deliver twelve hours per student per year—or zero for the

AT&T online model that eliminated personal attention. (The budget for student support suggested something close to eighty-seven.) This confusion may have been a feature rather than a bug: Udacity would appeal to the corporate belief that the future of teaching is no teachers, while hiring quasi-teachers to suppress that belief's bad results.

Let's turn from price to cost. MOOC advocates led investors to expect the spreadsheets to show that MOOCs offer an automation of teaching like the "rise of the robots" in manufacturing. But in the budget, the category of "student support" grew in lockstep with revenue (up 13.8 times and 13.9 times, respectively) over three years. One simple reason was that the Georgia Tech faculty wanted the OMS CS to have "world-class quality." Fully online courses are cheaper, but they generate the highest attrition rates in the history of higher education. I inferred that Georgia Tech had decided that their MOOCs would always be "blended" MOOCs, and blended MOOCs need lots of what we normally call teaching assistants, which means Georgia Tech's MOOCs weren't actually MOOCs in the sense of the imagined near-zero personnel costs that set the business and policy worlds on fire.

This was an important admission that a MOOC is "as good or better" than hands-on instruction only by paying for hands-on instruction. Although online support for instruction can, over time, help to control costs, the Georgia Tech demand to match existing instructional quality cancelled the cost revolution.

Continuing to pore over the spreadsheets, I had an unpleasant surprise in the equally relentless growth of "Operations, Materials, & Supplies." This is where Udacity's proprietary technology was to rescue teaching budgets from the supposedly medieval methods that had always bloated them. In fact, looking at the budget, its platform did nothing to cut operating costs. The MOOC examinations were particularly expensive. The big savings were to come in two ways. First, payments to faculty course creators flattened out, which meant reducing content innovation. Second, in exchange for shouldering most of the early costs, Udacity would leverage Georgia Tech facilities and personnel. But there's nothing novel in these practices. It's easy to reduce expenses by giving the same lecture over and over, which is what existing online courses are designed to do. This is also true for running more volume through the same plant, which is another time-honored university tactic.

A Promise of Market Position

The Udacity-GTRC contract raised the question of what exactly Udacity brought to the table. It certainly brought its platform. Yet its platform was not transformative—not visibly better, faster, or cheaper than what Georgia Tech's computer science department had already created or could create with new resources.

Second, there were some net revenues. Were it to achieve a profit of $1,665 per degree, the program would earn $14.5 million on the unlikely 8,700 students, or about $4.8 million per year. Sixty percent of this total (or $2.9 million) would go to Georgia Tech's operating unit (GTRC). This would amount to a bit over 1 percent of GTRC's annual research revenues, even with this very high number of enrollments. On top of this, GTRC would get 20 percent of gross revenues and 20 percent of gross profits for non-OMS students that took Georgia Tech courses through Udacity. But these would be MOOC students who would in general not pay anything. Georgia Tech probably had better margins on its existing extension programs, and could also support its institutional needs with new, smaller programs that it would run on its own. Three years after Rivard's and my analyses, Georgia Tech claimed to be breaking even on the program with fewer than half the 8,700 enrollments, with a fresh subsidy from AT&T and without disclosing budget data.[32]

What Udacity clearly brought to the table was platform branding. The company positioned itself as a first mover and dominant player in what it was describing as a new global market. Its founder was famous and influential: Sebastian Thrun was associated with Google's driverless car and with Stanford's artificial intelligence program. He had cosigned a deal to provide three entry-level courses to San José State University in the presence of the governor of California.

A similar story of brand dominance could be told about Coursera and its cofounder Daphne Koller, whose access to decision makers extended to the World Economic Forum conference at Davos. The three main MOOC companies had the clout to sign deals directly with a given institution's senior managers, over the heads of the faculty. Since Internet and communications technologies seem always to be controlled by a corporate oligarchy (Google/Bing/Yahoo! or Apple OS /Microsoft Windows/Linux), Udacity could pitch its platform as one of the very few ways for farsighted, "first mover" universities to win in a global online competition.

In exchange for presenting itself as an oligarch in waiting, Udacity extracted quite a bit of less quantifiable value from Georgia Tech. Udacity was to receive the intellectual content for a master's program of twenty courses at an upfront cost of $400,000. It would borrow Georgia Tech's reputation as its own, at a huge discount, in that it did not need to pay for the training of graduate students, for facilities and administration, or for decades of accumulated know-how through which Georgia Tech had earned its reputation. It acquired these courses for a proprietary platform: Georgia Tech could not offer these OMS CS courses, created by its own faculty, to a competing distributor. At the same time, Udacity expected Georgia Tech faculty members to maintain and update course material, whose latest version would be available to them. While requiring that Georgia Tech not compete with it, Udacity would take Georgia Tech-created courses and offer them to tens or hundreds of thousands of nonregistered students—and sell a program certificate for those courses. These courses would differ from Georgia Tech's in being "minimally staffed to rely on course assistants only for student assessment," but would use Georgia Tech's content to compete with Georgia Tech's and all other masters' programs. With these courses, Udacity could enter the master's certification business but without having to pay for a degree's physical infrastructure, professors, staff, collaboration time, intellectual ecology, and other sunk costs.

We have seen this model before on our tour of the decline cycle. A university, wholly or in part supported by the public, spends decades building its institutional and human capabilities. Then a sponsor, partner, or competitor, logically focused on their competitive advantage, comes along not to support but to *leverage* the existing public resources. Leveraging means incorporating the public institution's resources into the partner's "value proposition." This is how the corporate version of "open innovation" is designed to work: use other people's intellectual property, other people's human capital, and turn it into a proprietary product.[33]

This is a technique for enclosing the commons. But it is an everyday, routine business practice in which the commons comes in the form of innumerable local sectors of activity—"temporary autonomous zones"—that haven't yet been appropriated by anyone as part of a private value chain. It's good in the abstract for intellectual property (IP) to go to the people who can make the most use of it, but these new possessors need to compensate the original creators properly and keep the IP open enough for later improvers. In contrast, MOOC-style leveraging takes public resources with no compensation or prospects for nonowners to make future improvements. Leveraging means "free-riding," as private partners take out more than they put back in. This makes the devolutionary wheel spin.

For the first two years of the MOOC wave, claims about the cheapness of the MOOC format overcame widespread doubts about its educational and social effects. During this time, the main MOOC companies did not release specific financial projections. In mid-2013, we finally had two spreadsheets, and MOOC claims to cheapness were not confirmed. More information will emerge in the future to improve our sense of the MOOC financial picture.[34] The default mode is that MOOC profitability depends on direct subsidies (AT&T at Georgia Tech) and/or on using public universities to capture public cash flows and infrastructure value. Over the long run, this practice will not increase public college revenues, but siphon them off.

MOOCs Ignoring Social Difference

If cost savings were a bust, what about educational benefits? MOOC advocates were also asserting that "classes with online learning (whether taught completely online or blended) on average produce stronger student learning outcomes than do classes with solely face-to-face instruction." This claim appeared on Coursera's website with the imprimatur of the US Department of Education.[35] The Department of Education had sponsored a study of existing studies of online education, known as a meta-analysis. The study came with an abstract that declared, "students in online learning conditions performed modestly better than those receiving face-to-face instruction."[36] This was perhaps the most widely circulated sentence of an education article abstract in history.

Were it true, the claim would register a major change in US and international university outcomes. Educational attainment is dramatically skewed by income and, in the United States, by race. College graduation has been a tale of two nations, in which the top half of the United States by income has had the highest attainment rates in the world in a standard global sample, while the bottom half has had the second to worst rate.[37] Improvement in attainment rates since the late 1970s occurred overwhelmingly in this top income half: the bottom quartile had improved attainment by only 2 percent in thirty years.[38] Similarly, the graduation rates of students classed as members of US Underrepresented Minority Groups (UMGs) have been two-thirds to one-half that of whites (African Americans and Latinos, respectively).[39] In order to have the transformative educational impact it claimed, online technology would need to take the least-advantaged groups and bring them the largest distance. The poorest students abroad, and the least-well-served at home, would need to be at the front of the MOOC line.

MOOC advocates were of course aware that hundreds of millions of people were not getting the education they needed and deserved, yet they offered no meaningful analyses of how social, political, or historical obstacles to access would be specifically addressed by their learning technology.[40] They seemed to assume that the history of education consisted of insufficient use of technology until they came along, and now technology would conquer all.[41]

Decades of research has shown that poverty is a major source of reduced educational access in developing nations and in the United States. Poverty has been maintained by uneven development that many observers believe is intrinsic to capitalism itself, and has made economies like Pakistan's examples of neocolonial relations held in place by Western military strategies, resource wars, and other factors. Similar types of "structural adjustment" seem to be at work in the United States. How else can we explain the dramatic "two-nation" splits in attainment? The issue needed at least some serious engagement from firms claiming to cut through social problems with their technology in the "new digital age" that had, for example, supposedly brought democracy to the Middle East during the Arab Spring of 2011.[42] But on the home front, MOOC entrepreneurs were silent on questions of financing, preparation, poverty, and racialization that had been shown to cause performance gaps.[43] MOOC technology was to leapfrog social problems.

The educational claims were most clearly asserted by Coursera's lead apostle, Daphne Koller. Her TED Talk stated, among other things, that professors don't interact with their students but simply lecture at them.[44] This suggested that taking a MOOC with no human contact would not be much of a loss. Lecturing was the standard target of MOOC advocates, which they declared categorically obsolete. Koller explained the problem and the solution at the UCLA "Rebooting" conference:

> The insight that went into the design of this new generation of MOOCs came from a lot of the Stanford experiments on flipped classroom teaching where the idea was . . . let's take lecturing out of the classroom. Lecturing is not the way we want to teach our students in this day and age. It's a waste of time for me to come in to a lecture with 200 people and give the same lecture that I've been giving for 15 years telling the same jokes at the same time. It's just not a great experience for me. It's not a great experience for the students. Why not, instead come and talk to the students in class? Have a dialogue and have them talk to each other and have them do active things in the classroom so that they engage with

each other and with course material that's much deeper and in more meaningful ways. Very many people have talked about the benefits of that kind of active learning in the classroom.[45]

Elsewhere Koller described the bad model as the "sage on the stage," the professor who drones his students to sleep with notes first jotted down two decades earlier. Koller and others made three claims: college teaching consisted almost entirely of a professor lecturing and students passively taking notes; professors believed in this kind of passive learning and never supplemented it with seminars, discussions, and other forms of feedback; MOOCs had invented a new kind of teaching by "flipping the classroom" through technology, assigning the students to interact with material before class, and then using face-to-face time actively to discuss material rather than passively to receive it.

There were several odd things about these claims. The first was the aggressive dismissal of hundreds of thousands of work-a-day instructors without any evidence. A highlight of Koller's TED Talk was when she quoted Mark Twain saying, "College is a place where a professor's lecture notes go straight to the students' lecture notes without passing through the brains of either."[46] The joke expresses a kind of bigotry, and Koller took advantage of the stereotype of the boring professor to discredit the national faculty's pedagogical skill, which in turn helped senior managers to ignore faculty oversight procedures in signing teaching deals with MOOC companies. MOOCs could thus acquire a prestigious university partner by contracting with a vice president for extension learning, or an assistant provost for information technology, or something similar.[47] The categorical discrediting of faculty pedagogy made this bypass of faculty expertise and authority seem reasonable and necessary for the sake of progress.

Second, MOOC advocates were reinventing the wheel. The flipped classroom was what is normally called a seminar for which students read material beforehand and come to class prepared to discuss it. Two-to-one or one-to-one student-faculty ratios underwrite elite education in the tutorial system developed by the universities of Oxford and Cambridge; individualized instruction is also available to—indeed required of—all students at private universities like Princeton. This model has been adapted into standard seminar practice at private liberal arts colleges like Haverford, Oberlin, Grinnell, Millsaps, or Dickinson, which have student-to-faculty ratios as low as eight or ten to one.[48] My own BA is from Reed College, where, in three years, around four of my thirty courses were lectures that had thirty-five to seventy students; the rest had eight to twelve students. By comparison, at my current university, UC Santa Barbara, a public research university, our English majors are allowed to take exactly one fifteen-member seminar in four years. A limited number of the rest of their courses will be "discussions" of thirty-eight students, with the rest being one-hundred- to four-hundred-student lecture courses (with discussions run by teaching assistants). This type of mass instruction reflects funding limits rather than faculty or student preferences.

When Koller claimed MOOCs would offer "mastery learning," she was invoking an idea that had been developed by Benjamin Bloom and others in the 1950s and 1960s, and which seminars made much easier to achieve. Mastery learning is thought to require regular "formative tests" and "corrective feedback procedures" and was found in the 1980s to yield one standard deviation of improved learning. At the same time, one-on-one tutoring yields two standard deviations of improvement, and MOOC developers saw this "2-sigma problem" as one that MOOCs could solve.[49] The educational ambition is admirable, but MOOC advocates' claim to a novel goal and method was sheer pretense.

In effect, MOOC advocates were encouraging students to leave their state universities to attend liberal arts colleges, where they could go back to a future of intensive learning in the seminars that typify the "colleges that change lives."[50] But of course they weren't. Advocates were actually claiming MOOC ed tech could create liberal arts colleges all for next-to-no cost (Koller) or greatly lowered costs (Thrun). In making this claim, they ignored existing historical knowledge about learning at high-quality institutions, which made the technology seem original, when it was not.

Coursera Distorts the Federal Meta-Study

The third odd feature of the 2011–2013 MOOC campaign was that one leading advocate misstated crucial educational findings. The Department of Education meta-analysis is the most important case.[51] We've seen the abstract's famous quotation, which stated that "students in online learning conditions performed modestly better than those receiving face-to-face instruction." The catch is the phrase "online learning *conditions*." The study found that the conditions *associated with* online learning, rather than the technology itself, enhanced educational outcomes.

What are these conditions? The central clue comes from the widely recognized fact that "blended" or "hybrid" courses are better than purely online courses. The meta-analysis confirmed this: "Instruction combining online and face-to-face elements had a larger advantage relative to purely face-to-face instruction than did purely online instruction. . . . In fact, the learning outcomes for students in purely online conditions and those for students in purely face-to-face conditions were statistically equivalent."[52] Blending online technology with personal contact was, ironically, the only real source of online advantage. As we saw, the Georgia Tech–Udacity contract acknowledged this fact when they budgeted for a large number of "course assistants": this ensures that the online master's program is actually a series of blended courses with plenty of face-to-face guidance. When Daphne Koller and others called for replacing the "sage on the stage" with the "guide on the side," they were in fact summoning blended courses rather than MOOCs as such, where the personal interaction would consist of e-mail, peer-to-peer chats, and other mediated formats.

If "blended" creates courses that are better than both face-to-face and fully online courses, what are its defining features? Interestingly, adjusting the human-computer interface doesn't seem to make much difference. Though the data were weak here (and in some cases too old to instill confidence), it appeared that "variations in the way in which different studies implemented online learning did not affect student learning outcomes significantly."[53] In particular, "Elements such as video or online quizzes do not appear to influence the amount that students learn in online classes."[54] This is remarkable, since video is a MOOC's main instructional medium, and online quizzes are its core form of interactivity.

In my reading of the meta-analysis, four features turn out to determine educational value. The first is "giving learners control of their interactions with media and prompting learner reflection."[55] One great advantage of online materials is that each student gets as many swings at the ball as she wants and needs. If the first time isn't enough for real understanding, she can replay a topic two, three, or ten times, and focus on this or that element that is harder for her, even as a friend in the same course is working at the computer next to her on a completely different part of the material that he found hard—or interesting. Student control over the learning process allows individualized adaptation to material, which makes learning more effective.

The second positive feature is that benefits are proportional to "the amount of time the learners spent on task."[56] Online education could improve outcomes if it allowed or encouraged students to correct for the general decline in student study hours that is a major problem in the contemporary university.[57]

The third and fourth features are as follows: "Studies using blended learning also tend to involve . . . additional instructional resources, and course elements that encourage interactions among learners." You might miss that phrase "additional instructional resources," but it is important. Students with lower completion rates and other outcomes generally go to poorer colleges with fewer resources. Online experiments, and MOOCs in particular, inspired investment in programs that had often been starved of funds. The Udacity courses at San José State University were a case in point: MOOCs were competing against face-to-face courses that had been subject to the largest public funding cuts in the state's history.

The meta-analysis's real conclusion contradicted the one-liner lifted from the abstract, and read as follows: "This meta-analysis . . . should not be construed as demonstrating that online learning is superior as a medium. Rather, it is the combination of elements in the treatment conditions, which are likely to include additional learning time and materials as well as additional opportunities for collaboration, which has proven effective. The meta-analysis findings do not support simply putting an existing course online, but they do support redesigning instruction to incorporate additional learning opportunities online."[58]

The value of blended courses follows from four things: learner control, extra study time, more money, and interactive opportunities. The value, in other words, comes from more structured attention to the student's learning process, starting with greatly increased attention from the student herself. Online technology is often an *occasion* for upgrading the learning process, for the simple reason that, in a culture of privatization, university administrations that would not spend money on face-to-face improvements like smaller discussion sections *would* spend money for access to technology from a prestigious outside vendor. But the *means* to the student's learning upgrade was not technological in itself. It was upgraded studying—to repeat, learner control, more time, more learning resources, and more active learning, including feedback. The need to upgrade studying and feedback was in danger of getting lost in the focus on the technology.

Racial Impacts of MOOC Instruction

Were MOOCs approaching their egalitarian promise to distribute the best educational resources to all mankind, their failure to save money and increase learning would be seen as growing pains. I had hoped this would be the case. In early 2013, I organized a research group to look into the question of whether online instruction was improving outcomes across racial lines in California. We decided to compare similar types of institutions that used online strategies heavily or exclusively to those that did not. We included for-profits, and also took a special interest in community colleges.[59]

We were unable to get data on race and ethnicity from existing online companies. For colleges, the data did not break out graduation rates for different ratios of online/face-to-face instruction. The federal data did not include noncollege online providers. We requested this data from leading MOOC companies a number of times, but they did not provide it. In the fall of 2015, I discovered the most plausible reason why. At a conference at Teachers College, Columbia University, Al Filreis, a particularly engaging MOOC professor, described the benefits of his well-regarded Coursera MOOC, "Modern and Contemporary American Poetry." One of the benefits, he said, was the wide range of students who took the course. During the question session, I asked him whether he could share data on enrollment distribution by race and ethnicity. "No, we don't collect those data," he replied. He looked to someone in the audience for verification. This person was nodding vigorously and said, "it's true, we don't collect these data either." It turned out to be Anant Agarwal, the CEO of edX, another leading MOOC provider.

I spoke to Agarwal later about the data, saying that I thought it was hard to claim wide social benefits for MOOC courses when we don't actually know whether or not their enrollments include all racial groups, or in what proportion. "We don't ask that," he replied, "because if we ask more than 3 or 4 questions at registration, many students won't complete. But you're the fourth person to mention this issue to me, so I will think about it."[60] The goal of maximizing the headline enrollment number seems to conflict with keeping the racial and ethnicity data that would validate social claims.

Turning to pre-MOOC online companies, our research group first noted that virtually all of the mostly online higher education companies were for-profits.[61] In addition, a high proportion of their students were over the age of twenty-five–more than 80 percent of them, or about twice the proportion we found in our community college group.[62] These institutions are serving non-college-age learners, which is consistent with mass expansion.

The same is true for outreach to one underrepresented racial group, African Americans, and to lower-income students. The "distance-only" institutions had five to six times more African Americans in their student bodies than our set of community colleges, and a similarly larger proportion than all other types of not-for-profit colleges. (This was not the case for Latino and Asian Americans.) Distance-only institutions had more than twice the amount of Pell Grant recipients compared to community colleges and four-year colleges. The technology seemed to be reaching Black and low-income Americans who were not being served by traditional colleges.

But this is a good thing only if online learning without instructors offers quality that is equivalent to that of traditional classrooms. If online is worse, then we would be seeing a kind of racial dumping that leads to more of the problem ed-tech was supposed to solve—lower attainment for lower-income students. Online would be extending the known problems with for-profits, which have played the role of providing bad educational service for a very high price. Our second research question was, "How do online programs compare to face-to-face programs by standard metrics of educational quality?"

Here the results were discouraging. Distance-only institutions have one-third the proportion of full-time faculty compared to community colleges, and about one-eighth the share offered by public research universities. Student-faculty ratios were the highest (worst) in the business—worse even than community colleges, and three times higher than the gold standard of liberal arts colleges. Distance-only had the worst graduation rates—worse even than for-profits overall, at one-eighth the rate of public research universities and one-quarter the rate of community colleges. We concluded that existing distance learning colleges are at, or below, the bottom of the existing quality spectrum for colleges. They may be expanding access to higher learning, yet they are not providing much learning as such.

But surely, we thought, technology can make up for *some* socioeconomic disadvantages if applied on a large scale and in a not-for-profit context. So we asked whether existing assessments show that online technology overcomes the limitations of online's standard learning context—that is, when it is not accompanied by a Georgia Tech–type of premium TA support. We looked first at the most decisive recent study of a statewide community college system. This study, conducted by Columbia University researchers at the Community College Research Center, used a dataset containing about 500,000 courses taken by over 40,000 community and technical college students in Washington State.

The results were distressing. The online format did not help overall learning but in fact hurt it. And it hurt learning *more* for the underserved students that the MOOC boom is supposed to reach—in this case African Americans. The authors summarized their findings as follows.

> Overall, the online format had a significantly negative relationship with both course persistence and course grade, indicating that the typical student had difficulty adapting to online courses. While this negative sign remained consistent across all subgroups, the size of the negative coefficient varied significantly across subgroups. Specifically, we found that males, Black students, and students with lower levels of academic preparation experienced significantly stronger negative coefficients for online learning compared with their counterparts, in terms of both course persistence and course grade. These results provide support for the notion that students are not homogeneous in their adaptability to the online delivery format. . . . These patterns also suggest that performance gaps between key demographic groups already observed in face-to-face classrooms (e.g., gaps between male and female students, and gaps between White and ethnic minority students) are exacerbated in online courses. This is troubling from an equity perspective.

This is the largest study we could find, and it suggested as conclusively as any other study that online technology does not overcome learning problems that are known to correlate with sociocultural disadvantage. On the contrary, this study found that online education made racial disparity worse.

One of our group's members analyzed data from another large unit, the California Community College system, with a million and a half enrollments covering the full spectrum of the state's diverse population.[63] A large longitudinal dataset showed that, overall, online

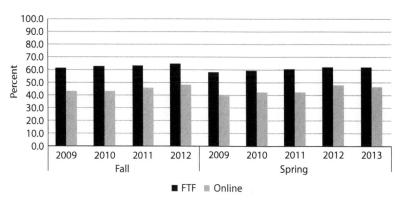

Figure 27. Online versus face-to-face course success rates, California Community Colleges. *Source:* Christopher Newfield and Cameron M. Sublett, "The Student Experience of Online Education: Interviews in a California Community College" (paper, "Learning with MOOCs II" conference, Teachers College, Columbia University, New York, October 2015). Data analysis conducted by Sublett.

achievement is lower than achievement in face-to-face contexts (figure 27).

In addition, the observed disparity in achievement varies sharply by race, with Asian American students exhibiting the smallest disparity, and Latinos and African Americans exhibiting greater disparity in outcomes than white students (figure 28).

We also confirmed that the disparity in achievement between online and face-to-face classes was greatest in so-called basic skills courses (that is, remedial courses) as compared to for-credit courses. The analysis suggests that online courses may increase long-term transfer and completion rates, but we interpret this to mean that online courses are better at helping students navigate curricular bottlenecks than they are at improving learning.

At the time of this writing, we were continuing to analyze the sources of these disparities. But one thing was already clear: online technology does not in itself overcome the racial disparities in educational achievement that are arguably the greatest challenge facing higher education today. MOOC advocates were at best incurious

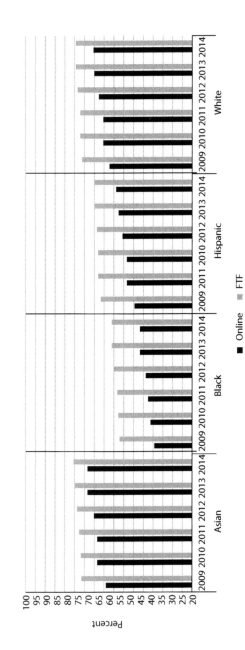

Figure 28. Face-to-face versus online course success rates by ethnic group (for-credit courses). *Source:* Newfield and Sublett, "The Student Experience of Online Education."

about using their famously big data to understand why. For reasons that the MOOC mental framework could not confront, online technology was more likely to lower the attainment of a minority majority state like California than to raise it.

Udacity Flunks Entry-Level Teaching

After two years of public relations triumphs, Udacity had an opportunity to show what they could do with a student population that looked much more like "everyone around the world" than did undergraduates at Stanford: entering students at San José State University (SJSU) who needed remedial work before they could start college.

Though it sits in the heart of Silicon Valley, SJSU is socially distinct from elite IT companies and their academic base, Stanford University, and serves a high proportion of first-generation college students, immigrant students, and students of color.[64] In the midst of the economic changes of the last thirty years, Silicon Valley's celebrated tech companies turned tax avoidance into a central business strategy, and this has hurt local public colleges. A major story on the subject noted that

> some, including De Anza College's president, [Brian] Murphy, say the philanthropy and job creation do not offset Apple's and other companies' decisions to circumvent taxes. Within 20 minutes of the financially ailing school are the global headquarters of Google, Facebook, Intel, Hewlett-Packard and Cisco.
>
> "When it comes time for all these companies—Google and Apple and Facebook and the rest—to pay their fair share, there's a knee-jerk resistance," Mr. Murphy said. "They're philosophically antitax, and it's decimating the state." "But I'm not complaining," he added. "We can't afford to upset these guys. We need every dollar we can get."[65]

While the valley's tech companies don't want to pay the taxes that support publics like two-year De Anza College and four-year San José State University, they *do* want to sell them learning tools like MOOCs. Can learning software help bridge the class divide that has been intensified through years of cuts that flow in part from Silicon Valley's prodigious influence over tax policy?

The theory was tested in September 2013, when a group funded by the National Science Foundation published a report on the SJSU–Udacity pilot of three college preparation and introductory courses.[66] The students in these courses were, by definition, underprepared. The project specifically targeted at-risk populations, largely those who had previously failed a face-to-face version of a basic math course. The participating faculty members were generally impressed with the materials. They believed that the content that was developed in collaboration with Udacity had tremendous potential to advance students' critical thinking and problem-solving abilities; courses were more contextualized and more inquiry-based, with added real life contexts.

The pass rates in the Udacity-developed courses were disappointing—an overall average of 33 percent, with fully matriculated students passing at 42 percent. This compared unfavorably to the 74 percent pass rate of the regular courses that Udacity's plan was meant to replace.[67] The switch to Udacity courses cut the SJSU pass rate in half.

The study confirmed that pass rates were linked not so much to the technology as to student effort. The clearest predictor of passing a course was the number of problem sets a student completed. Another major completion factor was the amount of time a student watched the video lectures, which offered a way of reviewing material, refining one's notes, and spending more time trying to understand more difficult material. These key activities are traditionally known as *studying*. For various reasons, including the need to meet rising tuition costs by increasing paid work, students have cut back on this important activity. No reader will be shocked to learn that students who studied early, often, steadily, and persistently were more likely to pass. The quality of the studying process was the main driver of the pass rate. The low pass rate suggested that the online format did not improve the learning practices of most of the students identified as needing exactly that kind of improvement.

The formal analysis of the Udacity pilot confirmed that technology cannot replace high-quality study time, but must enable or encourage it. Online technology can help increase study time and help increase persistence and regularity of study, both of which boost learning and retention of what is learned. It can be used to set up Socratic interrogations in which students become investigators of problems as they test and deepen their understanding of course material in the process of trying to put it to use. But in reviewing these studies and others, we have been unable to find evidence that a student's cognitive processes and learning activities are enhanced by the technology as such. Learning still takes time and effort, and MOOC programming does not appear to be offering technological short cuts. Concentration, focus, repetition, failure, self-correction, and practice—these are among the essential learning processes that good technology can assist but not replace.

Online technology can also be an obstacle and a distraction, and that was the case at SJSU, where students had to navigate two separate websites for materials and puzzle through confusing instructions. The online medium produces poor communication as readily as people do—MOOCs are a combination of writing, programming, and lecturing and are subject to the law of "garbage in, garbage out." This is a particularly vital issue when a course includes students who don't yet really know how to learn. Learning is a complicated cluster of many simultaneous processes that must be strengthened, aligned, and repeatedly practiced.[68] Online technology can help automate practicing learning like an academic batting cage. It can offer a higher-order version of, say, a Korean language lab where one has to spend hundreds of hours practicing Korean sounds, words, and sentences on top of studying textbooks, doing grammar exercises, writing short paragraphs, watching Korean-language movies or TV shows, and so on—all of which the learner needs for progress to occur. To repeat, online technology may structure and systematize some of the pathways to creating cognitive capabilities, and yet do this *without* replacing either the cognitive capabilities or the labor involved in creating them.

This is the reality of human learning: learning is a process that can be regularized and intensified but not bypassed or compressed algorithmically. The best learners are those who have sustained, systematized, and integrated their learning process. They do this by being reflective about their learning process, by organizing it carefully, by executing their study strategies consistently, and by putting in the hours it takes to be really good at anything—ten thousand hours to mastery, by one estimate.[69] Great learners don't learn by thinking that a particular medium is going to do their work for them.[70]

In working with SJSU, Udacity set up a group of "Online Support Providers" (OSPs). OSPs were quasi-instructors who functioned as teaching assistants. They were available online, but could offer help to individual students. One OSP described intended users as those "who have the right background or knowledge and are ready to succeed in class, but they are just confused about something or frustrated, and they get stuck on something and can't get past a certain point for whatever reason. Getting these students . . . unstuck—that is where we are most effective."[71]

Getting "unstuck." This is not an occasional issue in an otherwise smooth learning process: getting unstuck *is* the learning process. Stuck and unstuck describe polymorphous blockages and the small shifts that create understanding, at least for a few minutes, before the next moment of doubt, uncertainty, confusion, or total error appears and needs to be addressed in a somewhat different context. This has been the strength and weakness of educational practice throughout the ages. Results finally depend on the individual's intellectual labor, both its quantity and quality, and technology needs to work on the human terrain constituted by the learner's cognitive practices, which are in turn framed by her individual and social identities. This process is easier to undertake with the aid of other people. Udacity knew that it had no chance of succeeding without blending its online platform with the kind of face-to-face interaction that addresses the special features of any given learner's struggle.

In the process of selling their product, MOOC advocates damaged the public understanding of learning. Most of the xMOOC enthusiasts had a sincere interest in making good on the promise of mass quality at low cost to a global population that had more need for, and more interest in, university skills than ever before. Nothing I've written here questions their abstract idealism. What I've written here does question their strategy. Their strategy meant they

1. ignored social differences, particularly ethnic and racial differences;
2. stereotyped and dismissed working faculty, their intentions, and their experience;
3. overlooked the history of pedagogical research (and previous ed tech), with a few exceptions that became lodestars (mastery learning); and
4. cherry-picked a finding from the largest ed-tech meta-study while misrepresenting its larger results.

For the MOOC wave to rise the way it did, it had to commit errors that cultural, historical, and educational research exists to prevent. Yet in the decline cycle we've been analyzing, these bugs were features. They sped the technology's manifest destiny to move the core function of the public university—instruction—out of the universities and their faculties and into the hands of private vendors.

If this seems too harsh, consider Thrun's final statement about the racially and socially diverse students in his courses at San José State. "We have a lousy product," he declared after the SJSU+ results came in. His response was to drop the project. "These were students from difficult neighborhoods, without good access to computers, and with all kinds of challenges in their lives," he told *Fast Company* at the end of 2013. "It's a group for which this medium is not a good fit."[72] Thrun in effect said, oh well, we give up on the students who look like the country and the world. We'll do corporate training and offer "nanodegrees" to people who are self-selecting as already prepared to do programming work.[73] Thrun was right to conclude, "Online education that leaves almost everybody behind except for highly motivated students . . . can't be a viable path to education."[74] He was wrong to abandon the technology when it encountered racial and economic diversity, because equal education must be the primary goal of postsecondary systems. The private benefit of a Udacity nanodegree—focused on specific workplace training—may be significant.[75] Its public benefit is nanosized.

And yet, financially weakened by the decline cycle, and forgetting the basics of public good practice, many government and university officials continue to look to ed-tech providers as the private solution to public university woes. In the absence of the privatization frame, would officials have wanted online technology to be the magic budget bullet? Perhaps. But they would not have skipped the educational due diligence as they did.

Unequal Funding Cuts Attainment

We are now far along in our devolutionary cycle. Having camouflaged the university's public value (Stage 1), political and business actors came to expect public universities to seek private revenues and make money with them. This encouraged universities to ignore and conceal losses that needed internal subsidies for sponsored research, complex administration, and related activities (Stage 2). Universities covered their losses by increasing tuition (Stage 3), further privatizing their main revenue streams, which signaled to state legislatures that public funding was dispensable (Stage 4). Public university tuition became high enough to induce significant student debt, which financial aid policy sustained to serve the university's revenue needs (Stage 5). Having lived for years with cuts, austerity, and uncertainty, and drained of resources for major new investment in laboratories, libraries, computing, and arts and humanities infrastructure, public universities were easy pickings for private firms who promised to use their technology to deliver more education with less money. Stage 6 brought the outsourcing of core educational functions to private firms who promised more for less through private sector efficiencies. In Stage 7, the growing dependence of public college budgets on private funds, particularly net tuition, relentlessly widened the instructional resource gap among university types. Since this gap was not closed by education technology (Stage 6), the cycle led to a well-known decline in US college attainment, in large part by damaging the colleges attended by most low-income students and students of color.

Students for Educational Quality

When public university students are provoked, they say clear and unequivocal things about what's wrong with their education. Usually they are provoked by tuition hikes. In November 2014, the University of California offered yet another of these occasions, this time through a proposal to increase tuition 5 percent each year for five consecutive years. In response, students vividly described elements of declining educational quality on their public university campuses, then traced this decline to state underinvestment.

The UC Board of Regents meeting on November 18, 2014, was packed with the state's top political brass, including the governor, lieutenant governor, and Speaker of the Assembly, all Regents ex officio. They opposed the tuition hikes, but were unmoved by the students' call for major restoration of state funding. Governor Jerry Brown had cut the University of California's state allocation by 20 percent in 2011–2012. Four years later, that cut had still not been restored, and the university had made up less than half of it by doubling tuition for California residents and by a near doubling of the share of nonresident students in the system, who pay much higher tuition.[1] Teaching cuts were significant, and the most important loss, in my view, had been to the university's already limited ability to offer students individual attention—attention for specific weaknesses and for advanced projects that develop their special interests and capabilities. The governor's response this time was to propose the study of further reductions in teaching, which would result in offering three-year degrees, consolidating subjects across campuses, and the conversion of teaching into online courses.[2]

The proposal for further educational reductions prompted this response from student Regent Sadia Saisuddin:

> You've *done* studies. Students do not want an online classroom to supplant their education. We want a four-year university. We want to talk to our professors, and to our GSIs [graduate student instructors]. We want to be able to learn in real time. . . . This is not just another $612 increase

each year. This is an extra month of rent, and students are already having a hard time paying their rent. This is another 15–16 hours they need to work. This is another job they need to get. This is more things they cannot pay for. This is food they cannot buy. . . . Students are telling me that they're hungry. . . .

Students have always had to pay the price of economic mismanagement, by the Board [of Regents] and by the state. I think it's time that that stops. . . . Let's not compromise what the UC is about. The UC is about a four-year education. It is not about an online classroom. It is not about logging onto your computer screen. It is not a 2-year institution. It is a four-year university. . . . I am open to all sorts of new ideas, but I think that our quality cannot be compromised at any cost. Right now it is already being compromised. So let's build on what we have, rather than continuing to look at "new ideas" when our situation is already so fractured.[3]

Throughout the meeting's public comment session, student remarks ranged from identification of nontuition sources of revenue that the Regents had failed to pursue to testimony about students who, in spite of the vaunted financial aid program, went broke and dropped out of university, to descriptions of declining educational quality.[4]

On the radio that evening, UC Berkeley student Caitlin Quinn told a well-known California radio host, Warren Olney, that money worries are "a huge factor in how you do in school." Discussing costs, she said,

Students don't see the benefit of so many administrative positions. At UC Berkeley it seems like there's a new vice-chancellor of something-or-other every week. . . . I think students are fed up with what they see as administrative bloat. They aren't seeing this supposed quality education. I've been here for three years and ever since I've been here students have been struggling to see the value of a UC education. We're in huge classes. I've been in classes as big as 800 people. I don't think there are more than one or two professors who know me by name.[5]

Many years into the financial crisis, when austerity had become the public sector norm, university students were telling officials first, that their learning was endangered by declining teaching conditions; second, that public funding problems were the immediate cause; and third, that tuition hikes were not going to solve the crisis of educational quality.

How would state officials respond in this case? While in the past they'd turned a blind eye to tuition hikes, this time the governor and legislative Democrats blocked hikes for an additional two years. But this did not mean that they would address quality issues or rebuild public funding on the necessary scale.

But Do Students Want to Learn?

Student accounts of their own experiences contradicted a sudden policy orthodoxy that had appeared in the wake of publication of the higher education blockbuster *Academically Adrift* (2011), a study of college learning by the sociologists Richard Arum and Josipa Roksa.[6] That book argued that student learning had declined because students were barely studying and their instructors didn't really care.

On the day of the book's release, the senior higher education journalist Scott Jaschik summarized what would become its standard interpretation: "If the purpose of a college education is for students to learn, academe is failing."[7]

Jaschik identified the book's core findings as follows:

- Forty-five percent of students "did not demonstrate any significant improvement in learning" during the first two years of college.
- Thirty-six percent of students "did not demonstrate any significant improvement in learning" over four years of college.
- Those students who did show improvements tended to show only modest improvements.

We can add a further key claim that circulated far and wide:

- While college seniors in the 1980s had a full "standard deviation advantage over freshman" in critical thinking skills, this began to fall in the 1990s to its current level, in which seniors now progress about half as much beyond their freshman selves.[8]

More than any other recent article or book, *Academically Adrift* enflamed elite doubts about the value of college, whose costs had already charred the finances of middle-class and lower-income families.[9] Not only were families spending all they had (and more) helping their children get a basic bachelor's degree, it now appeared that all that money was buying very modest learning. The book triggered a media free-for-all of denunciations of American colleges.

But those who actually read the book could discover another message. It turned out that most college students in the study learned quite well. Furthermore, the data showed which students learned well and why. The problem was not that college students were in general not studying much and not trying hard enough. The problem was that structural changes were moving students from the liberal arts and sciences, where students learned well, to market-oriented fields where they did not. Was learning being reduced by adapting students to what the private sector seemed to expect from them and by shifting already limited resources in a market direction?

Limited Learning

The work of Arum and Roksa had a crucial advantage: it moved the spotlight away from the percentage of students who finish degrees toward what students learn in the process.

Degree completion is itself a problem in the United States, where a much higher share of students start college without finishing it than is the case in comparable countries.[10] Is the news much better for the learning levels of those who do persist and finish?

In arguing that the news is "limited learning" for graduates, Arum and Roksa relied in particular on the College Learning Assessment (CLA), which is an open-ended (non-multiple-choice) test designed to evaluate "core outcomes espoused by all of higher education—critical thinking, analytical reasoning, problem solving and writing."[11] The overall results did not flatter the twenty-four colleges that participated in the study Arum and Roksa discussed.[12] The study, they conclude,

> Provides vivid testimony of the extent to which many students have been left academically adrift on today's campuses. The typical student meets with faculty outside of the classroom only once per month. . . . Although 85 percent of students have achieved a B-minus grade point average or higher, and 55 percent have attained a B-plus grade point average or higher, the average student studies less than two hours per day. Moreover, half of students have not taken a single course that required more than twenty pages of writing, and approximately one-third have not taken any courses that required more than forty pages of reading per week during the prior semester.[13]

The reading and writing measures are important because they are the foundation of the "core outcomes" that the CLA measures. Reading and writing develop several major capacities: to take in and organize a great deal of data rather than just picking a few facts or details; to form independent judgments based on many particulars; and to express and evolve judgments in a sustained way. Students appear to go through college with much less than the needed practice at these intellectual techniques.

For many students in the study, college was not mainly about learning at all. Two-thirds of students work during college, on average thirteen hours a week, which is "an hour more than this subset of employed students spent preparing for classes."[14] Overall, these students' "inflated ambitions and high aspirations have not institutionally been met by equivalently high academic demands from their professors, nor have many of them found a sense of academic purpose or academic commitment at contemporary colleges. Instead, many of the students in our study appear to be academically adrift."[15] College unfolds here as a tragedy of great expectations and stunted skills, like a tale of an aspiring concert violinist who practices a half-hour a day. The dreams of even successful graduates, we are led to assume, will never get off the ground.

Who Brought Us This Fast-Food Service?

After 2008, most high-profile critics of university learning blamed the faculty—and the administrations of "faculty-centered" colleges that indulge them. In *Abelard to Apple*, the educational technologist Richard A. DeMillo claimed that the American college has followed the elitist Johns Hopkins model rather than the democratic example set by the University of Virginia in designing themselves so that "important decisions are made by elite bands of well-chosen professors whose focus is on the prevailing components of the *multiversity*: faculty research, faculty careers, and faculty tenure. It is for this reason that a faculty-centered university is at a fundamental disadvantage in the twenty-first century. Its value to students erodes and, in a competitive era, it is at a severe disadvantage."[16] In this view, university managers must step in to represent student interests against a professional guild—the faculty—that puts guild interests ahead of those of its clients: the students. Arum and Roksa also frontload their book with criticism of the faculty, citing education scholar George Kuh's claim that faculty and students have a "disengagement compact" in which I, the faculty member, "won't make you work too hard . . . so that I won't have to grade as many papers or explain why you are not performing well."[17]

Popular though it was, this explanation was vulnerable to critique. It overlooked faculty criticism of teaching environments they cannot change within current resource constraints, and did not offer empirical evidence of faculty neglect.[18] Contrary to DeMillo's premise, *no* university is "faculty-centered" in the sense that no American faculty members govern finance, facilities, fund-raising, administration, public relations, student affairs, or even student admissions. At several dozen elite research universities and liberal arts colleges, mostly wealthy privates, administrators make a visible effort to take faculty views seriously, but even at these places faculty groups are advisory, having no direct control over "important decisions" for the institution as a whole.

The majority of college instructors are contingent faculty who have neither research opportunities nor institutional authority, even over their own courses. If they are not nurturing students sufficiently, it's not because they don't see student learning as their job but because they don't have the resources to do the job completely. DeMillo's analysis greatly exaggerated the power of faculty governance and also smacked of a traditional managerial hostility to self-governed employees, whether they are shop mechanics or political science professors. No less insidiously, it assumed that quality would be improved were intellectual goals replaced by customer service.

The kicker, after all this criticism, was that faculty had all along been promoting studying rather than overlooking it. In a subsequent work, Arum and Roksa undermined the Kuh thesis by acknowledging that faculty members have consistently tried to get students to study about three times more than they actually do.[19]

Since "limited learning" couldn't be pinned on faculty alone, blame expanded to include students: "Beyond faculty offices and tenure review procedures . . . there are students, who spend far more time socializing than studying. Given the little time they spend studying, it is no surprise that they are not learning much on average."[20] At such moments, the entire melodrama of "our failed colleges" threatened to collapse into the alleged social problem of young Americans who are too confused, spoiled, immature, insecure, undirected, and anti-intellectual to study more than an hour or two a day. Good books have been devoted to what we might call "social college," books like *My Freshman Year* and *Paying for the Party*, both written by sociologists living among students in order to do undercover ethnography in class, at parties, and in dorms.[21] Many readers of these books might conclude that colleges need to crack down on their students, and if they can't, that they should lose even more funding.

Academically Adrift did give comfort to the political Right, which has been trying to downgrade public colleges for decades, to people who thought colleges should be run like corporations, to educational technologists like the 2012–2013 class of MOOC enthusiasts—to anyone who sought an alternative to paying more money to get better instruction.[22]

Known Conditions of Learning

In reality, the bulk of the CLA study's college students made major progress in their academic development. Arum and Roksa repeatedly generalized about students as a group, identifying them with statistical averages. The actual data show variation. This is easier to see if we start by splitting students into two groups. Those students who underwent what I'd call *full-service college,* defined below, learned quite a bit. Those who were treated to *fast-food college* didn't learn much at all.

The authors did not present their data so that we could see what percentage of their sample continued to learn at the higher 1980s or 1990s rates noted above. But pieces of their discussion suggest that those students who experienced the full-service elements showed about double the average improvement.[23] In spite of the national agonizing about why Johnny can't learn, even in college, the conditions of good learning are well known and were confirmed by this study.

For Johnny to learn higher-order thinking in college he must do all of the following:

1. Take many demanding courses (requiring twenty or more pages of writing per term *and* forty or more pages of reading per week).[24]
2. Spend much more than the current norm on his academics (class time and studying together now average 16 percent of a student's week, with studying averaging a total of twelve to thirteen hours a week).[25] He should probably double average study time.
3. Work with faculty members who have high expectations for his and her peers.[26]

A small set of institutional and practical conditions support these three elements:

4. Minimize non-academic social commitments: no fraternity and sorority membership, minimal off-campus socializing, minimal *group* study.[27]

5. Minimize work for pay, never work off campus, and never work more ten hours per week. (The current average is thirteen hours per week).[28]

6. Bring his net cost of college as close to zero as possible, with no loans.[29]

7. Major in a strong academic field in the liberal arts and sciences, *not* in a vocational or strictly "practical" field. Liberal arts and sciences rigor is of *fundamental* importance.

How should Johnny install elements 4, 5, 6, and 7 so that he can achieve factors 1, 2, and 3? Here the solutions are equally straight-forward:

8. Have strong academic preparation in K–12, and thus have experience handling major intellectual challenges. This then makes our student eligible to

9. Attend a wealthy, highly selective college that can cover his tuition and living costs so he doesn't have to work, maximizing his exposure to faculty who offer individualized attention and to other students who put academics first.[30] If our student does this, he will, for example, double the standard share of challenging courses.[31]

A student who can't go to MIT or Reed should find a less prestigious and perhaps more affordable college that tries to duplicate those conditions. There are many.[32] But there are obviously not enough for every deserving student. So Item 10 on our list would be to transform public colleges until they resemble liberal arts colleges and the Ivy League.

Arum and Roksa had nothing to say about funding and rebuilding, but with some effort the reader can extract a learning framework that goes well behind the headline news that students aren't learning. A student who follows this sequence has a good chance of neutralizing her socioeconomic liabilities and higher ed's structural limitations.

Although learning remains an active area of research, there's no deep mystery about which college students learn and why. When students are in an environment that defines them strictly as learners and offers the correct intellectual and financial infrastructure, they learn. Though all colleges, even elite full-service colleges, must continue to improve learning, the first steps are clear. A society needs to make all colleges like full-service colleges, and make all students like the fully served students who learn well.

The real problem with the college system is not that it doesn't know how to deliver great learning—it does deliver great learning to many students. The real problem is that it doesn't deliver great learning to *all* students, and particularly shorts the underserved and vulnerable students who most need to make significant progress.

The B-Side Call to the College Upgrade

The howls of outrage drowned out the latent findings of Arum and Roksa's book. Their data traced much of the learning deficit back to substandard high schools for which colleges cannot compensate. As we've started to see, what we can think of as the ignored "B-side" of *Academically Adrift* identified simple things that the majority of good learners in college did.

It turns out that to learn in college you have to read, write, and study—all with a professor! But didn't we already know this? What parent hasn't said more than once, "I'm not paying for college so you can party!" What self-supporting student hasn't said as much to herself, as she takes a third minimum-wage job to cover rent? Students constantly hear advice like "Challenge yourself." "Don't take gut courses." "Ask your TA to read a first draft." "Take notes like this. Do problem sets like that." Every student hears endless variations on RuPaul's old standard, "you better work."

Crucially, a good way for a student to *lower* her learning is to shift from an academic to a vocational major. Students who major in business, educational administration, health technologies, and the like learn less than students in the traditional liberal arts and sciences— chemistry, art history, microbiology, literature, physics, psychology, anthropology, philosophy, and so on. "Limited learning" is a problem all right—in practical majors. In traditional liberal arts and sciences majors, students learn fairly well.[33] This was the most grossly underreported finding in the book.

When I read through the *Academically Adrift*'s appendices and reviewed some CLA results at various universities, I got the strong impression that universities could close most of the gap between good 1980s learning and limited 2000s learning by moving all students from vocational to liberal arts majors—or, by raising all vocational courses to the more rigorous standard of the liberal arts and sciences. What if the solution to the learning crisis was for the country to turn its thousands of community colleges and state universities into large-scale versions of liberal arts colleges?

This remained an unthought possibility in the book. It certainly sounds cost prohibitive. But that is because Arum and Roksa, like most higher-ed scholars, didn't detail the costs of *not* investing or the concrete better practices that reinvestment would buy. They certainly didn't quantify the costs of converting lower-quality public colleges to liberal-arts-style quality. *Adrift* identified behaviors like fewer hours of studying for the same or higher overall grades and traced them to moral failures like disengagement. They should have traced them to teaching and learning conditions that have been degraded by years of underinvestment.

Student study hours are a case in point. Rising tuition and shifts in aid from grants to loans force students—particularly many who are most at risk of limited learning—to work eight, sixteen, or twenty-four hours a week for tuition, rent, books, and food. A second factor is academic labor. Tenure-track faculty members already work sixty or more hours per week, and much of this time consists of duties other than teaching.[34] University administrations have also been replacing permanent with contingent faculty: the 1970s ratio of two to one or three to one has been reversed, so that 70 percent of college courses are now taught by contingent faculty. Public systems like the California State University expect tenured professors to teach four or five courses at a time while grading papers for over one hundred students a term.[35] What happens when an overworked professor is also contingent, teaching multiple courses at three universities, and her rehire next term depends on high teaching evaluations? Can policymakers really expect her to assign twenty or more pages of writing to 100–150 students while giving each student meticulous comments week after week throughout the term?

Arum and Roksa also omitted the structural issue of budget cuts. After 2008, many colleges were forced to double or triple class sizes, eliminate discussions and grading assistance for many large lectures, and in general reduce contact hours between teachers and students. Reduced homework, less writing, shallow feedback: these things do limit learning, and yet they are not moral failures or a sign of a secret laxity deal, but are adaptations to resource constraints that have been deliberately imposed by governments.

Finally, in higher ed, de facto state policy is that poor colleges stay poor. This further limits the learning of the students who have gotten the least out of K–12. Limited learning is at its root not an attitude problem: it is a resource problem. *Adrift* helped weaken the case for reinvestment, since it did not trace the learning crisis to state under-investment but to bad teacher and student behavior.

And yet *Adrift* did offer a choice between two stories. The visible media story was that colleges keep jacking up prices on a shoddy product. The B-side tune was the reverse. Colleges aren't too far from business but too close. They have been making their students business-ready for years by adding vocational majors to the liberal arts and sciences core. It turns out that these vocational majors offer limited learning, which is the main college source of post-1980s declines. The college crisis is not that college is offering bad academic subjects, but that college has added a lot of non-academic subjects. The best way to fix academia would be to let it be academic again. It would renew its focus on the liberal arts and sciences, and judge vocational courses by *their* standards rather than the reverse.

It was of course "our failing colleges" that got the A-side listing. The B-side, "our failing commercialism," never got played.

Starving the Majority's Instruction

As we've seen, we *do* know what we need to do to help *any* student learn: give her the kind of feedback from peers and professors that increases retention of existing knowledge and the capacity to create new knowledge. We have seen learning attract national policy interest, including interest from Barack Obama, who has paid special attention to community colleges and their partnerships with local industry.[36] We also know that broadly equivalent services require broadly equivalent funding. One institution might find modest efficiencies here and there that others cannot, but the *variation* among expenditures needs to be relatively small in order to deliver roughly comparable educational outcomes.

This is the exact reverse of what the US university system does. The problem has been that a privileged minority of students gets the best instruction money can buy, while the disadvantaged majority have been getting much less.

The Delta Cost Project identified a startling investment skew that predated the 2008 crisis (figure 29). In 2006, the one-third of total US postsecondary enrollments that attended community college received a per-student investment of less than $10,000, which is about what they got in high school.[37] Meanwhile, each student in a private research university received over three times that amount—around $33,000 per year. These figures are averages. Estimates for leading private universities like Harvard are that they spend at least eight times a community college's per-student budget.[38] Note the fourth set of bars in the figure as well, for public research universities. These are universities like Michigan–Ann Arbor, North Carolina–Chapel Hill, Texas-Austin, SUNY-Buffalo, and Indiana University–Bloomington, which consider themselves the intellectual peers of the private research universities. Their students have better funding than do community college students, but receive less than one half the educational resources of their counterparts at private univer-

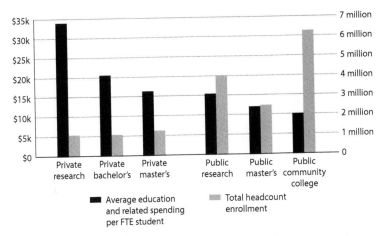

Figure 29. Institutions serving the most students spend the least amount on their education, enrollment vs. spending, AY2008 (in 2008 dollars). *Source:* Reproduced from *Trends in College Spending: 1998–2008* by D. M. Desrochers, C. M. Lenihan, and J. V. Wellman, 2010. Copyright 2010 American Institutes for Research (formerly Delta Cost Project), Washington, DC. Reprinted with permission.
Note: Delta Cost Project IPEDS database, 1987–2008, spending data from eleven-year matched set, enrollment data from unmatched set.

sities. Again, these are averages. University of California officials have estimated that Stanford spends four times more per student than does UC.[39]

How do we know that low spending levels matter to students' education—that it is not admirable efficiency? For starters, we can find evidence of a correlation between per-student resources and graduation rates within university systems. When a research assistant and I reviewed data from the Ann Arbor, Dearborn, and Flint campuses in the University of Michigan system, we found a direct correlation between student expenditures (lower at Dearborn and Flint) and student graduate rates (lower at those same campuses) (figure 30). The two regional campuses have far higher populations of Arab Americans and African Americans than does the flagship Ann Arbor campus. The Dearborn and Flint campuses are more focused on local workforce development than is the Ann Arbor campus. They

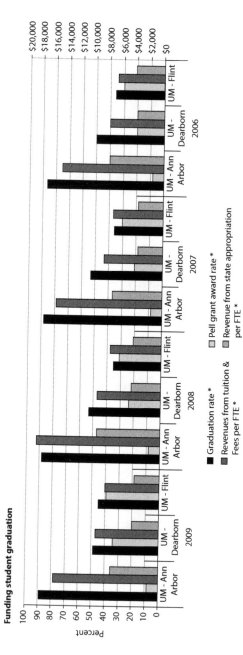

Figure 30. Comparison of graduation rates, Pell Grant awards, revenues from tuition and state funding on three University of Michigan campuses, 2006–2009. *Source:* Calculations by author and Jessica Cronin.

serve a far higher percentage of low-income students. They are given fewer public resources and generate fewer graduations. Less money does not equate to worse education in a one-to-one linear way, but such results suggest a tighter correlation than is usually admitted.

Officials continuously argue that the half-privatized American Funding Model (AFM) has not damaged access.[40] They can deploy studies like *Academically Adrift* to claim that the problems arise not from funding structures but from the behavioral defects of self-interested students and professors. This framework deflects attention from structural issues, making it harder to ask and answer this question: How does the combination of decreased public funding and high debt *cause* this lower attainment?

The full evidence and argument are both more complex than I can do justice to here, but I outline reasons supporting the claim that the shift toward private funding in public universities has indeed caused this decline in educational outcomes. In making this argument I rely particularly on data analyzed by William Bowen, Matthew Chingos, and Michael McPherson in a study entitled *Crossing the Finish Line* (*CFL*).[41] Their analysis rests on datasets that they constructed with unusual access to individual student records, which has allowed for unusually precise correlations and estimates of causality.[42] Their project also focused on public universities of varying positions in the US higher education hierarchy.

I'm going to make this case as a series of four propositions.

1. Large gaps in educational attainment persist among groups of students even after the effects of the students' secondary school outcomes are removed.[43]

While we normally assume that the students who do worse in college are those who weren't good in high school, the *CFL* analysis shows that large outcome gaps persist even after correcting for differences in high school test levels. These gaps in university attainment are not simply the effect of better and worse high school *preparation* for college, but are "systematically related to race/ethnicity and gender, as well as to the socioeconomic status (SES)" of students in college.[44]

We might think we know what this means: poor people are sent to bad schools, with bad results. For example, one study found that, although 71 percent of high school students graduate, only 34 percent have the academic prerequisites necessary for college.[45] Other studies have found that "the relatively modest educational gains that did occur [in bachelor's degree attainment between 1968 and 2007] were concentrated among the most advantaged groups."[46] But the point here is that socioeconomic status transcends individual performance: even if *you* individually do well in education, your lower socioeconomic status will lower your educational attainment. There is something of a mystery here to look into.

Part of the answer comes with our next step:

2. Larger shares of students with low SES—including racially underrepresented students—attend the less selective segments of public higher education.[47]

We might again assume this is because poorer students go to worse high schools and do worse, so they can only get into worse schools that will accept almost anybody. This is not what analysis shows. Recent studies have found a faulty "match" between the schools low-SES students are eligible to attend based on their individual qualifications and the less selective schools that these students actually *do* attend. Pioneering work on the Chicago Public Schools concluded that only one-third of students seeking to attend a university actually enrolled in an institution that matched their qualifications. "The dominant pattern of behavior for students [eligible for a good four-year college] who mismatch is not that they choose to attend a four-year college slightly below their match. Rather, many students mismatch by enrolling in two-year colleges or not enrolling in college at all."[48] Similarly large "undermatching" was found by the CFL study.[49]

Undermatching can be logical from a financial or social point of view—a strong African American female student may decline a prestigious liberal arts college where she would stand out as part of a 2 percent Black population and "undermatch" at a regional public college with a large, interesting peer group. She may discover that a wealthy liberal arts college admitted her with a "good" financial aid package that will still force her to take on $20,000 in debt. Undermatching is not a simple student mistake. But it does lower the educational resources available to many excellent students when they come from lower income levels.

Taking our first and second points together, we can say that poverty, structural racism, and related factors create a kind of double jeopardy: weaker secondary schools increase the chances of weak university preparation. Then, even when that doesn't happen, they incline their students to undermatch. This research undermines attempts by conservatives to tie American educational inequality to naturally unequal abilities, or to individual academic performance as such.[50]

Some observers might naturally wonder why this trend is a problem. More poor students of color go to less selective universities, and these universities have lower status, but does that mean they are inferior educationally? Unfortunately, it does. They are inferior not because they lack dedicated faculty and intelligent students, but because they are unable to deliver solid overall academic outcomes:

3. Less selective colleges and universities have lower continuation and graduation rates.

American degree attainment rates have stagnated for nearly thirty years, and as we've seen, most of the existing gains are concentrated among the wealthiest students.[51] It is well known that graduation rates vary by race, gender, and SES; poorer students, racial minorities, and males are all at greater risk of discontinuation during their university years. But for each social grouping, graduation rates also vary dramatically by the institution's selectivity. The *CFL* database shows that aggregate graduation rates (within six years) are 84 percent for their more selective university group and 56 percent for their less selective group.[52]

That is a significant difference. It is so large that it overwhelms the difference between private and public universities of similar selectivity, which is almost zero in their study. Selectivity is a better predictor of graduation rates than are other factors such as quality of the student's high school.[53]

A question naturally arises at this point: Doesn't this study support the standard choice of making a given college better by making it more selective? After all, selectivity eliminates weaker students, and the remaining better students would seem more likely to graduate in the first place, giving the college a higher graduation rate and thus making it higher quality in this sense.

This solution is in fact the dominant strategy in the United States as well as in countries that compete with it. Universities are now regularly ranked and compared with each other, and in prominent rankings such as that produced by the *U.S. News & World Report*, admissions selectivity is an influential proxy for quality.[54] The entrenched practices, the deep culture, the lived ideology, and the life-world of American higher education all point toward defining excellence through selectivity. This means that virtually all academic managers try to improve their universities, regardless of mission, by tightening their admissions standards.

Unfortunately for this conventional strategy, the CFL study found that selectivity as such does not improve college success rates. The authors ran an experiment by rejecting from their samples all students below a chosen threshold of high school grades. They then compared graduation rates for their "more qualified" remaining group. They found that "retrospectively rejecting" these weaker students did not change the graduation rates at all at the most selective universities, produced "only a tiny gain in the overall graduate rate" for the next group of schools, and increased the graduation rate by only six points at the least selective schools.[55]

This was a truly remarkable result that has not yet percolated into public debate. Most people assume that more selective colleges have better graduation rates for the simple reason that they take only the better students at the start. But that is not what this experiment found.

Instead, the surprising "reality is that graduation rates vary dramatically across universities even when we look [only] at students with good high school grades and impressive test scores."[56] In other words, students are *not* more likely to graduate at selective schools because they were stronger students to begin with. Graduation rates are higher at selective colleges because of something about the colleges themselves—something beyond their ability to reject more students.

What is it about selective schools that helps students graduate—other than this weeding out of students at the start? This is a mystery that the CLF study unfortunately did not address. It didn't address it because it didn't look at the elephant in the room. We've discussed this elephant: the highly unequal levels of instructional spending in different types of colleges and universities in the United States. The CLF authors say they fail "to find an institutional resource effect" that would explain graduation rates.[57] A better explanation is that they didn't look for one. Funding per student varies from college to college by up to a factor of ten. It's a linguistic convention and political fiction to use the terms "college" and "university" to refer to all these functionally and socially unrelated learning institutions.

Here I part company with the CLF study, since we *can* in fact identify large gaps in institutional resources across broad institutional types. Bowen and his coauthors did show correlations between improved outcomes and features like better access to community environments in honors colleges.[58] Well-staffed living arrangements, individual advising, tutoring staff, psychological and peer-counseling services, not to mention better-paid teaching assistants, departmental advising, and so on, are supports that cost money that most nonselective colleges don't have.

Indeed, the apparent mystery of selectivity's effects can be resolved by looking at funding levels:

4. *The least selective segment of public higher education spends the least money per student.*

We have already noted the expenditure gaps between private and public sectors, which we saw is enormous. Similarly large differences exist within the public system between research universities and two-year colleges. We use averages, which minimize differences by folding the richest and poorest schools of each type in with more typical ones: research universities spent on average $8,711 per student in 2006, while two-year colleges spent $4,609.[59] In other words, the better-funded end of the *public* university system spends nearly twice per student on "Education and Research" as what a two-year college spends—again, on average. Selectivity improves graduation rates not because it rejects weaker students, *CFL* confirms, but *because selectivity is accompanied by higher investment per student.*

Our Racist Funding Model

Another detailed study did find a causal connection between higher per-student investment and higher graduation rates. The Georgetown Center for Education and the Workforce controlled for test scores, so that they were comparing students at a group of 468 "most selective" colleges to academically similar students at the United States' more than 3,200 "open-access" colleges. The selective schools averaged $13,400 per student in instructional expenditures, while the open-access schools averaged less than half that ($6,000).[60] In many cases, the study confirmed, the gap is much larger.

The Georgetown group found that gaps in completion rates are equally large. Well-qualified students with SAT scores above 1,200 out of 1,600 have an 87 percent completion rate at the most selective colleges, but equally well-scoring students graduate at a rate of only 58 percent at the open-access colleges.[61] For African American and Latino students with above-average SAT/ACT scores, the gap is 73 percent versus 40 percent for completion at the two types of colleges.[62] The Georgetown report drew a clear conclusion: "The 468 most selective colleges spend anywhere from two to almost five times as much per student. Higher spending in the most selective colleges leads to higher graduation rates, greater access to graduate and professional schools, and better economic outcomes in the labor market, when comparing with white, African-American, and Hispanic students who are equally qualified but attend less competitive schools."[63] The "white students concentrated in the 468 most selective colleges" receive lifelong advantages—greater earnings, "as well as careers that bring personal and social empowerment." To repeat, these advantages follow directly from receiving greater resource investment while in college.

The Georgetown report reflected another vital theme of research that has not had enough impact on the debate about college costs and college quality. Its core insight was that the normalization of grossly unequal college funding has locked in racial inequality of college attainment. The title did not mince words: *Separate and Unequal: How Higher Education Reinforces the Intergenerational Reproduction of White Racial Privilege.* In case anyone missed the reference to the Jim Crow era of racial segregation, the report's first sentence was, "White flight from the center city to better neighborhood schools in the leafy green suburbs has finally arrived on the nation's ivy-covered college campuses." The report went on to quantify this white flight from everyday publics to "the 468 most selective colleges": "Since 1995, 82 percent of new white enrollments have gone to the 468 most selective colleges, while 72 percent of new Hispanic enrollment and 68 percent of new African-American enrollment have gone to the two-year and four-year open-access schools."[64] Students at those open-access schools receive fewer resources, which means that even the strongest students have a heightened chance of failing. Since a student is more likely to go to a poorer (open-access) school if she is a Black or Latino or Native American student, and since the American Funding Model allocates resources according not to need but to ability to pay, the AFM is a machine for producing racial disparity.

The Georgetown report is too polite to call this system racist. But they do plainly state that the American college system is "separate and unequal" like the K–12 system was on the eve of the *Brown v. Board of Education of Topeka* decision in 1954 (and still is today). The AFM takes white students and students of color of similar achievement and sends large majorities of each group to two distinct though parallel systems, one of which has much more money than the other to spend on students. Hence the term "separate and unequal." This separate and unequal system gives African American and Latino students a significantly lower chance than similarly accomplished whites of graduating and succeeding later on. The result is racial stratification in the American present as in the American past, with the likely continuation into the future. What we do is a kind of racial dumping. The funding model systematically gives different levels of educational quality to different racial groups. In this situation, we must say that the AFM is a racist funding model. It is not Ku Klux Klan racist, but structurally racist.

We have seen that the AFM does the same thing by income: attainment has barely increased for the bottom half of the US population over the decades in which attainment came close to doubling for the top income quartile.[65] In effect, the United States has an upside-down funding system, in which the students with the greatest learning challenges get the least amount of money. Meanwhile, the most selective schools lavish opportunities on students who, by and large, have been getting outsized educational benefits all their lives. The data on these expenditure differentials are quite clear and abundant. What they mean is that the students with the greatest need for the deployment of educational resources are the least likely to get them. To top things off, poor schools take good students who could have gone to a wealthier, more selective school, and help cut their attainment down to size. The AFM means the educational rich get richer. The AFM forces colleges to reinforce American plutonomy rather than fulfilling their desired role of making the United States more equal in opportunity and outcome.[66]

To conclude: while we cannot make a crude linear argument from "doubling the money" to "doubling the completion rate," we can assemble the four points in our argument into this claim:

The best way to increase American educational attainment is to improve completion rates for low-income and racially underrepresented students. This requires that we dramatically increase expenditures at the low-spending colleges, where most of those students go.

How can we do this? The one thing low-spending colleges *cannot* do to increase revenues is to raise tuition. The majority of their students cannot pay and should not borrow. Unfortunately, the AFM wants colleges to raise tuition, given its focus on private funds, and since they can't or won't, the AFM settles for impoverishing them. The purpose of privatization is to move resources toward those willing to pay for them, which in practice means giving more to those with more, and giving less to those with less. The AFM does this brilliantly, and solidifies structural racism and income inequality.

The real solution to the AFM's racial and income stratification is to get rid of the AFM, and *equalize public funding*. A simple goal would be to bring the per-student funding of poor schools up to the median of public research universities, which would mean, over time, reducing the funding gap between selective and open-access institutions to zero. This would cost very little additional money.[67] It would gradually equalize graduation rates among white students and underrepresented students of color, and equalize rates among low-, middle-, and high-income students.[68] Increasing public allocations is the only way that poor colleges can improve instruction and graduate rates *without* increasing their students' debt. We have tried privatizing revenue streams to open-access public colleges. Socially and educationally, it has failed.

Universities have taken the low road to self-preservation by silencing themselves about educational quality. University presidents, fundraisers, and boards of trustees talk about everything except the actual learning processes for which the university exists. Real learning always involves research, but a convergence of short-term self-interests means that there are virtually no prominent university officials speaking out for *mass quality* of instruction—great capabilities instilled in all students and not just the fortunate top 0.7 or 2.4 percent.[69] The result is that neither state legislatures nor core publics can tell the difference, once we correct for prestige, between a seminar-based liberal arts BA from, say, Occidental College in Los Angeles, where President Obama began his higher education, and a BA from an underfunded state college that has been earned in part online. They certainly have no idea about the difference in cost, or where the money goes. The further result is that the public and their legislators have *no* compelling need to restore public funds for instruction because they don't know what substantive difference to the individual and to the economy that *mass* access to top-quality instruction would actually make. In the absence of prominent university officials tying limited learning to limited funding, stereotypes of inadequate students and professors proliferate. Universities are to blame for this public lack of understanding about what universities do for regular people. Public universities will never again be properly funded unless they fix this. And the majority of students will never properly learn.

Universities Build the Post–Middle Class

I've been calling our public university policy a devolutionary cycle, a doom loop, a wheel of decline. But why does this wheel turn so easily? We seem to move without resistance from sidelining the public mission to subsidies for outside partners, to tuition hikes, state cuts, debt bloat, outsourced teaching, and funding inequalities that reduce attainment. It seems crazy, for example, that expenditures on instruction have stayed flat or fallen for students at most colleges, even as *net* tuition has doubled in constant dollars between 2000 and 2012.[1] But one person's pain is another's pleasure. One person's loss is another's gain. The cycle explains how public universities decline. But the decline has a coherent logic. The current, highly stratified college system fits with and sustains the increasingly unequal society we have right now, and promises to keep it unequal into the future.

Here in Stage 8, we arrive at the solution to the mystery of why a wealthy knowledge economy would degrade and destabilize its "knowledge factories." A downgraded and unevenly funded network of public universities speeds the transition from a large, culturally dominant middle class to a smaller, more insecure one. It supports *plutonomy*, meaning economies "where economic growth is powered by and largely consumed by the wealthy few."[2] Though I see no conspiracy of plutocrats aimed at an economic coup d'état, I do see a long sequence of anti-egalitarian policy choices in which a downsized public university plays a starring role. As the United States becomes a post-middle-class society, an anti-egalitarian public university system can help reduce the share of national wealth and income going to the increasingly multiracial majority.

Building Middle-Class Productivity

To understand this, we have to remember the economic bargain behind the middle-class economy whose image still dominates our thinking about Western societies. It was a productivity bargain: capitalism would reward individual productivity with good wages, because increased individual productivity increased productivity overall. As the individual's labor productivity increased, she generated more value for her company, and this would be recognized by a rising wage. "Human capital" theory, developed in the early 1960s by the conservative economist Gary Becker and others, helped economists theorize a policy deal that was fairly new at the end of World War II.[3] This deal regulated capitalism's traditional minimization of wages, sometimes known as the exploitation of labor. Since capitalist firms make their financial goals paramount, they tend to exclude consideration of negative impacts on employees or the surrounding society.[4] In the postwar period, employee interests came to have more impact on policy. We can think of the postwar bargain as hinging on a *productivity wage*.

College played an official role in the middle-class economy by increasing the productivity of its graduates. College was the central place where the individual could systematically develop her human capital to help place her in a white-collar job. No one's capability was fixed, and formal education tried to evolve this capability in the most systematic way.

Increased individual welfare had a simple metric. This was a better wage—a wage that was higher than the wage of noncollege graduates and that rose steadily year after year. Throughout the post-2008 crisis, college grads continued to earn about twice as much each year as high school graduates.[5] This "wage premium" has long been a reliable private market benefit of completing college.[6] The sources of this premium are complicated, but in general, the college wage rose by tracking a college-induced increase in both individual and collective productivity.

The *public* benefit of college education was also clear. As a larger share of a population acquired a higher level of education, the over-

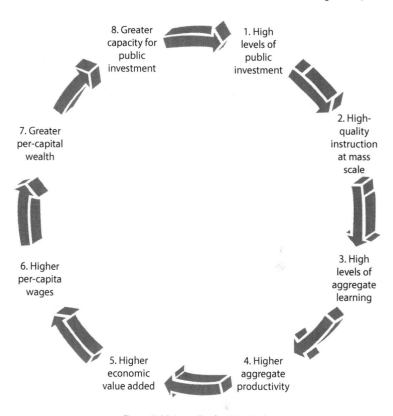

Figure 31. Virtuous Productivity Cycle

all productivity of the society increased. Since improved productivity is the only way to increase society's real wealth, higher levels of education meant greater general prosperity. Recent economic analysis has confirmed this relationship between more college degrees and greater national wealth.[7] Individual citizens saw one benefit of college as a larger paycheck. Society could contemplate the virtuous cycle pictured in figure 31. Continuous public investment supported continuous economic growth, which supported the continuous reduction of economic inequality and the expansion of a middle-class standard of living.[8] Although debates raged about the valid role and real effects of the public sector, and although social factors like racism remained fundamental, the overall cycle was at least tacitly accepted by mainstream conservatives as well as liberals. For the three decades after the end of World War II, wages increased as productivity increased.

In the 1970s and 1980s, this relationship was broken. Countless books and articles have argued that the US middle class was hurt by technological change and globalization, particularly wage competition that forced manufacturing workers to go head-to-head with their low-wage counterparts in Mexico, Brazil, Taiwan, Poland, China, and so on.[9] Regardless of how one models the interaction of various factors, the changes relentlessly transformed American society. They appear in trends like these:

- Real family income has risen largely for the top-level wage earners, slightly for the middle levels, and not at all for the bottom.[10]
- The bottom 70 percent of workers by income has not had a raise since the late 1970s.[11]
- Nearly all increases in college attainment have gone to the top half of the population by income, and the attainment gap between affluent and poor students has widened.[12]
- The United States is now the most unequal of wealthy nations, with a wealth distribution like those of undemocratic "banana republics."[13]
- Upward mobility in the United States is lower than that in all other nations in a comparison group—with the exception of the United Kingdom.[14]
- Inequality has increased. Starting in the mid-1980s, the top 1 percent increased their share of their national incomes in most wealthy nations. But US elites increased their share far more, and now have two to three times the share of national income of their counterparts in Australia, Denmark, France, Germany, Japan, and the United Kingdom. Only the United States has returned the income share of the top 1 percent back to the level of 1920.[15]

- The post-2007 housing price crash erased thirty years of gains in the net worth of the median family, highlighting the fragility of their economic position.[16]
- From 2009 to 2011, as a weak recovery began, "Top 1% incomes grew by 11.2% while bottom 99% incomes shrunk by 0.4%. Hence, the top 1% captured 121% of the income gains in the first two years, and 95% of gains from 2009 to 2012."[17]
- Five years into the crisis, in 2012, analysts at the US Census Bureau found that nearly half of the US population can be defined as poor or near poor.[18]

Though the United States was never an "affluent society" overall, these and related changes marked an epochal shift. Given the sacred stature of the middle class in US political discourse, how could this middle-class decline have happened?

A Neoliberal Prescription

The leading American explanation is that globalization changed the rules for poor and wealthy countries alike. Lower-skilled workers were now in competition with their global counterparts, most of whom lived in low-income countries and worked for lower wages. The blue-collar portion of the US middle class was threatened by the "great doubling" of the low-wage global labor pool.[19] "Semi-skilled" and "unskilled" labor was now a global commodity, and the output of workers in the United States was interchangeable with that of their Singaporean, Mexican, Chinese, or Vietnamese counterparts. (Labor in each of these latter countries had also, in turn, become too expensive in relation to even poorer ones.)

And yet, according to this theory, there was still hope. While people with interchangeable skills would see their wages fall and their jobs move abroad, those with advanced skills would benefit from global demand and see their wages rise.[20]

Mainstream economists of recent decades have described globalization as a force beyond the reach of domestic policies. Their argument has been that no country can change the rules of the global game, and each must focus on adaptation instead. This has meant that New Deal-type regulatory and development policies were outdated and should be replaced by lower tax burdens and deregulated market pressures that would force an increase in skills. The dominant assumption was that in a global economy, nations must give up trying to regulate economic competition and instead give themselves over to competing to win.[21] The framework for this view came to be called *neoliberalism*. In the system that gained momentum in the 1970s and consolidated itself in the following decades, the government's role was dialed back to smoothing the way for business to compete via lower taxes and more modest social provision, infrastructural investment, and support for education.[22]

Nearly everyone assumed that neoliberalism's shift from public to private investment would *increase* investment in public higher education rather than hurt it. This was because neoliberalism defined market-governed competitiveness as an educational imperative: each individual in this new globalized economy was obliged to continuously increase her productivity through advanced technical training, higher education, and the like.

In a characteristic formulation, Thomas L. Freidman wrote, "This is the march of progress. It eliminates bad jobs, empowers good jobs, but always demands more skill and creativity and always enables fewer people to do more things. We went through the same megashift when our agricultural economy was replaced by the industrial economy in the late 19th and early 20th centuries."[23] Using public policy to intervene in market forces would, in Friedman's view, delay the shift to Knowledge Economy 3.0, in which every employee will take responsibility for acquiring a flexible set of creative abilities. The highly innovative US workforce would steadily increase its productivity, defined as output per unit of labor. That continuous increase in productivity would, in turn, enable American victory in the global competition for the highest value-added goods. Progress and prosperity would be assured.

Neoliberalism has become a reigning paradigm, or worldview, in the United States, United Kingdom, Canada, and elsewhere. And yet it has not ensured high wages for highly skilled workers. As the business journalist Steven Greenhouse concluded, "It is often thought that college graduates can escape these unfortunate wage trends. But college graduates—hit by the bursting of the tech bubble in the late 1990s and then by the deep recession—have been hit hard, too. Seventy percent of the nation's college grads have had their after-inflation hourly wages decline since 2000, according to the Economic Policy Institute, with the typical graduate experiencing a 3.1 percent decline."[24] This was still true for the Class of 2016: "Young college graduates have average wages of $18.53—roughly the same as in 2000 (only 0.7 percent higher)."[25]

The neoliberalism framework offers a number of explanations for this stagnation. It points to excessive taxation and regulation, but effective corporate taxes are not higher in the United States than elsewhere.[26] It emphasizes inadequate levels of human capital—often called a "skills gap" or a "skills mismatch"—suggesting that American (or British) workers have fallen behind in the productivity race.[27] Without overstating the quality of the US workforce, which certainly needs better schools and vocational training programs, the importance of the "skills gap" has also been exaggerated.[28] US productivity increases have been holding up well against the global competition, even if rates have declined in recent decades from their levels earlier in the twentieth century.[29] American workers are not losing jobs and wage gains because they have failed to upgrade their skills or increase their productivity overall. College grads have fulfilled their end of the neoliberal bargain, but the economy has not upheld its end by matching their higher skills with higher wages.

If stagnating wages do not reflect stagnating skills or productivity in a globalized economy, why have wages stagnated?

Ending the Productivity Wage

The economist Lawrence Mishel offered a simpler and more accurate explanation, illustrated in a chart sometimes called the Mishel Wedge (figure 32). Mishel's data suggested that American business had continued to receive productivity increases from its core workforce but stopped paying their full value.[30] The ever-widening wedge seen in figure 32 signifies a breaking of the relationship between the

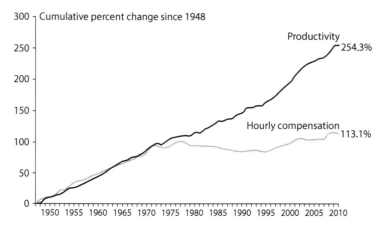

Figure 32. Growth of real hourly compensation for production/nonsupervisory workers and productivity, 1948–2011. *Source:* Lawrence Mishel, "The Wedges between Productivity and Median Compensation Growth," Issue Brief #330, Economic Policy Institute, April 26, 2012, accessed October 30, 2014, http://www.epi.org/publication /ib330-productivity-vs-compensation/.

Note: Supervisory workers and other types are excluded; this chart covers about 80 percent of the workforce. A more recent version of the figure has slightly lower values for each line (240.4 percent increase in productivity and a 108.3 percent increase in hourly compensation). For a critique of the Mishel Wedge that includes a series of gap-closing charts, see Robert Z. Lawrence, "The Growing Gap between Real Wages and Labor Productivity," Peterson Institute for International Economics, July 21, 2015, accessed August 13, 2015, http://blogs.piie.com/realtime/?p=5112.

effort people put into increasing their personal capabilities and business's material recognition for that effort.[31] For thirty years after World War II, when Americans increased their productivity, they also increased their pay. After the mid-1970s, they didn't. We can think of this as the end of the postwar *productivity wage*, in which wages had risen in keeping with the value that workers actually created. Now they no longer do.[32] Business took advantage of changing conditions to pay less for more, middle-class policymakers justified that, and politicians made laws encouraging it.

The most obvious social result is the decline of the middle class—expressed through both the incredible rise of wealth and

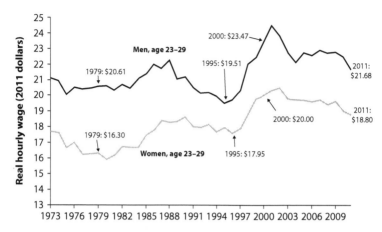

Figure 33. Entry-level wages of male and female college graduates, 1973–2011. *Source:* Lawrence Mishel, "Entry-level Workers' Wages Fell in Lost Decade," Issue Brief #327, Economic Policy Institute, March 7, 2012, accessed September 7, 2013, http://www.epi.org/publication/ib327-young-workers-wages/.

income at the top and through stagnation or decline for nearly everyone else.

Thinking within the neoliberal paradigm, commentators claim that globalization punishes low-skill workers yet rewards high-skill ones: we have just read Friedman saying this, when he stated that an affluent society must simply scramble quickly, eagerly, and without much regulation up the knowledge ladder.[33] This paradigm would attribute the gap between good productivity increases and flat or falling wages to the (deservedly) low earning power of low-skill workers, for which the productivity increases of high-end workers would not compensate. But this is not what we find in the data pictured in figure 33. College graduates do much better than high school grads. At least the former's earnings don't fall as high school grads' earnings do.[34] And yet, wages of college graduates are flat and do not keep up with productivity gains.[35] Even those who have followed prevailing advice and finished college are not rewarded for the additional value that they put into the economy.

For many years, the neoliberal paradigm has assured everyone that capitalism's market forces punished obsolete blue-collar jobs but rewarded high-skill knowledge jobs. This has been acceptable to much of the middle class and to policy elites—perhaps not coincidentally because for those decades they seemed immune to its "creative destruction." Destruction was aimed at non-college-educated blue-collar workers, while prosperity was the reward of the "creative class," those who became what Robert B. Reich called "symbolic analysts" via their status as technical and professional workers.[36] But in fact the typical college graduate was not seeing continuous increases in real wages. By 2000, high-skill jobs were being outsourced as well, first as a trickle and later as a flood. Although few US analysts understood this at the time, most high-skill jobs could move abroad as easily as low-skill jobs. The wages of high-skill workers could stagnate or fall as did those of low-skill workers.

A bipartisan lineage of distinguished authors sounded the alarm, from Kevin Phillips, who laid out a threat to US middle-class prosperity in *The Politics of Rich and Poor* (1989); through Louis Uchitelle, *The Disposable American* (2007) and Steven Greenhouse, *The Big Squeeze* (2008); to younger writers discussing the bad new deal for recent college grads, including Anya Kamenetz, *Generation Debt* (2006), and David Brook, *The Trap* (2007).[37] And yet mainstream commentators and policymakers continued to hold that sufficiently educated workers would enjoy the postwar wage bargain in which high skills would be rewarded with high pay.[38]

After 2008, more researchers turned against the assumption that "learning equals earning." One particularly clear analysis was *The Global Auction*, by three sociologists based in the United Kingdom—Philip Brown, Hugh Lauder, and David Ashton. Cutting against the Reich-Friedman paradigm, they describe the main educational strategy of Western countries as ineffective. Calling it the "neoliberal opportunity bargain"—"the state's role was limited to creating opportunities for people through education to become marketable in the global competition"—they showed that it was no longer working.[39]

Even as Americans have continued dutifully to increase their educational levels and their productivity, the rest of the world has been doing exactly the same thing. "Our analysis," Brown, Lauder, and Ashton wrote, "reveals a doubling in the number of university-level enrollments around the world in just 10 years."[40] The obvious effect of a rapid rise in the supply of knowledge workers, particularly in low-wage countries, has been a fall in the price of wages that those knowledge workers can command. Policymakers responded to this price pressure by helping it along. The *global* standard for knowledge workers has become not high-skill high-wage jobs, but *high-skill low-wage jobs.*

We are now in a better position to understand the deeper meaning of the Mishel wedge. It reflects two important trends. First, there is a new global mean in which high skills continue to produce strong increases in productivity but do *not* produce matching increases in the wages of high-skill workers. Second, there is the policy-enabled reversion of the United States to this global mean. The Mishel wedge shows the United States losing its exceptional status and becoming a normal (though still outsized) economy, which in the current age delivers low-wages for most workers, even those of very high skill. The United States has, since the mid-1970s, *not* been on the road to remaining an affluent middle-class economy by ensuring a link between high skills and high wages, but to becoming a *normal* country with plenty of low-wage jobs that require high skills, deployed under precarious conditions. The post-2009 recovery typifies this trend. Universities pioneered this high-skill/low-wage trend by spending the last forty years converting permanent faculty posts into adjunct positions.

Global Taylorization

Most of us still assume that access to knowledge work will shelter us and our children from the global economy's downward wage spiral. We might accept that General Electric's new "competitive" wage, of one-half to two-thirds that of its long-term workers, "threatens to undo the middle-class status of even the best-paid blue-collar jobs still left in manufacturing."[41] But that is because we believe there's some safety in white-collar work.

Middle-class affluence was always exaggerated. Richard Parker mocked as quasi-delusional a *New York Times* headline, "Opulence Becoming a Way of Life for the Middle Class," in his book *The Myth of the Middle Class*, which appeared in 1972.[42] Middle-class opulence seemed like it was getting closer for more people. Now it seems like it's getting farther away. Brown, Lauder, and Ashton explain that the global "reverse auction" puts equivalent downward pressure on *every* job, regardless of how much college, knowledge, or digitality is involved. We should, in their view, regularly read coverage showing that global competition in architectural design, radiology, case law analysis, commercial website maintenance, electron microscopy, research assistance in financial history, and so on threatens to undo the middle-class status of even the well-paid jobs in the knowledge economy.

This statement may at first seem overblown. The digital economy has been from the start a university-based economy and depends on the continuous creative inputs of college graduates. Isn't America a place that has always treated its college grads well and rewarded exceptional skill?

America is also a place that has always tried to automate or Taylorize skill, and the situation is the same today. "Mechanical Taylorism was to the 20th century what *digital Taylorism* is to the 21st," wrote Brown, Lauder, and Aston. Digital Taylorism "involves translating the knowledge work of managers, professionals, and technicians into working knowledge by capturing, codifying, and digitalizing their work in software packages, templates, and prescripts that can be transferred and manipulated by others regardless of location."[43] Information technology offers new scope for individual creativity, as technology in principle always does. But it also offers new and "prodigious powers of measurement, monitoring, and control."[44]

Harold Wilensky had already written ominously in 1960, "The line between those who decide, 'what is to be done and how' and those who do it—that dividing line would move up. The men who once applied Taylor to the proletariat would themselves be Taylorized."[45] Brown, Lauder, and Aston produce numerous examples of global knowledge businesses in which bankers, brokers, designers, client relations managers, and consultants saw their "expertise and judgment in making decisions" replaced by software systems for automated assessment.[46] Growing use of government and corporate programs for bulk data collection and performance tracking confirms that there is nothing inherent in white-collar or digital work that blocks Taylorization.

This potential for *total* Taylorization has not been, however, ignored by business consultants. In the 1990s, the increasing importance to information businesses of the "creative class"—many of whose members were programmers, designers, engineers, and artists just graduated from college—spawned attempts to minimize the firm's commitment to its very large proportion of college-educated knowledge workers. In *Unmaking the Public University*, I wrote about a version of digital Taylorism called "knowledge management" (KM), which was a successful attempt to separate the knowledge workers who could be treated as commodities from those with "proprietary skills" who needed to be retained at any cost.[47] A firm could have 100 percent brilliant, creative, college-educated knowledge workers, but might regard only 5 percent as having the proprietary knowledge that differentiated the firm's key products and contributed directly to its bottom line. In the typical case, one saved the juicy end of the payroll for one's proprietary creatives; meanwhile, one's commodity geniuses could be overworked, outsourced, or underpaid. Thanks to the gigantic higher education system of the United States, every industry had plenty of "microserf" brainworkers to spare.[48] US management theory was consciously and systematically working to commoditize the majority of its knowledge workers at least fifteen years before the 2007–2008 crisis.

To oversimplify, the policy result of this discrimination between brilliance that supports monopoly and brilliance that supports everything else is that most knowledge workers in wealthy nations are subject to the global wage auction. Outside of a small elite, the deal for most knowledge workers, *regardless* of personal capability, is that they are relegated to being *high skill, low pay.*

The Sorting Function

If most major policy players either openly embrace or quietly accept plutonomy, would they still want to expand and upgrade public colleges and universities? Wouldn't a highly unequal economy prefer college to offer "the ability with relatively modest investments of effort to earn a credential" that leads to modest success?[49]

During the rise of the dot-com economy in the 1990s, the sociologist David Labaree pointed in this direction:

> The payoff for a particular credential is the same no matter how it was acquired. So it is rational behavior to try to strike a good bargain, to work at getting a diploma, like a car, at a substantial discount. The effect on education is to emphasize form over content—to promote an educational system that is willing to reward students for formal compliance with modest performance requirements rather than for demonstrating operational mastery of skills deemed politically and socially useful.[50]

Students respond to social cues by picking up adaptive, low-effort behaviors expressed in sayings like "Cs get degrees." Policymakers who, year-in and year-out, support the impoverishment of mass-access universities force students to put the simplicity of the credential ahead of the creative capabilities that come with learning. The result is a university system through which "students are allocated to occupational positions based on their credentials, not their skills."[51] If most jobs you can obtain with a BA degree are going to offer mediocre wages, then the public college system can logically provide basic credentials and sociability without spending too much money on each individual student. Students then, first and foremost, comply with performance goals that are both modest and easily monitored. As my research assistant commented when she reviewed this text in draft, "Yup. Every 'A' paper I wrote at Cal, I wrote the night before. I'm no dummy, but I'm also not so gifted that I couldn't have used a couple of draft revisions to get that high a grade." The conclusion, which mainstream commentators avoid, is that by offering "limited learning," in which some students learn a lot while half learn little, public colleges overall are not letting elites down but giving them what they want.

The eclipse of learning by sorting expresses itself in our fixation on university brand. College sports are outside of my scope here, but they play a dominant role in marketing colleges as places that compete endlessly to move up in the standings. Their relationships to one another *are* standings—a rank order. University administrations spend lavishly on brand-management activities that help students acquire a school identity and become invested in its prestige. These activities focus not on boosting learning but on increasing rankings. University admissions is structured this way, and the higher education scholar Robert Samuels noted in a discussion of *U.S. News & World Report's* popular rankings:

> The universities are not ranked on what they actually do once the students get to them; instead, they are rated on who attends the schools and how many people are excluded from attending. Universities and colleges thus have a perverse incentive to recruit students so that they can reject them and thus raise their school's selectivity rating. . . . Even the universities that reject the vast majority of interested students spend lavishly on trying to attract more students so they can reject more students.[52]

There's no point in universities practicing high-quality instruction for all when their status derives from rejecting most of them. University leaders grumble about particular methodologies in the pervasive global rankings industry but accept the principles behind "rank merit," which measures the merit of an individual or institution by position in a vertical hierarchy.[53] Universities continue to sell themselves to society as rankers and sorters, feeding the presumption that they rate people according to measured performance, starting at the point of admission or rejection. There is another model of meritocracy, a democratic model focused on the full development of each member of the population. But universities cannot focus on engendering mass creativity when they are about team, brand, and building a campus that is superior to its rivals.

Limited learning is the effect of this system, and also the practice that *constitutes* that system. By this I mean that the limits of learning in poorer colleges with less-prepared students lead to stratified educational outcomes that express "merit," understood as a ranking of lesser or greater quantities of achievement. Where learning is limited and outcomes hugely unequal, as in the current system, the system *creates* the lesser merit of most students. By generating these inequalities, universities replicate and validate the large inequalities that distinguish contemporary US society from its wealthy peers.[54] And when universities do this, they justify the post-middle-class status of the majority as based on its limited skills.

Underfunding that leads to limited learning sorts the college population into three major grades. Note that I refer only to those with at least some college, so this is already the best-educated subset of the population.

First, there's a minority that learns a great deal and then graduates with high levels of skill that will continue to evolve. Members of this group have above all *learned to learn,* quickly and accurately and repeatedly. They will go on to be successful members of the "creative class," often accumulating advanced professional and research degrees, and to perform difficult, complex brainwork for a range of industries, sometimes, but not always, for top-tier pay.

Second, there's a large middle group who finished with limited learning and decent skills. They generally can't initiate or self-direct multistep projects and will not be put in leadership positions, but they can be trained in a particular job on the basis of their capacity, reinforced in college, "for formal compliance with modest performance requirements." They are prime candidates for serving as routine administrators and middle managers, conducting a range of sales and marketing functions, or populating academia's burgeoning administrative ranks, along with the massive bureaucracies of the health, finance, insurance, and other service industries. They are classic twentieth-century white-collar employees whose functions are still needed in an economy ruled by overly complicated organizations and preoccupied with employee control. Though still necessary, these "organization men" and women are no longer esteemed by US business culture, and they will not enjoy the job security, high wages, affordable health care, and solid retirements of their twentieth-century forebears.

Finally, there is the large portion of the college-starting population—more than half—that either didn't finish a four-year degree or finished it with substandard academic skills.[55] Their job prospects are little better than those of high school grads who have no college at all.

Under plutonomic drift, public universities are succeeding at something big, which is to use limited learning to knock lots of college-educated people out of the middle class. While a lucky minority gets full-service college, the majority gets the fast-food version. We may consider this not just inefficient but also unjust and unethical. I certainly do. But it does fit very well with the hierarchical structure of the late capitalist workforce and a "winner-take-all" society that doesn't need a solid working or middle class.[56]

The Default Purpose of the Public University

With the decline of knowledge work in mind, we can see limited learning in a new light. It applies the rules of the global auction at the college level. Limited learning implements passive learning and testing to deliver commodity skills to the great majority, and seminar-based, active learning to deliver creativity skills to the students who will go on to join a small elite. Obviously there are many individual exceptions, but this hierarchy of skills helps the economy to offer stagnant or falling real wages to a majority of the college educated. Once the United States slid into subjecting its citizens to a globalization that includes a reverse auction in wages, limited learning is a feature, not a bug.

The university system is perfectly suited to this project because it *constitutes* the subjects of globalization in advance of their entry into the workplace. It does this by lavishing world-leading education on a small university elite who have a much better than average chance of going on to develop proprietary knowledge. This elite will indeed have the creative capabilities to do this, *not* because they are innately smarter than the majority, but because they will, in their elite colleges, couple concentrated, high-end active learning with the kinds of social networks and institutional connections that will help place them at the top of the economy later on.[57] I am oversimplifying here, but students admitted to the "Double Ivies," a small number of public flagships, and the top liberal arts colleges, combine superb opportunities for individual cultivation with forms of cultural capital not available in the overall public system.[58] Although their hundreds of thousands of counterparts at the UCSBs and Iowa States and SUNY Stony Brooks and University of Texas–El Pasos of the world are in a deep biological, cultural, and existential sense just as creative, just as brilliant, just as morally deserving, the global knowledge economy has stopped pretending to have a place on the A-team for them. Rather than using caste or class or race or some similar, blatantly unjust marker, limited learning has been able to do the inequality job by generating a rank-meritocracy marker, a classification system that is not *only* structured by brand—Michigan–Ann Arbor, not Dearborn—but also structured by lower levels of learning. The college system provides not an objective sorting of people by "ability"—Stanford grads here, San Jose State grads there—but an "objective" *reduction of ability* through limited learning. Conveniently, society can then point to these limited or commodity skills in explaining why even *good* students who *finished* college aren't getting a raise and have no guaranteed shot at staying middle class. In the global auction, it can then be said, this great American majority just isn't all that good. And we can thank underfunded public universities for objectifying this reality.

This may seem like a particularly dismal interpretation of the current middle-class crisis. Aren't we the people who built fantastic public colleges after the Great Depression and World War II? But that was then, when elites mostly took for granted that wages should track productivity gains. This is now, when elites mostly read the global order as granting high wages to the few.

We have here an answer to the mystery of why public college teaching isn't as good as it could be. The answer is that it is exactly as good as it needs to be to produce masses of *post-middle-class workers* with the commodity version of "high skill" that entitles them to low wage.

We also have an answer to the related mystery of why policy-makers have been cutting resources to public colleges as though they now have a lower social value. The answer is that they *do* have a lower social value in a post-middle-class society. In the postwar period, we could expect public funds to pay for a version of higher education that improves everyone's wages. Now, we can expect private funds (tuition) to pay for a version of higher education that allows a minority of college graduates to increase their wages while everyone else's stagnate.[59] If even public colleges offer an economic and social benefit only to a minority, politicians will quite logically reduce their public funding.

The bad news for colleges and universities is also the good news. The bad news in our developing, post-middle-class society is that public colleges have lost their core cluster of social missions. They are less generally associated with the progress of thought, with democratic management, with the most humane workplaces, with cultural enlightenment, with creative capability for all, or even with economic invention, which has been arrogated by the tech industries. This loss of confident purpose is the sociocultural basis for years of declining state funding and popular support. Downsized public universities are perfectly appropriate for the second- and third-class citizens from whom plutonomy withholds the spoils.

The good news is that higher education has no choice now but to confront the global political economy that removes this core mission and its public funding. In confronting this core issue, universities will finally have to join the legions of social critics and scholars of racial and other forms of structural inequality who have been warning for decades that already inadequate cures were being withdrawn.[60] Nothing less will do than stark opposition to the entire devolutionary cycle. That is the subject of my final chapter.

Part III: The Recovery Cycle

Reconstructing the Public University

I am my own avatar. Means I paid for it all.

—Saul Williams

For years now, our public colleges have been cut, squeezed, trimmed, neglected, overstuffed, misdirected, kludged, and patched. As a logical result, they do their core educational jobs less well than they used to—in a period when society needs them more than ever. We can't patch the public systems any more. We need to reconstruct them.

When I came back to California in 2011 from France, where I'd worked as a faculty director of the University of California's study-abroad centers, I began to give lectures about the public university's "devolutionary cycle" that form the basis of this book. One of the things being sacrificed in the ritual rounds of budget cuts, research constraints, and pedagogical placebos, I said, was the ability to expand intensive, personalized teaching from elite private colleges to the mass-access publics where most of today's multiracial majority get their bachelor's degrees.[1] I meant PhD students as well as under-graduates, and biochemistry majors as much as classicists. When taking questions at the end of the lectures, I noticed a split in the more skeptical audience comments. Some people said, "Well of course, this is what we are doing already—we know our students need to learn creativity." Other people said, "This isn't realistic; the states have to pay for lots of things besides college; you need to give us practical solutions." This split was between "we already do this" and "we can't do this"—lined up, respectively, with the private and the public university audiences.

I have been haunted by this split, and have written this book because the growing gap between the private and public sectors is ethically and intellectually unacceptable to me. It is also economically stupid. It is a waste of humanity. It is a waste of the rising generation that we are sending down Devolution Road toward being less well educated than their parents.[2] I sometimes feel that national elites in the United States and the UK have decided to float the ship by throwing most of its passengers over the side—to drown the middle class in pieces, having tossed away the working classes in earlier decades. From day to day my metaphors change for the voluntary devolution I've been describing. The trend does not.

Debating the Results

As I was reviewing final copy-edits for this book, I had a long phone call with a new friend in higher-education studies, who serves as dean of a school of education.

"When we had dinner last month," I began, "I had the sense that you had mixed feelings about the ending of the version of *The Great Mistake* that my editor sent you. But it sounded like you were saying two different things—that the solutions weren't practical, since they were too far from political reality, and also that they weren't provocative, since they didn't go far enough."

"That's right," he laughed. "I was saying both of those things. Here's what I think that means.

"You're right about the systemic nature of the neoliberal shift to market forces in public universities, and the damage that does. But what then? To be provocative you need to give us practical solutions. But you don't give us much we can work with, Chris. I thought when I got to the last chapter that I was going to read a plan. Where's the plan?"

"True," I agreed. "It's not a plan, it's principles for developing the plan. And there will be lots of plans, depending on the state."

"Yes. Of course. But you can't ignore the context, Chris. We're not just in a cycle here. Grover Norquist won. He did shrink it to the size where he could 'drown it in the bathtub.'" We don't have the public resources anymore. We can't sustain the public university investment—it's like a rule of physics. Your calling for public reinvestment isn't helping us here."

"What you're describing," I said, "is the context of my whole adult life. The money for my first 'merit raise' as an assistant professor was taken away in the 1992–1995 round of budget cuts, and we had to sue to get it back years later—it was about six hundred bucks. That's why I focus on the reframing. The entire paradigm is wrong. We have twenty-five or thirty years of solid evidence. It needs to go."

"Let's say I'm a college president," he responded. "What can I take away from this to help me with the state legislature?"

"Principles. A better paradigm."

"Or say I'm a state legislator chairing a higher education subcommittee. I say, 'Sure, I like free college. But I have six or eight different things to pay for with public money. I also sit on the corrections committee. How much am I supposed to cut prisons for free colleges? And by the way, why not free health care? Why not free mass transit? That's urgent in the cities. Why should free college come first?' I'm a legislator and you're a policy analyst, and I need to feel like you have a clue about realities on the ground."

"I hear you loud and clear. And the times I've joined faculty groups in our legislature, we heard this same thing. 'Why should I put you first? Ahead of people who need wheelchairs.' That's what happens as we let one public good get played against another."

"How are you going to stop that? That's the reality on the ground. I'm a college president, I need a blueprint. I'm not seeing a blueprint at the end of your book."

"There's no one blueprint," I said. "We don't have the right frame in place. The private good frame allows all these public goods to seem like add-ons that we really can't afford, which is false, except that it's true in the current frame. There are blueprints out there, many written by college presidents. My book is about why the current framework will keep any of them from working. They start with higher ed as a kind of private investment with some public benefits and then move to the kinds of tweaks and efficiencies that got us to the decline we're in today. And to the need to accept reality, which unfortunately will keep things in the same state they're in today, or worse."[3]

"That's right," he said. "Your book is convincing on that. You don't want to get in the weeds of policy detail."

"I try to link policy details, like how student debt is built into financial aid, back to existing principles that keep them in place. So the book points toward new principles, a countercycle, without which real policy change will neither happen nor make any sense."

"Yes," he replied. "If you said something like, 'by embracing these five principles (or some other number) then every state would be in a better position to work on fixing its public colleges.'"

"As long as they are looking at them from the next paradigm, based on higher ed as a public good."

And so we continued for quite a while. We never converged on a single level of analysis, but the debate clarified what I think about the purpose and limits of my approach here.

This book is not only about policy errors but about the framework or paradigm that enables them. The great mistake is not this or that specific surrender, much as the ensemble of these has unjustly deprived important sectors of the population of what their society should provide—and for which, as citizens, they have already paid. The great mistake is the private good framework, which is itself predetermined by that constellation of axioms and practices we call neoliberalism, and which takes its life from the institutional practices I've described here. The great mistake is to have relinquished the power of the public sector as a society. The great mistake is to have given up on the full democratization of intelligence.[4]

There is also something else, lying behind this loss of collective understanding of collective capability. That is the loss of a feeling for it, of a sense of attachment to it, or commitment, or a right to it—the loss of the common feeling that a complete education to the highest level is a part of who we are. We face many policy obstacles, but I found in my travels around the country that we face more fundamentally a loss of confidence and vision. I became most concerned about privatization as an *ethos*. To bend the term somewhat, I have been concerned about the weakened character of the collective practice of higher education that separates us emotionally and psychologically from the public vision of full participation in higher learning across all economic and racial groups.[5]

This is a book about changing the framework, the fundamental values, the paradigm under which we labor together. Our problem isn't actually lack of money. It's that lack of confidence and vision, including the confidence and vision to think outside the framework that our increasingly backward leaders use to contain public feelings about common resources.[6] Policy errors express the limitations of an antipublic paradigm that itself depends on its surrounding ethos, structured by common affects, with their shaping mixtures of desires and taboos. The United States can afford a fully reconstructed public university system. But "we" have to want to, and want it with enough conviction to force the political system to deliver it.

My analysis reflects the fact that I am a humanities scholar who is particularly focused on the cultural and psychological preconditions of public policy. This book is an example of an emerging field called Critical University Studies, an interdisciplinary field encompassing culture, institutions, policy, and political economy, and might be seen as a kind of "cultural economics."[7] My discussion with my friend, the dean of education, expressed my effort here to address three spheres or systems at the same time. These are the policy system, the private-good framework or paradigm that underlies it, and the cultural psychology or ethos that underlies the paradigm and keeps it in place. Ethos. Paradigm. Policy. The order goes from depth to surface, and yet these levels are systems that interact continuously.

So what practical thing does this book say to its audience—maybe college presidents and legislators, but especially students, parents, staff, all types of professors, and the public interested in fixing public colleges? It says, *You can't get there from here.*

Starting from Somewhere Else

The recovery cycle starts from the public good conception of higher education, and rests on positive feedback among the stages.

Figure 34. The Recovery Cycle

It can be pictured as shown in figure 34. I briefly summarize each of these recovery stages. Each undoes or reverses its equivalent in the devolutionary cycle I've analyzed in detail. No stage has guaranteed effects, and the causality from one stage to the next is imperfect and uncertain. But in each case, recovery processes are already under way, though generally off camera and out of view.

New Stage 1: University Recognized as a Public Good

We saw that the road to the public university's decline was paved with a long, diffuse campaign against its status as a public good. The practical effects were disastrous. The demotion of public good status forced university managers to pare their institutions' overall value to a narrow and fragile private fraction of the total (the wage premium over high school graduation). This paring undermined the university's ability to deliver the indirect, nonmarket, and social benefits that make up the majority of its total value, and its ability to deliver the *emerging* private market good, which were creative capabilities, which paradoxically could not be supported by private good market calculations. The failure to make a strong case for both individual and mass creativity, which depended on rebuilt support for research as well as instruction, weakened the case for rebuilt public funding. Collateral damage includes weaker understanding of the public value of academic freedom for faculty, of due-process-based job security for all university employees, and of the need to convert student work time to study time.

The solution requires restoring the university's public good status. A first step would be basic accounting reform that quantifies the value of indirect effects, nonmarket value, and social benefits with the same dutiful attentiveness that accounting applies to the private market benefit of higher salaries. One of the most hopeful trends from within economics is the conjunction represented by the McMahon and Goldin and Katz books I have discussed: both reject, from within a mainstream tradition, the dualism of private and public benefits that blinds us to the latter. Over time, *only* strong public funding has created the capabilities in a society that enable its economic health (Goldin and Katz), since more than half of educational benefits are public (McMahon). This work needs to be amplified inside the fields of economics and accounting. And yet the indirect, nonmarket, and social benefits are social and cultural stories that are going to have to be told by sociologists, cultural scholars, historians, literary critics, musicologists, architectural critics, novelists, playwrights, and poets.

One instance of the social benefit of artistic training and cultural scholarship is the installation of mimes in place of traffic cops in Bogotá, Colombia, which reduced accidents and violence, whose effects were then told by participants and cultural scholars. Transmission and improvement of such practices—conceiving of the concept of "cultural agency" to explain how mimes could be better than traffic cops—is part of the social benefits of the university.[8] Massive spillover effects for society are hard to measure and must be brought to life in narrative form.

We also need to shift philosophically away from the current incomplete definition of public goods that has been devised by the economics profession.[9] Economics asks us to treat higher education as a private market good because it is "excludable" and "rivalrous" at the point of consumption—you can reject applicants from your university or charge admits more than they can afford, and when you add more students to a classroom you subtract instructor attention and probably learning gain from each student there. We can and do treat higher education this way. But it is a conceptual and political choice, and it is wrong. Most of higher education's total benefits are neither rivalrous nor excludable. Educational effects, ranging from greater individual cognitive capabilities to more knowledge about racial conflicts, are non-excludable and nonrivalrous—everyone can use them, and their effects are not used up. Public goods benefit from "network effects" that are well understood in the private sector, but are generally ignored in the public sphere. In Stage 1, I defined a public good as a good whose benefit continues to increase as it approaches universal access. No doubt this definition could be improved, but it allows us to see the necessity of funding higher education as a public good rather than a private one. The fact that higher education is now set up to be rivalrous and excludable is not a reason to enforce the ensuing market framework that economics associates with these features. It is a reason to set up higher education differently—as a public good, on the grounds of its effects.

Outside of mainstream economics, the intellectual and activist worlds have generated a large supply of public good concepts, ranging from open-source conceptions of intellectual property to models of collective cognitive labor from autonomist Marxism, to varieties of antiprivatization and decolonization movements. "Culture" itself *is* indirect, nonmarket, and social. It encompasses simultaneously public-private goods like pleasure, fulfillment, well-being, non-exclusion, copresence, mutual respect, self-determination, and communal enjoyment. The current generation of university managers have a wide range of postcapitalist or Marxian or racially egalitarian or autonomist or ethnocultural or mainstream economic models to draw on. There is no reason for them to keep missing the boat. A wide range of society has rejected the private good model of higher education.

When we correctly understand university education as a public good, it becomes possible to grasp the virtuous cycle that public investment creates (figure 35). This cycle is reductively economic, and is *not* meant to suggest direct, certain causality but instead a series of positive influences within the existing system. It takes place *within* the new Stage 1 of the larger evolutionary cycle. I am speaking in economic terms here, but the components are sociocultural and psychological. There is an especially important linkage between Step 5, the addition of higher economic value, and Step 6, its yielding of higher wages. We saw in Stage 8 of the decline cycle that US policymakers gradually broke the link between economic value and wages after 1975. Here, Steps 1 through 5 carried on for years afterward, using still-high public investment to continue to generate relatively high productivity growth (which included gains rooted in public investment in the Internet). But the broken link between Steps 5 and 6 began to take a toll on later stages. Income shortfalls were veiled for years by the stock market boom, the debt boom, and the housing bubble. The 2007–2008 financial crisis made these shortfalls visible to all, but post-2008 policy has done nothing to relink higher productivity (Step 5) and higher wages (Step 6). My view is that this relinkage can happen politically when people can see clearly what a battle for it will get them—both higher personal income and a society thriving on public benefits.

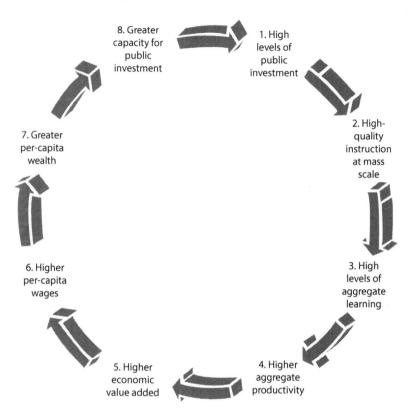

Figure 35. The Cycle of Economic Benefits of the Public Good University

New Stage 2: Reduce Public Subsidies to Outside Partners to Zero

The founding claim of privatization is that increasing market activities increases net revenues. Our review of major examples of university privatization suggested otherwise. Sponsored research increases gross revenues—while also increasing net losses. The situation is bad for research, and bad for other educational activities that must subsidize it. Privatization allows individuals and firms to externalize their costs onto universities. Individual sponsors and recipients gain, while the whole loses. Various problems ensue, including a loss of resources for the educational core and the poverty of arts, humanities, and qualitative social science (SASH) fields, which reduces sociocultural research on public crises. State legislatures can't try to fill budget holes that they don't even know exist.

All this can be fixed. The first requirement is for universities to stop treating research accounting as though it involves commercial secrets, and open the books. The principal investigators on major grants should be able to find out what happens to the indirect funds that come with their grants but are removed from them by the central administration. The same is true for the university community, which lives in the dark about fund flows. Faculty should be able to see, understand, debate, and participate in setting research funding policy. Their tuition contributions to research should earn students a place at the table, where they can understand how their payments underwrite the overall academic operation. University communities have the right to understand why so much teaching is done by adjuncts, why administrative budgets grow more quickly than instructional budgets, and what the return on investments in private partnerships really is. Universities should be exemplary open-book circulators of information rather than concealers thereof.

As is the case at the end of any artificial information embargo, officials will not be able to control people's reactions, which will include shock and anger. They will be more cross than ever that universities have built marquee projects and dodged tough negotiations with funders by surcharging students and impoverishing sociocultural fields. But where there is truth there can be reconciliation. That will include clear justifications of mutual aid and cross-subsidies, including continuing modified versions of current practices, but this time based on the general understanding of, and consent to, what is happening.

The second major reform is to take most of the large share of federal R&D money now going to businesses and redirect it to universities. It may have been tolerable for 40 percent of public sector R&D money to go to corporations when that money was growing steadily and when many corporations were conducting basic research.[10] Now each small annual funding increment is contested, and corporations have offloaded the vast majority of research (and much development) onto universities—but without the necessary federal funding. The struggle to cover existing STEM research is now endangering science's rising generation, and industry has not stepped up to replace public funds at the correct scale. Since businesses have reduced their internal R&D expenditures, the corporate share of federal R&D is a public subsidy to shareholders who need research but no longer want to support it with company funds.[11] Ending all public subsidies to private sector R&D, other than those with a direct public benefit, will increase the funds available to universities. For example, federal funding of industry research and basic research amounted to about $14.3 billion in FY 2015. Redirecting these funds to universities would replace nearly all of the approximately $15 billion of "institution funds" that private and public universities spent supporting extramural research.[12] To minimize disruption, lawmakers could decide to restructure federal research investments toward public universities from various funding categories over a number of years.

Increasing gross federal funding to universities will enable the third reform, which is the full costing of sponsored research. This means that, over time, the share of a university's institutional funds devoted to subsidizing extramural research would head to zero. The internal subsidy for extramurally funded research was a system that grew topsy-turvy in response to multiple pressures, and that also grew in the dark, since virtually no one affected by this system understood how it worked or the amounts of money involved. The current structure wreaks structural injustice on fields that are not in the STEM areas in which 99 percent of public funding occurs.

Were extramural sponsors, including corporations, to cover the full university costs of the research they support, institutional funds would be freed up for many other things, including the sociocultural fields that produce many, if not most, of the university's indirect private and social benefits.[13] These SASH disciplines would cease being impoverished like second-class citizens. We might see a renaissance in the sociocultural research that is critical to the solution of the world's environmental, social, political, military, cultural, and religious crises. These fields could finally take advantage of the collaborative infrastructures that allow the existence of modern science.

One understandable fear is that if corporations lose the deep discounts they receive for sponsoring research on US campuses, they will find those discounts abroad, meaning that they will offshore more basic research to countries like India and China. In fact this is already happening, both because the United States lost its partial monopoly on mass scientific talent and because universities are insufficiently funded. Improved funding will help public universities retain local research partners by improving the overall research environment, and thus the scientific return on investment, even if that improved environment means a higher upfront investment from each partner. Full costing of their sponsored research would not prevent corporations from conducting basic research at universities more efficiently than they can in house.

I've already identified the fourth reform, which is the adequate funding of the SASH fields that have been budgeted as amateur disciplines. Most universities confront the mixture of sociocultural and scientific-technical problems that haunt the world with their SASH arm tied behind their back. Both social benefits and global problem solving would be improved by funding SASH fields at a level where they can use data and collaborative networks as the STEM fields have long been able to do—without abandoning their own forms of qualitative knowledge steeped in history, interpretation, narrative, emotions, subjectivity, and the experience of everyday life.

Ending public university subsidies for private partners need not end those partnerships. Many of them are mutually beneficial. But it would put these partnerships on an equitable basis. Postprivatization partnerships would acknowledge that for-profit companies act rationally when they try to make university revenues their own, and these new partnerships would guard explicitly against leverage that drains the university's public resources rather than supporting them.

**New Stage 3. Public University Tuition Is Capped
and Reduced to Zero
New Stage 4. Public Funding Is Reset to Replace Tuition
New Stage 5. Student Debt Is Reduced to Zero**

These three stages of decline are so interconnected that they must be solved as a group. The long-term trend of annual tuition increases, of two to four times the consumer price index, has to stop. Public university tuition should be capped and allowed to decline slowly through inflation and, over a fixed period of years, be rolled back to near-zero levels. Next, public funding needs to rise to levels that allow public universities to reduce tuition without cutting educational quality. This will mainly involve state government but could include the federal government as well. Finally, three decades of debt funding of higher education through student borrowing needs to be ended and reversed. No one of these factors can be made less destructive without the other two being fixed at the same time.

The most important post-2008 change in public attitudes toward universities has been the new hostility to student debt. Nearly everyone used to see public colleges as the affordable alternative to private colleges. They assumed that they were more or less as good. Though it has taken many years, people now realize that policymakers and businesses have turned public colleges into debt machines that hum along with their private counterparts. Reports continue to emerge that debt is downgrading the fortunes of the millennial generation. A bachelor's degree now *increases* the disparity in economic security between African American and Latino graduates on the one hand and white and Asian American graduates on the other.[14] Young graduates with student debt have a fraction of the household wealth enjoyed by graduates without debt.[15] Nearly a third of the student borrowers who have started repayment are a month or more behind on this bill.[16] Student debt continues to erode the benefits of the weak economic recovery. Finally, in 2015, national political candidates began to float the concept of "debt-free college" and proposed some increases in public investment.[17]

The political center on public university policy has begun to move, and it is moving left, away from privatization, away from letting market forces continue to pile up student costs and student debt. Free community college was endorsed by the US president. Calls for free four-year colleges followed on its heels. The higher education analyst Robert Samuels notes that when his book *Why Public Higher Education Should Be Free* came out in 2013, he was a "lone, crazy voice in the wilderness." Two years later, "free" was a respectable part of mainstream debate.[18]

The move toward free recognizes the interconnection among our new Stages 3, 4, and 5. Democratic plans sought to lower debt payments by reducing public college tuition so that less debt is incurred in the first place, which would require giving federal money directly to state colleges to offset lost tuition income, while giving state legislatures incentive to rebuild public funding.[19] The overall political climate took tuition increases for resident BA students off the political table.

This combination of elements is a very big deal. National political proposals have finally jumped the tracks of the privatization cycle. They are trying to reverse decades of pushing the public costs of higher education onto private accounts. The plans are sure to produce massive resistance in the states, since they mean, as with ObamaCare, expanding a public service many conservatives don't like, with new federal money that will require cost sharing from them. There will be political blood. But in 2015, the country finally hit a milestone that might be like those that were on the road to Medicare, which established the public good principle of full health care coverage in retirement, which then made meaningful coverage the responsibility of public funding. The conceptual and ethical arguments for public good funding are being rebuilt. They are converging. And their political costs are coming down.

There are many standards that might define the right public good funding for universities. The new Stage 3 sets a sharply reduced tuition level for public colleges and universities. A starting point is to cap tuition at current levels. A better idea is a tuition "reset" to the inflation-adjusted amount at which it had not yet started to produce high levels of student debt. In Stage 4, I discussed the Council of University of California Faculty Associations' reset of tuition in California's university systems. At UC, resident undergraduate tuition would drop from $12,300 to about $5,400 per year.[20]

The best idea of all is a multiyear, incremental return to free tuition, which was proposed by one of the 2016 Democratic presidential candidates, Bernie Sanders, in his "College for All Act."[21] The federal government would split the cost with the states, buying out all tuition charged at a state's public colleges and universities. Sanders estimated the annual cost at about $70 billion, which is in the ballpark of other estimates.[22] If the federal government pays half, this would add about 6 percent to total US nondefense discretionary spending in 2017.[23] This is real money, but is a small price for an affordability revolution in public universities.

The new Stage 4 is reliable, rebuilt public funding. It might be guided by a different but compatible rule of thumb, which is that public universities should "grow with the state" in which they are located. As personal income increases, university budgets would also increase, meaning that they would retain at least the same share of state personal income over the years. When the citizenry has less money, universities would have less. The reverse would also be true. This is the least we should do—average budget treatment—to support arguably the most important driver of a knowledge society that is now leaving its majority behind.

"Growing with the state" is a simple rule, but it has not been practiced. States cut their universities way out of proportion to actual declines in personal income during downturns, and more deeply than other state functions.[24] Were the University of California to have followed the grow-with-the-state principle, it would have had over $5 billion in state general funding in 2014–2015, or about $2.2 billion more than it actually had.[25] The additional amount would buy out about 75 percent of UC's total tuition bill. It would not replace cut operating funds, but the point is that were UC to have simply kept up with state personal income, it would be three-quarters of the way to free UC.

The new Stage 4 can establish a base for this principle for future growth while also supporting tuition reductions to zero, at a surprisingly low cost. To stick with the UC example, rebuilding state general funding to 2000–2001 levels (prior to the last two recession-period cuts) would cost about $1.2 billion (a 38 percent increase, compared to the 4 percent annual increases the state is currently providing).[26] Getting all the way to free UC for undergraduates would require buying out something less than the $3 billion UC receives annually from all tuition sources, including nonresident and professional school tuition.[27] A rough estimate for the total bill for a decently funded free UC would then be an additional $4 billion per year. This is about 70 percent of the cost of the "reset" for the entire California public higher education system, which suggests that the additional cost to the median taxpayer for a free UC would be twenty-two dollars per year. Doing the same for the state's other two postsecondary systems would cost the median taxpayer an additional forty dollars a year.[28]

We can alarm the political system by pointing out that this more than doubles the state's current allocation to UC and CSU of about $6.3 billion. Or we can push the debate toward more sophisticated metrics and a higher vision of the public university's role. The more sophisticated metrics include public higher education's declining share of state personal income and of state government expenditures; the 5 percent share of state general funds the additional higher ed money would involve; and the affordability of the additional tax for all taxpaying state residents. To repeat, free UC and CSU, with reset operating funding, would cost taxpayers a vanishingly small amount of money as a share of their income. Stage 4 in our evolutionary cycle would constantly announce this affordability—the affordability of both solid operating budgets and free tuition for all public university undergraduates.

The new Stage 5 is student debt reduced to zero, over some set period of years. Aggregate US student debt was more than $1.3 trillion by 2015, and the extraordinary burden, particularly for younger graduates, was prompting calls for action across the political spectrum. Some groups proposed rule-of-thumb caps on student and parental payments as a way of limiting future obligations.

An example was the Lumina Foundation's "Rule of 10": "Students should pay no more for college than the savings generated through 10 percent of discretionary income for 10 years and the earnings from working 10 hours a week while in school."[29] The goal was to replace student debt with limited family savings, with the understanding that families with incomes under 200 percent of the poverty rate would be exempt. A family of four at that level ($48,500 in 2015, in the fifty-fifth percentile from the top) would save $1,500 over ten years, and the student could earn $3,625 per year. This means an "affordable" college would cost this student and his family about $4,000 per year—for everything.[30] Since total cost of attendance at a public university for an in-state student averaged around $23,000, state and federal governments would need to come up with $19,000 per year, or $80,000 for a degree, for this student from the third income quartile. A similar *zero*-debt plan would cost more per student for the bottom-quartile students that society most needs to get to a BA degree, and less per student for those with more means, as college saving capacity increases with income.

Plans focusing on reducing future debt to zero should be accompanied by debt reduction for existing borrowers. The best way to do this would be to peg repayment to income, perhaps with another Rule of 10: repayment should last for no more than ten years, and should not exceed 10 percent of "discretionary income," meaning income beyond a basic threshold of gross pay of 200 percent of the poverty line. Individual debt above this limit would be bought out by a combination of federal and state governments. This would alleviate the concern that high-income professionals wouldn't pay their fair share, while giving everyone both a manageable total debt and a light at the end of a relatively short debt tunnel—one from which most new borrowers would emerge before their mid-thirties. Additional work would need to be done to manage the high debt generated by postbachelor degrees, but the same basic principles would apply. The basic goal should be zero student debt.[31]

Public university officials will fight two of these three goals—free tuition and zero debt—and the third—rebuilt state funding—won't happen without some version of the first two. In the current paradigm, their opposition makes sense. Precedent suggests that if state and federal governments pay public college operating costs, they will pay as little as they can get away with, and shortages, deterioration, overcrowding, and the rest will continue until state colleges look like run-down urban high schools, with learning outcomes to match. Legislators mostly have no clue about the costs of research, so free tuition and zero debt could doom every public university in the country. Or so it seems from inside our current broken model. But in this model public tuition has already been capped, without funding restoration or the goal of zero debt. The three problems can only be solved together, and can be solved by aiming for the public benefits while telling the budget truth.

New Stage 6: Universities Rebuild Educational Core for Creative Capabilities

Our new Stage 6 involves upgrading public university instruction to deliver mastery learning and creativity learning. What I mean takes a bit of explaining.

In the devolutionary cycle, university learning is a compromise between teaching as a profit center and learning focused on degree completion. Under the American Funding Model, universities need to use a share of teaching revenues to cover the costs of research, administration, and other non-instructional activities. Public college and university faculty have always tried to help students to have the best possible skills and knowledge of subject matter, but funding conditions cut against it. There is no way around the limits imposed by a straightforward problem like one professor grading multiple papers for 150 students per term. Over time, educational results will decline.

In recovery, public colleges will help every student integrated their learning across disciplines and various cognitive activities. One somewhat unattractive term that captures the aspiration, and that spread with the MOOC craze of 2012–2013, is "mastery learning." The core idea is fundamental: "*all* students should learn *all* the material." This can happen when teaching adapts to the learning capacities of the students, whatever they are, while also monitoring the progress of each student and giving each student the specific help they need. This might mean offering additional time, or repeating material for class meeting 6 while most of the class needs help with class meeting 5, or giving Ramona more theory while giving Gilbert more concrete examples, and so on. Mastery learning is complicated and expensive because it adapts the learning process to individual students rather than treating each class as a group of functionally identical people. The basic ideas of this form of pedagogy go back to Rousseau and Pestalozzi, Alcott and Mann, if not to Socrates, but they were further developed in the twentieth century in many countries and cultures. In the American postwar period, mastery learning has often been associated with education researcher Benjamin S. Bloom. In a canonical set of studies, he got the following results: "90% of the tutored students and 70% of the mastery learning students attained the level of summative achievement reached by only the highest 20% of the students under conventional instructional conditions."[32] Mastery learning moved regular classrooms a long way toward all students learning all the material all of the time.

Since public universities must achieve results on a mass scale, they have an obvious interest in such techniques. The MOOC advocates claimed that online technology actually implemented mastery learning at a mass scale. That was wrong. And yet the goal was good, and the effort did push many faculty to imagine new ways to make mastery learning a public university reality.

This is an important short-term project, but it should be seen as laying the foundation for the real goal—*creativity learning* on a mass scale. I'll use an example from my teaching at UC Santa Barbara to 'explain what I mean.

One of my students there, whom I'll call Jasmine, was taking her second course with me, "Global California." She was a sophomore and was in that course's honors section, where I could track her progress in detail. Each student could have one-on-one tutorial time with me, which I encouraged. As in all of my courses these days, students were asked to learn through research. To do research learning, they first needed to identify their personal, overall research question for the course. I tell my students that college is about developing their abilities to absorb subject matter, but also to learn much more about learning itself. That means at least three things: analyzing complex information independently, integrating knowledge from various courses, and inventing and sustaining creative projects—both their own and collaborative projects of the kind they might be required to do in a future job.

I start this process with a small step. In the first weeks of the quarter, I ask students to post an item of personal significance on the course blog. It can be any small thing—a photo of their third-grade class when they were an English as a Second Language student, two sentences about why California's weather is such a big deal, a map of taco stands in Los Angeles in 1951, a paragraph about Rose of Sharon in *The Grapes of Wrath*, or a link to a video of a short monologue by Paulo Freire (all real examples). I am often surprised by the high percentage of students who struggle with this low-key and yet open assignment. "It's not a trick question," I say. "You really can post anything you want." This comment doesn't help them at all.

Jasmine puzzled over this and then came up with a newspaper story about the day her high school won a football game against its big rival team for the first time in twenty-seven years. The topics she identified were "Importance of sports in small towns. Development of team rivalries between different types of high schools. Social media and its influence on mentalities/rivalries." The assignment for the first paper was to take a topic and research it, and develop a thesis. Jasmine talked about this issue several times in class, and I suggested elements that she might research. Next thing I knew, she had written her paper about suicide barriers on bridges in California.

"Interesting," I said, "but what happened to your football story?" "I couldn't decide what it was really about," she replied.

I am now used to the difficulty that most good students have with picking topics and then sticking with them. Picking and sticking is apparently not so easy. I've found that my public school students are very bright and generally motivated—Jasmine worked on a campus newspaper, became an editor, and helped restart a literary journal in her junior year—but they are not trained to see themselves as society's future leaders or to assume their ideas are important and worthy. So one of my core teaching activities is helping them get started, first by picking a project topic.

Two issues appear immediately: *topic* and *project*. Picking a topic is a form of self-starting that is hard for most students, at least outside of the carefully curated elites who end up at universities like Stanford and Yale—though my colleagues at those schools think they have the same problems. As soon as a topic becomes something more than what can fill five pages, choosing one becomes intimidating. The student's search needs a *personal interest*, which involves figuring out what she is really interested in; a question about that interest, which evolves into a *research question*; and a *method of address*—not a methodology exactly, but a way of approaching the topic.

When Jasmine defined her topic as a football rivalry, she finally wasn't interested in it. Is there something interesting about losing again and again for years, or what a nerd school does to non-nerdy students, or the effects of different degrees of racial integration, or high school's impacts on people who want to be writers and editors? Maybe, maybe not. How is she supposed to find the issue that really matters—really matters to her, much less to the rest of the world? How is she supposed to approach it?

The same goes for turning the topic into a project. This involves a series of steps, including forming a research question, sorting through research materials that may be relevant, and developing a process for deciding what to include and exclude. My students often ask me, "What's our prompt for this paper?" They assume that I will give them the topic and the materials they are supposed to use to discuss it. I always say, "You need to make your own prompt—that's the first step for writing this paper." When a college professor says, "I've listed the topics for the mid-term paper that is due in week 5," he describes a known entity. When he says, as I do each term, "your mid-term paper, due in week 5, is the research phase of a ten-week investigation about something that matters to you," the known entity disappears. The student needs to construct the project—its process—before the entity in the assignment actually exists. This is the point at which mastery learning ends and creativity learning begins. More accurately, it's the point when mastery learning serves as the starting point for a creative process that involves reflection, analysis, and discovery, all assembled into an undergraduate project.

Projects require planning. Planning means sequencing a series of steps and then performing them. Performing steps means keeping records about them, keeping the relationships among the steps more or less in one's conscious mind, and tracking the results. Tracking the results requires the ability to describe and analyze incomplete information, uncertainty, ambiguity, contradiction, incoherence, or refutation of one's hypothesis. All this is for writing a nonroutine five-page paper.

How do we learn how to do this? How do we sustain the attention and the ability to find, assess, organize, and synthesize information? A paper topic can produce an existential crisis, and often does. Uncertainty recurs throughout the process, and it's easy enough to experience oneself as basically stupid.

Feelings of stupidity are what universities need to help masses of people overcome. Universities teach two inseparable things at the same time. The first is how to structure thinking into research projects that address major topics that emerge from personal interests, whether we call that "instruction" or "research," art or science. The second is self-awareness of one's identity as a person and thinker, which enables project thinking to proceed.

We often try to use technology to present material and rehearse learning it. Some help does come from external and internal audits. Advocates of online instruction pitched it, in large part, as an audit mechanism; if you are partial to external controls, then you will be more impressed with online than otherwise. But studies of motivations and incentives generally conclude that *internal* motivation is more important. An emerging biopsychological strain of cognitive research suggests that learning is always structured and propelled by personal identity and interest. To improve learning, we don't want to weaken individuality, but to develop and strengthen it.

The problem is that public universities do not now have enough money to offer the personalized instruction that forms the strong personalities on which creative capabilities rest. The work that was most often cited to prove that colleges aren't teaching anything—*Academically Adrift*—actually showed that most students lack intellectual advising, study time, and coherent curricula.[33] As one example, the chancellor of the California Community College system, which serves a million and a half students, elicited a gasp of surprise from a jaded radio host when he stated that the CCCs have a student to advisor ratio of 2,000:1.[34] Students who have advising and coherent *academic* majors advance quite well—it's just that few public systems have the money to give this to their students.

With an undergraduate like Jasmine, whom I saw once a week, I tried to help her construct a "roadmap" that at every turn reflected her awareness both of her research question and of her personal interests. "What's interesting to you," I would ask, "about your high school winning a game against a team that had beaten you twenty-six times?" Her abandonment of this topic reflected the fact that the true answer to this question was finally, "Nothing." But nothing can take a while to uncover.

In insisting that college is about both personal interests and personal projects, I am drawing on a venerable humanistic definition of the uses of the university. This humanism has always seen the liberal arts and sciences as central to higher education. They are "liberal" because all of their disciplines, from linguistics to history to sociology to biology to astrophysics, focus simultaneously on subject expertise *and* the formation of the self that is acquiring the expertise. Vocational training cannot be separated from self-development. The training is only as good as the self that grasps it. Every liberal arts and sciences course in a university is in principle about intellectual development and self-development at the same time. The practice is simultaneously individual and collective, personal and social, private and public. This nondualistic practice acknowledges the united fates of individuals and society and is the hinge of the development of society as a whole.

The liberal arts vision of combining intellectual and self-development seems limited at first, but it covers the political spectrum from the "pedagogy of the oppressed" and radically democratic grassroots educational movements to Christian colleges' interest in the spiritual welfare of their students. Universal higher learning was an animating vision of the engineering professors who founded the MOOCs of 2012. The nineteenth century had already put self-development at the center of higher learning, and when I say this I invoke radical visionaries like Walt Whitman as well as establishment university presidents. The University of Chicago's founding president, William Rainey Harper, an intimate of the Rockefeller donors and their circles, praised the university's practical career focus by noting it produced graduates who could "develop their own methods of work." Similarly, the conservative president of the University of California, Benjamin Wheeler, said in 1900 that the university "proposes to rescue men from slavery and make them free . . . free from the bondage of routine . . . A freeman is a man who can initiate."[35] In an earlier book of mine, *Ivy and Industry,* I showed that a consensus version of university humanism has long consisted of "five interwoven concepts: the free self, experiential knowledge, self-development, autonomous agency, and enjoyment."[36] University philosophers and administrators did not simply espouse these concepts as ideals, but institutionalized them. These concepts remained central to daily academic practice—to the pleasures and struggles of learning in both teaching and research—even during the advent of the corporate "multiversity" that UC president Clark Kerr described somewhat unhappily in 1963.[37] There has always been general agreement that universities created and transmitted knowledge, and also fashioned selves.

Our current emphasis on creativity and innovation was already present in the mid-twentieth-century awareness that democracy required widespread higher learning. The "Report of the Harvard Committee" of 1945, entitled *General Education in a Free Society*, argued that the university must "reflect two characteristic facets of democracy: the one, its creativity, sprung from the self-trust of its members; the other, its exposure to discord and even to fundamental divergence of standards precisely because of this creativity, the source of its strength."[38] Here self-trust is the essential prerequisite of creativity, as is working with contradiction, dissonance, and what we would now call cultural conflict and racial diversity. Democratic citizens had to have knowledge and skills *and* the personal capabilities that would enable them, without anguish and hostility, to interpret ambiguous information, find new data, and undertake continuous revision, all in conjunction with people not much like themselves. Democratic citizens had to be as familiar with the process of knowledge creation as with established knowledge itself. They had to see learning and research as permanently combined. They had to see that all learning is research learning *and* then be the kind of people that could practice this.

What we sometimes call the innovation economy should instead be called the knowledge society or the creative society. It only works if it is a classless society in the sense defined by C. L. R. James, Christopher Lasch, and others as the democratization of intelligence. The *means* to this society is to universalize as much as humanly possible every university student's development of creative capabilities.[39] The condition of individual life and consciousness is more important in humanistic traditions than are economic requirements. The core assumption of the university humanities is that creative capabilities serve at least three core missions—self-development, democratic citizenship, and sustainable economic development.

The obvious next question is, "What are those creative capabilities today?" We already have the answer in the project process I just described, which I'll informally codify in a longish list.

1. Basic subject knowledge in a field
2. Knowledge of a field's major questions (including of what a research question is)
3. Developed capacity for being interested in questions where the answer is "nonobvious"
4. Formation of a project topic via practical inquiry into one's own core interests
5. Development of the project topic research question (including self-awareness of the course's and one's own paradigm or interpretative framework—and its limits)
6. Identifying a thesis or hypothesis about the topic, one that is interesting and nonobvious
7. Planning the investigation (identification of steps; ongoing revision of methods)
8. Organized research, including recording and sorting of conflicting information
9. Interpretation of research results. This includes analyzing conflicting, divergent information; interpreting tacit, informal, unsanctioned, or disorganized information; interpreting anomalous information, meaning information that is incommensurable with the paradigm or framework.
10. Development of analysis and narrative into a coherent story line, with acknowledgment of gaps and internal tensions
11. Presentation of findings and responding to criticism, skepticism, new contexts
12. Ability to reformulate conclusions and narrative in response to new information
13. Ability to fight opposition, to develop within institutions, to negotiate, to struggle—in general to make one's knowledge interactive with society

There is much that could be said about this list. It may seem too ambitious and irrelevant to teaching students to accept functional positions in the economy. It may seem too demanding for the "academically adrift" who are "paying for the party." It is neither too ambitious nor too demanding. Over the past two generations we have seen the culture and the high end of the economy shift their official demand from *do what you're told* to *tell yourself what to do.* It is discriminatory *not* to teach the other 96 percent how to respond.

Of course, this demand for creative capabilities is mostly honored in the breach—only part of the contemporary economy is a knowledge economy, the knowledge economy is relentlessly managerial, and most of the fastest-growing jobs are medium-skill jobs at best. In addition, a large part of the political spectrum sees mass creativity, or even basic self-management, as subversive and will never pay taxes to support it.

None of this changes the basic direction of history toward higher learning. None of it changes the need for universities to provide the higher-order skills I put under the umbrella of *creativity learning.* None of it changes the need for society to pay the high cost of developing them.

I have spent my entire career at research universities, and some of my tenure-track colleagues will read this and think I want to take faculty away from their research so they can spend more time correcting basic mistakes in writing and math. To the contrary, I want teaching to be more like research, done in smaller groups, but not to become a larger proportion of research faculty's time—or dumped on an even larger proportion of adjunct instructors. That is the cut-rate teaching model that we've used in public research universities for eighty to a hundred years. It has reached the end of its useful life. We've tried to extend it with technology. Instead we need to set the massification model aside. We need more instructional hours from larger instructional staffs, not sped-up research faculty in the classroom. This means paying for the classroom.

Why can't we have creativity learning through privatization? Because privatization blocks its mass application, in two ways: by limiting deep education to people who can pay the full cost, and by tying expenditures to calculations to a private return on investment, which suppresses investment in public goods, which cost money now for mostly nonmonetizable gains later. Creativity learning must now occur on a mass scale and must therefore be paid for publicly. There is simply no other way to get it.

New Stage 7: Equal and Higher Overall Learning across Race and Class

The creativity learning I've just described must be extended from elite colleges and universities to public regional and community colleges.

It would be nice to be able to start with basic parity between elite private universities and the best-funded publics, but we don't even have that. This was brought home to me again when I was reading a *New York Times Magazine* piece about Stanford University called "The Stanford Undergraduate and the Mentor." The story was a potboiler about accusations of sexual misconduct in a relationship between a student and the young company founder who was one of the mentors in a university course. Most people focused on the guilt or innocence of the mentor-lover, the student's helicopter mother, the structural inequality between the mentor figure and the student, or the student's mixture of vulnerability and anxious striving. I, on the other hand, became obsessed with this passage, which was the setting for the relationship:

> Clougherty [the student] and Lonsdale [the mentor] had been dating over the previous couple of weeks, while he was her assigned mentor for an undergraduate course at Stanford called Technology Entrepreneurship, Engineering 145. The limited-enrollment class offered a combination of academics, business skills and access to Silicon Valley that has made Stanford the most-sought-after university in the country, with the most competitive undergraduate admissions and among the highest donations. . . . Lonsdale, who also went to Stanford, made much of his fortune by helping to start Palantir Technologies, a major data-mining company. He was among the "top entrepreneurs and venture capitalists," according to the course description, many of them alumni, who came to campus as mentors for E145. "Students will learn how to tell the difference between a good idea in the dorm and a great scalable business

opportunity," the E145 handbook for mentors says. "Guide them and challenge them." Stanford students are well aware of how valuable these contacts are. Around the time Clougherty took E145, another student's project, a virtual-payment app, attracted an investment from a Google board member who was a guest speaker in the course. It became the start-up Clinkle, with initial financing of $25 million.

Well, actually that wasn't the passage—that's standard boilerplate about Stanford's unique social networks at the top of the global tech world. This is the passage:

The following January, Clougherty started E145, which was part of her self-designed major in management science and neuroengineering. She imagined some day starting a company that would find a socially responsible application of neurological research. The E145 professor matched Clougherty's team of four students with two mentors.[40]

I read these lines many times. Recall the UC Berkeley student saying her classes all had hundreds of students in standard major structures. Her Stanford counterpart can match her big ambition to a customized major that leads to a course that will not only link her to a business network but develop her ideas through a two-to-one student-to-faculty ratio, which puts in place Benjamin Bloom's "mastery learning" tutorial. This is one-tenth of UC's official student-faculty ratio, and one-hundredth of operational reality for UC undergraduates. Many UC lecture courses have no discussion sections. Most UC majors require some kind of senior seminar for graduation, meaning one course in four years with a ratio of fifteen to one.

During the last round of cuts, as we saw, many UC departments were forced to drop even that requirement. Many majors operate most courses with machine-graded tests, and nearly all do a majority of a major's grading with graduate students. I am regularly asked to write reference letters for students from other majors who say to me, "You're the only professor I've talked to at UCSB." Stanford and UC Berkeley admit students of comparable previous achievement, and all UC campuses have, in my experience, a large majority of what

I call "everyday smart people," meaning they lack custom development with private tutors and sports coaches but are full of energetic intelligence and good skills that put them at the top of their public high schools. And yet they are not only not getting two-on-one attention from professors and researchers: they can spend years without taking a seminar in which they speak in class at least once a week.

We saw that the American university system is "separate and unequal," that attainment is lower for African American, Latino, and Native American students than for whites and Asian Americans, that attainment is lower for lower-income students, and that the current laissez-faire approach to attainment is helping to make it worse. Privatization has increased public college dependence on tuition revenues and other private funds, which has increased resource inequality between universities whose students can pay more and those whose students cannot. The public university system now sustains rather than decreases the racial isolation and class polarization that over several decades has produced educational decline.

Decades ago, the courts began to force states to equalize funding among rich and poor school districts that had been spending grossly different amounts of money per student and were producing widely different educational outcomes. The country's K–12 system remains unequally funded and unjust and skews results by race and income, but the problem is well understood and there are efforts to make it better. This is not the college case. Will university students need to start suing university systems to equalize academic resources between, say, the University of Michigan's Ann Arbor flagship and its Flint campus, or between UC Riverside and UCLA, where completion rates track resources per student? Public colleges and universities should start equalizing the distribution of resources before it comes to that.

There are plenty of excuses for why this equalization can't and shouldn't happen. One is that some universities do things that cost more money than others—like STEM research—and need to spend more money per student. That is true, and that would be a reason why Ann Arbor would spend more money per student *overall* than

Flint. It could not be a reason why Ann Arbor would spend more money per student on instruction, which if anything should be the reverse, with the well-prepared Ann Arbor students needing less tutorial-style attention than Flint students, in theory. And it could not be a reason why a development fund would not be supplied to Flint to help it provide the same research-learning experience to its lower-income and minority-majority student body that they would receive at Ann Arbor. The goal must be equality of educational intensity.

Another excuse for inequality is that most people aren't able and/or willing to benefit from high-end creativity learning, and that if anything, too many people are in college already. This argument falsely applies past and present practice to future possibility. It commits the mistake of what critical theorists call "essentialism," in which the contingent, unnecessary result of a (faulty) changeable system is wrongly thought to be an intrinsic quality or essence of a group—the majority of university students. In reality, people aren't mediocre. Most people receive a mediocre education from our highly stratified primary, secondary, and public university systems. This can and must be fixed.

Another excuse for tolerating unequal university funding is that the economy can't really use the number of graduates with bachelor's degrees that we already have, much less vastly more. I agree that we can't really use a vastly greater number of graduates with factory-style college degrees, ones that don't deliver mastery learning, much less creativity learning. But I am talking about mass *quality* in degree production, and conventional wisdom doesn't apply. A mass supply of high-end degree-bearers would flood the narrow channels we fit them into now, in ways we can't yet imagine.

The general investment in research-based instruction has to be built mostly with new money. Imagine a society in which excellent liberal arts and sciences educations are given not just to the 4 percent who go to Ivy League or liberal arts colleges or their equivalent, or to those plus the additional 15 percent who go to research-oriented public universities, but to a third, a half, the whole 100 percent of people in university. Society's powers to solve problems and resolve conflicts would be revolutionized. There is no excuse for not making our public universities the places that get the capability revolution going.

New Stage 8: Creative Capabilities Increase Pressure for Productivity Wage

This stage is out of the control of universities. The repair will require a wholesale shift in economic philosophy and policy. At the same time, it will be helped by redefining universities as public goods, funding them accordingly, noting the intellectual flourishing that results, and rebuilding the entitlement of cognitive labor to the fruits of production.

In this phase, employee wages once again increase in step with increases in productivity. As workers add more value to firms because their work time is more productive, their pay increases accordingly.

This has not been happening. University graduates have continued to receive a wage premium over high school graduates, and their pay has come closer than that group to reflecting their productivity increases. At the same time, university graduates and professional employees have lost their forty-hour week—professors work fifty hours or more, the equivalent of an additional day per week.[41] They have also for decades been subject to continuous demands to work with more focus and intensity during each of these longer hours.

One of Karl Marx's key contributions to the understanding of capitalism was the idea that the employer can extract "surplus-value" from the employee, defined crudely as the difference between the value her labor produces and what she is paid to produce it. Marx noted that three principal ways of increasing surplus value are to increase the length of the working day, the intensity of the work, and the productivity of the work.[42] These practices became explicit virtues in the New Economy of the 1990s, famously encapsulated by Amazon.com CEO Jeff Bezos's statement to shareholders in 1997, "It's not easy to work here (when I interview people I tell them, 'You can work long, hard, or smart, but at Amazon.com you can't choose two out of three.)"[43] Amazon employees must choose all three, meaning a working week that is longer and more intense and supposedly more inventive. In addition, the "at will" firing that typified the factory floor in Marx's day is increasingly common in the workplaces occupied by university graduates. As I was writing this book, a detailed story about Amazon's exhausting, sometimes humiliating, and always highly controlling workplace led to a general consensus that Amazon was on the more extreme end of what is now standard white-collar practice.[44] Most of us assume that university graduates must now expect continuous monitoring, pressure, job insecurity, and exploitation in the classical sense of producing quite a bit more than what they are paid for. The main sign of commitment is an eagerness to be exploited in this sense. The productivity wage must be restored, and that starts with university people—employees and graduates—developing a new sense of the value of what they create, what their working lives should be like, and what share of it must be returned to them.

This topic is beyond the scope of this book. It will be a complicated, difficult struggle over many decades. But the current situation emerges from a set of reversible policy mistakes that have been embedded in our institutions and can therefore be extracted from them. After World War II, the United States built the best industrial-era public universities in the world. In the next era—the Soviet launch of the Sputnik satellite in 1957 is a convenient starting point—"post-Fordist" capitalism and social transformation (the civil rights and feminist movements at home, decolonization abroad) all in their different ways required new levels of mass creativity to sustain the production of new goods, services, technologies, arts, letters, and politics. But the country failed to upgrade the bulk of its public colleges and universities. Attainment rose more slowly than before, and the majority of American public university students continued to receive factory educations for a postfactory economy. In the moment in which good jobs became less routine and our sociocultural worlds more complex, culture wars and budget cuts forced universities to narrow their aims and to sustain the routinization of higher learning.

We knew in the fifties, sixties, and seventies—and eighties and nineties—that we needed more overall creativity in society, business, government, schools, everywhere, and creativity of every kind. But we stuck with our biases and affirmed our errors.

First, we continued to assume that real creativity belongs to the few, who in the economy came to be called entrepreneurs. So this ersatz creative society would gorge the top and ration the rest—and that is what we have done. Second, we believed that most, if not all, value lay in private and not public goods. Private wealth thus accurately measured degrees of creativity and contribution to society, and public goods like health, housing, and educational infrastructure could be neglected. Third, we assumed that external pressure automatically elicits creativity in those who have it. So we managerialized everything, now with bulk data collection at work. Finally, we assumed that the economically important forms of creativity were scientific and technological. So we underfunded and sidelined the arts, humanities, and social sciences (SASH), which meant underdeveloping both our social systems and ourselves. We became dependent on importing creative technological labor from poorer countries with strong educational systems, while denigrating the liberal arts of personal and social formation. Ethnic studies were seen as a sidelight compared to electrical engineering.

We are now undoing the pieces of the great mistake. The recovery cycle sketches the working principles: a public good vision focused on nonmarket and social educational benefits; zeroed-out private subsidies and their replacement with equitable partnerships; rebuilt public funding that eliminates student debt; elite training on a mass scale for regular students; and the reconstruction of the productivity wage.

If you think all this is impossible, you are right—inside the current paradigm. We can't get there from here. But we can get there from another ethos and paradigm, both of which have been coming into view. Everything we need to achieve—sustainable economics, racial equality, cross-cultural accommodation, environmental justice, radically reduced warfare—depends in some real measure on ending the scarcity of transformative public higher education. We do have to bite the bullet of paying for it. The good news is that we can.

There are no guarantees in the recovery cycle I've outlined here—except for one. It will work a lot better than what we are doing now.

Notes

Holding Back Public Colleges

1. One eminent example is William F. Massy, *Reengineering the University: How to Be Mission Centered, Market Smart, and Margin Conscious* (Baltimore, MD: Johns Hopkins University Press, 2016).

2. Tyler Cowen, *Average Is Over: Powering America beyond the Age of the Great Stagnation* (New York: Dutton, 2013); Phillip Brown, Hugh Lauder, and David Ashton, *The Global Auction: The Broken Promises of Education, Jobs, and Incomes* (New York: Oxford University Press, 2010).

3. Author's calculations. For the very small number of US college students who attend what are increasingly called student-centered colleges, see similar calculations in Victor E. Ferrall, *Liberal Arts at the Brink* (Cambridge, MA: Harvard University Press, 2011), table 1.1. Ferrall shows that the 225 private liberal arts colleges described in *America's Best Colleges* enroll 349,000 students, which is the same number of students that attend just three large urban community college systems (Miami-Dade College, Northern Virginia Community College, and the Houston Community College System).

4. For the derivation of these figures, based on actual UC Santa Barbara financial aid packages for 2014–2015, see Christopher Newfield, "The Impact of Tuition Hikes on Undergraduate Debt," *Remaking the University* (blog), November 26, 2015, http://utotherescue.blogspot.co.uk/2014/11/the-impact -of-tuition-hikes-on.html; and Stage 5 in this volume.

5. Richard Arum and Josipa Roksa, *Academically Adrift: Limited Learning on College Campuses* (Chicago: University of Chicago Press, 2011); Elizabeth A. Armstrong and Laura T. Hamilton, *Paying for the Party: How College Maintains Inequality* (Cambridge, MA: Harvard University Press, 2013).

6. Christopher Newfield, "The End of the American Funding Model: What Comes Next?," *American Literature* 82, no. 3 (September 2010): 611–35.

7. Andrew P. Kelly and Mark Schneider, *Getting to Graduation: The Completion Agenda in Higher Education* (Baltimore, MD: Johns Hopkins University Press, 2012).

8. Thomas Bailey, "Can Community Colleges Achieve Ambitious Graduation Goals?," in Kelly and Schneider, *Getting to Graduation,* 92.

9. Andrew P. Kelly and Mark Schneider, "Introduction," in Kelly and Schneider, *Getting to Graduation,* 6. The passage continues, "While experimentation with small-scale interventions is important, we must be sure to emphasize scalability and comprehensive approaches to institutional

reform. Finally, we must look to the states." States have done little but cut public higher education in recent years.

10. Eric Bettinger, "Financial Aid: A Blunt Instrument for Increasing Degree Attainment," in Kelly and Schneider, *Getting to Graduation*, 157–74. The best-studied financial aid program, Georgia's HOPE, increased attendance by 3.7 to 4.2 percent for students who, having gotten a B average in high school, can attend a Georgia public university for free. The chapter concludes,

> In sum, we have two key concerns about the role of financial aid policies in increasing retention and completion rates. First, we do not know how much of the gap in college completion and retention between socio-economic groups is attributable to financial factors. Given that the effects of need-based and merit-based aid are positive, it is clear that more generous financial policies can help, but we do not know the size of the gap that can be attributed to financial aid factors. At what point does increasing aid lose its effectiveness? The second and more severe problem is the magnitude and the potential cost-effectiveness of expanded grant aid policies. We have to make significant assumptions to get a positive rate of return on these programs. (165)

11. Kevin Carey, *The End of College: Creating the Future of Learning and the University of Everywhere* (New York: Riverhead Books, 2015).

12. The "why" of public university decline is the subject of my *Unmaking the Public University: The Forty-Year Assault on the Middle Class* (Cambridge, MA: Harvard University Press, 2008).

The Price of Privatization

1. This section is based on the introductory section of my essay "Humanities Creativity in the Age of Online," *Occasion Journal* (2013), accessed April 20, 2015, http://arcade.stanford.edu/sites/default/files /article_pdfs/OCCASION_v6_Newfield_100113.pdf.

2. State Higher Education Executive Officers Association (SHEEO), *SHEF: FY 2014: State Higher Education Finance* (Boulder, CO: SHEEO, 2015), fig. 2.

3. Claudia Goldin and Lawrence F. Katz, *The Race between Education and Technology* (Cambridge, MA: Belknap Press of Harvard University Press, 2008).

4. Organisation for Economic Co-operation and Development (OECD), "Indicator A4: How Many Students Complete Tertiary Education?," *Education at a Glance 2013: OECD Indicators* (Paris: OECD Publishing, 2013), chart A4.2; OECD, *Education at a Glance 2015: OECD Indicators*, chart A1.2, accessed May 14, 2016, http://www.keepeek.com/Digital-Asset

-Management/oecd/education/education-at-a-glance-2015_eag-2015
-en#page34.

5. Tom Mortenson, "Family Income and Unequal Educational Opportunity, 1970 to 2011," *Postsecondary Education Opportunity*, no. 245 (November 2012): 1–20.

6. College Board, Trends in Student Aid 2014, fig. 14B, accessed May 10, 2016, https://secure-media.collegeboard.org/digitalServices/misc/trends /2014-trends-student-aid-report-final.pdf. The costs of financial aid complexity have become a staple of discussions of the byzantine and largely privatized financial aid system. For one vivid example of the challenges faced by a low-income student, see Jason DeParle, "For Poor, Leap to College Often Ends in a Hard Fall," *New York Times*, December 22, 2012, http://www .nytimes.com/2012/12/23/education/poor-students-struggle-as-class-plays -a-greater-role-in-success.html?pagewanted=all&_r=0.

7. *Knowledge industries* was already a term in circulation by the time Clark Kerr helped popularize it in *The Uses of the University* (Cambridge, MA: Harvard University Press, 1963). Nonstandardized labor was a central concept in Alvin Toffler's *Future Shock* (1970; repr., New York: Bantam, 1984). A watershed exploration of the rise of customized production and flexible problem solving in manufacturing is Michael J. Piore and Charles F. Sabel, *The Second Industrial Divide: Possibilities for Prosperity* (New York: Basic Books, 1984).

8. The problem is sometimes called "Baumol's cost disease," and Baumol has updated his discussion of the issue in William J. Baumol et al., *The Cost Disease: Why Computers Get Cheaper and Health Care Doesn't* (New Haven, CT: Yale University Press, 2012).

9. Lawrence Mishel, *The Wedges between Productivity and Median Compensation Growth*, Economic Policy Institute Issue Brief, no. 330 (April 26, 2012), http://www.epi.org/publication/ib330-productivity-vs-compensation/.

10. The economist Richard Vedder has been effective in disseminating this view in the mainstream media. See Richard Vedder and Matthew Denhart, "Why Does College Cost So Much?," *CNN*, December 2, 2011, http://www .cnn.com/2011/12/02/opinion/vedder-college-costs/index.html; and Richard Vedder, "Reducing State Higher Ed Spending Is Not Foolhardy," *Forbes*, March 17, 2011, http://blogs.forbes.com/ccap/2011/03/17/reducing-state -higher-ed-spending-is-not-foolhardy/.

11. Bob Meister, "They Pledged Your Tuition: An Open Letter to UC Students," Council of UC Faculty Associations, October 11, 2009, http://www .cucfa.org/news/2009_oct11.php; Andrew McGettigan, *The Great University Gamble: Money, Markets, and the Future of Higher Education* (London: Pluto Press, 2013), 143.

12. Jeffrey J. Selingo, *College (Un)bound: The Future of Higher Education and What It Means for Students* (Boston: Houghton Mifflin, 2013), 58–61.

13. Republican Party, "Addressing Rising College Costs," *We Believe in America: 2012 Republican Platform,* accessed April 21, 2015, http://www.presidency.ucsb.edu/ws/index.php?pid=101961.

14. Scott Jaschik, "Trump's Campaign Co-Chair Describes Higher Education Policies Being Developed," *Inside Higher Ed,* May 13, 2016, https://www.insidehighered.com/news/2016/05/13/trumps-campaign-co-chair-describes-higher-education-policies-being-developed.

15. See, for example, Christopher Newfield, "Gov Gives UC Just About Nothing, Continuing the Gradual Termination of UC," *Remaking the University* (blog), January 6, 2012, http://utotherescue.blogspot.com/2012/01/gov-gives-uc-just-about-nothing.html.

16. For a description of perma-austerity's impacts on the University of California, see Christopher Newfield, "Confronting Our Permanent Public University Austerity," *Remaking the University* (blog), July 17, 2014, http://utotherescue.blogspot.co.uk/2014/07/confronting-our-permanent-public.html.

17. Christopher Newfield, Henning Bohn, and Calvin Moore, *Current Budget Trends and the Future of the University of California* (UC Academic Council, UC Committee for Planning and Budget, May 2006), chart 2d, 8, accessed April 21, 2015, http://www.universityofcalifornia.edu/senate/reports/AC.Futures.Report.0107.pdf.

18. SHEEO, *SHEF: FY 2014,* fig. 2.

19. Ibid., table 2.

20. Ibid.

21. Cheryl Lee et al., *State Government Tax Collections Summary Report: 2014* (Washington, DC: US Census Bureau, 2015), 1, accessed May 14, 2016, http://www2.census.gov/govs/statetax/G14-STC-Final.pdf.

22. Alan Scher Zagier, "For-Profit Colleges Respond to Increased Scrutiny," Associated Press, August 6, 2011, http://www.deseretnews.com/article/700169000/For-profit-colleges-respond-to-increased-scrutiny.html?pg=all.

23. Christopher Newfield, "Messing with the Wonkblog College Story," *Remaking the University* (blog), September 11, 2013, http://utotherescue.blogspot.co.uk/2013/09/messing-with-wonkblog-college-story.html.

24. The opening piece was Dylan Matthews, "Introducing 'The Tuition Is Too Damn High,'" *Washington Post,* August 26, 2013, http://www.washingtonpost.com/blogs/wonkblog/wp/2013/08/26/introducing-the-tuition-is-too-damn-high/.

25. My discussion is based on Newfield, "Messing with the Wonkblog College Story."

26. American Association of University Professors, *Losing Focus* (March 2014), http://www.aaup.org/sites/default/files/files/2014%20 salary%20report/Figure%201.pdf.

27. Howard R. Bowen, *The Costs of Higher Education: How Much Do Colleges and Universities Spend Per Student and How Much Should They Spend?* (San Francisco: Jossey-Bass, 1980), 19.

28. Dylan Matthews, "The Tuition Is Too Damn High, Part III—The Three Reasons Tuition Is Rising," *Washington Post*, August 28, 2013, http:// www.washingtonpost.com/blogs/wonkblog/wp/2013/08/28/the-tuition-is -too-damn-high-part-iii-the-three-reasons-tuition-is-rising/.

29. This is the title of arguably the strongest recent effort by education economists to answer this question: Robert B. Archibald and David Henry Feldman, *Why Does College Cost So Much?* (New York: Oxford University Press, 2011).

30. "Public choice theory" helped conceptualize the failings of public sector incentives and motives, which included seeing public officials as "self-interested utility maximizers" like any private sector economic agent. Although its theoretical foundations are traced to works such as James M. Buchanan and Gordon Tullock, *The Calculus of Consent: Logical Foundations of a Constitutional Democracy* (Ann Arbor: University of Michigan Press, 1962), its premise was most famously articulated by Ronald Reagan: "Government is not the solution to our problem [government is the problem]" ("Address by Ronald Reagan, 1981," accessed May 14, 2016, http://www.inaugural.senate.gov/swearing-in/address/address-by-ronald -reagan-1981).

31. For a good overview of this understanding of privatization that reflects its pertinence to 1980s economic policy in the United States and the United Kingdom, see Paul Starr, "The Meaning of Privatization," *Yale Law and Policy Review* 6 (1988): 6–41, http://www.princeton.edu/~starr/articles/articles80 -89/Starr-MeaningPrivatization-88.htm.

32. Text available at http://www.railwaysarchive.co.uk/documents/HMG _Act001.pdf, accessed July 21, 2014. UK privatization has become increasingly contested, often on grounds that it failed to improve efficiency and reduce prices. For coverage of a possible Labour Party call for the "end of Tory privatization," see Toby Helm, "Labour Reaches New Deal for Overhaul of 'Failed' Railways," *The Guardian*, July 19, 2014, http://www .theguardian.com/uk-news/2014/jul/20/labour-party-overhaul-failed -railways.

33. Andrew McGettigan and Aditya Chakrabortty, "Student Loans Sell-Off Abandonment Raises Tension in Cabinet," *The Guardian*, July 20, 2014, http://www.theguardian.com/money/2014/jul/20/vince-cable-cabinet -tensions-scrap-student-loan-sell-off. More details are available in Andrew McGettigan, "Project Hero Deserves a Zero: Comment on Our Student Loans Interest Increase Story," *False Economy* (blog), June 14, 2013, http:// falseeconomy.org.uk/blog/project-hero-deserves-a-zero-comment-on-our -student-loans-interest-increase. One subsidy would take the form of a government-funded "synthetic hedge" to indemnify investors from low interest rates. The report makes it clear that many investors don't want to buy student loans if the interest rate continues to be capped at "the lower of the Retail Price Index . . . or 1 per cent above the highest base rate of a nominated group of banks. [Under this plan], the government would agree to compensate investors for the difference between the cash flow actually received from the student loans, and the estimated cash flow that would have been received without the Base Rate cap."

34. As I was completing this book, the University of Warwick in England announced that it had created a kind of Manpower Inc. to supply itself and other universities with temporary instructors—perhaps to recapture some of the revenues lost in its own instructional outsourcing. See Craig McVegas, "Coming to a University Near You: Casualisation through Internal Outsourcing," *openDemocracy UK*, April 9, 2015, https://www.opendemocracy.net /ourkingdom/craig-mcvegas/coming-to-university-near-you-casualisation -through-internal-outsourcing.

35. Kerr, *Uses of the University*.

36. Anne Case and Angus Deaton, "Rising Morbidity and Mortality in Midlife among White Non-Hispanic Americans in the 21st Century," *Proceedings of the National Academy of Sciences* 112, no. 49 (December 8, 2015): 15078–83, doi:10.1073/pnas.1518393112.

37. Walter W. McMahon, *Higher Learning, Greater Good: The Private and Social Benefits of Higher Education* (Baltimore, MD: Johns Hopkins University Press, 2009), chaps. 4–5.

38. Wendy Brown, *Undoing the Demos: Neoliberalism's Stealth Revolution* (New York: Zone Books, 2015), 36. See also Michel Feher, "Self-Appreciation: Or, The Aspirations of Human Capital," *Public Culture* 21, no. 1 (2009): 21–41.

39. Here and elsewhere I will use the term *leverage* to mean the use of other people's resources to multiply one's own returns. In general, the profit from an investment is equal to the size of the asset multiplied by the asset's return. Investors often borrow large parts of the asset they are investing, thereby increasing their lending. Private sponsors who use university personnel or facilities to conduct research for the ten cents on the dollar they would have

spent in house (an informal estimate I often heard from technology transfer officials), have effectively borrowed nine units for the one they have spent. This multiplies the effective return on their investment, which has thus been leveraged.

40. Suzanne Mettler, *The Submerged State: How Invisible Government Policies Undermine American Democracy* (Chicago: University of Chicago Press, 2011).

41. John Smyth, *Academic Work: The Changing Labour Process in Higher Education* (Buckingham: Open University Press, 1995); Neil Tudiver, *Universities for Sale: Resisting Corporate Control over Canadian Higher Education* (Toronto: James Lorimer Publishers, 1995); James Turk, ed., *The Corporate Campus: Commercialization and the Dangers to Canada's Colleges and Universities* (Toronto: James Lorimer & Company, 2000); Simon Marginson and Mark Considine, *The Enterprise University: Power, Governance and Reinvention in Australia* (Cambridge: Cambridge University Press, 2000).

The tradition that focuses on business influence over the research university's technology transfer is encapsulated in a book by one of its founders, Henry Etzkowitz, *The Triple Helix: University-Industry-Government Innovation in Action* (New York: Routledge, 2008). See also Henry Etzkowitz and Loet Leydesdorff, eds., *Universities and the Global Knowledge Economy* (New York: Continuum, 2002).

42. Sheila Slaughter and Larry L. Leslie, *Academic Capitalism: Politics, Policies, and the Entrepreneurial University* (Baltimore, MD: Johns Hopkins University Press, 1997).

43. Core texts include Robert Rhoads and Carlos Torres, eds., *The University, State, and Market: The Political Economy of Globalization in the Americas* (Stanford, CA: Stanford University Press, 2005); Sheila Slaughter and Gary Rhoades, *Academic Capitalism and the New Economy: Markets, State, and Higher Education* (Baltimore, MD: Johns Hopkins University Press, 2009); Stephen J. Ball, *Global Education Inc.: New Policy Networks and the Neoliberal Imaginary* (New York: Routledge, 2012); Brian Pusser, Ken Kempner, Simon Marginson, and Imanol Ordorika, eds., *Universities and the Public Sphere: Knowledge Creation and State Building in the Era of Globalization* (New York: Routledge, 2013); Brendan Cantwell and Ilkka Kauppinen, eds., *Academic Capitalism in the Age of Globalization* (Baltimore, MD: Johns Hopkins University Press, 2014).

44. Study of the university ecosystem is clearly articulated by the European Union research project Universities in the Knowledge Economy (UNIKE) with which I have been involved (http://unike.au.dk/).

45. *Ambivalent*: Archibald and Feldman, *Why Does College Cost So Much?*; *Enthusiastic*: Andrew Policano and Gary Fethke, *Public No More: A New Path*

to Excellence for America's Public Universities (Stanford, CA: Stanford Business Books, 2013). For a good overview of the Policano and Fethke argument for a necessary privatization, see Ronald G. Ehrenberg, "What's the Future of Public Higher Education? A Review Essay on Gary C. Fethke and Andrew J. Policano's Public No More: A New Path to Excellence for America's Public Universities," *Journal of Economic Literature* 52, no. 4 (2014): 1142–50.

46. Jacob S. Hacker and Paul Pierson, *Winner-Take-All Politics: How Washington Made the Rich Richer—and Turned Its Back on the Middle Class* (New York: Simon & Schuster, 2011); Larry M. Bartels, "Economic Inequality and Political Representation" (working paper, Department of Politics and Woodrow Wilson School of Public and International Affairs, Princeton University, August 2005), http://www.princeton.edu/~bartels/economic .pdf; Larry M. Bartels, *Unequal Democracy: The Political Economy of the New Gilded Age* (Princeton, NJ: Princeton University Press, 2010); Carina Engelhardt and Andreas Wagener, *Biased Perceptions of Income Inequality and Redistribution* (CESifo Working Paper Series No. 4838, June 12, 2014), http://papers.ssrn.com/abstract=2463129.

The Devolutionary Cycle

1. Privatization often operates as what the literary theorist Fredric Jameson once called the "*ideology of form*, that is, the symbolic messages transmitted to us by the coexistence of various sign systems which are themselves traces or anticipations of modes of production." Fredric Jameson, *The Political Unconscious: Narrative as a Socially Symbolic Act* (Ithaca, NY: Cornell University Press, 1981), 56.

2. Since this chapter offers a summary of the overall devolutionary cycle, I have kept supporting notes to a minimum.

3. Claudia Goldin and Lawrence F. Katz, *The Race between Education and Technology* (Cambridge, MA: Belknap Press of Harvard University Press, 2008).

4. David L. Kirp, "Teaching Is Not a Business," *New York Times*, August 16, 2014, http://www.nytimes.com/2014/08/17/opinion/sunday/teaching-is-not -a-business.html.

5. Walter W. McMahon, *Higher Learning, Greater Good: The Private and Social Benefits of Higher Education* (Baltimore, MD: Johns Hopkins University Press, 2009).

6. See, for example, Eugenie Samuel Reich, "Thrift in Store for US Research," *Nature News* 476, no. 7361 (August 23, 2011): 385, doi:10.1038/476385a. For an overview of the issue, see Christopher Newfield, "How Can Public Research Universities Pay for Research?," *Remaking the University* (blog), August 5,

2014, http://utotherescue.blogspot.co.uk/2014/08/how-can-public-research
-universities.html.

7. National Science Board, *Science and Engineering Indicators 2012*, fig. 4-18, "Academic R&D financed by business, for selected countries, 1981–2009," accessed April 20, 2015, http://nsf.gov/statistics/seind12/figures.htm#c5.

8. I discuss this relationship in detail in Christopher Newfield, *Ivy and Industry: Business and the Making of the American University, 1880–1980* (Durham, NC: Duke University Press, 2003). For a detailed analysis of post–World War II university-industry relations, see Elizabeth Popp Berman, *Creating the Market University: How Academic Science Became an Economic Engine* (Princeton, NJ: Princeton University Press, 2012).

9. Martin Kich, "A Real Numbers-Cruncher Weighs in on the Campos Article," *The Academe Blog*, April 7, 2015, http://academeblog.org/2015/04/07/a-real-numbers-cruncher-weighs-in-on-the-campos-article/.

10. National Science Foundation, *Higher Education Research and Development Survey: Fiscal Year 2013*, table 18, "Higher education R&D expenditures, ranked by all R&D expenditures, by source of funds: FY 2013," accessed April 12, 2015, http://ncsesdata.nsf.gov/herd/2013/html/HERD2013_DST_18.html.

11. Reich, "Thrift in Store for US Research."

12. Nathan Brostrom, "Soaring College Tuition: What Is to Blame?," *New York Times*, April 10, 2015, http://www.nytimes.com/2015/04/10/opinion/soaring-tuition-what-is-to-blame.html.

13. Nanette Asimov, "UC: Millions Lost in Research Costs from Grants," *San Francisco Chronicle*, June 16, 2010, http://www.sfgate.com/education/article/UC-Millions-lost-in-research-costs-from-grants-3185121.php.

14. John W. Curtis and Saranna Thornton, "Losing Focus: The Annual Report on the Economic Status of the Profession, 2013–14," *Academe* (March–April 2014): 4–38.

15. Tuition increase figures are from "Tuition and Fees and Room and Board over Time, 1975–76 to 2015–16, Selected Years," *Trends in Higher Education*, College Board, 2016, accessed May 12, 2016, http://trends.collegeboard.org/college-pricing/figures-tables/tuition-and-fees-and-room-and-board-over-time-1975-76-2015-16-selected-years.

For state funding for the 1980s and 1990s, see SHEEO, *State Higher Education Finance, FY 2005*, fig. 2, accessed April 21, 2015, http://archive.sheeo.org/finance/shef_fy05_full.pdf. A recent attempt to identify the causal relation between public cuts and tuition hikes found a correlation between the two after 2008 but not before, by which time, I argue, the public university's ability to raise tuition was well established. Rajashri Chakrabarti, Maricar

Mabutas, and Basit Zafar, "Soaring Tuitions: Are Public Funding Cuts to Blame?," accessed October 11, 2012, http://libertystreeteconomics .newyorkfed.org/2012/09/soaring-tuitions-are-public-funding-cuts-to-blame .html#.UFnZJAauLvQ.twitter.

16. Christopher Newfield, *Unmaking the Public University: The Forty-Year Assault on the Middle Class* (Cambridge, MA: Harvard University Press, 2008), 266.

17. Center on Budget and Policy Priorities, "State-by-State Fact Sheets: Higher Education Cuts Jeopardize Students' and States' Economic Future," March 5, 2015, http://www.cbpp.org/cms/index.cfm?fa=view&id=5278. These figures are corrected for inflation (in constant 2013 dollars), but not for enrollments.

18. Daniel Indiviglio, "Obama's Student-Loan Order Saves the Average Grad Less Than $10 a Month," *Atlantic*, October 26, 2011, http://www .theatlantic.com/business/archive/2011/10/obamas-student-loan-order-saves -the-average-grad-less-than-10-a-month/247411/.

19. Charlie Eaton, Jacob Habinek, Adam Goldstein, Cyrus Dioun, Daniela García Santibáñez Godoy, and Robert Osley-Thomas, "The Financialization of US Higher Education," *Socio-Economic Review*, February 8, 2016, doi:10.1093 /ser/mwv030.

Stage 1. The University Retreat from Public Goods

1. For example, the Middle Income Student Assistance Act of 1978 began to move federal student aid from grants to loans, and academic leaders largely acquiesced. See F. King Alexander, "Student Tuition and the Higher Education Marketplace: Policy Implications for Public Universities," *Journal of Staff, Program, and Organization Development* 17, no. 2 (Summer 2000): 79–93.

2. "Higher Education Compact: Agreement between Governor Schwar-zenegger, the University of California, and the California State University 2005–2006 through 2010–2011," accessed April 22, 2015, http://people.ucsc .edu/~bmalone/Data_files/compact.pdf.

3. Ibid., 2.

4. Christopher Newfield, Henning Bohn, and Calvin Moore, *Current Budget Trends and the Future of the University of California* (UC Academic Council, UC Committee for Planning and Budget, 2006), 11, accessed April 22, 2015, http://senate.universityofcalifornia.edu/reports/AC.Futures .Report.0107.pdf.

5. Ibid.

6. Paul Pierson and Jacob S. Hacker, *Winner-Take-All Politics: How Washington Made the Rich Richer—and Turned Its Back on the Middle Class* (New York: Simon & Schuster, 2010), 187. The failure of policy decisions to

reflect actual public opinion is detailed in Larry M. Bartels, *Unequal Democracy: The Political Economy of the New Gilded Age* (New York and Princeton, NJ: Princeton University Press, 2010).

7. Pierson and Hacker, *Winner-Take-All Politics,* 208.

8. Ibid., 214–15.

9. Ibid., 224.

10. Ibid., 236. On the reasons why the Democratic Party failed to realign itself away from business influence, see Paul Heideman, "It's Their Party," *Jacobin* (Winter 2016): 23–39. On the Democratic Party failure to retain populist themes after Watergate, see Kevin P. Phillips, *Post Conservative America: People, Politics, and Ideology in a Time of Crisis* (New York: Random House, 1982), chaps. 3, 9. Academia allowed itself to be positioned with the elites in these political narratives.

11. Andrew Leonard, "America's Worst Colleges," *Salon,* June 5, 2012, http://www.salon.com/2012/06/05/americas_worst_educators/singleton. The most thorough examination of the sector is Suzanne Mettler, *Degrees of Inequality: How the Politics of Higher Education Sabotaged the American Dream* (New York: Basic Books, 2014).

12. Kevin Carey, "Let's Put 'Gainful Employment' Ruling in Perspective," *Brainstorm* (blog), *Chronicle of Higher Education,* July 2, 2012, http://chronicle .com/blogs/brainstorm/lets-put-gainful-employment-ruling-in-perspective /49203?cid=at&utm_source=at&utm_medium=en.

13. Mary Nguyen, "Degreeless in Debt: What Happens to Borrowers Who Drop Out," Education Sector, February 2012, http://educationpolicy.air.org /sites/default/files/publications/DegreelessDebt_CYCT_RELEASE.pdf.

14. See, for example, Bill Alpert, "Clever Is as Clever Does," *Barron's,* April 14, 2012, http://online.barrons.com/article/SB50001424053111904857404577333971078578982.html.

15. The Institute for College Access & Success, *Student Debt and the Class of 2014* (October 2015), http://ticas.org/sites/default/files/pub_files /classof2014.pdf. For a breakdown of different types of federal student aid that go to for-profits, see College Board, *Trends in Student Aid 2011,* fig. 7, accessed January 29, 2012, http://trends.collegeboard.org/student_aid.

16. Alan Scher Zagier, "For-Profit Colleges Respond to Increased Scrutiny," Associated Press, August 6, 2011, http://www.deseretnews.com/article /700169000/For-profit-colleges-respond-to-increased-scrutiny.html?pg=all.

17. Chris Kirkham, "For-Profit Colleges Spend Much Less on Educating Students Than Public Universities," *Huffington Post,* May 25, 2011, http://www .huffingtonpost.com/2011/05/26/for-profit-colleges-spend_n_867175.html; US Senate Health, Education, Labor and Pensions Committee, "Executive Summary," *For Profit Higher Education: The Failure to Safeguard the Federal*

Investment and Ensure Student Success, Staff Report, July 30, 2012, http://www
.help.senate.gov/imo/media/for_profit_report/ExecutiveSummary.pdf.

18. Suevon Lee, "The For-Profit Higher Education Industry, By the
Numbers," *ProPublica*, August 9, 2012, http://www.propublica.org/article
/the-for-profit-higher-education-industry-by-the-numbers.

19. Goldie Blumenstyk, "Key Congressman Begins Inquiry into Executive
Pay at For-Profit Colleges," *Chronicle of Higher Education*, December 12, 2011,
http://chronicle.com/article/Key-Congressman-Begins-Inquiry/130090/
?sid=pm&utm_source=pm&utm_medium=en.

20. Zagier, "For-Profit Colleges Respond."

21. US Senate Health, Education, Labor and Pensions Committee,
"Executive Summary," *For Profit Higher Education: The Failure to Safeguard
the Federal Investment and Ensure Student Success*, Staff Report, July 30, 2012,
http://www.help.senate.gov/imo/media/for_profit_report/Executive
Summary.pdf.

22. Jennifer Gonzalez, "Community-College Chiefs Are Underpaid
Relative to Their 4-Year Peers," *Chronicle of Higher Education*, January 3, 2010,
http://chronicle.com/article/article-content/63382/.

23. For school-by-school percentages, see US Department of Education,
"Proprietary School 90/10 Revenue Percentages," *Federal Student Aid*,
accessed July 11, 2012, http://federalstudentaid.ed.gov/datacenter/proprietary
.html.

24. Goldie Blumenstyk, "For-Profit Colleges Show Increasing Dependence on Federal Student Aid," *Chronicle of Higher Education*, February 15,
2011, http://chronicle.com/article/For-Profit-Colleges-Show/126394/?sid=at
&utm_source=at&utm_medium=en.

25. Jonathan R. Laing, "What a Drag!," *Barron's*, April 16, 2012, http://
online.barrons.com/article/SB50001424053111904857404577333842637459600
.html.

26. "Cracking down on For-Profit Colleges," *The Week*, September 16, 2011,
http://theweek.com/articles/481805/cracking-down-forprofit-colleges.

27. Paul Fain, "Corinthian's Cloudy Future," *Inside Higher Ed*, June 20, 2014,
http://www.insidehighered.com/news/2014/06/20/major-profit-chain-faces
-bankruptcy-feds-turn-heat#sthash.QoroKEem.dpbs; Goldie Blumenstyk,
"For-Profit Colleges Still Cash In on Post-9/11 GI Bill, Harkin Report Says,"
Chronicle of Higher Education, July 30, 2014, http://chronicle.com/article/For
-Profit-Colleges-Still-Cash/147977/?cid=at&utm_source=at&utm_medium
=en; Goldie Blumenstyk, "U. of Phoenix Looks to Shrink Itself with New
Admissions Requirements and Deep Cuts," *Chronicle of Higher Education*,
June 30, 2015, http://chronicle.com/article/U-of-Phoenix-Looks-to-Shrink

/231247/?cid=at&utm_source=at&utm_medium=en; Patricia Cohen and Chad Bray, "University of Phoenix Owner, Apollo Education Group, Will Be Taken Private," *New York Times*, February 8, 2016, http://www.nytimes.com /2016/02/09/business/dealbook/apollo-education-group-university-of -phoenix-owner-to-be-taken-private.html; Andy Thomason, "Federal Court Upholds Gainful-Employment Rule, Dealing For-Profit Group Another Loss," *Chronicle of Higher Education Blogs: The Ticker*, March 8, 2016, http:// chronicle.com/blogs/ticker/federal-court-upholds-gainful-employment-rule -dealing-for-profit-group-another-loss/109294.

28. See "Public Good," *Wikipedia,* https://en.wikipedia.org/wiki/Public _good.

29. Kenneth J. Arrow, "Economic Welfare and the Allocation of Resources for Invention," in *The Rate and Direction of Inventive Activity: Economic and Social Factors,* ed. Universities-National Bureau Committee for Economic Research and Committee on Economic Growth of the Social Science Research Council (Princeton, NJ: Princeton University Press, 1962), 609–24; Milton Friedman, "The Role of Government in Education," in *Economics and the Public Interest*, ed. Robert A. Solo (New Brunswick, NJ: Rutgers University Press, 1955).

30. Cited in Michael L. Whalen, *A Land-Grant University* (Ithaca, NY: Cornell University 2002), accessed July 31, 2014, http://web.archive.org/web /20080228163104/http://www.cornell.edu/landgrant/resources/Land_Grant _Univ_Whalen.pdf.

31. Claudia Goldin and Lawrence F. Katz, *The Race between Education and Technology* (Cambridge, MA: Belknap Press of Harvard University Press, 2008).

32. Ibid., 26.

33. Angel Gurría, "Fifty Years of Change in Education," *OECD Education at a Glance* (Paris: Organization for Economic Co-operation and Development, 2011), chart 3, accessed September 17, 2013, http://www.oecd.org/edu/skills -beyond-school/48642586.pdf.

34. Goldin and Katz, *Race between Education and Technology,* 41.

35. Ibid., 15.

36. Ibid., title of chapter 7, emphasis added.

37. Ibid., 134–35.

38. Christopher Newfield, *Ivy and Industry: Business and the Making of the American University, 1880–1980* (Durham, NC: Duke University Press, 2003), chaps. 3–5; Christopher Newfield, *Unmaking the Public University: The Forty-Year Assault on the Middle Class* (Cambridge, MA: Harvard University Press, 2008), Introduction, chaps. 1–2.

39. Walter W. McMahon, *Higher Learning, Greater Good: The Private and Social Benefits of Higher Education* (Baltimore, MD: Johns Hopkins University Press, 2009), 45.

40. Ibid., chap. 4.

41. Ibid., 49.

42. Margaret Thatcher, "Interview for *Woman's Own*," Margaret Thatcher Foundation, September 23, 1987, accessed April 24, 2015, http://www.margaretthatcher.org/document/106689.

43. McMahon, *Higher Learning*, 193.

44. Ibid.

45. McMahon discusses the dark matter metaphor on page 192.

46. Ibid., 195–201.

47. Ibid., 240.

48. Ibid., 244.

49. Ibid., 252.

50. Andrew Policano and Gary Fethke, *Public No More: A New Path to Excellence for America's Public Universities* (Stanford, CA: Stanford Business Books, 2013).

51. McMahon, *Higher Learning*, 65.

52. Ibid., 12–13.

53. Ibid., 44, 176.

54. Ibid., 326.

55. An example of the former was UC president Mark G. Yudof's response to California governor Arnold Schwarzenegger's midyear cuts in 2008–2009: " 'I am compelled to note that the proposed cuts to the university, while serious, do not appear to be disproportionate,' Mark G. Yudof, president of the University of California, wrote in a letter to its regents on Tuesday. 'Indeed, I believe the Governor and the Legislature have helped to protect the university's base budget from potentially even deeper cuts.' " Doug Lederman, "A Bad Budget That Could Have Been Worse," *Inside Higher Ed*, February 20, 2009, https://www.insidehighered.com/news/2009/02/20/california.

After the massive cuts later that year, Yudof did publicly state that the missing state money was "vital if UC is to avoid declining educational quality, access and research." He sometimes echoed his predecessor's claim that budget cuts can compromise "our ability to preserve this institution's world-class quality and continue making a major contribution to California's economy." Robert Dynes, cited in Christopher Newfield, "Same Flat Revenues, Same Flat Pitch: How to Do Better," *Remaking the University* (blog), June 6, 2010, http://utotherescue.blogspot.co.uk/2010/06/same-flat-revenues-same-flat-pitch-how.html.

56. Alvin Toffler, *Future Shock* (1970; repr., New York: Bantam, 1984); Michael J. Piore and Charles F. Sabel, *The Second Industrial Divide: Possibilities for Prosperity* (New York: Basic Books, 1984); David Harvey, *Condition of Postmodernity* (Oxford, UK: Blackwell Publishers, 1989); David M. Gordon, *FAT AND MEAN: The Corporate Squeeze of Working Americans and the Myth of Managerial "Downsizing"* (New York: Free Press, 1996); Giovanni Arrighi, *Adam Smith in Beijing: Lineages of the Twenty-First Century* (London: Verso, 2007).

57. McMahon, *Higher Learning*, 63.

58. Margaret Heffernan, *Willful Blindness: Why We Ignore the Obvious at Our Peril* (New York: Walker & Company, 2011), 20–21.

Stage 2. Subsidizing the Outside Sponsors

1. For a list of CLA departments, see http://cla.umn.edu/departments/.

2. Figures are for 2012–2013, in that year's dollars. This is a 16 percent increase from 2008–2009 in constant dollars ("Minnesota Tuition and Fee Trends," Minnesota Office of Higher Education, accessed February 21, 2014, http://www.ohe.state.mn.us/dPg.cfm?pageID=812). Information about indirect costs for the university's STEM programs can be found at http://www.budget.umn.edu/other.htm, but, as is generally the case with research cost information, it is not public.

3. The institute has "decided to provide free domestic long distance rather than require that an index number be typed in for every 12 cent phone call so that it could be directly charged to a grant. Now there's another miracle—the director decided to use some internal funds to provide basic computer support to everyone free of charge"—not for purchases but for maintenance, and support at the "low rate of only $60 per hour" (correspondence in author's files).

4. Katherine Mangan, "Texas A&M System Will Rate Professors Based on Their Bottom-Line Value," *Chronicle of Higher Education*, September 2, 2010, https://chronicle.com/article/Texas-A-M-System-Will-Rate/124280/; Katherine Mangan, "Texas A&M's Bottom-Line Ratings of Professors Find That Most Are Cost-Effective," *Chronicle of Higher Education*, September 15, 2010, https://chronicle.com/article/Texas-A-Ms-Bottom-Line/124451/. The original Texas A&M report is not available online. The authors obtained the document though an open-records request.

5. Brent Gustafson, "CLA Budget 1001—Part 7: Grants & External Funding—College of Liberal Arts E-News," University of Minnesota, 2013, accessed October 26, 2013, http://blog.lib.umn.edu/cla/enews/2013/04/cla-budget-1001--part-7-grants-external-funding.html.

6. National Science Board, *Diminishing Funding and Rising Expectations: Trends and Challenges for Public Research Universities* (Arlington, VA: National Science Foundation, 2012), http://www.nsf.gov/nsb/publications/2012/nsb1245.pdf.

7. Ibid., 14.

8. Ibid., 16.

9. National Science Foundation (NSF), *Higher Education Research and Development (HERD) Survey: Fiscal Year 2011,* Detailed Statistical Tables, NSF 13-325 (July 2013), table 1, http://www.nsf.gov/statistics/nsf13325/pdf/tab1.pdf.

10. John P. Hutton, *University Research: Policies for the Reimbursement of Indirect Costs Need to Be Updated* (Washington, DC: US Government Accountability Office, September 8, 2010), accessed October 27, 2013, http://www.gao.gov/products/GAO-10-937.

11. One technical issue that may explain some of the variation is that indirect cost recovery is calculated as a share of modified total direct costs (MTDC), and the MTDC figure reflects the exclusion of a range of expenditures. One typical summary of exclusions is Dartmouth College's: "Modified total direct costs shall exclude equipment, capital expenditures, charges for patient care, tuition remission, rental costs of off-site facilities, scholarships, and fellowships as well as the portion of each subgrant and subaward in excess of $25,000," accessed August 22, 2015, http://www.dartmouth.edu/~osp/faq/modifiedtotal.html. But there are many other factors affecting the variability with which universities resort to institutional backfilling. For the document that governs these calculations, see Office of Management and Budget Circular A-21, accessed August 22, 2015, https://www.whitehouse.gov/omb/circulars_a021_2004/.

12. NSF, *HERD Survey,* FY 2013, table 18, Higher education R&D expenditures, ranked by all R&D expenditures, by source of funds: FY 2013, accessed April 12, 2015, http://ncsesdata.nsf.gov/herd/2013/html/HERD2013_DST_18.html.

13. Rhonda Britt, "Universities Report Continuing Decline in Federal R&D Funding in FY 2014," November 17, 2015, http://www.nsf.gov/statistics/2016/nsf16302/.

14. NSF, *HERD Survey,* FY 2011, table 14, http://www.nsf.gov/statistics/nsf13325/pdf/tab14.pdf; NSF, *HERD Survey,* FY 2013, table 18, https://ncsesdata.nsf.gov/herd/2013/html/HERD2013_DST_18.html.

15. Council on Governmental Relations (COGR), "Finances of Research Universities," June 2014, http://cogr.edu/COGR/files/ccLibraryFiles/Filename/000000000267/Finances%20of%20Research%20Universities_June%202014.pdf.

16. Financial Sustainability Strategy Group, "The Sustainability of Learning and Teaching in Higher education in England," March 2015, fig. 6, accessed May 5, 2015, http://www.hefce.ac.uk/media/HEFCE,2014/Content /Funding,and,finance/Financial,sustainability/Pubs/sustain_LT_HE _England_web.pdf.

17. Cynthia Lee, "UCLA Researchers Bring in Record $966 million in Contract and Grant Awards," *UCLA Today,* July 9, 2009, http://today.ucla.edu /portal/ut/ucla-researchers-break-record-95636.aspx.

18. Nanette Asimov, "UC: Millions Lost in Research Costs from Grants," *San Francisco Chronicle,* June 15, 2010, http://www.sfgate.com/education /article/UC-Millions-lost-in-research-costs-from-grants-3185121.php.

19. Ibid. These figures do not exactly reflect totals for any specific year in the UC Accountability Reports.

20. Mary Croughan and Henry Yang, et al., "Recommendations of the Research Strategies Working Group to the UC Commission on the Future," March 8, 2010, 111, accessed October 27, 2013, http://ucfuture .universityofcalifornia.edu/files/pdf/cotf_first_recs_research.pdf.

21. Eugenie Samuel Reich, "Thrift in Store for US Research," *Nature* 476 (August 25, 2011): 385.

22. *UC Annual Accountability Report 2014,* Indicator 10.1.1, accessed May 2, 2016, http://accountability.universityofcalifornia.edu/documents /accountabilityreport13.pdf. Direct research expenditures by source Universitywide 1997–1998 to 2012–2013. The data tables on which these statements are based have been removed from their original URL, accessed May 2, 2015, http://accountability.universityofcalifornia.edu/index.php?in=10 .1.1&source=uw. The figures for the spreadsheet available as of this writing are lower, ranging from 19.5 percent to 24.3 percent of total research expenditures coming from "University Funds." The trend is the same, toward higher institutional expenditures. The published Accountability Reports for 2014 and 2015 no longer use this graphic, which allows each funding source to be compared to another; figure 4 was provided to me directly by the UC Office of the President.

23. Following the removal of earlier data tables, I recalculated proportions of University Funds based on the spreadsheet available at University of California, Accountability Report 2015, chap. 9, accessed March 17, 2016, http://accountability.universityofcalifornia.edu/2015/chapters/chapter-9 .html#9.1.1. From FY 2010 through FY 2014, those percentages are 20.29, 19.48, 21.8, 22.64, and 24.33. The increase in the university's research support obligations is the same in both sets, around 19 percent. I cannot account for the discrepancy in each annual ratio between prior and current spreadsheets, but have retained both sets of calculations.

24. Personal correspondence, in author's files.

25. For an example of the calculation of the difference between UC's "benchmark" budget and its actual budget, see Stanton A. Glantz and Christopher Newfield, "Gov Brown Could Take an Important Step towards Fixing Higher Ed," *Remaking the University* (blog), February 11, 2013, http://utotherescue.blogspot.co.uk/2013/02/gov-brown-could-take-important-step.html. The methodology was developed in Christopher Newfield, Henning Bohn, and Calvin Moore, *Current Budget Trends and the Future of the University of California* (UC Academic Council, UC Committee for Planning and Budget, 2006), 11, accessed April 22, 2015, http://senate.universityofcalifornia.edu/reports/AC.Futures.Report.0107.pdf.

26. Thanks to Ruth Wilson Gilmore, who got me thinking about "externalization" as a key mechanism of privatization, or even a function that is prior to it.

27. Jane V. Wellman et al., *Trends in College Spending: Where Does the Money Come From? Where Does It Go? What Does It Buy?* (Delta Cost Project, 2009), 12, accessed December 14, 2013, http://www.deltacostproject.org/resources/pdf/Trends2011_Final_090711.pdf.

28. Our planning and budget group developed a "core fund model" for the University of California, and a version of it is now used in UC's official budget reports (Newfield, Bohn, and Moore, "Appendix A: Core UC Fund Model," *Current Budget Trends,* 37–39). This model was largely the creation of Calvin Moore: in this report, "core funds" are only about 26 percent of total revenue when the accountants exclude items like medical and other sales revenues, along with direct contracts and grants expenditures. The university now defines its version of core funds as "comprised of State General Funds ($2.64 billion), student tuition and fee revenue ($3.03 billion), and UC General Funds ($929 million). The latter category includes Nonresident Supplemental Tuition revenue, cost recovery funds from research contracts and grants, patent royalty income, and fees earned for management of Department of Energy laboratories." University of California, *Budget for Current Operations, 2014–15,* S-5, accessed May 3, 2015, http://regents.universityofcalifornia.edu/regmeet/nov13/f6attach.pdf.

29. "UC general funds include revenue from nonresident tuition, portions of the overhead on federal and state contracts and grants, Department of Energy lab management fees and overhead, a portion of the patent royalties earned on UC inventions, application and other fees and interest earnings." "How the Budget Works," *University of California Budget News,* accessed October 30, 2013, http://budget.universityofcalifornia.edu/?page_id=1120.

30. Might it in some cases be possible that some surplus revenues from non-educational activities like clinical practices are transferred to help support instruction and research? I have found no evidence of this in the records that I have reviewed. University officials generally deny that it's possible, given the restricted nature of most nontuition and nongeneral fund sources, and their own accounting does not include these funds as core revenues. This may be changing in auxiliary enterprises like student housing, but that would increase the student share of cost coverage rather than generating an independent revenue stream.

31. "The UC Budget: Myths and Facts," October 30, 2013, http://budget .universityofcalifornia.edu/files/2011/07/myths_facts071411.pdf.

32. NSF, *HERD Survey*, FY 2013, table 18, row 53, http://ncsesdata.nsf.gov /herd/2013/html/HERD2013_DST_18.html.

33. ASU's summary budget shows large auxiliary and other revenues without defining how they are spent: Arizona State University, "FY 2016 Annual Operating Budget Allocation by Fund," accessed May 4, 2015, http://www.asu.edu/pb/documents/AOB%20FY15.pdf.

34. I owe special thanks in this arena to Gene Lucas and Joel Michaelson at UC Santa Barbara, to Calvin Moore at UC Berkeley, and to Stanton Glantz at UC San Francisco.

35. For examples early in the financial crisis, see "Public Universities at Risk: 7 Damaging Myths," *Chronicle of Higher Education*, October 31, 2008, A128; "A Teachable Crisis" (the California Budget Crisis), *Chronicle of Higher Education*, September 29, 2009, A30; "Ending the Budget Wars: Funding the Humanities during a Crisis in Higher Education," *Profession 2009* (Modern Languages Association), 270–84; and "The End of the American Funding Model: What Comes Next?," *American Literature* 82, no. 3 (September 2010): 611–35; "La fin du modèle de financement américain : comment le remplacer?" *L'economie et societé* 40, no. 4 (2010): 603–35.

36. For example, see Ronald G. Ehrenberg, Michael J. Rizzo, and George H. Jakubson, "Who Bears the Growing Cost of Science at Universities?," NBER Working Paper no. 9627, April 2003, accessed April 17, 2015, http://www.nber.org/papers/w9627.pdf. Ehrenberg, Rizzo, and Jakubson polled department heads to quantify the high and rising cost of start-up packages in selected STEM fields and identified a robust correlation between increased research expenditures and above-average increases in tuition charges.

37. Wellman et al., *Trends in College Spending*.

38. I base this summary on my post "Notes on the UC Commission's First Meeting," September 9, 2009, *Remaking the University* (blog), accessed

November 1, 2013, http://utotherescue.blogspot.co.uk/2009/09/notes-on-uc
-commissions-first-meeting.html.

39. Dennis Jones and Jane Wellman, "Rethinking Conventional
Wisdom about Higher Ed Finance," Delta Cost Project, accessed November
1, 2013, http://www.deltacostproject.org/resources/pdf/advisory_10
_Myths.pdf.

40. Jack Kadden, "Questioning a College President about the High Cost of
College," *The Choice* (blog), *New York Times,* September 4, 2009, http://
thechoice.blogs.nytimes.com/2009/09/04/questioning-a-college-president
-about-the-high-cost-of-college/.

41. Spencer Michaels, "College Tuition Hike in California Sparks Protests,"
PBS NewsHour, 2009, accessed November 1, 2013, http://www.pbs.org
/newshour/bb/education/july-dec09/feehikes_11-20.html.

42. "The Ten Best College Presidents," *Time,* November 11, 2009, accessed
November 1, 2009, http://content.time.com/time/specials/packages/article
/0,28804,1937938_1937933_1937940,00.html.

43. Robert N. Watson, "The Humanities Really Do Produce a Profit,"
Chronicle of Higher Education, March 21, 2010, http://chronicle.com/article
/The-Humanities-Really-Do/64740/.

44. Mark Yudof, "U. of California's Problem Is Unreliable State Support,"
Chronicle of Higher Education, May 2, 2010, http://chronicle.com/article/U-of
-Californias-Problem-Is/65346/.

45. University Committees on Planning and Budget and Research Policy,
"Report of the 2009–10 Joint UCORP-UCPB Committees on Indirect Cost
Recovery," University of California Office of the President, April 2010,
accessed March 18, 2016, http://senate.universityofcalifornia.edu/reports
/HP_MGY_ICR.pdf.

46. National Research Council, *Research Universities,* 125.

47. "Colleges and Universities Rate Agreement," UC Davis, August 19,
2013, accessed November 2, 2013, http://research.ucdavis.edu/pgc/d/spo/f-a
-rate-agreement.

48. COGR, "Finances of Research Universities," 23.

49. Ibid., 19.

50. "Humanities Indicators, Indicator IV-10b: Academic Research and
Development Expenditures in the Humanities and Other Selected Fields,
Fiscal Years 2005–2014 (Adjusted for Inflation)," http://www.humanities
indicators.org/content/indicatordoc.aspx?i=386.

51. Overall federal totals are from National Science Foundation, *Higher
Education Research and Development Survey,* Fiscal Year 2014, table 1, "Higher
education R&D expenditures, by source of funds and R&D field: FYs
1953–2014," https://ncsesdata.nsf.gov/herd/2014/html/HERD2014_DST

_01.html; humanities totals are from "Humanities Indicators, Indicator IV-10a: Academic Research and Development Expenditures in the Humanities," accessed June 1, 2016, http://www.humanitiesindicators.org /cmsData/pdf/IV-10a.pdf. Some additional humanities research occurs away from universities. At the same time, one major funding source for this work, state humanities councils, gets nearly two-thirds of its funding from the National Endowment from the Humanities, which is now spending only 13 percent of its revenues on general humanities research ("Indicator IV-3c," http://www.humanitiesindicators.org/cmsData/pdf /IV-3c.pdf).

52. "Humanities Indicators, Indicator II-1aa: Bachelor's Degree Completions in the Humanities as a Percentage of All Bachelor's Degree Completions, 1948–2014," http://www.humanitiesindicators.org/content/indicatordoc.aspx ?i=197.

53. "Humanities Indicators, Indicator IV-10d: Sources of Funding for Academic Research and Development in the Humanities and Other Selected Fields, Fiscal Year 2014," http://www.humanitiesindicators.org/content /indicatordoc.aspx?i=388.

54. These reimbursements have been capped at 26 percent since 1991, though only for universities.

55. Figures for FY 2012 are available at NSF, *HERD Survey,* FY 2012, table 4, "Higher education R&D expenditures, ranked by all R&D expenditures, by source of funds: FY 2012," http://ncsesdata.nsf.gov/herd /2012/html/HERD2012_DST_04.html. Figures for FY 2013 are at table 18, "Higher education R&D expenditures, ranked by all R&D expenditures, by source of funds: FY 2013," accessed May 5, 2015, http://ncsesdata.nsf.gov /herd/2013/html/HERD2013_DST_18.html. After the drafting of this book was complete, the NSF released the results of its "Higher Education Research and Development Survey: Fiscal Year 2014," https:// ncsesdata.nsf.gov/herd/2014/. Also see Britt, "Universities Report Continuing Decline in Federal R&D Funding in FY 2014." The NSF's breakdown of uses of institutionally funded R&D expenditures is in figure 2.

56. COGR, "Finances of Research Universities," 18.

57. Ibid., 20, chart 13, referring to a "Private Research University, Southeast." This university spent $505 million on research but received $390 million in revenues, which required it to chip in $115 million of its own money, meaning that 23 percent of this university's total research costs came from institutional funds.

58. Corporate indirect cost recovery rates are apparently considered proprietary information and not disclosed. Technology transfer experts have

told me the assumed figure is 100 to 120 percent or more, or double the indirect cost recovery rate allowed for universities. The issue is discussed in "Issue 1: Comparison of F&A Rates Across Sectors," in Charles A. Goldman, Traci Williams, David M. Adamson, Kathy Rosenblatt, *Paying for University Research Facilities and Administration* (Santa Monica, CA: Rand Corporation, 2000), accessed May 9, 2015, http://www.rand.org/content/dam/rand/pubs /monograph_reports/MR1135-1/MR1135-1-chap3.pdf. Thanks to Gerald Barnett for this reference, who also wrote to me, "Although data are maintained on F&A rates for universities, no comparable government or private data exist for commercial enterprises. Corporate indirect cost rates are considered proprietary information that companies are sensitive about disclosing, because these rates have important effects on competitiveness. To our knowledge, government agencies do not maintain a centralized registry of corporate indirect cost rates" (private correspondence, May 5, 2015).

59. "Report of the Humanities Task Force, December 2009," author's files, Appendix B: Spreadsheet (Cost-Revenue Analysis), Summary table.

60. NSF, *HERD Survey,* FY 2013, table 24, "Higher education R&D expenditures funded by institutional funds, ranked by all R&D expenditures, by R&D field: FY 2013," accessed May 6, 2015, https://ncsesdata.nsf.gov/herd /2013/html/HERD2013_DST_24.html.

61. Examples of fields in "Psychology, Social Sciences, and Other Sciences Fields of R&D" are given in the sample HERD survey form, 15, accessed May 5, 2015, http://www.nsf.gov/statistics/srvyherd/surveys/srvyherd_2012.pdf. "Non-S&E Fields of R&D" are defined on page 16.

62. The range of non-S&E institutional expenditures at public universities is wide: the University of North Carolina at Chapel Hill spends 4.6 percent in this category. The figure at the University of Texas at Austin is 18.4 percent. Open discussion of research costs could shed light on these differences.

63. UCLA Council on Research Annual Reports, accessed May 5, 2015, http://www.senate.ucla.edu/committee/COR/CORreports.htm.

64. See the topics listed in Council on Research, "2013–14 Annual Report," Appendix 1, accessed May 6, 2015, http://www.senate.ucla.edu/committee /COR/documents/2013-14CORAnnualReport.pdf.

65. UC Office of the President, Campus Financial Schedules 2012– 2013, Los Angeles Current Funds Expenditures By Department, Schedule 4-C, 14-15, accessed May 6, 2015, http://www.ucop.edu/financial -accounting/financial-reports/campus-financial-schedules/12-13/la -combined.pdf.

66. My tabulation is as follows (from the schedules in note 65):

	Total	Unrestricted	Restricted
Arts & Architecture –	644	164	480
GEIS	12,444	1745	10,699
SEAS (engineering)	63,393	3371	60,022
Law	1,049	74	975
L&S	120,73	14,603	106,132
GSM (Anderson)	4,788	1,878	3,270
Public Affairs	3,826	515	3,311
Theater, Film, TV	585	92	493
Campus Research*	29,674	18,533	11,142
TOTALS	237,139	40,975	196,524

*minus Biomed & Neuropsychology

This list excludes the schools of Dentistry, Medicine, Nursing, Public Health

67. This is sometimes called "departmental research." Independent UC budget expert Charles L. Schwartz defines the two categories I am including as follows: "Unrestricted General Funds are State appropriations (State General Funds) plus UC General Funds (mostly Nonresident tuition and a major portion, 44 percent, of Federal ICR [Indirect Cost Recovery from extramural contracts and grants]). Unrestricted Designated Funds are monies collected by the Regents and not under state control—student tuition and fees and other revenues, especially big in the medical industries. Restricted Funds are mostly sponsored research and endowments and gifts" (Private correspondence with author, May 6, 2015). Note that I am not counting the share of faculty salaries that would be allotted to research as research funding.

68. In my attempt to validate my analysis here, I contacted UCLA budget analysts. One wrote back as follows:

I wish there were a way to break out the expenditure of institutional funds between overhead in the broad sense and departmental research. The financial system at UCLA (and I suspect this applies to all such systems across the UCs) does not distinguish these expenditures in separate pots (through different accounts or codes of any kind). For example, direct matching funds from the dean for a grant will be sent to the faculty's research account as will funds from the dean/chair to help the faculty directly with a research project. Both types of funds can be spent, for example, on a graduate student researcher, and there is no way to distinguish that graduate student A was covered by the matching funds and B by just regular department research funds. The dean/chair could have used general funds or ICR return funds to pay for both instances, and both instances are spent from the same faculty account.

I am aware throughout that much of the accounting evidence is indeterminate—and that these problems would have been corrected before, were administrators actively pursuing interdepartmental equity. My hope is that my argument here will encourage the accounting reforms that could provide more definitive answers.

69.

L & S breakout	Unrestricted	Restricted	72% of R	Surplus
Anthro	166	146		60.8k
Art History	155	50	36	119k
As Am	34	0	0	34k
C Jewish St	208	496	357	—
C MedivRenn	615	333	239.8	375k
C 17th/18th	498	64	46	452k
C Women	491	134	96.5	394.5k
Classics	59	361	260	—
Comp Lit	27	0	0	27
East Asian Lang	158	78	56.2	102k
Econ	49	186	134	—
English	209	154	111	98k
French	184	0	0	184
Germanic	7	95	68.4	—
History	245	79	57	188k
Inst SS	1489	6244	4496	—
I Archeol	456	877	631	—
I IndustRel	1812	112	80.6	1731
I Env Sust	338	3232	2327	—
Interdept	174	17	12.2	162k
Italian	4	0	0	4
Ling	83	40	28.8	54.2
Musicology	43	0	0	43
Near East	92	517	327	—
Phil	40	62	44.6	—
Poly Sci	94	136	67.7	26.3
Scand	10	0	0	10
Slavic	48	0	0	48
Sociology	97	69	49.7	47.3
SpanPort	33	5	3.6	29.4
Speech	12	0	0	12
TESL	14	0	0	14
Total				4,215k

Adding back in

Arts & Arch	164	480	345.6	—
GSEIS	1745	10699		—
Law	74	975		—

L & S breakout	Unrestricted	Restricted	72% of R	Surplus
GSM	1518	3270		—
Public service	515	3311	—	—
Film	92	493		—
Grand T SASH =				$4,215,000

"Surplus" of unrestricted over restricted minus full indirect cost recovery, the result defined as "internal research funding." True overhead costs for SASH research are much lower than 72 percent, but I am maintaining the convention for the sake of consistency. L & S = Letters and Sciences; C = Center; I = Institute; GSM = Graduate School of Management.

70. Survey data from American Society for Biochemistry and Molecular Biology, *Unlimited Potential, Vanishing Opportunity: Nondefense Discretionary Science 2013 Survey* (2013), question 10, accessed November 2, 2013, http://www.asbmb.org/uploadedFiles/Advocacy/Events/UPVO%20Survey%20Data.pdf.

71. Battelle, *2012 Global R&D Funding Forecast* (December 2011), 8, accessed November 2, 2013, http://battelle.org/docs/default-document-library/2012_global_forecast.pdf.

72. Battelle, *2013 Global R&D Funding Forecast* (December 2012), 6, accessed November 2, 2013, http://www.rdmag.com/sites/rdmag.com/files/GFF2013Final2013_reduced.pdf.

73. COGR, "Finances of Research Universities," chart 12: Research & Development (R&D) Expenditures by Funding Source as a Percentage of All R&D Expenditures.

74. National Science Foundation, *Survey of Federal Funds for Research and Development, Fiscal Years 2014–16,* table 2, "Summary of federal obligations and outlays for research, development, and R&D plant, by type of R&D, performer, and field of science and engineering: FYs 2013–16," accessed June 1, 2016, https://ncsesdata.nsf.gov/fedfunds/2014/html/FFS2014_DST_002.html.

75. NSF, *HERD Survey,* FY 2013, table 18.

76. University Committees on Planning and Budget and Research Policy, "Report of the 2009–2010 Joint UCORP-UCPB Committees on Indirect Cost Recovery," 6.

77. William Lazonick, *Sustainable Prosperity in the New Economy: Business Organization and High-Tech Employment in the United States* (Kalamazoo, MI: W. E. Upjohn Institute, 2009).

78. Charles Duhigg and David Kocieniewski, "How Apple Sidesteps Billions in Taxes," *New York Times,* April 28, 2012, accessed June 8, 2012, http://www.nytimes.com/2012/04/29/business/apples-tax-strategy-aims-at-low-tax-states-and-nations.html.

79. Eric Walker and Jayne Standley, "Koch Foundation Memorandum of Understanding, Ad Hoc Committee Review Report" (original draft), Florida State University (2011), accessed May 12, 2015, https://ia600509.us.archive.org /24/items/2015FSUKoch/FSSC%20Report%20Standley.pdf.

80. Ralph Wilson, *A Student Review of FSU Gift Acceptance Policy: Undue Influence and Charles Koch Foundation*, May 2015, FSU Progress Commission and Unkoch My Campus, accessed May 12, 2015, http://static1.squarespace .com/static/5400da69e4b0cb1fd47c9077/t/5565ddb6e4b0c699861fc0c6 /1432739254835/UnKochGiftReportMay2015.pdf.

81. General press coverage with key examples includes G. Jeffrey MacDonald, "Donors: Too Much Say on Campus Speech?," *Christian Science Monitor*, February 10, 2005, http://www.csmonitor.com/2005/0210/p11s01-legn.html; Seth Lubove and Oliver Staley, "College Gifts Now Coming with Strings Attached," *Washington Post*, May 8, 2011, https://www.washingtonpost.com/business /college-gifts-now-coming-with-strings-attached/2011/05/08/AF9TEf3G _story.html; Elizabeth Redden, "Return to Sender," *Inside Higher Ed*, February 22, 2016, https://www.insidehighered.com/news/2016/02/22/uc -irvine-moves-reject-endowed-chair-gifts-donor-strong-opinions-about -study; Dave Levinthal, "Universities Getting Koch Cash for Libertarian Economics," *Aljazeera*, October 30, 2016, http://america.aljazeera.com /articles/2015/10/30/koch-foundations-invest-in-higher-education-indepth .html.

82. For a mainstream press overview, see William J. Broad, "Billionaires with Big Ideas Are Privatizing American Science," *New York Times*, March 15, 2014, http://www.nytimes.com/2014/03/16/science/billionaires-with-big -ideas-are-privatizing-american-science.html.

83. I cite the original title (2008), which in 2009 was modified: Matthew Bishop, Michael Green, and President Bill Clinton, *Philanthrocapitalism: How Giving Can Save the World* (repr., New York: Bloomsbury Press, 2009).

84. Cassie Hall and Scott L. Thomas, "'Advocacy Philanthropy' and the Public Policy Agenda: The Role of Modern Foundations in American Higher Education" (paper prepared for the Ninety-third Annual Meeting of the American Educational Research Association, Vancouver, Canada, April 2012), 12.

85. Ibid., 17.

86. Robin Rogers, "The Price of Philanthropy," *Chronicle of Higher Education*, July 14, 2013, http://chronicle.com/article/The-Price-of -Philanthropy/140295/.

87. Newfield, Bohn, and Moore, *Current Budget Trends*, 22–23.

88. See, for example, Newfield, "The Old State Funding Model Is Dead: What Will Replace It?," *Remaking the University* (blog), November 14, 2013,

http://utotherescue.blogspot.com/2013/11/the-old-state-funding-model-is
-dead.html.

89. Merrit Kennedy, "Nike Co-Founder Donates $400 Million to Stanford
University," *NPR.org*, February 24, 2016, http://www.npr.org/sections
/thetwo-way/2016/02/24/467937476/nike-co-founder-donates-400-million
-to-stanford-university. This account is based on Newfield, "The New Normal
Isn't Normal—It Erodes Democracy," *Remaking the University* (blog),
February 26, 2016, http://utotherescue.blogspot.com/2016/02/the-new
-normal-isnt-normal-it-erodes.html.

90. "U.S. and Canadian Institutions Listed by Fiscal Year (FY) 2014
Endowment Market Value and Change in Endowment Market Value from
FY2013 to FY2014," National Association of College and University Business
Officers, February 2015, http://www.nacubo.org/Documents
/EndowmentFiles/2014_Endowment_Market_Values_Revised.pdf.

91. Michael Gioia, "Stanford Launching Knight-Hennessy Scholarship
to Attract Top Graduates," *Stanford Daily*, February 24, 2016, http://www
.stanforddaily.com/2016/02/24/stanford-launching-knight-hennessy
-scholarship-to-attract-top-graduates/.

92. Donna M. Desrochers and Steven Hurlburt, *Trends in College Spending:
2003–2013* (Washington, DC: American Institutes for Research, 2016), fig. A2,
http://www.deltacostproject.org/sites/default/files/products/15-4626%20
Final01%20Delta%20Cost%20Project%20College%20Spending%2011131.406
.P0.02.001%20....pdf.

93. Michael Krasny, "Stanford Creates Largest Graduate Scholarship
Program with $400 Million Donation from Nike Co-Founder," *KQED Public
Media*, February 24, 2016, http://www.kqed.org/a/forum/R201602241000.

94. Calculations based on Allan Brettman, "Phil and Penny Knight,
Thanks to Nike Fortune, Have given More than $1 Billion in Philanthropy,"
OregonLive.com, August 12, 2014, http://www.oregonlive.com/playbooks
-profits/index.ssf/2014/08/phil_and_penny_knight_thanks_t.html.

95. "Private Financial Gifts to Higher Education Colleges & Universities,"
Dilemma-X, October 1, 2013, http://dilemma-x.net/2013/10/01/private
-financial-gifts-to-higher-education-collegesuniversities/.

96. UCOP, *Accountability Report 2014,* "Indicator 12.2.1: Current Giving, by
Purpose," accessed June 1, 2016, http://accountability.universityofcalifornia
.edu/2014/documents/accountabilityreport14.pdf.

97. UCOP, *Accountability Report 2014,* 12.2 Development, "A campus's
ability to raise money is related to its age, number of alumni and presence of
health science programs, which attract nearly half of all private support at
UC," http://accountability.universityofcalifornia.edu/2015/chapters/chapter

-12.html#12.2.2. The national pattern is similar, in which half of large gifts go to medicine (Marts & Lundy, "$1m+ Gifts to Higher Education," February 2015, accessed June 1, 2016, http://www.martsandlundy.com/wp-content/uploads /2015/04/Big_Gifts_Higher_Ed_Feb2015.pdf. I have been unable to find general breakdowns of higher education giving by discipline or topic area.

98. The first is a report of a study by Gi-Yong Koo and Stephen W. Dittmore cited in Allie Grasgreen, "Athletic Giving Crowds out Academic Donations, Research Finds," *Inside Higher Ed*, April 27, 2012, https://www .insidehighered.com/news/2012/04/27/athletic-giving-crowds-out-academic -donations-research-finds. The second is a paper by the same two researchers: Koos and Dittmore, "Effects of Intercollegiate Athletics on Private Giving in Higher Education," *Journal of Issues in Intercollegiate Athletics* 7 (2014): 1–16, which finds spillover effects from athletic to academic giving.

99. See, for example, the *Chronicle of Philanthropy*'s, "Top Donors" tool, accessed May 6, 2015, https://philanthropy.com/factfile/gifts/1 ?DonorDisplayName_cu=&Category=Colleges+and+universities &GiftRecipients_RecipOrgDateline_c=&GiftRecipients_RecipStateFull =any&GiftDonors_SourceWealth_cu=&GiftDonors_aStateFull=any &GiftYear=any.

100. Referenced in Melissa Korn, "For U.S. Universities, the Rich Get Richer Faster," *Wall Street Journal*, April 16, 2015, http://www.wsj.com/articles /for-u-s-universities-the-rich-get-richer-faster-1429156904.

101. Charlie Eaton, Jacob Habinek, Adam Goldstein, Cyrus Dioun, Daniela García Santibáñez Godoy, and Robert Osley-Thomas, "The Financialization of US Higher Education," *Socio-Economic Review* (February 8, 2016), doi:10.1093/ser/mwv030: "The weighted mean endowment asset values per student at public systems between the 50th and 89th percentile was just $13.7 thousand in 2012, only $3.9 thousand higher than in 2003. In contrast, endowment asset values per student for the eight private institutions in the 99th percentile were $886 thousand in 2012, $178 thousand higher than 2003 levels. In 2012, these nine institutions controlled 27% of all endowment assets, but enrolled around 1% of FTE students attending public and private schools" (9).

102. On the gap between selective and open access colleges, see Anthony P. Carnevale and Jeff Strohl, *Separate and Unequal: How Higher Education Reinforces the Intergenerational Reproduction of White Racial Privilege,* Center on Education and the Workforce, Georgetown Public Policy Institute, July 31, 2013, part 2, http://cew.georgetown.edu/separateandunequal. I discuss this report in Stage 7.

103. UCLA Foundation, "Endowment and Finances," accessed May 6, 2015, https://www.uclafoundation.org/finances.aspx; California State University,

Fullerton, Philanthropic Foundation, "Endowments," accessed May 6, 2015, http://foundation.fullerton.edu/about/endowments.asp.

104. Ken Stern, "Why the Rich Don't Give to Charity," *The Atlantic*, April 2013, accessed May 5, 2015, http://www.theatlantic.com/magazine/archive /2013/04/why-the-rich-dont-give/309254/.

105. Abby Jackson, "Malcolm Gladwell Just Went Nuts on a Wall Street Billionaire's $400 Million Donation to Harvard," *Business Insider*, June 3, 2015, http://www.businessinsider.com/malcolm-gladwell-goes-nuts-on-john -paulsons-harvard-donation-2015-6.

106. Matt Rocheleau, "Lawmakers in Congress Query Colleges on Endowments," *BostonGlobe.com*, February 11, 2016, https://www.bostonglobe .com/metro/2016/02/11/lawmakers-ask-wealthy-colleges-for-details-their -billion-dollar-endowments/OsD8TXJ4eyUi4UBcIYiC6O/story.html.

107. Brettman, "Phil and Penny Knight."

108. "MEMORANDUM OF AGREEMENT made as of this 23rd day of November 2009 between The Peter and Melanie Munk Charitable Foundation (the 'Donor') and the Governing Council of the University of Toronto (the 'University')," http://individual.utoronto.ca/paul_hamel/Documents /Munk_MoA-Global_Affairs.pdf.

109. Larry Gordon, "UCLA gets $100-million Donation," *Los Angeles Times,* January 26, 2011, http://articles.latimes.com/2011/jan/26/local/la-me -ucla-gift-20110126.

110. UC Board of Regents, "Amendment of the Budget and Approval of External Financing and Standby Financing, Luskin Conference and Guest Center, Los Angeles Campus," March 28, 2012, 2, http://regents.university ofcalifornia.edu/regmeet/mar12/gb1.pdf.

111. See, for example, "Discussion of the 2014–15 Budget," UC Board of Regents, September 18, 2013, 5, accessed November 2, 2013, http://regents .universityofcalifornia.edu/regmeet/sept13/f5.pdf.

112. UC Board of Regents, "Authorization to Create a Separate $501(C)(3)$ Nonprofit Corporation to Oversee the Management of Intellectual Property and Industry-Sponsored Research Contracting, Los Angeles Campus," accessed November 2, 2103, http://regents.universityofcalifornia.edu/aar /mayf.pdf.

113. Christopher Newfield, *Unmaking the Public University: The Forty-Year Assault on the Middle Class* (Cambridge, MA: Harvard University Press, 2008), 343.

114. Darwin BondGraham, "Public Research for Private Gain," *East Bay Express*, 2013, accessed June 27, 2013, http://www.eastbayexpress.com/oakland /public-research-for-private-gain/Content?oid=3619535.

115. Walter W. McMahon, *Higher Learning, Greater Good: The Private and Social Benefits of Higher Education* (Baltimore, MD: Johns Hopkins University Press, 2009), 280.

116. For attacks on science under the George W. Bush administration, see Chris Mooney, *The Republican War on Science* (New York: Basic Books, 2006). Science has not been immune in the Obama proscience administration. The National Nanotechnology Initiative renewal was tabled by Senator Kay Bailey Hutchinson in 2010 and has never been renewed via comprehensive legislation. See John F. Sargent Jr., "The National Nanotechnology Initiative: Overview, Reauthorization, and Appropriations Issues," *Congressional Research Service*, December 16, 2014, Summary, https://www.fas.org/sgp/crs/misc/RL34401.pdf. In 2013, one senator managed to block all NSF appropriations for the discipline of political science except for work "promoting national security or the economic interests of the United States." See Scott Jaschik, "NSF Releases Guidelines for Complying with Law Barring Support for Political Science," *Inside Higher Ed*, June 10, 2013, accessed December 14, 2013, http://www.insidehighered.com/news/2013/06/10/nsf-releases-guidelines-complying-law-barring-support-political-science.

Stage 3. Large, Regular Tuition Hikes

1. An early use is Andrew Gillen, *A Tuition Bubble? Lessons from the Housing Bubble* (Washington, DC: Center for College Affordability and Productivity, April 2008), accessed November 23, 2013, http://files.eric.ed.gov/fulltext/ED536280.pdf.

2. Scott Bland, "Obama Aims to Lift College Graduation Rates, but His Tools Are Few," *Christian Science Monitor*, August 9, 2010, http://www.csmonitor.com/layout/set/r14/USA/Education/2010/0809/Obama-aims-to-lift-college-graduation-rates-but-his-tools-are-few.

3. For example, I appeared on Warren Olney's radio broadcast, "Student Loan Debt Surpasses Credit Card Debt," *To the Point*, KCRW, September 3, 2010, http://www.kcrw.com/news/programs/tp/tp100903student_loan_debt_su.

4. Barack Obama, "President Obama's Blueprint for Keeping College Affordable and within Reach for All Americans," White House press release, January 27, 2012, http://www.whitehouse.gov/the-press-office/2012/01/27/fact-sheet-president-obama-s-blueprint-keeping-college-affordable-and-wi.

5. National Center of Education Statistics, "Tuition Costs of Colleges and Universities," 2012–2013), *Fast Facts*, accessed June 11, 2015, http://nces.ed.gov/fastfacts/display.asp?id=76.

6. Larry Gordon, "UC Ready to Raise Student Fees by 32%," *Los Angeles Times*, November 19, 2009, http://articles.latimes.com/2009/nov/19/local

/me-ucfees19. For reporting that acknowledged the uneven pattern, see Mary Beth Marklein, "Public Colleges, Universities Grapple with Tuition Hikes," *USA Today*, May 25, 2010, accessed June 8, 2016, https://www.wvhepc.org /news/News_Clippings/2010/Weekly%20News%20Clippings%20(5-24-10) .pdf.

7. Alex Usher and John Medow, *Global Higher Education Rankings 2010: Affordability and Accessibility in Comparative Perspective* (Higher Education Strategy Associates, October 2010), table 5, accessed November 19, 2013, http://www.ireg-observatory.org/pdf/HESA_Global_Higher _EducationRankings2010.pdf.

8. While the comparative report listed US college tuition costs as $13,856 (with data from 2007–2008), the College Board calculated private college average tuition for the following year as $27,920. College Board, *Trends in College Pricing 2013*, fig. 11, accessed June 27, 2013, http://trends.collegeboard .org/college-pricing.

9. College Board, *Trends in College Pricing 2014*, 3, accessed March 4, 2016, https://secure-media.collegeboard.org/digitalServices/misc/trends/2014 -trends-college-pricing-report-final.pdf.

10. State Higher Education Executive Officers Association (SHEEO), *State Higher Education Finance FY 2012* (2013), fig. 3, accessed May 12, 2015, http://www.sheeo.org/sites/default/files/publications/SHEF%20FY%2012 -20130322rev.pdf.

11. Ibid., fig. 4.

12. National Center of Education Statistics, "Tuition Costs of Colleges and Universities."

13. The causality is assumed by most higher education journalists. See Katherine Long, "UW Tuition: What's behind the Rising Costs?," *Seattle Times*, September 21, 2013, http://www.seattletimes.com/seattle-news/uw -tuition-whatrsquos-behind-the-rising-costs/. See also Gary Fethke, "Why Does Tuition Go Up? Because Taxpayer Support Goes Down," *Chronicle of Higher Education*, April 1, 2012, http://chronicle.com/article/Why-Does -Tuition-Go-Up-/131372/. Fethke was previewing a book he co-authored called *Public No More*, which used declining public funds as the core reason to privatize public universities.

14. For example, a Wisconsin legislator agreed that the University of Wisconsin system had underfunded the urban Milwaukee campus compared to the flagship Madison campus. " 'I've always contended that the funding gap needed to be addressed,' Darling said. 'If UWM is to be an economic engine like Madison, UWM should get more funding.' That doesn't mean the Republican senator from suburban Milwaukee is willing to consider giving the UW System overall more money, though. Instead, Darling said campuses

should explore ways to share costs by collaborating and eliminate duplication of degree programs." Karen Herzog, "Amid Rough Seas for UW System, Wave of Challenges Hits UWM," *Milwaukee Journal Sentinel*, March 5, 2016, http://www.jsonline.com/news/education/amid-rough-seas-for-uw-system -wave-of-distinct-challenges-hits-uwm-b99678457z1-371174451.html.

15. SHEEO, *SHEF FY 2014* (2015), fig. 2, accessed April 1, 2015, http://www .sheeo.org/sites/default/files/project-files/SHEF%20FY%202014-20150410 .pdf; Charles I. Jones, "Useful Macro Graphs," Stanford Graduate School of Business, January 12, 2015, 12, accessed August 27, 2015, http://web.stanford .edu/~chadj/Chad-UsefulGraphs.pdf.

16. SHEEO, *SHEF FY 2014*, fig. 2.

17. Speaker John Pérez told the UC Board of Regents, "The possibility of increased funding right now: it doesn't exist. . . . There is no significant amount of money to backfill previous cuts. We've made roughly $900 million in cuts and you've increased fees $1.4 billion dollars. The [tuition] increases were disproportionate to the level of disinvestment by the state." Christopher Newfield, "Privatization Hits the Wall," *Remaking the University* (blog), January 24, 2013, http://utotherescue.blogspot.co.uk/2013/01/privatization -hits-wall.html.

18. Cited in Dylan Matthews, "The Tuition Is Too Damn High, Part VI—Why There's No Reason for Big Universities to Rein in Spending," *Washington Post*, September 9, 2013, http://www.washingtonpost.com/blogs/wonkblog/wp /2013/09/02/the-tuition-is-too-damn-high-part-vi-why-theres-no-reason-for -big-universities-to-rein-in-spending/. See Howard Rothmann Bowen, *The Costs of Higher Education: How Much Do Colleges and Universities Spend per Student and How Much Should They Spend?* (San Francisco: Jossey-Bass Publishers, 1980).

19. Christopher Newfield, "Confronting Our Permanent Public University Austerity," *Remaking the University* (blog), July 17, 2014, http://utotherescue .blogspot.co.uk/2014/07/confronting-our-permanent-public.html.

20. Bowen, *Costs of Higher Education*, 19.

21. Dylan Matthews, "Introducing 'The Tuition Is Too Damn High,'" *Washington Post*, August 26, 2013, http://www.washingtonpost.com/blogs /wonkblog/wp/2013/08/26/introducing-the-tuition-is-too-damn-high/. These paragraphs are based on my post, "Messing with the Wonkblog College Story," *Remaking the University* (blog), September 11, 2013, http:// utotherescue.blogspot.co.uk/2013/09/messing-with-wonkblog-college-story .html.

22. Dylan Matthews, "The Tuition Is Too Damn High, Part III—The Three Reasons Tuition Is Rising," *Washington Post*, August 28, 2013, http://

www.washingtonpost.com/blogs/wonkblog/wp/2013/08/28/the-tuition-is
-too-damn-high-part-iii-the-three-reasons-tuition-is-rising/.

23. Ibid.

24. James C. Garland, *Saving Alma Mater: A Rescue Plan for America's Public Universities* (Chicago: University of Chicago Press, 2009), Kindle edition, 267–76.

25. Eric Hoover, "3 Key Findings about College Admissions," *Chronicle of Higher Education*, May 7, 2015, http://chronicle.com/article/3-Key-Findings -About-College/229983/.

26. James C. Garland, *Saving Alma Mater,* 280–85.

27. Newfield, "Messing with the Wonkblog College Story."

28. Philip Mirowski, *Science-Mart: Privatizing American Science* (Cambridge, MA: Harvard University Press, 2011), 27, 29.

29. Laurence R. Veysey, *The Emergence of the American University* (Chicago: University of Chicago Press, 1965), 337–38.

30. Sheila Slaughter and Larry L. Leslie, *Academic Capitalism: Politics, Policies, and the Entrepreneurial University* (Baltimore, MD: Johns Hopkins University Press, 1997).

31. Author's interviews and correspondence with principal investigators; American Association for Biochemistry and Molecular Biology (ASBMB), "Nondefense Discretionary Science 2013 Survey: Unlimited Potential, Vanishing Opportunity," accessed June 8, 2016, http://www.asbmb.org/uploadedFiles /Advocacy/Events/UPVO%20Report.pdf.

32. Christopher Newfield, "Surprising Office Politics at UCSF Mission Bay," *Remaking the University* (blog), November 24, 2013, http://utotherescue .blogspot.co.uk/2013/11/surprising-office-politics-at-ucsf.html.

33. Elizabeth F. Farrell and Martin Van Der Werf, "Playing the Rankings Game," *Chronicle of Higher Education*, May 25, 2007, A11, http://chronicle.com /article/Playing-the-Rankings-Game/4451/.

34. W. J. Baumol, and W. G. Bowen, *Performing Arts: The Economic Dilemma* (New York: Twentieth Century Fund, 1966).

35. William J. Baumol et al., *The Cost Disease: Why Computers Get Cheaper and Health Care Doesn't* (New Haven, CT: Yale University Press, 2012), 20–21.

36. Robert E. Martin and Carter Hill, "Baumol and Bowen Cost Effects in Research Universities," March 2014, 21, Social Science Research Network, http://papers.ssrn.com/abstract=2153122.

37. American Association of University Professors (AAUP), *A Very Slow Recovery: The Annual Report on the Economic Status of the Profession, 2011–12,* table B, "Change in Inflation-Adjusted Published Tuition and Fee Prices and Full-Time Faculty Salaries, by Type of Institution, 1981–82 to 2011–12,"

accessed November 30, 2013, http://www.aaup.org/NR/rdonlyres /C2BAFA70-057E-4097-908B-6E4A6B5A6D38/0/TABB.pdf.

38. Ibid., fig. 3, "Trends in Instructional Staff Employment Status, 1975–2009," http://www.aaup.org/NR/rdonlyres/4EF6F3E2-98B2-477E -AAD9-E105ABD3C0D7/0/Figure3.pdf.

39. Ibid., http://www.aaup.org/reports-publications/2011-12salarysurvey.

40. Donna M. Desrochers, Colleen M. Lenihan, and Jane V. Wellman, *Trends in College Spending, 1998–2008* (Washington, DC, Delta Cost Project, 2010), 22, accessed November 30, 2013, http://www.deltacostproject.org/sites /default/files/products/Trends-in-College-Spending-98-08.pdf.

41. Robert B. Archibald and David H. Feldman, *Why Does College Cost So Much?* (New York: Oxford University Press, 2011), 76.

42. H. Moses III et al., "The Anatomy of Health Care in the United States," *JAMA* 310, no. 18 (November 13, 2013): 1947–64, doi:10.1001/jama.2013.281425.

43. Walter W. McMahon, *Higher Learning, Greater Good: The Private and Social Benefits of Higher Education* (Baltimore, MD: Johns Hopkins University Press, 2009), 63.

44. Ibid., 75.

45. Ibid.

46. Brad Hayward, "Gov. Schwarzenegger and UC, CSU Leaders Announce Multi-Year Compact Addressing Funding and Accountability," UC Newsroom, May 11, 2004, accessed December 4, 2013, http://www .universityofcalifornia.edu/news/compact/ucpressrelease.html. UC also agreed to return 20 to 33 percent of the new money to financial aid.

47. Christopher Newfield, Henning Bohn, and Calvin Moore, *Current Budget Trends and the Future of the University of California* (UC Academic Council, UC Committee for Planning and Budget, May 2006), charts 5a, 5b, 5c, accessed May 14, 2015, http://www.universityofcalifornia.edu/senate /reports/AC.Futures.Report.0107.pdf.

48. Jack Stripling, "After a Contentious Year, Chancellor Martin Is Leaving Madison," *Chronicle of Higher Education,* June 14, 2011, http://chronicle.com /article/After-Contentious-Year-Martin/127919/?sid=at&utm_source=at &utm_medium=en.

49. Richard Grusin, "Is the UW System Selling Its Birthright for a Mess of Pottage?," *Ragman's Circles,* November 30, 2012, accessed January 14, 2013, https://ragmanscircles.wordpress.com/2012/11/30/is-the-uw-system-selling -its-birthright-for-a-mess-of-pottage/.

50. Richard Grusin, "Public Authority: The End of Public Higher Education in Wisconsin?," *Ragman's Circles,* January 28, 2015, accessed February 7, 2015, https://ragmanscircles.wordpress.com/2015/01/28/public -authority-the-end-of-public-higher-education-in-wisconsin/.

51. Rebecca Blank and Frederica Freyberg, "Rebecca Blank on Proposed UW System Cuts, Autonomy," Wisconsin Public Television, January 30, 2015, accessed February 2, 2015, http://wpt.org/Here_and_Now/rebecca-blank-proposed-uw-system-cuts-autonomy.

52. "UW System Emails Regarding Budget Cuts," *Madison.com*, January 6, 2015, accessed February 24, 2015, https://docs.google.com/viewerng/viewer?url=http://bloximages.chicago2.vip.townnews.com/host.madison.com/content/tncms/assets/v3/editorial/1/7f/17fdd220-86a4-57c5-9a0f-acd95db17c5c/54da9de8cd9c9.pdf.pdf.

53. This outlook is not new. Thorstein Veblen criticized the nineteenth- and early twentieth-century university for loading up on an excessive number of undergraduates for the sake of a "large showing of turnover and output" that would raise their prestige and resources in competition with their rivals. Thorstein Veblen, *The Higher Learning in America: The Annotated Edition; A Memorandum on the Conduct of Universities by Business Men*, ed. Richard F. Teichgraeber III, annot. ed. (Baltimore, MD: Johns Hopkins University Press, 2015), 105.

54. Dean E. Murphy, "Harvard Scholar to Lead California Law School," *New York Times*, December 11, 2003, http://www.nytimes.com/2003/12/11/education/11BERK.html?pagewanted=print&position.

55. "A Conversation with Berkeley's New Law School Dean, Christopher Edley Jr.," *UC Berkeley News*, December 15, 2003, http://www.berkeley.edu/news/media/releases/2003/12/15_edley.shtml.

56. Ronald Roach, "A New Mountain to Climb," *Black Issues in Higher Education* 21, no. 12 (July 29, 2004): 22–25. On the institutional mission, Edley said, "I can tell you that I think the financial challenges facing the school mean that I have to devote a substantial amount of my time to fund raising to maintain the inclusivity of the student body, to expand the research activity and the size of the faculty, to build a new building, to tackle major social policy questions—all of this requires resources."

57. Christopher Edley Jr., "A Needy Boalt Hall Looks to Private Money," *Los Angeles Times*, January 17, 2005, http://articles.latimes.com/2005/jan/17/opinion/oe-edley17.

58. Ibid.

59. UC Regents Committee on Finance, Attachment C, "Planning for Professional School Fee Increases, 2007–2008 and 2008–2009," November 16, 2005, accessed December 4, 2013, http://regents.universityofcalifornia.edu/regmeet/jan07/303attach.pdf.

60. UC Regents Committee on Finance, Attachment B, "Draft Guiding Principles for Professional School Fees," accessed December 4, 2013, http://regents.universityofcalifornia.edu/regmeet/jan07/303attach.pdf.

61. UC Regents Committee on Education Policy, "Proposed Revision to the Policy on Fees for Selected Professional School Students," January 17, 2007, accessed December 4, 2013, http://regents.universityofcalifornia.edu /regmeet/jan07/303.pdf.

62. Jonathan D. Glater, "At Berkeley Law, a Challenge to Overcome All Barriers," *New York Times,* January 17, 2007, http://www.nytimes.com/2007 /01/17/education/17face.html.

63. "Stop the Cuts," text available at Christopher Newfield, "Sign UC Petition—Stop the Cuts!," *Remaking the University* (blog), July 12, 2009, http://utotherescue.blogspot.com/2009/07/sign-uci-petition-for-cuts -postponement.html.

64. Christopher Newfield, "Berkeley Law Dean Tees off on Petition Writers," *Remaking the University* (blog), July 13, 2009, http://utotherescue .blogspot.co.uk/2009/07/berkeley-law-dean-tees-off-on-petition.html.

65. Christopher Newfield, "Petition Writer's Response to Law Dean Chris Edley's Critique," *Remaking the University* (blog), July 14, 2009, http://utotherescue.blogspot.co.uk/2009/07/petition-writers-response-to -law-deans.html.

66. Berkeley Law, "Fees and Cost of Attendance 2015–2016," https://www .law.berkeley.edu/admissions/jd/financial-aid/fees-cost-of-attendance/.

67. Melissa Peerless, "Regents to Decide Tuition Increase," *Michigan Daily Summer Weekly,* July 15, 1992, 1, accessed December 2, 2013, http://news.google .com/newspapers?nid=2706&dat=19920715&id=5NtJAAAAIBAJ&sjid =zBoNAAAAIBAJ&pg=2688,576225; Larry Gordon, "Incoming UC President Warns of Fee Increases: Education: Peltason Says Costs Could Go up or Enrollment Could Be Limited to Cover Budget Shortfall," *Los Angeles Times*, October 16, 1992, accessed December 2, 2013, http://articles.latimes .com/1992-10-16/news/mn-340_1_state-budget-crisis.

Stage 4. The States Cut Public Funding

1. See, for example, Catherine Rampell, "Why Tuition Has Skyrocketed at State Schools," *Economix* (blog), *New York Times*, March 2, 2012, http:// economix.blogs.nytimes.com/2012/03/02/why-tuition-has-skyrocketed-at -state-schools/.

2. Legislative Analyst's Office, "Growth in General Fund Spending by Program Area," *The 2008–2009 Budget: Perspectives and Issues. Report from the Legislative Analyst's Office to the Joint Legislative Budget Committee* (2008), part IV, fig. 4, 76, accessed December 15, 2013, http://www.lao.ca.gov/analysis _2008/2008_pandi/pandi_08.pdf.

3. For an analysis of higher education cuts in the state budget context, see Christopher Newfield et al., "The Cuts Report," UC Academic Council,

March 2008, accessed December 15, 2013, http://www.universityofcalifornia
.edu/senate/reports/cuts.report.04.08.pdf.

4. Christopher Newfield, "Pay Even More to Get Even Less," *Remaking the
University* (blog), January 12, 2011, http://utotherescue.blogspot.co.uk/2011
/01/pay-even-more-to-get-even-less.html; on budget framing, see Christopher Newfield, "Ending a Bad UC Week: What Points Might Help Turn
Things Around?," *Remaking the University* (blog), January 16, 2011, http://
utotherescue.blogspot.co.uk/2011/01/ending-bad-uc-week-much-remains-to
-be.html.

5. Al Rodda, "Tuition: Considerations of Interest to Democratic Legislators" (March 1, 1970), republished in *The Back Bench*, accessed May 19, 2015,
http://thebackbench.blogspot.co.uk/2007/08/tuition-at-university-of
-california.html.

6. One article on the impact of better state budgets for 2014 began, "For
the first time in 20 years, there will be no tuition hike at the University of
Arizona, Arizona State University or the University of Northern Arizona."
Tyler Kingkade, "Tuition Hikes in Higher Education around the Country at
Public Colleges in 2012," *Huffington Post*, June 25, 2012, accessed December 10,
2013, http://www.huffingtonpost.com/2012/06/25/higher-ed-tuition-hikes
-2012_n_1446559.html. Similarly, a news item at the University of Michigan
noted that the FY 2014 tuition increase of 1.1 percent was the smallest since
1985. Rick Fitzgerald, "U-M Tuition Increase for Coming Year Is Smallest in
Nearly 30 Years," *The University Record,* June 24, 2013, accessed May 19, 2015,
http://ur.umich.edu/1213/Jun24_13/4682-u-m-tuition-increase. In the 1980s,
the University of Michigan at Ann Arbor made the understandable but costly
decision that their future depended on decoupling from state funding through
continuous hikes in tuition. In 1987–1988, its in-state tuition was $1,554 per
year. Nonresidents paid $4,782. *University of Michigan Bulletin,* February 18,
1987, accessed June 8, 2016, http://www.umich.edu/~bhlumrec/um-fees/1987
_fees.pdf. By 1997–1998, UM's undergraduate tuition was $3,130 for resident
and $9,500 nonresident students. "The University of Michigan Student Fees
and Fee Regulations Effective August 1996," accessed December 2, 2013,
http://www.ro.umich.edu/tuition/archive/documents/9697FEES.pdf.
Students had complained throughout. One editorial, on the heels of the
8.4 percent/9.7 percent tuition increase (in-state/nonresident) for 1987–1988,
said that tuition hikes were destroying class and race diversity on campus—
that they showed that the administration "considers students to be an
inexhaustible supply of funds to fill budget gaps." Editorial, *The Michigan
Daily,* September 10, 1987, 4, accessed December 2, 2013, http://news.google
.com/newspapers?nid=2706&dat=19870910&id=4g1KAAAAIBAJ&sjid
=vh4NAAAAIBAJ&pg=1131,19574. It just didn't matter. Tuition was a revenue

source that bypassed the declining public sector, and state officials learned that cuts to university funding were the least worst option.

7. ModernEsquire (Brian Hester), "Ohio's Colleges and Universities Pray Kasich Will Allow Them to Increase Tuition by Double Digits Again," Plunderbund, November 9, 2010, accessed December 10, 2013, http://www .plunderbund.com/2010/11/09/ohios-colleges-and-universities-pray-kasich -will-allow-them-to-increase-tuition-by-double-digits-again/.

8. Jan Murphy, "Corbett's Proposed Higher-Education Cuts Have College Students, Parents Bracing for Worst," *Pennlive.com,* March 13, 2011, accessed December 18, 2013, http://www.pennlive.com/midstate/index.ssf/2011/03 /corbetts_proposed_higher-educa.html/.

9. "The 2014–2015 Budget: California's Fiscal Outlook," *Legislative Analyst's Office,* 2013, Section on Higher Education: Assumptions, accessed December 10, 2013, http://www.lao.ca.gov/reports/2013/bud/fiscal-outlook/fiscal -outlook-112013.aspx#Higher_Education.

10. Author's transcript, from Christopher Newfield, "Privatization Hits the Wall," *Remaking the University* (blog), January 24, 2013, http://utotherescue .blogspot.co.uk/2013/01/privatization-hits-wall.html.

11. State Department of Finance, "California State Budget: Higher Education," fig. HED-01, accessed December 10, 2013, http://www.ebudget.ca .gov/2013-14/pdf/BudgetSummary/HigherEducation.pdf; Christopher Newfield, "The Old State Funding Model Is Dead: What Will Replace It?," *Remaking the University* (blog) November 14, 2013, http://utotherescue .blogspot.co.uk/2013/11/the-old-state-funding-model-is-dead.html.

12. Jerry Brown, "Statement to Committee on Finance, UC Board of Regents," September 18, 2013, recording at "Listen to First Segment of Afternoon Session of UC Regents: 9-18-2013," *UCLA Faculty Association,* September 19, 2013, accessed May 19, 2015, http://uclafacultyassociation .blogspot.de/2013/09/listen-to-first-segment-of-afternoon.html; author's transcript.

13. Office of the President, "UC's President Jack W. Peltason Ends Extended Administrative Leaves," Oakland, University of California, April 6, 1994, in author's files.

14. Robert B. Archibald and David Henry Feldman, *Why Does College Cost So Much?* (New York: Oxford University Press, 2011), chap. 5.

15. University of California Office of the President, "UC Mandatory Student Charge Levels," December 2011, accessed June 8, 2016, http://ucop .edu/operating-budget/_files/fees/201415/documents/Historical_Fee _Levels.pdf.

16. Todd Wallack and Tanya Schevitz, "No. 2 Official at UC Quits Suddenly: University Probes Possibility of Favoritism in Hiring of Friend

and Son of Provost," *San Francisco Chronicle,* November 5, 2005, http://www
.sfgate.com/education/article/No-2-official-at-UC-quits-suddenly-University
-2562136.php.

17. Ákos Róna-Tas, "Growth Trends in UC Administration," *Remaking
the University* (December 10, 2009), accessed December 19, 2013, http://
utotherescue.blogspot.com/2009/12/growth-trends-in-uc-administration
.html.

18. "The University of California Academic and Non-Academic Personnel
Growth FY 1997–1998 to FY 2008–2009," UC Office of the President, author's
files. The relevant full-time equivalents (FTEs) by budget area were 11 percent
to instruction, 11 percent to research, and another 11 percent to academic
support.

19. Donna M. Desrochers, Colleen M. Lenihan, and Jane V. Wellman,
*Trends in College Spending, 1998–2008: Where Does the Money Come From?
Where Does It Go? What Does It Buy?* (Delta Cost Project, 2010), 22, accessed
June 1, 2016, http://www.deltacostproject.org/sites/default/files/products
/Trends-in-College-Spending-98-08.pdf.

20. "Before the Fall," *The Economist,* August 6, 2009. Similar coverage
included Erika Check Hayden and Rex Dalton, "Cuts Bite in California:
University Faces Hard Times as Budget Gets Squeezed," *Nature* 460, 441
(2009), doi: 10.1038/460441a.

21. "Employee Furloughs," *University of California Budget News,* 2009, copy
in author's files.

22. UC Santa Barbara faculty member, e-mail dated August 10, 2009,
author's files.

23. UC Irvine faculty e-mail, October 18, 2009, author's files.

24. Mary Croughan, "Implementation of Furlough Days on Instructional
Days," memo, UC Academic Senate, August 5, 2009, accessed December 24,
2013, http://senate.universityofcalifornia.edu/reports/MC2Pitts_Furlough%
20Days%20Implementation_080509.pdf. Their two key statements: "While
Council members acknowledge that students are already being negatively
impacted through increased fees, staff reductions, and loss of services on
furlough days, the Academic Council unanimously supported the concept
that furloughs should affect instructional days." And "following a lengthy
debate, the Academic Council makes the following request and recommendation: (1) that the Executive Vice President for Academic Affairs institute a
systemwide standard of six furlough days assigned to days of instruction over
the nine month academic calendar; and (2) that he approve campus requests
for changes to their academic calendars that place furloughs on specified
instructional days for up to ten days." I discussed furloughs as a form of public
outreach in "Emerging Furlough Standards and Goals," Remaking the

University (blog), August 11, 2009, http://utotherescue.blogspot.co.uk/2009 /08/emerging-furlough-standards-and-goals.html.

25. Lawrence H. Pitts to UC Chancellors and Academic Council Chair Croughan, reprinted in Christopher Newfield, "UCOP on Furloughs: We're the Deciders!," *Remaking the University* (blog), August 23, 2009, http:// utotherescue.blogspot.co.uk/2009/08/ucop-on-furloughs-were-deciders .html.

26. I criticized administrative policy in Christopher Newfield, "What's the Matter with UCOP?," *Remaking the University* (blog), August 26, 2009, http://utotherescue.blogspot.co.uk/2009/08/whats-matter-with-ucop .html.

27. I refer to the updated version of the 2009 report, Stanton A. Glantz and Eric Hays, "How Much Will It Cost Us to Restore Public Higher Education in 2013–14," *Keep California's Promise*, December 2013, accessed December 24, 2013, http://keepcaliforniaspromise.org/3553/restore-2013-14.

28. My comments here are based on my post on the first version of the report, Christopher Newfield, "Saving Public Higher Ed: Cheaper than Christmas Shopping," *Remaking the University* (blog), December 22, 2009, http://utotherescue.blogspot.co.uk/2009/12/saving-public-higher-ed -cheaper-than.html.

29. Stanton A. Glantz and Eric Hays, "How Much Will It Cost Us to Restore Public Higher Education in 2015–16," *Keep California's Promise*, February 2015, accessed July 20, 2015, http://keepcaliforniaspromise.org /473424/reset-2015-16.

30. Brad Delong, "Well, It's the End of Nicholas Dirks's First Semester as Berkeley Chancellor, so Why Not Offer Him Some Unsolicited Advice?," *Berkeley Blog*, December 11, 2013, http://blogs.berkeley.edu/2013/12/11/well -its-the-end-of-nicholas-dirkss-first-semester-as-berkeley-chancellor-so-why -not-offer-him-some-unsolicited-advice/.

31. These are 2015–2016 figures. Undergraduate FTE totals are from Community College League of California, "Fast Facts 2015," accessed June 8, 2016, http://www.ccleague.org/files/public/Publications/FF2015.pdf.

32. This presentation was based on Christopher Newfield, Henning Bohn, and Calvin Moore, *Current Budget Trends and the Future of the University of California* (UC Academic Council, UC Committee for Planning and Budget, May 2006), accessed December 9, 2013, http://www.universityofcalifornia .edu/senate/reports/AC.Futures.Report.0107.pdf. I discussed the findings of this report in some detail in my *Unmaking the Public University: The 40 Year Assault on the Middle Class* (Cambridge, MA: Harvard University Press, 2008), chap. 11.

Stage 5. Increased Student Debt, College as Burden

1. Annette Smith Parker, "Why Tuition at Highly Selective Colleges Is So High and Why the Cost to the Institution Is Even Higher: Dickinson College, a Case Study of a Community in Constant Transformation," Dickinson College, 2010, accessed November 19, 2013, http://www.dickinson.edu/about /president/special-report/. Dartmouth College offers another example. The Dartmouth College fund first cites an alumni comment: "Dartmouth creates a world-class product, discounts the price 51 percent, gives an additional discount for certain buyers . . . then begs for money." The college proclaims that this is true: Dartmouth discounts the price by 51 percent—for everybody. Dartmouth charges $61,947 for undergraduate tuition, room, and board, even though it spends $126,058 per student per year. The college then goes on to give "need-based financial aid" to nearly half of its students, averaging $43,287 per student in 2014–2015. It then "begs for money" because "charitable gifts and endowment income underwrite 36 percent of the cost of a year at the College; tuition, room, and board cover only 42 percent of the cost of a Dartmouth education." See "You Wouldn't Run a Business This Way: Here's Why Dartmouth Does," Dartmouth College, accessed August 1, 2016, http://www.dartmouthcollegefund.org/why-give/dartmouths-wacky-busi ness-model. See also Andrew Gillen, Matthew Denhart, and Jonathan Robe, *Who Subsidizes Whom?,* Center for College Affordability and Productivity, March 2011, accessed November 4, 2014, http://centerforcollegeaffordability .org/uploads/Who_Subsidizes_Whom.pdf; Andrea Santiago, Gerardo Largoza, and Conchada (Mitzie Irene), "What Does It Cost a University to Educate One Student?," *International Journal of Education Policy and Leadership* 2, no. 2 (2007).

2. Harvard Management Company, "Harvard Management Company Endowment Report: Message from the CEO, September 2013, accessed December 30, 2013, http://www.hmc.harvard.edu/docs/Final_Annual _Report_2013.pdf.

3. "Harvard at a Glance," Harvard University, accessed December 30, 2013, http://www.harvard.edu/harvard-glance; Higher Education Statistics Agency, "Free Online Statistics: Students and Qualifiers," accessed December 30, 2013, http://www.hesa.ac.uk/content/view/1897/239/.

4. "Liftoff: Harvard Campaign Details and Analysis," *Harvard Magazine*, September 2013, accessed December 30, 2013, http://harvardmagazine.com /2013/09/harvard-campaign-details-and-analysis.

5. Drew Gilpin Faust, "To Seize an Impatient Future," speech, Harvard University, September 21, 2013, accessed December 30, 2013, http://www .harvard.edu/president/the-harvard-campaign.

6. "Liftoff," *Harvard Magazine.*

7. Steven Hurlburt and Rita J. Kirshstein, *Spending Update: Where Does the Money Go? A Delta Data Update, 2000–2010* (Washington, DC: Delta Cost Project-American Institutes for Research, n.d.), fig. 1, accessed February 13, 2014, http://www.deltacostproject.org/sites/default/files/products/Delta -Spending-Trends-Production.pdf.

8. The first two figures are from "Quick Facts about Student Debt," The Institute for College Access & Success, March 2014, http://ticas.org/sites /default/files/pub_files/Student_Debt_and_the_Class_of_2010_NR.pdf; the third is from "Average Student Debt Tops $25,000 for Class of 2010 in Tough Job Market," The Project on Student Debt, November 3, 2011, accessed February 13, 2014, http://ticas.org/sites/default/files/pub_files/Student _Debt_and_the_Class_of_2010_NR.pdf.

9. "Trends in Higher Education: Average Cumulative Debt of Bachelor's Degree Recipients at Public Four-Year Institutions over Time," College Board, 2014, accessed August 11, 2015, http://trends.collegeboard.org/student-aid /figures-tables/average-cumulative-debt-bachelors-recipients-public-four -year-time.

10. "FICO Labs: U.S. Student Loan Delinquencies Climbing Fast, Showing No Signs of Slowing," FICO, January 31, 2013, accessed February 13, 2014, http://www.fico.com/en/newsroom/fico-labs-us-student-loan -delinquencies-climbing-fast-showing-no-signs-of-slowing-01-30-2013.

11. Jeffrey Sparshott, "Congratulations, Class of 2015. You're the Most Indebted Ever (For Now)," *Real Time Economics* (blog), *Wall Street Journal,* May 8, 2015, http://blogs.wsj.com/economics/2015/05/08/congratulations -class-of-2015-youre-the-most-indebted-ever-for-now/.

12. Mary Pilon, "Student-Loan Debt Surpasses Credit Cards," *Wall Street Journal,* August 8, 2010, http://blogs.wsj.com/economics/2010/08/09 /student-loan-debt-surpasses-credit-cards/.

13. Total annual loan volume increased 139 percent after inflation from 2000 to 2011–2012. Sonia Garrison, "The State of Lending in America & Its Impact on U.S. Households," Center for Responsible Lending, December 2012, fig. 1, accessed November 4, 2014, http://www.responsiblelending.org /state-of-lending/reports/6-Student-Loans.pdf. For another measure, see William G. Bowen, Matthew M. Chingos, and Michael S. McPherson, *Crossing the Finish Line: Completing College at America's Public Universities* (Princeton, NJ: Princeton University Press, 2009), 154.

14. Daniel Indiviglio, "Obama's Student-Loan Order Saves the Average Grad Less Than $10 a Month," *Atlantic,* October 2011, http://www.theatlantic .com/business/archive/2011/10/obamas-student-loan-order-saves-the -average-grad-less-than-10-a-month/247411/.

15. Alan Michael Collinge, *The Student Loan Scam: The Most Oppressive Debt in U.S. History—and How We Can Fight Back* (Boston: Beacon Press, 2009), vii.

16. Ibid., ix–x.

17. Collinge started a web-based project, StudentLoanJustice.Org, which continues to collect the debt stories of graduates across the country.

18. New York Federal Reserve, "Quarterly Report on Household Debt and Credit," August 2012, 2, accessed June 4, 2016, https://www.newyorkfed.org /medialibrary/interactives/householdcredit/data/pdf/DistrictReport _Q22012.pdf.

19. Federal Reserve, "Statistical Release G19: Consumer Credit, April 2016" (December 6, 2013), accessed June 1, 2016, http://www.federalreserve.gov /releases/g19/Current/g19.pdf.

20. John W. Schoen, "Student Loan Debt Piles up to $1.16 Trillion: NY Fed," *CNBC*, February 17, 2015, http://www.cnbc.com/2015/02/17/student -loan-debt-piles-up-to-116-trillion-ny-fed.html; Andrew Haughwout, Donghoon Lee, Joelle Scally, Wilbert van der Klaauw, "Student Loan Borrowing and Repayment Trends, 2015," New York Federal Reserve Bank, April 16, 2015, accessed July 24, 2015, https://www.newyorkfed.org /medialibrary/media/newsevents/mediaadvisory/2015/Student-Loan-Press -Briefing-Presentation.pdf.

21. College Board, *Trends in College Pricing, 2010*, 3, accessed January 1, 2014, http://trends.collegeboard.org/sites/default/files/CP_2010.pdf.

22. Author's compounding calculations.

23. This source of rising debt consists not of rising net tuition as such but of the different rates at which tuition and income have increased (higher and lower, respectively). For an example of this argument, see James L. Doti, "In Praise of Federal Loans for College," *Chronicle of Higher Education*, July 21, 2015, http://chronicle.com/article/In-Praise-of-Federal-Loans-for/231505 /?cid=at&utm_source=at&utm_medium=en. Noting that debt rose more quickly than tuition during a recent period, Doti wrote, "the increases in Stafford loans, accommodated by more-liberal federal borrowing standards, were not used to cover excessive tuition increases at nonprofit colleges. Rather, they were used to make up for the slow growth in family income brought about by weak economic growth." In fact, increased loans *are* covering tuition increases, "excessive" or not, as a function of family income.

24. Grants and Work Study Consortium, "Beyond Pell: A Next-Generation Design for Federal Financial Aid," *The Education Trust* (October 2014), 5, accessed June 3, 2016, http://edtrust.org/wp-content/uploads/2013/10 /BeyondPell_FINAL.pdf.

25. College Board, *Trends in Student Aid,* fig. 4A, "Grants and Loans as a Percentage of Funds from Total Aid and Nonfederal Loans for Undergraduate Students, 1992–93 to 2012–13," accessed June 9, 2014, http://trends .collegeboard.org/sites/default/files/student-aid-2013-full-report.pdf.

26. The Middle Income Student Assistance Act (1978) and other legislation "began to emphasize student loan aid over federal grant aid by again expanding student eligibility for loans. For example, in 1979 two-thirds of federal assistance to students came in the form of grants and work-study jobs, with the remaining one-third in the form of subsidized loans. Today the reverse is true." James J. Duderstadt and Farris W. Womack, *The Future of the Public University in America: Beyond the Crossroads* (Baltimore, MD: Johns Hopkins University Press, 2004), 39.

27. Collinge, *Student Loan Scam,* 9. Collinge relies in part on Larry L. Leslie and Gary P. Johnson, "The Market Model and Higher Education," *Journal of Higher Education* 45, no. 1 (January 1974): 1–20.

28. Suzanne Mettler, *Degrees of Inequality: How the Politics of Higher Education Sabotaged the American Dream* (New York: Basic Books, 2014), 67.

29. Ibid., 80.

30. Duderstadt and Womack, *Future of the Public University.*

31. For a survey of private-public partnerships in three major UK sectors, see Andrew Bowman et al., *The End of the Experiment?* (Manchester: Manchester University Press, 2014).

32. Collinge, *Student Loan Scam,* 10

33. Ibid.

34. Ibid., 12.

35. Ibid., 66–68.

36. The legislated prohibitions were accompanied by a set of practices revealed by three mid-2000s investigations: one by *60 Minutes* ("Sallie Mae," broadcast May 7, 2006); another by the Office of the Attorney General of the State of New York (for an overview, see Doug Lederman, "Inside the Cuomo Probe," *Inside Higher Ed,* July 30, 2007, accessed January 1, 2014, http://www.insidehighered.com/news/2007/07/30/cuomo); and a third conducted by the US Senate Committee on Health, Education, Labor and Pensions, Edward M. Kennedy, chairman, issued in "Report on Marketing Practices in the Federal Family Education Loan Program," US Senate, June 15, 2007, accessed November 4, 2014, http://eric.ed.gov/?id =ED497127.

37. Collinge found that Sallie Mae had turned loan defaults into their fastest growing revenue stream. "Sallie Mae's fee income increased by 228 percent (from $280 million to $920 million) between 2000 and 2005,

while its managed loan portfolio increased by only 82 percent (from $67 billion to $122 billion) during the same time period." Collinge, *Student Loan Scam*, 5. Sallie Mae's Net Interest Income and Net Interest Income—loss provisions, increased from 2000 to 2013 by 393 percent and 281 percent, respectively. Fee and collections income also ballooned over the same period (Sallie Mae's Annual Form 10-K report: Consolidated Statements of Income Filings, https://www.salliemae.com/about/investors/stockholderinfo /annualreports).

38. Other sanctioned practices were "revenue-sharing" between the lender and the university when university officials sent a student to that lender (these payments are more commonly known as kickbacks); denial of choice of lender, in which lenders would offer a university "consideration" in exchange for the university abrogating the right of students to choose their lender "by stating or strongly implying that borrowers were limited to the lenders on the list"; "exclusive consolidation loan marketing agreements"; "undisclosed sales of loans to another lender"; and "call centers" that students thought were official university providers of neutral financial information, but were actually staffed with lender employees. "Assurance of Discontinuance," Attorney General of the State of New York, in the matter of Nelnet, Inc., n.d., accessed January 2, 2014, http://www.ag.ny.gov/sites/default/files/pdfs/bureaus /student_loan/aod_nelnet.pdf.

39. Ruth Simon, Rachel Louise Ensign, and Al Yoon, "Student-Loan Securities Stay Hot," *Wall Street Journal*, March 3, 2013, http://online.wsj.com /article/SB10001424127887323293704578334542910674174.htmla. I discussed this piece and the overall issue in Christopher Newfield, "The Current Cost Debate Will Do Nothing Except Hurt Students," *Remaking the University* (blog), March 4, 2013, http://utotherescue.blogspot.co.uk/2013/03/the -current-cost-debate-will-do-nothing.html.

40. Matt Taibbi, "U.S. Student Loan Bubble Saddles a Generation With Debt and Threatens the Economy," *Democracy Now!*, August 20, 2013, http://www.democracynow.org/2013/8/20/matt_taibbi_us_student_loan _bubble.

41. "Report Urges Bankruptcy Protection for Risky Student Loans," *Inside Higher Ed*, August 21, 2013, accessed December 31, 2013, http://www .insidehighered.com/quicktakes/2013/08/21/report-urges-bankruptcy -protection-risky-student-loans.

42. Natalie Kitroeff, "Loan Monitor Is Accused of Ruthless Tactics on Student Debt," *New York Times*, January 1, 2014, http://www.nytimes.com /2014/01/02/us/loan-monitor-is-accused-of-ruthless-tactics-on-student-debt .html.

43. US Government Accountability Office, *Federal Student Loans: Borrower Interest Rates Cannot Be Set in Advance to Precisely and Consistently Balance Federal Revenues and Costs,* GAO-14-234 (January 2014), accessed February 6, 2014, http://www.gao.gov/assets/670/660548.pdf.

44. See, for example, Peter Baker and David M. Herszenhorn, "Obama Signs Overhaul of Student Loan Program," *New York Times,* March 30, 2010, http://www.nytimes.com/2010/03/31/us/politics/31obama.html.

45. See, for example, Barack Obama, "FACT SHEET: President Obama's Blueprint for Keeping College Affordable and within Reach for All Americans," White House, January 1, 2012, accessed January 28, 2012, http://www.whitehouse.gov/the-press-office/2012/01/27/fact-sheet-president-obama-s-blueprint-keeping-college-affordable-and-wi; and Goldie Blumenstyk, "Obama Calls for Control of College Costs and Renewed Support for Higher Education," *Chronicle of Higher Education,* January 27, 2012, http://chronicle.com/article/Obama-Calls-for-Control-of/130496/?sid=pm&utm_source=pm&utm_medium=en.

46. White House, "Ensuring That Student Loans Are Affordable," accessed June 11, 2014, http://www.whitehouse.gov/issues/education/higher-education/ensuring-that-student-loans-are-affordable.

47. Indiviglio, "Obama's Student-Loan Order."

48. Andrew Ross, *Creditocracy: And the Case for Debt Refusal* (New York: OR Books, 2014); Robert Samuels, *Why Public Higher Education Should Be Free: How to Decrease Cost and Increase Quality at American Universities* (New Brunswick, NJ: Rutgers University Press, 2013).

49. Stephanie Gleason, "Former Corinthian Students Seek $2.5 Billion Bankruptcy Claim," *Wall Street Journal,* July 22, 2015, http://www.wsj.com/articles/former-corinthian-students-seek-2-5-billion-bankruptcy-claim-1437588632; Kelly Field, "Debt Protesters Disrupt Student-Aid Group's Parade," *Chronicle of Higher Education,* July 21, 2015, http://chronicle.com/article/Debt-Protesters-Disrupt/231771/?cid=at&utm_source=at&utm_medium=en.

50. Ben Rooney, "Bernie Sanders Wants College to Be Free," *CNNMoney,* May 20, 2015, http://money.cnn.com/2015/05/20/news/bernie-sanders-free-college/index.html.

51. F. King Alexander, "Student Tuition and the Higher Education Marketplace: Policy Implications for Public Universities," *Journal of Staff, Program, and Organization Development* 17, no. 2 (Summer 2000): 83.

52. Rachel Nathanson, "What Wisconsin Can Learn from Louisiana's Budget Debates," *WISCAPE,* July 9, 2015, accessed July 24, 2015, https://wiscape.wisc.edu/wiscape/home/blog/wiscape-blog/2015/07/09/what-wisconsin-can-learn-from-louisiana-s-budget-debates.

53. Mark G. Yudof, "A Baker's Dozen Myths about Higher Education," speech to California Chamber of Commerce Board Meeting, San Francisco, CA, December 2, 2011, accessed January 4, 2014, https://www.facebook.com /notes/uc-for-california/a-bakers-dozen-myths-about-higher-education /10150402368604542.

54. University of California, "Indicator 3.6, Undergraduate Hours of Work, Universitywide and UC campuses, 2005–06, 2007–08, 2009–10 and 2011–12," *Accountability Report 2013,* accessed January 5, 2013, http://accountability .universityofcalifornia.edu/index/3.6.

55. Student Debt Project, "Student Debt and the Class of 2012," December 2013, table 2, accessed January 14, 2014, http://projectonstudentdebt.org/files /pub/classof2012.pdf.

56. "The 2013–14 Budget: Analysis of the Higher Education Budget," Legislative Analyst's Office, Sacramento, CA, February 12, 2013, fig. 7, accessed January 16, 2014, http://www.lao.ca.gov/analysis/2013/highered/higher -education-021213.aspx.

57. Bowen, Chingos, and McPherson, *Crossing the Finish Line,* 157–58.

58. Ibid., 180–81.

59. Jim Miller, "Napolitano Makes Case for University of California Tuition Increase," *Sacramento Bee,* November 14, 2014, http://www.sacbee .com/news/politics-government/capitol-alert/article3938256.html.

60. This section is based on Christopher Newfield, "The Impact of Tuition Hikes on Undergraduate Debt," *Remaking the University* (blog), November 26, 2014, http://utotherescue.blogspot.co.uk/2014/11/the-impact-of-tuition -hikes-on.html.

61. Public Affairs, "Regents Approve Five-Year Tuition-Hike Plan for UC Students," *Berkeley News,* November 20, 2014, accessed July 25, 2015, http:// newscenter.berkeley.edu/2014/11/20/regents-approve-five-year-tuition-hike -plan-for-uc-students/.

62. Robert J. Birgeneau, "Who Pays More? Who Pays Less?," *The Daily Californian,* November 18, 2014, http://www.dailycal.org/2014/11/18/pays -pays-less/.

63. US Census Bureau, "Quick Facts: California," accessed July 25, 2015, http://quickfacts.census.gov/qfd/states/06000.html.

64. Among the webpages devoted to helping students and their families read these letters, see Mark Kantrowitz, "Guide to Financial Aid Award Letters," *FinAid,* 2015, accessed July 25, 2015, http://www.finaid.org/fafsa/awardletters.phtml.

65. See the charts of both UC Berkeley borrowing and national borrowing in Christopher Newfield, "Free Speech and Free UC," *Remaking the University* (blog), October 12, 2014, http://utotherescue.blogspot.co.uk/2014/10/free -speech-and-free-uc.html.

66. On study time and other issues regarding student attainment, see Christopher Newfield, "Is College Still Worth It?," *Los Angeles Review of Books*, September 29, 2014, http://lareviewofbooks.org/review/college-still-worth/.

67. Carly Stockwell, "Gapping Is a Controversial Practice That Remains Commonplace in Many Universities," *College Factual Insights*, September 24, 2014, accessed July 25, 2015, http://insights.collegefactual.com/gapping-controversial-practice/.

68. Scott Jaschik, "Need Blind, but 'Gapping,'" *Inside Higher Ed*, November 26, 2008, accessed June 1, 2016, https://www.insidehighered.com/news/2008/11/26/aid.

69. UC Berkeley Financial Aid and Scholarships, "Middle Class Access Plan," accessed July 25, 2015, http://financialaid.berkeley.edu/middle-class-access-plan.

70. Christopher Newfield, "The Old State Funding Model Is Dead: What Will Replace It?," *Remaking the University* (blog), November 14, 2013, http://utotherescue.blogspot.co.uk/2013/11/the-old-state-funding-model-is-dead.html. See also Newfield, "Privatization Hits the Wall," *Remaking the University* (blog), January 24, 2013, http://utotherescue.blogspot.co.uk/2013/01/privatization-hits-wall.html; Katy Murphy, "University of California: The Hidden Cost of Tuition Hikes," *San Jose Mercury News*, November 23, 2015, http://www.mercurynews.com/education/ci_26998525/hidden-cost-ucs-tuition-hike.

71. Combining data at University of California, *Statistical Summary of Students and Staff, Fall 2013*, table 1A, http://legacy-its.ucop.edu/uwnews/stat/statsum/fall2013/statsumm2013.pdf; University of California, "Accountability Report 2015," table 2.2.2, "Undergraduate income distribution, University-wide and UC campuses, 2013–14," accessed July 25, 2015, http://accountability.universityofcalifornia.edu/2015/chapters/chapter-2.html#2.2.2.

72. University of California Office of the President, *Budget for Current Operations, 2013–14*, S-9, accessed July 27, 2015, http://www.ucop.edu/operating-budget/_files/rbudget/2013-14-budget.pdf.

73. Newfield, "The Old State Funding Model Is Dead."

74. Department of Finance (California), *Budget Summary: Higher Education*, fig. HED-01, accessed July 27, 2015, http://www.ebudget.ca.gov/2013-14/pdf/BudgetSummary/HigherEducation.pdf.

75. Health insurance costs seem very high for this generally young population, suggesting profits from this service may flow to other parts of the university, most likely its medical centers, particularly now that the university has moved to medical self-insurance. On-campus housing costs are also very high. Universities can take advantage of their long "college roommate"

tradition of two or more students to a room that would be considered substandard overcrowding by most students in Europe. This allows them to charge by the bed rather than the room, and for the neighboring private sector landlord to do the same. The UCSB aid packages assume that the university will charge each student $4,000 a year *more* than would the famously price-gouging Isla Vista landlords next to UCSB's campus. Rather than focusing on minimizing student costs, the campus may be using on-campus housing as a profit center to generate cross-subsidies for other activities or purchases. Suspicions that this is indeed what's happening were strengthened in 2015, when UCSB spent $156 million to buy three local apartment buildings from a Chicago real estate investment trust. See Elijah Brumback, "UCSB Buys up Apartment Complexes for Student Housing," *Pacific Coast Business Times*, July 14, 2015, http://www.pacbiztimes.com/2015/07/14/ucsb-buys-up -apartment-complexes-for-student-housing/. The university's cost per bed was about $156,000, and the funding source was identified as Housing and Residential Services. See "Funding Source Revealed in UC Tropicana Purchase," *Santa Barbara Independent*, July 25, 2015, http://www.independent .com/news/2015/jul/23/funding-source-revealed-uc-tropicana-purchase/. Plowing housing profits back into housing is rational in itself, but it conflicts with the mission of minimizing student costs and with constructing new housing that might offer more privacy for better learning.

Stage 6. Private Vendors Leverage Public Funds: The Case of the MOOCs

1. David Siders, "Capitol Alert: How Udacity's Leader Met 'a Guy Named Jerry Brown,' " *Sacramento Bee*, November 29, 2013, http://blogs.sacbee.com /capitolalertlatest/2013/01/how-udacity-sebastian-thrun-met-jerry-brown .html.

2. Laura Pappano, "The Year of the MOOC," *New York Times*, November 2, 2012, http://www.nytimes.com/2012/11/04/education/edlife/massive -open-online-courses-are-multiplying-at-a-rapid-pace.html?pagewanted=all &_r=0.

3. See, for example, Coursera's launch coverage: Liz Games, "Stanford Professors Launch Coursera With $16M From Kleiner Perkins and NEA," *All Things D*, April 18, 2012, accessed January 21, 2015, http://allthingsd.com /20120418/stanford-professors-launch-coursera-with-16m-from-kleiner -perkins-and-nea/.

4. Katherine Mangan, "MOOC Mania: It's Raising Big Questions about the Future of Higher Education," *Chronicle of Higher Education*, October 5, 2012, B4, cited in Derek Bok, *Higher Education in America* (Princeton, NJ: Princeton University Press, 2013), Kindle ed., 9529–9531.

5. Bok, *Higher Education in America*, Kindle ed., 4118–4125.

6. Richard A. DeMillo, *From Abelard to Apple: The Fate of American Colleges and Universities* (Boston: MIT Press, 2011), 142–43; Daphne Koller, "What We're Learning from Online Education," *TED Talks*, June 2012, accessed January 21, 2015, http://www.ted.com/talks/daphne_koller_what_we_re_learning_from_online_education/transcript?language=en#t-1205549.

7. Cathy N. Davidson, "Year of the MOOC: Rsp to NY Times, A Student-Made MOOC by Dan Ariely and Me," *HASTAC*, November 3, 2012, accessed January 21, 2015, http://www.hastac.org/blogs/cathy-davidson/2012/11/03/year-mooc-rsp-ny-times-student-made-mooc-dan-ariely-and-me.

8. Christopher Newfield, "MOOCs Have Become a Straight Business Play," *Remaking the University* (blog), March 18, 2013, http://utotherescue.blogspot.com/2013/03/moocs-have-become-straight-business-play.html.

9. National Center for Education Statistics, "Expenses of Postsecondary Institutions," accessed January 21, 2015, http://nces.ed.gov/programs/coe/indicator_cue.asp.

10. The other three elements of privatization are private revenues covering costs (tuition), control, and mission (see chapter 2).

11. National Center for Education Statistics, "Digest of Education Statistics," table 334.10, "Expenditures of public degree-granting postsecondary institutions, by purpose of expenditure and level of institution: 2005–06 through 2011–12," accessed January 21, 2015, http://nces.ed.gov/programs/digest/d13/tables/dt13_334.10.asp.

12. José Medina, *The Epistemology of Resistance: Gender and Racial Oppression, Epistemic Injustice, and Resistant Imaginations* (New York: Oxford University Press, 2012). Thanks to Madelyn Detloff for pointing me to this work.

13. Anant Agarwal, president of edX, in "edX: The Future of Online Education is Now," May 12, 2012, accessed July 31, 2015, https://www.youtube.com/watch?v=MJZN7ooYSoo.

14. See, for example, the overview statement of how the Internet was transforming higher education, written by leading "new learning" advocate Cathy N. Davidson, "Five Ways the Open Web Can Transform Higher Education," *cathydavidson.com* (blog), December 4, 2011, accessed December 6, 2011, http://www.cathydavidson.com/2011/12/five-ways-the-open-web-can-transform-higher-education/.

15. Pappano, "Year of the MOOC."

16. Universities UK, *Massive Open Online Courses: Higher Education's Digital Moment?* (London: Universities UK, May 2013), accessed May 10, 2016, http://www.universitiesuk.ac.uk/highereducation/Documents/2013/MassiveOpenOnlineCourses.pdf; Department for Business, Innovation &

Skills, "The Maturing of the MOOC," BIS Research Paper, no. 130 (September 2013), accessed May 10, 2016, https://www.gov.uk/government/uploads /system/uploads/attachment_data/file/240193/13-1173-maturing-of-the -mooc.pdf.

17. A short summary is George Siemens, "Connectivist Learning Theory," *P2P Foundation*, accessed January 25, 2015, http://p2pfoundation.net /Connectivist_Learning_Theory_-_Siemens.

18. Alexander McAuley, Bonnie Stewart, George Siemens, and Dave Cormier, *The MOOC Model for Digital Practice* (2010), accessed May 10, 2016, http://www.elearnspace.org/Articles/MOOC_Final.pdf.

19. Alex Usher, "The Future of MOOCs: Coursera and EdX," *Higher Education Strategy Associates*, November 19, 2013, accessed August 4, 2015, http://higheredstrategy.com/the-future-of-moocs-coursera-and-edx/; Xarissa Holdaway, "Major Players in the MOOC Universe," *Chronicle of Higher Education*, April 29, 2013, http://chronicle.com/article/The-Major -Players-in-the-MOOC/138817/.

20. An important resource of expert critique was the Hack Education blog, authored by independent analyst Audrey Watters at http://hackeducation .com/.

21. Ed-tech analyst Phil Hill disputed the claim that MOOC experiments with public colleges were aimed primarily at cost savings. Phil Hill, "You Know What Would Help MOOC Articles? Getting the Facts and Goals Right before Analyzing," *e-literate,* August 20, 2013, accessed January 21, 2015, http://mfeldstein.com/you-know-what-would-help-mooc-articles-getting -the-facts-and-goals-right-before-analyzing/. He was correct that this aim was not as such written into the partnership or regulatory language he cites, but the larger motives and political aims are as I describe them in the text. For an example of the link between cost cutting and access from someone imagining a transformation of global higher education, see Cathy N. Davidson, "If We Profs Don't Reform Higher Ed, We'll Be Re-Formed (and We Won't like It)," *HASTAC,* January 13, 2013, accessed July 31, 2013, http://hastac.org/blogs /cathy-davidson/2013/01/13/if-we-profs-dont-reform-higher-ed-well-be-re -formed-and-we-wont-it#.UPbcPOhXLFc.

22. "Rebooting Higher Education" conference, UCLA, January 8, 2013, unofficial draft transcript prepared by Jenna Joo, UC Santa Barbara, for the Online Study Group, in author's files.

23. Ibid., 3–4.

24. Ibid., 28–29.

25. See, for example, Richard A. DeMillo, *Abelard to Apple: The Fate of American Colleges and Universities* (Cambridge, MA: MIT Press, 2011); Ann Kirschner, "Innovations in Higher Education? Hah!," *Chronicle of Higher*

Education, April 8, 2012, http://chronicle.com/article/Innovations-in-Higher
/131424/.

26. Michael Meranze, "Paved with Good Intentions," *Remaking the
University* (blog), April 7, 2013, http://utotherescue.blogspot.co.uk/2013/04
/paved-with-good-intentions.html; Michael Meranze, "Amended Steinberg
Is Still Privatization," *Remaking the University* (blog), April 18, 2013, http://
utotherescue.blogspot.co.uk/2013/04/amended-steinberg-is-still
-privatization.html.

27. Ry Rivard, "Documents Shed Light on Details of Georgia Tech-
Udacity Deal," *Inside Higher Ed*, May 28, 2013, http://www.insidehighered
.com/news/2013/05/28/documents-shed-light-details-georgia-tech-udacity
-deal.

28. This section is based on my analysis in Christopher Newfield, "Where
Are the Savings?," *Inside Higher Ed*, June 24, 2013, accessed March 16, 2016,
http://www.insidehighered.com/views/2013/06/24/essay-sees-missing
-savings-georgia-techs-much-discussed-mooc-based-program. The contract
and appendix spreadsheets are posted at https://www.documentcloud.org
/documents/703593-udacity-gtrc-amendment-5-13-2013.html#document/p3
/a104046.

29. Stuart Zweben, "Computing Degree and Enrollment Trends:
Undergraduate Enrollment in Computer Science Trends," Computing
Research Association, 2009, accessed August 4, 2015, http://archive2.cra.org
/uploads/documents/resources/taulbee/CS_Degree_and_Enrollment
_Trends_2008-09.pdf.

30. Year 3 expenses, the final year for which the contract offered cost
estimates, were about $14.4 million total, of which nearly $12 million was to be
spent by Udacity.

31. The Georgia Tech College of Computing reported 2,841 students
enrolled in the OMS CS program in spring 2015 (Year 2), accessed March 16,
2016, http://omscs.gatech.edu/prospective-students/numbers, and 3,358
a year later on the splash page http://www.omscs.gatech.edu/.

32. Carl Straumsheim, "Georgia Tech Plans Next Steps for Online Master's
Degree in Computer Science," *Inside Higher Ed*, April 27, 2016, https://www
.insidehighered.com/news/2016/04/27/georgia-tech-plans-next-steps-online
-masters-degree-computer-science.

> The program has not been a "big revenue stream," [Georgia Tech
> President G. P.] Peterson said. With 3,358 students, the program is a
> "positive cash flow at this point" and the institute is "beyond break even,"
> but he expressed doubt that the program will reach the 10,000-student
> mark. . . . The institute did not share specific information about the

program's finances, but [an associate dean] indicated that the fixed costs of running the program are due to drop. Course development has been a major expense—Peterson said the institute spends about $350,000 to create each course—but with 20 courses in its inventory and another seven or eight lined up for this fall, the institute will soon have "more than enough" to satisfy student demands. . . . AT&T subsidized the program's launch with a $2 million investment, then later made an additional $1.9 million commitment.

33. Henry William Chesbrough, *Open Innovation: The New Imperative for Creating and Profiting from Technology* (Cambridge, MA: Harvard Business Press, 2003); Christopher Newfield, "Corporate Open Source: Intellectual Property and the Struggle over Value," *Radical Philosophy* 181 (September/October 2013), http://www.radicalphilosophy.com/commentary/corporate-open-source.

34. Rather typically, a follow-up piece on the Georgia Tech–Udacity partnership stressed the low, low price without offering new data on costs (Carl Straumsheim, "One Semester in, Students Satisfied with Unfinished Georgia Tech Online Degree Program," *Inside Higher Ed,* June 6, 2014, http://www.insidehighered.com/news/2014/06/06/one-semester-students-satisfied-unfinished-georgia-tech-online-degree-program#sthash.OWzg94Mi.6GVwebfh.dpbs).

35. https://www.coursera.org/about/.

36. Barbara Means et al., *Evaluation of Evidence-Based Practices in Online Learning: A Meta-Analysis and Review of Online Learning Studies* (Washington, DC: Department of Education, Center for Technology in Learning, 2009), accessed May 10, 2016, http://files.eric.ed.gov/fulltext/ED505824.pdf.

37. The Pell Institute for the Study of Opportunity in Higher Education, *Developing 20/20 Vision on the 2020 Degree Attainment Goal: The Threat of Income-Based Inequality in Education* (Washington, DC: Pell Institute, 2011), fig. 4, accessed August 2, 2015, http://www.pellinstitute.org/downloads/publications-Developing_2020_Vision_May_2011.pdf; this report refers to the standard group of twenty-four nations studied by the OECD.

38. Ibid., fig. 3.

39. US Census, "Educational Attainment in the United States: 2014—Detailed Tables," table 3, accessed August 2, 2015, http://www.census.gov/hhes/socdemo/education/data/cps/2014/tables.html. Rounded-off percentages for bachelor's degrees only are 24 (Asian American), 16 (non-Hispanic white), 10 (African American), and 8 (Hispanic any race). Native Americans are omitted from this table. For a summary, see Christopher Newfield, "How Unequal State Support Diminishes Degree Attainment,"

Chronicle of Higher Education, April 15, 2012, http://chronicle.com/article/How-Unequal-State-Support/131536/.

40. Koller, "What We're Learning from Online Education," accessed August 2, 2015, https://www.youtube.com/watch?v=U6FvJ6jMGHU.

41. See the introduction to Anant Agarwal, Andrew Ng, Andrea Mitchell, and Shirley Jackson, *Full Session: Will Massively Open Online Courses Transform the Way We Learn?* (Aspen Institute, 2013), accessed May 10, 2016, https://www.youtube.com/watch?v=VAlu1HUiUg8.

42. Eric Schmidt and Jared Cohen, *The New Digital Age: Reshaping the Future of People, Nations and Business* (New York: Knopf, 2013).

43. Koller, "What We're Learning from Online Education," at 12′30″.

44. Ibid. at 19′.

45. "Rebooting Higher Education," 4–5.

46. Koller, "What We're Learning from Online Education," at 18′20″.

47. For example, the Coursera contract with UC Irvine was an "online course hosting and services agreement" between Coursera and "The Regents of the University of California, a California constitutional corporation, on behalf of University Extension at the University of California, Irvine." Document in author's files.

48. Official student-to-faculty ratios can be found at "National Liberal Arts College Rankings," *U.S. News & World Report,* accessed August 5, 2015, http://colleges.usnews.rankingsandreviews.com/best-colleges/rankings/national-liberal-arts-colleges.

49. Benjamin S. Bloom, "The 2 Sigma Problem: The Search for Methods of Group Instruction as Effective as One-to-One Tutoring," *Education Researcher* 13, no. 6 (June–July 1984): 4–16.

50. Loren Pope, *Colleges That Change Lives: 40 Schools That Will Change the Way You Think About Colleges,* rev. ed. (New York: Penguin, 2007).

51. Means et al., *Evaluation of Evidence-Based Practices,* n. 36.

52. Ibid., xv, 51.

53. Ibid., xv, 48.

54. Ibid., xvi, 46.

55. Ibid., xvi, 46.

56. Ibid., xiv, xviii.

57. See the discussion of Richard Arum and Josipa Roksa, *Academically Adrift: Limited Learning on College Campuses* (Chicago: University of Chicago Press, 2011), in Stages 7 and 8 in Chapter 11 of this book.

58. Means et al., *Evaluation of Evidence-Based Practices,* 51.

59. A total of ninety-seven national bachelor's-level schools and twenty California associate-level schools were selected for comparison. The schools were classified into one of the following institution types: (1) Public Research

Universities, (2) Regional Colleges, (3) Liberal Arts Colleges, (4) For-Profit Institutions, (5) For-Profit Institutions with Distance Learning Only, and (6) California Community Colleges. Schools for the first three groups were selected from the top forty *U.S. News & World Report*'s 2013 Best Colleges Rankings (http://colleges.usnews.rankingsandreviews.com/best-colleges). Identifying and selecting schools for the fourth category was rather challenging since their rankings were not available. Furthermore, many for-profit institutions are subsidiaries of larger parent companies and are located in multiple locations throughout the country, making selection difficult. Twenty schools that had comparable data available on the National Center for Education Statistics website were selected from the list of for-profit institutions in Wikipedia (http://en.wikipedia.org/wiki/List_of_for-profit _universities_and_colleges). The fifth group had the smallest number of institutions throughout the country, as there were only twenty-seven of them. Seventeen schools that had comparable data in the National Center for Education Statistics were selected and included in the dataset. Lastly, twenty California Community Colleges were selected from the list on a website (http://www.schools.com/articles/top-25-community-colleges-in-california) and entered into the dataset.

Since almost all schools in our dataset, except those in the Public Research University category, didn't have a significant number of research and public service faculty (according to NCES), only the percentages of instructional faculty were used for comparison. Percentage of full-time instructional faculty could be a useful metric to surmise educational quality of an institution.

60. Author's notes on response and conversation, "Learning with MOOCs II," Teachers College, Columbia University, New York, October 3, 2015.

61. Note that we sought to identify data about for-profits that did and did not use distance learning in their strategies, and we compared two types of for-profits. Highly ranked online programs (per *U.S. News & World Report*) are a mixture of for-profit and not-for-profit institutions. We sought to track changes in data as we moved from "for-profit institutions (distance learning only)" to "distance learning only (for-profit and not-for-profit)." Available data were insufficient to complete this analysis.

62. Online Research Group calculations, conducted by Jenna Joo.

63. California Community College Chancellor's Office 2015.

64. For campus demographics in fall 2012, see http://www.sjsu.edu /careercenter/employers/about-our-students/demographics-irene-2012.pdf, accessed August 4, 2015.

65. Charles Duhigg and David Kocieniewski, "Apple's Tax Strategy Aims at Low-Tax States and Nations," *New York Times*, April 28, 2012, http://www

.nytimes.com/2012/04/29/business/apples-tax-strategy-aims-at-low-tax
-states-and-nations.html.

66. Elaine D. Collins, *SJSU+ Augmented Online Learning Environment
(AOLE) Pilot Project Report* (Research and Planning Group of California
Community Colleges, September 2013), accessed January 21, 2015, http://
www.sjsu.edu/chemistry/People/Faculty/Collins_Research_Page
/AOLE%20Report%20-September%2010%202013%20final.pdf.

67. Ry Rivard, "Udacity Project on 'Pause,'" *Inside Higher Ed*, July 18, 2013,
https://www.insidehighered.com/news/2013/07/18/citing-disappointing
-student-outcomes-san-jose-state-pauses-work-udacity; Collins, "Preliminary
Summary," in *SJSU+ Augmented Online Learning Environment Pilot Project*.

68. For an accessible overview of these and related conceptions of
learning, see Peter C. Brown, Henry L. Roediger III, and Mark A. McDaniel,
Make It Stick: The Science of Successful Learning (Cambridge, MA: Belknap
Press of Harvard University Press, 2014).

69. Malcolm Gladwell, *Outliers: The Story of Success* (New York: Little,
Brown, 2008), chap. 2.

70. See Brown, Roediger, and McDaniel, *Make It Stick.*

71. Collins, "Preliminary Summary," 31.

72. Max Chafkin, "Udacity's Sebastian Thrun, Godfather of Free Online
Education, Changes Course," *Fast Company*, November 30, 2013, accessed
August 4, 2015, http://www.fastcompany.com/3021473/udacity-sebastian
-thrun-uphill-climb.

73. Eduardo Porter, "Udacity-AT&T 'NanoDegree' Offers an Entry-Level
Approach to College," *New York Times*, June 17, 2014, http://www.nytimes
.com/2014/06/18/business/economy/udacity-att-nanodegree-offers-an
-entry-level-approach-to-college.html.

74. Eric Westervelt, "The Online Education Revolution Drifts Off
Course," *NPR.org*, December 31, 2013, http://www.npr.org/2013/12/31
/258420151/the-online-education-revolution-drifts-off-course.

75. Udacity received a new round of funding for this project: Lizette
Chapman, "E-Learning Startup Udacity Raises $35M to Launch 'Nanode-
grees,'" September 24, 2014, http://blogs.wsj.com/venturecapital/2014/09
/24/e-learning-startup-udacity-raises-35m-to-launch-nanodegrees/.

Stage 7. Unequal Funding Cuts Attainment

1. UC Board of Regents, "Agenda, Committee on Long Range Planning,
July 16, 2014," accessed November 23, 2014, http://regents.universityofcalifornia
.edu/minutes/2014/lrp7.pdf; UC Office of the President, "UC Mandatory
Student Charge Levels," accessed November 22, 2014, http://ucop.edu
/operating-budget/_files/fees/documents/history_fees.pdf; UC Office of

the President, "University of California Accountability Report," Indicator
2.5.2, "Percentage of full-time-equivalent undergraduate enrollees classified as
nonresidents for tuition purposes, universitywide, 1999–2000 to 2012–13,"
accessed November 22, 2014, http://accountability.universityofcalifornia.edu
/index/2.5.2.

2. Edmund G. Brown Jr., "Request from Edmund G. Brown, Jr., President
of the Regents of the University of California," accessed November 22, 2014,
https://www.scribd.com/doc/247214287/BrownJerry5PointPlanUC
-1114Regents.

3. University of California Board of Regents Meeting, Committee for
Long-Range Planning, November 19, 2014, author's transcript; original audio
recording removed.

4. University of California Board of Regents Meeting, Committee for
Long-Range Planning, November 19, 2014. One speaker in public comment
said, "I have friends who say I can't afford to live here anymore therefore
I'm not going to school any more. People are not going to school any more.
People like me are saying can I really make it to senior year." Author's
transcript; original audio recording removed.

5. Warren Olney et al., "UC Committee Moves forward with Tuition
Hike," *Which Way LA?* KCRW radio show, November 19, 2014, 13′, 16′00″–
16′28″; http://www.kcrw.com/news-culture/shows/which-way-la/uc
-committee-moves-forward-with-tuition-hike.

6. Richard Arum and Josipa Roksa, *Academically Adrift: Limited Learning
on College Campuses* (Chicago: University of Chicago Press, 2011).

7. Scott Jaschik, " 'Academically Adrift,' " *Inside Higher Ed*, January 18, 2011,
http://www.insidehighered.com/news/2011/01/18/study_finds_large_numbers
_of_college_students_don_t_learn_much.

8. Arum and Roksa, *Academically Adrift,* 35–36.

9. Total revolving credit debt in 2010 was $840.7 billion (down from
$1,005.2 billion in 2008) versus total student loan debt of $912.4 billion (up
from $730.7 billion in 2008). As of the third quarter of 2013, revolving debt
was down to $820.3 billion and student loan debt was up to $1,213.0 billion.
See http://www.federalreserve.gov/releases/g19/Current/#fn11b. Also see
http://www.fastweb.com/financial-aid/articles/2589-total-college-debt-now
-exceeds-total-credit-card-debt.

10. The graduation rate for a first tertiary nonvocational education
degree in the United States is just 39 percent, versus 60 percent for Australia,
50 percent for Denmark, 63 percent for Iceland, 58 percent in Poland,
and 43 percent for the United Kingdom. The European Union group of
twenty-one countries (EU21) averages a 38 percent graduation rate. OECD,
Education at a Glance 2013: OECD Indicators, chart A3.3, January 12, 2015,

http://www.oecd.org/edu/eag2013%20%28eng%29—FINAL%2020%20
June%202013.pdf.

11. Citing the CLA's developers, Arum and Roksa, *Academically Adrift*, 21.

12. The study is described in Arum and Roksa, *Academically Adrift*,
"Methodological Appendix," 145.

13. Arum and Roksa, *Academically Adrift*, 88.

14. Ibid., 89.

15. Ibid.

16. Richard A. DeMillo, *Abelard to Apple: The Fate of American Colleges and
Universities* (Cambridge, MA: MIT Press, 2011), 21.

17. Arum and Roksa, *Academically Adrift*, 5.

18. Abraham Flexner criticized the overreliance on lecture formats and the
absence of clear educational goals in *The American* College (New York: The
Century Company, 1908). In the modern period, the authors of a thorough sociological study, *The Academic Marketplace*, concluded that faculty shortchange
teaching for the sake of pursuing their careers—in 1958. See Theodore Caplow
and Reece McGee, *The Academic Marketplace* (New York: Science Editions,
1961). Fifty years later, one could find former Harvard University president Derek
Bok lamenting *Our Underachieving Colleges*, noting that although there is no
evidence that faculty neglect their students, they don't seem to be going beyond
normal "conscientiousness" either. See Derek Bok, *Our Underachieving Colleges:
A Candid Look at How Much Students Learn and Why They Should Be Learning
More* (Princeton, NJ: Princeton University Press, 2007), 32, 34.

19. Richard Arum and Josipa Roksa, *Aspiring Adults Adrift: Tentative
Transitions of College Graduates* (Chicago: University of Chicago Press, 2014),
Kindle location 798.

20. Ibid., 120.

21. See Rebekah Nathan, *My Freshman Year: What a Professor Learned
by Becoming a Student* (New York, Penguin Books: 2006); and Elizabeth A.
Armstrong and Laura T. Hamilton, *Paying for the Party: How College Maintains
Inequality* (Cambridge, MA: Harvard University Press, 2013).

22. Richard Vedder, "The Real Reason College Costs So Much," *Wall Street
Journal*, August 26, 2013, http://online.wsj.com/article/SB10001424127887324
619504579029282438522674.html?mod=WSJ_Opinion_LEADTop; Steve
Kolowich, "California State U. System Will Expand MOOC Experiment,"
Wired Campus (blog), *Chronicle of Higher Education*, April 10, 2013, http://
chronicle.com/blogs/wiredcampus/california-state-u-system-will-expand
-mooc-experiment/43361.

23. I extrapolate from the statement that the average CLA performance
improvement was 34 points, and that high faculty expectations and more

rigorous coursework improve achievement by another 27 and 23 points, respectively. A query to one of the book's authors confirmed that they did not analyze their data in this way.

24. Arum and Roksa, *Academically Adrift,* 72, 94–95.

25. Ibid., 69, 97–98.

26. Ibid., 93.

27. Ibid., 103–4, 100–101.

28. Ibid., 102, 85–86.

29. Ibid., 109.

30. For a concise tribute to the value of individual attention in college, see Charles M. Blow, "In College, Nurturing Matters," *New York Times,* May 7, 2014, http://www.nytimes.com/2014/05/08/opinion/blow-in-college -nurturing-matters.html.

31. Arum and Roksa, *Academically Adrift,* 115.

32. An influential list is found in Loren Pope, *Colleges That Change Lives: 40 Schools That Will Change the Way You Think About Colleges* (New York: Penguin, 2007).

33. Richard Arum, Josipa Roksa, and Esther Cho, "Improving Undergraduate Learning: Findings and Policy Recommendations from the SSRC-CLA Longitudinal Project (New York: Social Science Research Council, 2014), fig. 6, accessed November 30, 2014, https://s3.amazonaws.com/ssrc-cdn1 /crmuploads/new_publication_3/%7BD06178BE-3823-E011-ADEF -001CC477EC84%7D.pdf.

34. Christopher Newfield, "Good and Bad in the Teaching Report," *Remaking the University* (blog), May 14, 2013, http://utotherescue.blogspot .com/2013/05/good-and-bad-in-teaching-report.html.

35. See Katherine D. Harris, "Drowning and No One Cares," *TriprofTri* (blog), December 19, 2013, http://triproftri.wordpress.com/2013/12/19 /drowning-workload/; and Joanne Barker, "The Beginning and End of Ethnic Studies," *Tequila Sovereign* (blog), February 22, 2016, https:// tequilasovereign.wordpress.com/2016/02/22/the-beginning-and-end-of -ethnic-studies/.

36. Andrew P. Kelly and Mark Schneider, eds., *Getting to Graduation: The Completion Agenda in Higher Education* (Baltimore, MD: Johns Hopkins University Press, 2012), 6, and esp. the chapters by Brian Bosworth, Diane Auer Jones, and Bridget Terry Long; see also Barack Obama, "Remarks by the President on College Affordability—Buffalo, NY," press release, White House, August 22, 2013, accessed August 23, 2013, http://www.whitehouse .gov/the-press-office/2013/08/22/remarks-president-college-affordability -buffalo-ny.

37. National Center for Education Statistics, table 236.55, "Total and current expenditures per pupil in public elementary and secondary schools: Selected years, 1919–20 through 2011–12," accessed August 10, 2015, https://nces.ed.gov/programs/digest/d14/tables/dt14_236.55.asp. Total expenditure per pupil in fall enrollment for 2005–2006 was $10,603.

38. Estimate of Harvard expenditure of $60,000 per student in 2005–2006 courtesy of Calvin Moore, in author's files.

39. Nathan Brostrom, discussion of UC Regents, "Approval of Long-Term Stability Plan for Tuition and Financial Aid," November 19, 2014, UC Board of Regents Item L3, accessed November 29, 2014, http://regents.university ofcalifornia.edu/regmeet/nov14/l3.pdf. Video archived at http://uclafaculty association.blogspot.de/2014/11/listen-to-regents-morning-meeting-of.html, accessed November 29, 2014.

40. Christopher Newfield, "The End of the American Funding Model: What Comes Next?," *American Literature* 82, no. 3 (September 2010): 611–35. This section is derived from this article.

41. William G. Bowen, Matthew M. Chingos, and Michael S. McPherson, *Crossing the Finish Line: Completing College at America's Public Universities* (Princeton, NJ: Princeton University Press, 2009). Hereafter, *CFL*.

42. Ibid., ix.

43. Ibid., 22–25, also 32–56.

44. Ibid., 224.

45. Jay P. Greene and Marcus A. Winters, "Tougher Standards Are Already Yielding Results," *USA Today*, May 31, 2005, 13a.

46. *CFL*, 27. The low academic level of American high school graduates became a topic of national debate, and it prompted the Obama Administration to formulate its controversial "Race to the Top" program. See William Branigin, "Obama Launches 'Race' for $4 Billion in Education Funds," *Washington Post*, July 24, 2009, www.washingtonpost.com/wp-dyn/content /article/2009/07/24/AR2009072402203.html. However, the *CFL* study shows that most of the lingering gap is tied to social position, including economic position.

47. Danette Gerald and Kati Haycock, *Engines of Inequality: Diminishing Equity in the Nation's Premier Public Universities* (Washington, DC: Education Trust, 2006), accessed January 17, 2010, www.edtrust.org/dc/publication /engines-of-inequality-diminishing-equity-in-the-nation's-premier-public -universities; Kati Haycock, Mary Lynch, and Jennifer Engle, *Opportunity Adrift: Our Flagship Universities Are Straying from Their Public Mission* (Washington, DC: Education Trust, 2010); Department of Education, "2007–08 Federal Pell Grant End of Year Report," table 13, accessed January 17, 2010, www.ed.gov /finaid/prof/resources/data/pell-2007–08/pell-eoy-07–08.pdf.

48. Melissa Roderick et al., *From High School to the Future: Potholes on the Road to College* (Chicago: Consortium on Chicago School Research at the University of Chicago, 2008), 5, accessed November 3, 2014, http://ccsr .uchicago.edu/sites/default/files/publications/CCSR_Potholes_Report .pdf.

49. *CFL*, 112–33. Formative studies of undermatching include Christopher Avery et al., "Cost Should Be No Barrier: An Evaluation of the First Year of Harvard's Financial Aid Initiative," NBER Working Paper no. 12029 (Cambridge, MA: National Bureau of Economic Research, February 2006), http://www .nber.org/papers/w12029; and Caroline M. Hoxby and Christopher Avery, "The Missing 'One-Offs': The Hidden Supply of High-Achieving, Low-Income Students," NBER Working Paper no. 18586 (Cambridge, MA: National Bureau of Economic Research, December 2012), http://www.nber .org/papers/w18586.

50. Charles Murray, *Real Education: Four Simple Truths for Bringing America's Schools Back to Reality* (New York: Three Rivers Press, 2009).

51. *CFL*, 27; Thomas G. Mortenson, "Family Income and Unequal Educational Opportunity, 1970 to 2011," *Postsecondary Education Opportunity* (November 2012): 1.

52. *CFL*, 202–3.

53. Ibid., 202–3, 90–93.

54. The most selective universities in the United States—Harvard, Yale, Princeton, Stanford, and so on—form the academic gold standard for most of the public as well as for educational leaders. In this view, to improve ranking and hence competitiveness and quality requires that an institution increase selectivity. According to *U.S. News & World Report*, 2013 sample admission rates are: Stanford—5.7 percent; Harvard—5.8 percent; Yale—6.9 percent; Princeton—7.4 percent; University of Chicago— 8.8 percent; Penn—12.2 percent; Duke—12.4 percent; Northwestern— 14 percent; Cornell—15.6 percent; NYU—32.4 percent. Brooklyn College admits only one-third of its applicants, and traditionally less prestigious private universities like Bucknell and Trinity accept about 30 percent of applicants or fewer, http://colleges.usnews.rankingsandreviews.com/best -colleges/rankings/lowest-acceptance-rate?src=stats, accessed November 4, 2014.

55. *CFL*, 197.

56. Ibid., 198.

57. They add that they may miss the institutional resource effect "due to the lack of measures of resources that are truly comparable across universities." *CFL*, 200. But, such measures do exist.

58. *CFL*, 196.

59. Donna M. Desrochers, Colleen M. Lenihan, and Jane V. Wellman, *Trends in College Spending, 1998–2008* (Washington, DC: Delta Cost Project, 2010), 26, 28, accessed March 16, 2016, http://www.deltacostproject.org /resources/pdf/Trends2011_Final_090711.pdf.

60. Anthony P. Carnevale and Jeff Strohl, *Separate and Unequal: How Higher Education Reinforces the Intergenerational Reproduction of White Racial Privilege* (Center on Education and the Workforce, Georgetown University, July 31, 2013), part 2, accessed February 17, 2014, http://cew.georgetown.edu /separateandunequal.

61. Ibid., fig. 10.

62. Ibid., fig. 11.

63. Ibid., "Introduction."

64. Ibid., 9. The report focuses on Underrepresented Minorities (URMs), which does not include Asian Americans, who in most locations qualify for university at higher rates than whites.

65. Tom Mortenson at *Postsecondary Opportunity* has traced income divergence for years. His work lies behind a good compendium of these trends: Margaret Cahalan and Laura Perna, *Indicators of Higher Education Equity in the United States: 45-Year Trend Report* (Philadelphia: University of Pennsylvania-Penn Ahead, 2015).

66. The term *plutonomy* is generally traced to Ajay Kapur, Niall Macleod, and Narendra Singh, "Plutonomy: Buying Luxury, Explaining Global Imbalances," *Citigroup Equity Strategy: Industry Note,* October 16, 2005, accessed August 10, 2015, http://delong.typepad.com/plutonomy-1.pdf. I discuss this concept in chapter 11, Stage 8.

67. Estimates vary, but the numbers for gross state tuition money and total federal subsidies to the financial aid system are close enough to suggest that the latter, if converted to direct payments, could buy out the former. See Jordan Weissmann, "Exactly How Much Would It Cost to Make Public Colleges Tuition-Free? (An Update)," *Slate,* January 14, 2015, http://www.slate .com/blogs/moneybox/2015/01/14/free_college_here_s_how_much _public_college_students_pay_in_tuition.html; Robert Samuels, *Why Public Higher Education Should Be Free: How to Decrease Cost and Increase Quality at American Universities* (New Brunswick, NJ: Rutgers University Press, 2013).

68. See Hoxby and Avery, "The Missing 'One-Offs'"; and Avery et al., "Cost Should Be No Barrier."

69. These are the proportions of undergraduates served, respectively, by what I call the Double Ivies (the Ivy League plus MIT, Caltech, Stanford, Duke, Emory, Carnegie Mellon, NYU, and Northwestern) and by these sixteen schools plus the Annapolis Group of liberal arts colleges.

Stage 8. Universities Build the Post–Middle Class

1. In 2000 Educational Appropriations (EA) per Full Time Equivalent (FTE) student were $8,427 to Net Tuition per FTE of $3,486. In 2005, EA per FTE was $7,152 versus $4,031 in Net Tuition per FTE. In 2010 these figures were $6,729 versus $4,468. In 2012 they were almost equal, with EA per FTE at $5,906 and Net Tuition per FTE at $5,189. Aggregate spending on Educational Appropriations dropped from $72.5 billion in 2000, to $70.8 billion in 2005, rose to $76.4 billion in 2010, and then plummeted back down to $68.2 billion in 2012. Over this same time period, Net Tuition rose from $30.0 billion in 2000, to $39.9 billion in 2005, $51.8 billion in 2010, and $60.0 billion in 2012. Calculated using SHEEO's State Higher Education Finance 2012 data, available for download under "All States Wavechart 2012" on their website: http://www.sheeo.org/resources/publications/shef-%E2%80%94 -state-higher-education-finance-fy12.

2. Ajay Kapur, Niall Macleod, and Narendra Singh, "Plutonomy: Buying Luxury, Explaining Global Imbalances," Citigroup Equity Strategy: Industry Note (October 16, 2005), accessed August 10, 2015, http://delong.typepad .com/plutonomy-1.pdf.

3. Gary Stanley Becker, *Human Capital: A Theoretical and Empirical Analysis, with Special Reference to Education* (Chicago: University of Chicago Press, 1993).

4. Extraction of surplus value was most influentially discussed in Karl Marx, *Capital,* vol. 1, *A Critique of Political Economy,* trans. Ben Fowkes (London: Penguin Books, 1976, 1990). (The original work was published in 1887, by Samuel Moore and Edward Aveling, edited by Frederick Engels, Progress Publishers, Moscow.)

5. See *The State of Working America* for exact figures, http://www .stateofworkingamerica.org/chart/swa-wages-table-4-14-hourly-wages -education/.

6. For mainstream media evidence, see Dylan Matthews, "The Tuition Is Too Damn High, Part II: Why College Is Still Worth It," *Washington Post,* August 27, 2013, http://www.washingtonpost.com/blogs/wonkblog/wp/2013 /08/27/the-tuition-is-too-damn-high-part-ii-why-college-is-still-worth-it/. See also Katie Zaback, Andy Carlson, and Matt Crellin, "The Economic Benefit of Secondary Degrees: A State and National Level Analysis," *State Higher Education Executive* Officers, December 2012, accessed May 1, 2015, http://www.sheeo.org/sites/default/files/publications/Econ%20Benefit%20 of%20Degrees%20Report%20with%20Appendices.pdf.

7. Claudia Goldin and Lawrence F. Katz, *The Race between Education and Technology* (Cambridge, MA: Belknap Press of Harvard University Press, 2008).

8. Three key contemporary texts were John Kenneth Galbraith, *The Affluent Society* (Boston: Houghton Mifflin, 1958); David Potter, *People of Plenty: Economic Abundance and the American Character* (Chicago: University of Chicago Press, 1958); and Clark Kerr, *The Uses of the University* (Cambridge, MA: Harvard University Press, 1963).

9. A particularly useful anatomy of the change as the end of "Fordist" capitalism and the arrival of "post-Fordism" remains David Harvey, *The Condition of Postmodernity: An Enquiry into the Origins of Cultural Change* (London: Blackwell, 1992).

10. "The median worker saw an increase of just 5 percent between 1979 and 2012, despite productivity growth of 74.5 percent, while the twentieth percentile worker saw wage erosion of 0.4 percent and the eightieth percentile worker saw wage growth of just 17.5 percent." Lawrence Mishel and Heidi Shierholz, "A Decade of Flat Wages: The Key Barrier to Shared Prosperity and a Rising Middle Class," EPI Briefing Paper #365, Economic Policy Institute, August 21, 2013, accessed September 4, 2013, http://www.epi.org/publication /a-decade-of-flat-wages-the-key-barrier-to-shared-prosperity-and-a-rising -middle-class/.

11. Lawrence Mishel, "Entry-level Workers' Wages Fell in Lost Decade," Issue Brief #327, Economic Policy Institute, March 7, 2012, accessed September 7, 2013, http://www.epi.org/publication/ib327-young-workers-wages/.

12. Tom Mortenson, "Family Income and Unequal Educational Opportunity, 1970 to 2011," *Postsecondary Education Opportunity* (November 2012): 1–20.

13. As the World Bank explains, the "Gini index measures the extent to which the distribution of income or consumption expenditure among individuals or households within an economy deviates from a perfectly equal distribution. . . . [A] Gini index of 0 represents perfect equality, while an index of 100 implies perfect inequality." Gini coefficients from about 40 and up signal unusually unequal economies. In 2010, China stood at 42, Nigeria at 43, Mexico about 47, Paraguay at 52, and Brazil at 53, and Namibia at over 61. On the other hand, Slovenia stood at 25, Iceland at 26, Germany at 30.6, Ireland at 32, Canada at 34, Poland at 34, the UK at 38. The US is closer to the more unequal societies with a Gini coefficient of 41 (in 2010), http://data.worldbank .org/indicator/SI.POV.GINI/countries/1W?order=wbapi_data_value _2010%20wbapi_data_value&sort=asc&display=default, accessed October 30, 2014.

14. Isabel Sawhill and John E. Morton, *Economic Mobility: Is the American Dream Alive and Well?* (Washington, DC: Economic Mobility Project, Pew Charitable Trusts, May 2007), accessed April 26, 2009, http://www.brookings .edu/papers/2007/05useconomics_morton.aspx.

15. Thomas Piketty et al., "The World Top Incomes Database," multiple comparisons generated at http://topincomes.g-mond .parisschoolofeconomics.eu/#Graphic, accessed September 6, 2013.

16. Jeff Keans, "Fed Says U.S. Wealth Fell 38.8% in 2007–2010 on Housing," *Bloomberg Personal Finance News,* June 12, 2012, http://www.bloomberg.com /news/2012-06-11/fed-says-family-wealth-plunged-38-8-in-2007-2010-on -home-values.html. Also see Alissa Anderson, "Census Data Show That Gains during the Recovery Have Failed to Reach Middle-Income Families," California Budget Project, September 18, 2012, http://californiabudgetbites .org/2012/09/18/census-data-show-that-gains-during-the-recovery-have -failed-to-reach-middle-income-families/.

17. Emmanuel Saez, "Striking It Richer: The Evolution of Top Incomes in the United States (Updated with 2011 Estimates)," *Elsa Berkeley,* January 23, 2013, http://elsa.berkeley.edu/~saez/saez-UStopincomes-2011.pdf. Saez's claims are contested by Stephen Rose, "The False Claim That Inequality Rose during the Great Recession," The Information Technology and Innovation Foundation, February 2015, accessed August 13, 2015, http://www2.itif.org /2015-inequality-rose.pdf.

18. Kathleen Short and Timothy Smeedling, "Understanding Income-to-Threshold Ratios Using the Supplemental Poverty Measure: People with Moderate Income," SEHSD Working Paper Number 2012-18 (August 21, 2012), fig. 1 (using the Supplemental Poverty Measure), accessed August 28, 2013, http://www.census.gov/hhes/povmeas/methodology/supplemental /research/SEHSD2012-18.pdf.

19. Richard Freeman, "The Great Doubling: The Challenge of the New Global Labor Market," August 2006, accessed September 8, 2013, http:// emlab.berkeley.edu/users/webfac/eichengreen/e183_sp07/great_doub.pdf.

20. The most lucid version of this argument was Robert B. Reich, *The Work of Nations: Preparing Ourselves for 21st-Century Capitalism* (New York: Knopf, 1991).

21. An influential advocate of competing to win a global economic race where the other runners are faster than ever before has been the *New York Times* columnist Thomas Friedman, *The Lexus and the Olive Tree: Understanding Globalization* (New York: Anchor, 2000), and *The World is Flat: A Brief History of the Twenty-first Century* (New York: Farrar, Straus and Giroux, 2005).

22. Two particularly good, comprehensive syntheses of neoliberal theory and practice are Wendy Brown, *Undoing the Demos: Neoliberalism's Stealth Revolution* (New York: Zone Books, 2015), and Philip Mirowski, *Never Let a Serious Crisis Go to Waste: How Neoliberalism Survived the Financial Meltdown* (London: Verso, 2013). See also Mirowski's useful summary, "The Thirteen

Commandments of Neoliberalism," *The Utopian*, June 19, 2013, http://www.the-utopian.org/post/53360513384/the-thirteen-commandments-of-neoliberalism.

23. Thomas L. Friedman, "I Made the Robot Do It," *New York Times*, August 25, 2012, http://www.nytimes.com/2012/08/26/opinion/sunday/i-made-the-robot-do-it.html.

24. See Steven Greenhouse, "Our Economic Pickle," *New York Times*, January 12, 2013, http://www.nytimes.com/2013/01/13/sunday-review/americas-productivity-climbs-but-wages-stagnate.html.

25. Teresa Kroeger, Tanyell Cooke, and Elise Gould, "The Class of 2016: The Labor Market Is Still Far from Ideal for Young Graduates," Economic Policy Institute, April 21, 2016, accessed June 1, 2016, http://www.epi.org/publication/class-of-2016/.

26. "Although the US statutory tax rate is higher, the average effective rate is about the same, and the marginal rate on new investment is only slightly higher." Jane G. Gravelle, "International Corporate Tax Rate Comparisons and Policy Implications," *Congressional Research Service*, January 6, 2014, https://www.fas.org/sgp/crs/misc/R41743.pdf. See also Chad Stone, "Putting U.S. Corporate Taxes in Perspective," *Center on Budget and Policy Priorities*, October 27, 2008, http://www.cbpp.org/cms/?fa=view&id=784#_ftn1.

27. Thomas L. Friedman, "If You've Got the Skills, She's Got the Job," *New York Times*, November 17, 2012, http://www.nytimes.com/2012/11/18/opinion/sunday/Friedman-You-Got-the-Skills.html. See also Thomas L. Friedman, "New Rules," *New York Times*, September 8, 2012, http://www.nytimes.com/2012/09/09/opinion/sunday/friedman-new-rules.html: "The truth is, if you want a decent job that will lead to a decent life today *you* have to work harder, regularly reinvent yourself, obtain at least some form of postsecondary education, make sure that you're engaged in lifelong learning and play by the rules. . . . More than ever now, lifelong learning is the key to getting into, and staying in, the middle class. . . . *You have to work harder and smarter and develop new skills faster*" [emphasis in original].

28. Peter Cappelli, *Why Good People Can't Get Jobs: The Skills Gap and What Companies Can Do About It* (Philadelphia: Wharton Digital Press, 2012).

29. A leading productivity "bear" is Robert J. Gordon, "Is U.S. Economic Growth Over? Faltering Innovation Confronts the Six Headwinds," NBER Working Paper no. 18315 (August 2012), accessed August 13, 2015, http://www.nber.org/papers/w18315; "The Demise of U.S. Economic Growth: Restatement, Rebuttal, and Reflections," NBER Working Paper no. 19895 (February 2014), accessed August 13, 2015, http://www.nber.org/papers/w19895; and

The Rise and Fall of American Growth: The U.S. Standard of Living since the Civil War (Princeton, NJ: Princeton University Press, 2016).

30. Mishel identifies three factors that contribute in varying ratios in different periods: inequality of compensation, shifts in labor's share of income, and divergence of consumer and output prices. From 1973–2011, the first factor accounted for 45 percent of the divergence. Lawrence Mishel, "The Wedges between Productivity and Median Compensation Growth," Issue Brief #330, Economic Policy Institute, April 26, 2012, 5–6, http://www .excellentfuture.ca/sites/default/files/The%20Wedges%20Between%20 Productivity%20and%20Meidian%20Compensation%20Growth.pdf.

31. As another example, "In 2011, the hourly wage of entry-level college-educated men was slightly more than $1 higher than in 1979, a rise of only 5.2 percent over 32 years." Mishel, "Entry-level Workers' Wages Fell in Lost Decade."

32. On the pre-1970s systems "of wage payment which gear earnings to production," see John T. Dunlop, "Productivity and the Wage Structure," in *Income, Employment and Public Policy* (New York: W. W. Norton, 1948), 341–62; and Joseph W. Garbarino, "The Productivity-Wage Relationship: Comment," *Industrial and Labor Relations Review* 7, no. 4 (July 1954): 608. On the centrality of productivity and the slowing of its growth, see Jeffrey G. Madrick, *Why Economies Grow: The Forces That Shape Prosperity and How We Can Get Them Working Again* (New York: Basic Books, 2002); Gordon, "Is U.S. Economic Growth Over?"; Gordon, "The Demise of U.S. Economic Growth."

33. Friedman, *The Lexus and the Olive Tree.*

34. Mishel, "Entry-level Workers' Wages Fell in Lost Decade," fig. B.

35. Gains to college graduates persisted through the 1990s, see, for example, Jennifer Cheeseman Day and Eric C. Newburger, "The Big Payoff: Educational Attainment and Synthetic Estimates of Work-Life Earnings," US Census Bureau, July 2002, http://smccd.edu/accounts/wongk/Value%20 of%20College.pdf. The authors mostly look at the 1997–1999 snapshot and then educational attainment against HS grads from 1975 to 1990, which shows a clear advantage and increase in earnings with educational attainment.

These wage gains may have reflected a temporary tightening of the job market rather than a restored connection between productivity gains and wage gains. Controversy has always existed on the question of what the connection is. For example, "signaling theory" doubts that wage gains for college grads ever tracked productivity gains that depended on university learning: "To the extent that the signaling theory of education wage premiums is true, rising educational attainment does not reflect increasing levels of human capital, but merely indicates an ongoing signaling 'arms race' in which talented workers need to spend more and more time in school in order to demonstrate their higher quality to potential employers . . . it may be possible to improve growth prospects by reducing the average number of years workers spend in school—years they could spend being productive in the workplace and honing actual skills through on-the-job experience." Brink Lindsey, "Why Growth Is Getting Harder," *Policy Analysis* 737 (October 8, 2013): 9, http://object.cato.org/sites/cato.org/files/pubs/pdf/pa737_web _1.pdf. My argument here does not depend on a claim that productivity increases *caused* wage gains at any point in the past: the connection rests on a cultural correlation that creates the reality of wage gains in conjunction with a range of policies (legal protections for unionization, etc.).

36. Reich, *Work of Nations*; Richard Florida, *The Flight of the Creative Class: The New Global Competition for Talent* (New York: HarperBusiness, 2007).

37. Kevin Phillips was a kind of middle-class Paul Revere of plutocracy warnings. See, for example, the reference to his "Millennial Plutographics" in Paul Krugman, "Plutocracy and Politics," *New York Times,* June 14, 2013, http://www.nytimes.com/2002/06/14/opinion/plutocracy-and-politics .html.

38. For a brief example of the zeitgeist that enfolded conservatives and progressives alike, see Jillian Berman blaming a skills gap for income equality in "Alan Greenspan: Don't Blame Capitalism for All This Income Inequality," *Huffington Post,* January 26, 2012, http://www.huffingtonpost.com/2012/01 /26/alan-greenspan-income-inequality_n_1234253.html.

39. Phillip Brown, Hugh Lauder, and David Ashton, *The Global Auction: The Broken Promises of Education, Jobs, and Incomes* (Oxford: Oxford University Press, 2010), Kindle ed., 134–39.

40. Ibid., 193–94.

41. Louis Uchitelle, "U.S. Manufacturing Gains Jobs as Wages Retreat," *New York Times,* December 29, 2011, http://www.nytimes.com/2011/12/30 /business/us-manufacturing-gains-jobs-as-wages-retreat.html.

42. Richard Parker, *The Myth of the Middle Class: Notes on Affluence and Equality* (New York: Liveright, 1972), 153.

43. Brown, Lauder, and Ashton, *Global Auction,* 1377–79.

44. Ibid., 1394, citing Simon Head.

45. Harold Wilensky, "Work, Careers, and Social Integration," *International Social Science Journal* 12 (1960): 557, cited in Brown, Lauder, and Ashton, *Global Auction,* 1546–47.

46. Ibid., 1447–48.

47. Christopher Newfield, "Facing the Knowledge Managers," in *Unmaking the Public University: The Forty-Year Assault on the Middle Class* (Cambridge, MA: Harvard University Press, 2008).

48. Douglas Coupland, *Microserfs* (New York: HarperCollins, 1995).

49. Richard Arum and Josipa Roksa, *Academically Adrift: Limited Learning on College Campuses* (Chicago: University of Chicago Press, 2011), 137.

50. David Labaree, *How to Succeed in School without Really Learning: The Credentials Race in American Education* (New Haven, CT: Yale University Press, 1997), 32, cited in Arum and Roksa, *Academically Adrift,* 17.

51. Arum and Roksa, *Academically Adrift,* 125.

52. Robert Samuels, *Why Public Higher Education Should Be Free: How to Decrease Cost and Increase Quality at American Universities* (New Brunswick, NJ: Rutgers University Press, 2013), 4–5.

53. For an explanation of the two major forms of meritocracy, see Newfield, *Unmaking the Public University,* chap. 6.

54. The Distributions of Income index–GINI–shows the following figures for 2000, where higher is less equal: Austria–29, Belgium–33, Canada–33, Finland–27, Germany–28, Greece–34, Ireland–34, Italy–36, Luxembourg–31, Norway–26, Spain–35, Sweden–25, Switzerland–34, US–42. http://wdi .worldbank.org/table/2.9, accessed November 12, 2014.

55. For 25 to 34-year-olds, more than 60 percent have "some college" according to Pew. "Is College Worth It? College Presidents, Public Access Value, Quality and Mission of Higher Education," Pew Research Center: Social & Demographic Trends, May 16, 2011, 23, accessed November 12, 2014, http://online.wsj.com/public/resources/documents/HigherEdReport.pdf. According to the 2012 US Census Data, of the total population of 18- to 34-year-olds, 27 percent have "some college, no degree." Thirty-five percent have "some college, no degree," an occupational associate's degree, or an academic associate's degree. Calculated using US Census data from "Educational Attainment in the United States: 2012—Detailed Tables," All Races, accessed December 11, 2013, http://www.census.gov/hhes/socdemo /education/data/cps/2012/tables.html.

56. Robert H. Frank and Philip J. Cook, *Winner-Take-All Society* (New York: Free Press, 1995).

57. For a journalistic appraisal of this aspect of elite universities, in this case, Stanford University, see Ken Aluetta, "Get Rich U.," *New Yorker,* April 30, 2012, http://www.newyorker.com/reporting/2012/04/30/120430fa_fact _auletta.

58. "The Double Ivies consist of the Ivy League plus MIT, Caltech, Stanford, Duke, Emory, Carnegie Mellon, NYU, and Northwestern." Christopher Newfield, "Humanities Creativity in the Age of Online," *Occasion* 6, accessed October 30, 2014, http://arcade.stanford.edu/sites/default/files /article_pdfs/OCCASION_v6_Newfield_100113.pdf. In 2014 William Deresciewicz drew broad attention to the possibility that Ivy League students

do not avail themselves of these cultivation opportunities and use universities like Columbia and Yale as brands to enhance their comparative advantage in conformity-inducing competition for high-paying posts in a narrow range of overcompensated professions. William Deresciewicz, *Excellent Sheep: The Miseducation of the American Elite and the Way to a Meaningful Life* (New York: Free Press, 2014).

59. Robert Meister, "Debt, Democracy, and the Public University," *Remaking the University* (blog), December 16, 2011, http://utotherescue .blogspot.fr/2011/12/debt-democracy-and-public-university.html.

60. Kevin Phillips, *The Politics of Rich and Poor: Wealth and the American Electorate in the Reagan Aftermath* (New York: Random House, 1990); Barack Obama, "Remarks by the President on the Economy—Knox College, Galesburg, IL," press release, White House, July 24, 2013, accessed September 5, 2013, http://www.whitehouse.gov/the-press-office/2013/07/24/remarks -president-economy-knox-college-galesburg-il.

Reconstructing the Public University

1. The concept of creative capabilities, or the "capability approach," emerges from the work of Sudhir Anand, Paul Anand, Martha Nussbaum, Amartya Sen, and others, and led to the formulation of the United Nation's human development indicators. The most pertinent formulation for this book appears in Nussbaum's *Not for Profit: Why Democracy Needs the Humanities* (Princeton, NJ: Princeton University Press, 2010).

2. Some of the earlier decline in the eighteen- to thirty-four-year-old demographic was identified in the "Measuring Up" reports; for representative conclusions, see Patrick M. Callan, "The 2008 National Report Card: Modest Improvements, Persistent Disparities, Eroding Global Competitiveness," The National Center for Public Policy and Higher Education, accessed May 12, 2016, http://measuringup2008.highereducation.org/commentary/callan.php. This decline was suspended in part by the attraction that higher education holds as an alternative to the job market during recessions. Recent projections continue to predict flat or falling attainment for younger Americans compared to their elders. See, for example, William G. Bowen and Michael S. McPherson, *Lesson Plan: An Agenda for Change in American Higher Education* (Princeton, NJ: Princeton University Press, 2016), 11–19.

3. I was thinking in particular of James C. Garland, *Saving Alma Mater: A Rescue Plan for America's Public Universities* (Chicago: University of Chicago Press, 2009), discussed in Stage 3, and Bowen and McPherson, *Lesson Plan*.

4. See also the concept of "democratic merit" in Lani Guinier, *The Tyranny of the Meritocracy: Democratizing Higher Education in America* (Boston: Beacon Press, 2015). My thinking is indebted to Guinier's many years of work on the

practical arrangements involved in democratizing voting, learning, and other collective practices.

5. I derive my understanding of ethos and of its importance to critical theory and public argument from Amanda Anderson, *The Way We Argue Now: A Study in the Cultures of Theory* (Princeton, NJ: Princeton University Press, 2006).

6. A large field of affect theory stands behind the concept of public feeling, which was pioneered by Feel Tank Chicago and related groups and particularly well embodied in Ann Cvetkovich, *Depression: A Public Feeling* (Durham, NC: Duke University Press, 2012), whose Part I provides a collective memoir of the genesis of the field.

7. Caitlin Rosenthal, "In the Money: Finance, Freedom, and American Capitalism," *American Quarterly* 68, no. 1 (March 2016): 161–75.

8. Doris Sommer, *The Work of Art in the World: Civic Agency and Public Humanities* (Durham, NC: Duke University Press Books, 2014).

9. Thanks to Aashish Mehta of UC Santa Barbara's Department of Global Studies for helping me clarify my thinking about public goods. He is of course not responsible for any ongoing errors.

10. National Science Foundation, *Survey of Federal Funds for Research and Development, Fiscal Years 2014–16*, table 2, "Summary of federal obligations and outlays for research, development, and R&D plant, by type of R&D, performer, and field of science and engineering: FYs 2013–16," accessed June 1, 2016, https://ncsesdata.nsf.gov/fedfunds/2014/html/FFS2014_DST_002.html.

11. For a definitive analysis, see William Lazonick, *Sustainable Prosperity in the New Economy: Business Organization and High-Tech Employment in the United States* (Kalamazoo, MI: W. E. Upjohn Institute, 2009).

12. NSF, *Survey of Federal Funds 2014–16*, table 2. Adding industry and industry research and development centers together in the two subcategories of "research" and "basic research."

13. Walter W. McMahon, *Higher Learning, Greater Good: The Private and Social Benefits of Higher Education* (Baltimore, MD: Johns Hopkins University Press, 2009), 284.

14. William R. Emmons and Bryan J. Noeth, "Why Didn't Higher Education Protect Hispanic and Black Wealth?," *In the Balance,* Federal Reserve Bank of St. Louis, August 2015, accessed August 26, 2015, https://www.stlouisfed.org/publications/in-the-balance/issue12-2015/why-didnt-higher-education-protect-hispanic-and-black-wealth.

15. Patricia Cohen, "Racial Wealth Gap Persists Despite Degree, Study Says," *New York Times*, August 16, 2015, http://www.nytimes.com/2015/08/17/business/racial-wealth-gap-persists-despite-degree-study-says.html.

16. Josh Mitchell, "The Student-Loan Problem Is Even Worse Than Official Figures Indicate," *Real Time Economics* (blog), *Wall Street Journal*, April 14, 2015, http://blogs.wsj.com/economics/2015/04/14/the-student -loan-problem-is-even-worse-than-official-figures-indicate/.

17. Christopher Newfield, "Hillary Clinton and Phyllis Wise: Signs of Better Things," *Remaking the University* (blog), August 17, 2015, http:// utotherescue.blogspot.co.uk/2015/08/hillary-clinton-and-phyllis-wise-signs .html. My comments here are based on this post.

18. Robert Samuels, "Free Public Higher Ed Goes Viral," *Changing Universities* (blog), June 9, 2015, http://changinguniversities.blogspot.com /2015/06/free-public-higher-ed-goes-viral.html.

19. See, for example, Jordan Weissmann, "The Big, Bold Idea at the Heart of Hillary Clinton's Plan to Make College Cheaper," *Slate*, August 10, 2015, http://www.slate.com/blogs/moneybox/2015/08/10/hillary_clinton_debt _free_college_plan_the_democrats_have_one_big_bold_idea.html.

20. For a discussion of tuition levels, see Stage 4.

21. "College for All Act," accessed August 27, 2015, http://www.sanders .senate.gov/download/collegeforall/?inline=file.

22. Another estimate of total tuition charged at public colleges and universities is $59 billion. Mark Kantrowitz, "Proposal for Free College Tuition & Required Fees and Free Textbooks," *Edvisors*, August 20, 2015, accessed August 27, 2015, https://www.edvisors.com/ask/student-aid-policy /free-tuition/.

23. Debt and spending projections in Josh Zumbrun, "The Legacy of Debt: Interest Costs Poised to Surpass Defense and Nondefense Discretion- ary Spending," *Real Time Economics* (blog), *Wall Street Journal,* February 3, 2015, http://blogs.wsj.com/economics/2015/02/03/the-legacy-of-debt -interest-costs-poised-to-surpass-defense-and-nondefense-discretionary -spending/.

24. For the California example, see Newfield et al., "The Cuts Report," UC Academic Council, March 2008, accessed September 1, 2015, http://www .universityofcalifornia.edu/senate/reports/cuts.report.04.08.pdf.

25. Christopher Newfield, "The Old State Funding Model Is Dead: What Will Replace It?," *Remaking the University* (blog), November 14, 2013, ·http://utotherescue.blogspot.co.uk/2013/11/the-old-state-funding-model-is -dead.html.

26. Author's calculations from Stanton Glantz and Eric Hays, "Financial Options for Restoring Quality and Access to Public Higher Education in California: 2015–16," *Keep California's Promise,* February 2015, table 1, accessed July 20, 2015, http://keepcaliforniaspromise.org/473424/reset-2015-16. See discussion in Stage 4.

27. State Department of Finance, "California State Budget: Higher Education," fig. HED-01, accessed December 10, 2013, http://www.ebudget.ca.gov/2013-14/pdf/BudgetSummary/HigherEducation.pdf.

28. The reset bought both rebuilt state funding and tuition reduction to about two-thirds of the way to zero, suggesting that a free UC and a free CSU (totaling over 600,000 undergraduates) would be about forty-two dollars per year for the median taxpayer (total cost of an additional $7.6 billion per year).

29. Lumina Foundation, *A Benchmark for Making College Affordable: The Rule of 10* (Indianapolis, IN: Lumina Foundation, 2015), 5, accessed August 28, 2015, http://www.luminafoundation.org/files/resources/affordability-benchmark-1.pdf.

30. Families USA, "Federal Poverty Guidelines," accessed August 28, 2015, http://familiesusa.org/product/federal-poverty-guidelines; Lumina, *A Benchmark for Making College Affordable, 6.*

31. Andrew Ross, *Creditocracy: And the Case for Debt Refusal* (New York: OR Books, 2014).

32. Benjamin S. Bloom, "The 2-Sigma Problem: The Search for Methods of Group Instruction as Effective as One-to-One Tutoring," *Educational Researcher* 13, no. 6 (June–July 1984): 4. The cofounder of the MOOC company Coursera, Daphne Koller, referred to the 2-Sigma problem in her widely circulated TED Talk on online education. See Daphne Koller, "What We're Learning from Online Education," August 1, 2012, accessed July 11, 2013, https://www.youtube.com/watch?v=U6FvJ6jMGHU. MOOC advocates regularly invoked mastery learning as their core goal.

33. Richard Arum and Josipa Roksa, *Academically Adrift: Limited Learning on College Campuses* (Chicago: University of Chicago Press, 2011).

34. Christopher Newfield, "How Public Universities Are Losing the Framing Wars," *Remaking the University* (blog), February 14, 2013, http://utotherescue.blogspot.com/2013/02/how-public-research-universities-are.html.

35. Christopher Newfield, *Ivy and Industry: Business and the Making of the American University, 1880–1980* (Durham, NC: Duke University Press, 2003), chap. 3, 56.

36. Ibid.

37. Clark Kerr, *The Uses of the University* (Cambridge, MA: Harvard University Press, 1963).

38. Report of the Harvard Committee, *General Education in a Free Society* (Cambridge, MA: Harvard University Press, 1945), 3–4. Thanks to Michael Meranze for this passage and related discussions of midcentury humanism.

39. See Martha C. Nussbaum, *Not For Profit: Why Democracy Needs the Humanities* (Princeton, NJ: Princeton University Press, 2010); and Martha C.

Nussbaum, *Creating Capabilities: The Human Development Approach* (Cambridge, MA: Belknap Press of Harvard University Press, 2011).

40. Emily Bazelon, "The Stanford Undergraduate and the Mentor," *New York Times Magazine,* February 11, 2015, http://www.nytimes.com/2015/02/15/magazine/the-stanford-undergraduate-and-the-mentor.html?_r=0.

41. Bryce Covert, "What Amazon Didn't Understand about Overwork," *The Nation,* August 27, 2015, http://www.thenation.com/article/relax-or-collapse/.

42. Karl Marx, *Capital,* vol. 1, *A Critique of Political Economy,* trans. Ben Fowkes (London: Penguin Books, 1976, 1990), chap. 17.

43. Jeff Bezos, "To Our Shareholders," Amazon.com, 1997, 4, accessed August 31, 2015, http://media.corporate-ir.net/media_files/irol/97/97664/reports/Shareholderletter97.pdf.

44. Jodi Kantor and David Streitfeld, "Inside Amazon: Wrestling Big Ideas in a Bruising Workplace," *New York Times*, August 15, 2015, http://www.nytimes.com/2015/08/16/technology/inside-amazon-wrestling-big-ideas-in-a-bruising-workplace.html.

Index

Italic page numbers indicate figures